Murat Halstead

A History of the national political Conventions

Of the current presidential Campaign

Murat Halstead

A History of the national political Conventions
Of the current presidential Campaign

ISBN/EAN: 9783337132729

Printed in Europe, USA, Canada, Australia, Japan

Cover: Foto ©ninafisch / pixelio.de

More available books at **www.hansebooks.com**

CAUCUSES OF 1860.

A HISTORY

OF THE

National Political Conventions

OF THE

CURRENT PRESIDENTIAL CAMPAIGN:

BEING A

COMPLETE RECORD OF THE BUSINESS OF ALL
THE CONVENTIONS;

WITH

SKETCHES OF DISTINGUISHED MEN IN ATTENDANCE UPON THEM,
AND DESCRIPTIONS OF THE MOST CHARACTERISTIC
SCENES AND MEMORABLE EVENTS.

Compiled from the Correspondence of the Cincinnati Commercial, written
"On the Circuit of the Conventions," and the Official Reports.

By M. HALSTEAD,
AN EYE-WITNESS OF THEM ALL.

COLUMBUS:
FOLLETT, FOSTER AND COMPANY.
1860.

PREFACE.

If I have a prejudice against or partiality for any political party, such that I am incapable of taking an impartial view of its proceedings, and of telling the truth of it irrespective of the antagonisms, that demand concealment on the one hand and perversion on the other, I am unconscious of the fact.

I know that in making the "Circuit of the Conventions," in the capacity of a journalist, I endeavored to pursue the path of candor; and that this was not only my personal feeling but the policy of the journal with which I am connected.

In the first letter of the correspondence from which this publication is largely made up, I promised to remember in my writings of the Conventions the entreaty of Othello, concerning information to be despatched from Cyprus to Venice:

> "I pray you, in your letters,
> When you shall these unlucky deeds relate,
> *   *   *   Nothing extenuate,
> Nor set down aught in malice"—

I should consider the displeasure and hostile criticisms of partisans of all persuasions and organizations, the best testimony that I have kept this promise. M. H.

CONTENTS.

	Page
The Charleston Convention	1
The Constitutional Democratic Convention at Charleston	97
The Baltimore National Constitutional Union Convention	104
The Chicago Convention	120
The Constitutional Democratic Convention at Richmond	154
The National Democratic Convention at Baltimore	159
Institute Hall ("Seceders") Convention	217
The Second Richmond Convention	231

ERRATA

Page 9, first line, second paragraph, for "*Magnolia* Hall" read "*Hibernia* Hall."
Page 31, last line, read "*equivocal*" for "*equivalent.*"
Page 101, last line of page, read "*leonine*" instead of "*canine.*"

THE CHARLESTON CONVENTION.

The Hon. Stephen A. Douglas was the pivot individual of the Charleston Convention. Every delegate was for or against him. Every motion meant to nominate or not to nominate him. Every parliamentary war was *pro* or *con* Douglas.

On the route to Charleston, delegates and others who were proceeding to attend the Convention, talked about Mr. Douglas. The questions in every car and at every station, were: Would he be? could he be? should he be nominated? Could he get a majority of the Convention? could he get two-thirds? Would the South support him if he should be nominated? Would the Administration acquiesce if he were nominated?

NOTES BY THE WAY.

[The following extract from a letter written at Atlanta, Ga., April 17th, will give an idea of the spirit of Southerners when *en route* for the Convention :]

ATLANTA, GA., April 17th.

We had interesting political talk on the cars this evening. Two Georgians were disputing as to the strength of Douglas in the State. One, a Charleston delegate, said he would not do. He might possibly vote for him if nominated, but it would be with great reluctance. He did not know but one man in favor of Douglas in his district. The other had been defeated as a candidate for Charleston delegate. He said Douglas men were thick as blackberries all through the region from which he came. Douglas would carry the State by twenty thousand majority. "Let him be nominated, and there will be such a war-whoop as never was heard in the land." The same man said the old-line Democrats of Georgia were for Douglas, and the old-line Whigs and the Americans, turned Democrats, were against him. This man was asked if he believed in Douglas's doctrine of popular sovereignty, which was no better than Abolitionism, and he said he "went the whole of it;" and he was backed up by a Douglas man from Kentucky. The Georgians and Kentuckians generally, on the train, considered that it would not do at all to run Douglas. Some man must be run who would unite the party—somebody not obnoxious to any section of it—somebody who had not been so recently as Douglas fighting side by side with the Black Republicans against the one and indivisible Democracy.

[The following from a letter written at Social Circle, Georgia, on the 18th April, is still farther illustrative:]

SOCIAL CIRCLE, GA., April 18th.

We have had warm times among the delegates to the Convention since our stop here. A conversation commenced at the dinner table about Douglas. There was a delegate from Indiana and an outsider from Kentucky, sitting very near a couple of Mississippians, delegates, friends of Jeff. Davis, and "fire-eaters," as we term them. Some private whisky was passed, and the Mississippians drank to "the health of the nominee." The question was asked whether that included Douglas. Mississippi said he did not consider him in the ring at all. He [Douglas] had no chance of being the nominee, and therefore, when he drank to the health of the nominee it did not include him. The Douglas man thought Douglas should be included, and proceeded to say that if he was nominated he must have the support of the entire Democratic party. 'A man could not go into a Convention and then bolt the nominee if not pleased with him—not at all, certainly not with honor. Now, the Mississippians do intend to bolt Douglas if he is nominated, and hence they were touched, and took fire. The controversy ran high. The Indianian was asked what he meant by "Southern fanatics and fire-eaters"—an expression he had used—and he said, "such men as Jeff. Davis." This was touching the Mississippians on a tender point. They demanded very explicitly to know in what respect Davis was fanatical—and the specifications were rather vague. Mississippi wanted to know whether Davis had ever demanded any thing but the rights of the South, and if so, what?—and said that certain allegations made against the conservatism of Davis were mere falsehoods. Indiana claimed the same right to criticise Davis that Mississippi had to criticise Douglas. Mississippi denied that. "Davis was a patriot, and Douglas was a traitor, d—d little better than Seward—that was the difference." Indiana talked about fighting the battles of the South in the North, and all that sort of thing. Mississippi did not thank the Northern Democracy for doing any such thing. The South was able to fight her own battles, and to protect her rights. She could do this out of the Union, if not in it. Indiana talked about returning fugitive slaves, and Mississippi laughed scornfully. And as the parties had to either bet or fight, a bet of one thousand dollars was made on the spot. The Mississippian bet that Douglas would not receive the electoral vote of that State if he were nominated. The Douglasite bet that he would. If Douglas is not nominated at Charleston, the stakes are, of course, to be withdrawn.* The feeling excited by this controversy, was warm and general. The delegates who did not mix in, shook their heads and talked of stormy times ahead, and the peril in which the party would be placed. It was manifest that if the Mississippian and the Indianian were joint representative men of their sections, there was little chance for the nomination of a candidate who could, by any possibility, be elected, or of the con-

* This bet was withdrawn at the solicitation of mutual friends from Kentucky.

struction of a platform that would be even superficially satisfactory. The Mississippians understood themselves to be of the class that dictates doctrine to the Democratic party, and talked as if the party was their property, "peculiar," at that, and rather a worn out old nigger, welcome to die. Indiana talked of love for the party, and devotion to it, and a determination to support the nominee, whoever he might be. Mississippi talked of principle, and "damn the party," if it was not placed squarely upon principle. In other words, if the party was not to serve the South, its mission was accomplished. My Indiana friend, was, I think, astonished to find a real live specimen of fire-eater—and was rather embarrassed by his discovery.

I have dwelt on this scene thus fully, because it is a preliminary symptom of the Charleston Convention, and is, indeed, the history of the Convention in miniature and wanting the climax. While the war went on, the Kentucky delegation, quiet, substantial gentlemen, who don't want office, and would not have it, stood back, and talked in business-like style of the great merits as a man and availability as a candidate, of their friend, the Hon. James Guthrie. The Mississippians have the Freeport speech of Douglas with them, and intend to bombard him in the Convention with ammunition drawn from it. The extract upon which they depend most, is that in which he said "no matter what may be the decision of the Supreme Court," the people of a Territory could abolish slavery while in a territorial condition. They will use this remorselessly. However great may be the weight of the Douglas men in the Convention, he will be assailed most bitterly. The fight against him involves, for a very large class of Southern politicians—indeed, the most influential class of the time—the issues of life, and those Southern men have a great advantage over the Douglas men in the fact that they are sincere. They have principles. They stand upon convictions, and will fight until from their bones the flesh be hacked. The Douglas men are not so stiff in their backs nor so strong in the faith. In a conversation with an Alabama delegate to-day, I told him I presumed the South would have to put up with another platform capable of a double construction ; he declared that impossible. I inquired —"Don't you see the Douglas delegates don't agree with you, and can't and won't agree with you? Do you not know that if they went home to make a fight on the platform you insist they shall place themselves upon, they would be beaten in every Northern State and every Northern township, and that the majority against them in all the Northern States would only be counted by tens of thousands?"

No, he did not know any such thing. Mayor Wood was a "sound man," and had carried the city of New York. He was as sound as any Southern man. Connecticut would have been carried by the Democracy if there had not been so much pandering to Douglasism. The way to fight a battle was to fight it on principle. If the North was not willing to stand squarely up for the Constitution with the South, it was high time the fact were known. This campaign was the test campaign. It must be fought on principle. There must be no Douglas dodges—no double constructions—no janus-faced lying resolutions—no double-tongued and doubly damned trifling with the people. The people were entitled to a fair fight, and must have it. What was the Democratic party for if it was not for the vindication of the great constitutional principles upon which our governmental fabric rests? [I stated I had for some time strongly suspected that the Democratic party was an organization for the purpose of obtaining federal offices—in other words, a political corporation—like a great lottery company—for the distribution of the spoils. I thought that I could safely speak for the party in the North, in that respect. He repudiated, with indignation—obviously sincere, too—all idea of the spoils. He was for Southern principle; and if the Democratic party was not for them it was against them—and if it was a spoils party, the sooner it was destroyed and sent to the devil, the better. As for the popular sovereignty doctrine, it was as bad as Sewardism; it was the real practical Black Republicanism doctrine ; it was the veritable " short cut"—as Gov. Wise said in his Donnelly letter—" to all the ends of Black Republicanism." "If the Republican party leaders had half sense (he said), they would adopt the Squatter Sovereignty platform at Chicago. It was the Chicago, not the Charleston card."

I thought so too, but the difficulty was, the Republican leaders hadn't half sense, and couldn't see their game. His confidence in their political sagacity was far greater than mine.

The chances of Mr. Douglas for the Charleston nomination, were next in order. I spoke of the great pressure that would be brought to bear from the North, for Douglas. He said the nomination of Douglas was not a possibility. He put the case in this way : The North has had two Presidents. The South is willing, so far as she is concerned, that she shall have another one. But the South will not allow the Northern man, who, of all men claiming to belong to the Democratic party, is most obnoxious, to be the candidate. The South has to perform the principal part in the election of the President; and her feelings must be respected. The nomination of Douglas would be an insult to her, which she must resent by defeating him at all hazards. And here our coversation subsided into observations concerning cypress swamps, the inky Edisto river—a ditch fifty yards wide, filled with black water—the lofty cypress trees—the yellow pines—the live oaks—the Spanish moss making the wilderness venerable—the white sand—the red clay, etc., etc.

PLACES, PERSONS AND POLITICS IN CHARLESTON BEFORE THE CONVENTION.

There was in Charleston, as usual in such cases, much that was important in the business preliminary to the Convention, and there are many places in the city intensified with the Convention in interest. Among those places, perhaps the most interesting are Institute Hall, where the Convention was held, and Hibernia Hall, which was the Douglas head-quarters.

CHARLESTON, April 20th.

The Institute Hall where the Convention is to be held, will contain about three thousand people. The floor is perfectly level, and the seats are all old-fashioned, wooden-bottomed chairs, which have been independent of each other heretofore, but which are now being screwed by the half-dozen to pine planks placed across the bottom. There is a good deal of gaudy and uncouth ornamentation about the hall. The frescoing is mere daubing. The principal effort in art is immediately over the stage. Three highly colored but very improperly dressed females are there engaged. One seems to be contemplating matters and things in general. Another is mixing colors with the apparent intention of painting something. The other is pointing with what seems to be a common bowie-knife, to a globe. The point of the dagger is plunged into the Black Sea. It may be held to be according to the proprieties, that the continent which is outlined most conspicuously on this globe is marked "Africa." There are rooms behind the stage, and two private boxes above it.

The Hall is situated on the principal thoroughfare and near the business centre of the city. The Hibernian Hall—the Douglas head-quarters is situated on the same street, a square and a half distant. This building has two large halls, and is two stories in height. The first floor is divided into two small rooms and one spacious hall, where a gigantic bard of Erin is holding a harp, such as was heard in Tara's Halls before the soul of music fled. The smaller rooms are furnished with long tables, plenty of chairs and writing materials, and a large supply of Sheahan's Life of Stephen A. Douglas. The second floor is one large hall, and is full of cots for the Northwestern delegations. There are several hundreds of them, with white spreads and pillows. They are arranged in rows and sections, numbered and marked for the different States.

The Douglas men are to be found for the most part at the "Mills House." The fire-eaters congregate at the "Charleston." The spacious passages and public rooms about these houses are already swarming with politicians. It must be admitted that the Southerners have the advantage in personal appearance. The strong men of the South are here in force, as they always are upon such occasions. There is sufficient wisdom among the oligarchy to be represented in Congress and Conventions by men of experience and intellect, and they attain weighty advantages in this way.

The arrival at the Charleston Hotel to-day, is that of the Hon. W. L. Yancey of Alabama, the prince of the fire-eaters. He is the man said to be charged with a three days' speech against Douglas. He is a compact, middle-sized man, straight limbed, with a square built head and face, and an eye full of expression. He is mild and bland in manner as Fernando Wood, and has an air of perfect sincerity which Wood has not. No one would be likely to point him out in a group of gentlemen as the redoubtable Yancey, who proposes according to common report to precipitate the cotton States into a revolution, dissolve the Union and build up a Southern empire. The strong point made against him by the Douglasites is that he is a disunionist. It will not frighten him, nor his Southern friends, however, to apply that epithet to him. I very much doubt whether the Douglas men have a leader competent to cope with him in the coming fight. It is quite clear that while the North may be strongest in votes here, and the most noisy, the South will have the intellect and the pluck to make its points. I do not think any importation of Douglas men can prevent the Convention from "wearing a southern aspect," as the *Mercury*, of this city, said it must. Prominent in the crowd at the Mills House, is the burly form of the far-famed Geo. N Sanders, New York navy agent. The politicians here are fond of inquiring whether he feels comfortable about the neck, it being rumored that the President is about to remove him for his audacity in coming down here as a Douglas man.

There are a great many men of distinguished personal appearance to be seen about the hotels, as usual during National Conventions, speakership contests, and other times of extraordinary commotion among politicians. A large number have the general characteristics of first class gamblers, and the probability is, there are keepers of the playful animal known as "ye tiger" to be found in this vicinity. There are great portly fellows, with protuberant stomachs and puffy checks, red foreheads, hair thin and grizzly, dressed in glossy black and fine linen, with the latest style of stove-pipe hats, and ponderous gold-headed canes—perspiring and smoking, and engaged in mysterious conversations, concerning caucus stratagems, of intense interest to themselves. Every body is talking about the Convention, and prophesying and wondering as to its action. The Douglasites claim prodigious things. The ultra Southern men sneer at the idea of Douglas's nomination, and inquire— "Where was he two years ago?"—and answer the question themselves —"Caucusing with Seward —leagued with the Black Republicans against a Democratic Administration." They say his pretenses in the Lecompton rebellion were false, and that his subsequent talk proves them to be so. They say his line of policy then, if honestly followed, would have carried him where John W. Forney is now—into the ranks of the Republican party. The Douglas men generally respond by speaking of their champion facing dreadful mobs of Black Republicans, and gazing into the mouths of pistols, in defense of the rights of the South. They inquire further, whether Illinois has not always been true to the Democratic party. I heard this question put to a fire-eater, and he said, "Did'nt Illinois elect a Black Republican Governor?" "Who was Bissell?" The response of the Douglas man was, that Bissell was not not elected by a majority vote. The Southern rejoinder was: "Did Douglas have a majority of the popular vote in his Senatorial contest with Lincoln?" And the Douglasite come back with a broadside, directed at the Danites, or Administration men, who gave Lincoln aid and comfort. And so the battle rages along the whole line.

The Douglas men came down here from their head-quarters in Washington, where whisky flows like a river.

> Like some vast river of unfailing source ;
> Rapid, exhaustless deep, * *

—they were full of enthusiasm—rampant and riotous—"hot as monkeys"—and proclaim that the universal world is for the Little Giant. They have a desperate fight before them, and are brim full of the sound and fury of boastfulness.

THE DOUGLAS DEMONSTRATION—SENATOR SLIDELL.

CHARLESTON, S. C., April 21st, 1860.

The principal hotels swarm like hives this morning. The greatest crowd is at the Mills House, which is the Douglas head-quarters The air is full of tobacco-smoke and rumors. There is nothing definite to be found out. The private consultation rooms are the centres of interest, but it is impossible to arrive at results. The friends of Douglas are by no means disposed to talk about their second choice. They swear they have none, and will stick to Dug while the hair is on their heads. They won't, however. Many of them would be weary after two days' balloting. The Administration and Southern U. S. Senators scout the idea of the success of Douglas. They consider his defeat a foregone conclusion. Slidell was urged last week to come down and attend to the extermination of his enemy, but said at first, he would not —for there was no danger of the nomination of the obnoxious individual. The Douglas men made such demonstrations in Washington, however, and indicated such power and confidence, that "Old Houmas," as his enemies style him, concluded to come. He will be here this evening, and will operate against Douglas. He is a matchless wire-worker, and the news of his approach causes a flutter. His appearance here means war to the knife. It means also, that the Administration is uneasy on the Douglas question—and feel constrained to exert every influence against the Squatty Giant of Illinois, whose nomination would be perdition to Buchanan, Slidell & Co.

There is not, however, for the moment, so much bitterness of denunciation in the talk of the Southern delegates here, as there was on the road. The Douglas element is so powerful, that it would be indiscreet to exasperate it. And the Douglasites repeat very few of those disparaging words so familiar in their mouths at home, about the Southern fire-eaters and fanatics. They sing low and roar gently about Southern sectionalism. All these ill humors must, however, have their breaking out in the heat of the Convention. In these piping times of private caucuses, the bad blood is diplomatically preserved for home consumption.

THE DAY PRECEDING THE CONVENTION—DOUGLAS STOCK UP.

CHARLESTON, S. C., April 22d.

The run of the current this morning is Douglas-ward. The friends of Douglas are encouraged by the events of last night. In the first place, the Executive Committee adjourned *sine die*, without repudiating the action of Judge Smalley, the Chairman, in issuing tickets to the Cagger, Cassidy and Dean Richmond New Yorkers, and to the Douglas Illinois delegation. Fernando Wood and Ike Cook and their delegations are full of wrath, and denounce Smalley in extreme terms. The fight in the Executive Committee on the question of adjournment *sine die*, was a small fight between the Douglas and Anti-Douglas men, and the former triumphed by one majority. The Committee, however, was not full, only eighteen States being represented. This sends Douglas stock up this morning. Another thing is, the Southern delegations have held caucuses and consultations for two or three days, to try to agree upon a candidate upon whom to concentrate their vote, and upon the points of the platform. They had a special meeting last night and failed to accomplish any thing, except to exhibit their incapacity to come together. The game of the Douglas men, just now, is one they are not well qualified to play. It is to be quiet and conciliatory. They try to think and act upon the presumption, that they have the Convention in their hands, and wish to make all the friends they can in the South. They say, and it is possible there is some truth in it, that the failure of the South to unite, arises from secret Douglas influences. The ultra Southerners are becoming more bitter. The delegations from Georgia, Alabama, Mississippi, Louisiana, Florida, Arkansas and Texas, have agreed to withdraw if Douglas should be nominated, and it is believed that a portion of the North Carolina, Virginia, Kentucky and Missouri delegations would follow. The Douglas men look a little wild at this, but say they don't care, and console themselves by assuming that this course on the part of the South would be great gain to them in the North. They assert their ability to carry all the Northern States, if this Southern withdrawal should take place. The South is not unwilling, if it fails to control the Convention, so far as to defeat Douglas, to accept the hazard. The ultras have no doubt of their ability to carry six or eight, perhaps more, Southern States.

They expect Douglas then to carry enough Northern States to carry the election into Congress, where they have no doubt the Senate would finally be called upon to elect. In case of the nomination of Douglas by the Convention, and the withdrawal of the Southern ultras—there would be a desperate battle fought in the ultra Southern States between the slave code and Douglas Democracy; and it might do the fire-eaters great good to be whipped in that way upon their own ground. They have, however, unlimited confidence in their ability to carry their own States.

Several incidents occurred last night to raise the spirits of the Douglasites.

The majority of the Pennsylvania delegation is against Douglas and proposing in the caucus last night that Pennsylvania should vote as an unit in the Convention; the Douglasites rebelled, and threatened to leave the caucus room if the movement of the majority were persisted in, whereupon the caucus adjourned, to meet at nine o'clock to-morrow morning, when the majority will experiment again on giving the vote of the State solid. The prospect of attaining this solidity, is by no means flattering. On the other hand, in the Indiana delegation, the Douglas majority triumphed, and the stiff-necked Administration district delegates, Develin of Wayne, and Tabot of Marion, knocked under, and agreed to go with their Douglas brethren and cast the vote of the State as a unit. My opinion still is that the chances are against the nomination of Douglas. I can see how he can get a majority vote— but I cannot figure out a two-thirds vote for him. The tide of affairs is, however, favorable to him to-day, and the capacity of the presuming and vehement bearers of the political fortunes of the Little Giant to realize their prophecies, may be very great.

THE NIGHT BEFORE THE CONVENTION.

CHARLESTON, S. C., April 22— 10 P. M.

The excitement in the city to-night is higher than heretofore. The politicians are in full blast. I think Douglas stock, which went up a little this morning, is now drooping.

Passing Magnolia Hall this evening, I saw the Douglas delegation of Congressmen from Illinois, seated mournfully on the steps. Their native resolution seemed sicklied o'er by the pale cast of thought, and to have lost the name of action. They were pensive and silent. There was Logan with his dark, narrow face, and black hair and eyes, gazing upon one of the pillars, his hat tilted far back on his head, his hands in his pockets, and his mouth full of tobacco. There was Col. McClernand, with peaked face, running to a hooked nose, sadly playing with his watch-guard. Presently there was Richardson, the Douglas leader in the Cincinnati delegation, and the champion in the House of Representatives, of the Little Giant, in the days of the Kansas Nebraska Bill. Poor Richardson has had a hard time of it. He left Congress, where he might have been a fixture, and made the canvass for Governor of Illinois against Bissell. He did this against his wishes, and to carry the State, where his popularity with his party is second only to that of Douglas. He was influential in carrying the State for Buchanan, but lost his own election. He was appointed Governor of Nebraska, and resigned after the Lecompton rebellion, to escape removal. He is a fine specimen of a strong, coarse man. He has an immense nose and mouth, and fine eyes, and amid such scenes as are here being enacted, he is second to none as a worker of sagacity and force.

The Mills House, where Douglas "men most do congregate," is as lively as a molasses barrel with flies. Here is where the outside pressure is brought to bear. It is here that "public opinion" is represented according to Douglas. Here they tell you Douglas must be the nominee —" all that is to be done is to ratify the voice of the people." There is nothing but a few ballots, and all is over—Douglas the nominee—South will come down—certain to be elected. The country safe—the party safe. They only want a "chance to raise the war-whoop for Douglas in the North-west—that's all. Carry every State North-west —carry Ohio? Lord, yes! Carry Ohio by twenty thousand. If somebody suggests, but where are your figures? How can you obtain the two-thirds vote requisite to nominate? And half a dozen of the makers of public opinion tell you all about it. Every thing North is claimed of course, and you hear that on certain ballots, Kentucky, Missouri, and Virginia, North Carolina, Tennessee, California and Oregon, are coming into line. "And suppose Alabama, Mississippi, Georgia and Louisiana, with scattering delegates in other States, go out—what then?" "What? why tremendous gains in the North, to be sure, just the thing we want." But if you suggest, "Douglas stock is drooping a little this evening. It is not at the high mark it was this morning. You have enthusiasm enough, but you have not the votes." You are told, "Not a bit of it. Douglas stock down—not possible. It can't go down."

There is "For God's sake Linder," of Illinois. He made a speech last night in Hibernia Hall to the faithful, something after the John Brough style of eloquence. His linen suffered in the effort, and he has not been at pains to conceal the evidences of his enthusiasm by the proper change. His collar and cravat have seen service evidently. He gets his name "For God's sake Linder," from a letter which Douglas once wrote him saying, "for God's sake, Linder, come down here, I need help." Some enterprising editor obtained a copy of the letter, and printed it, and it has not been forgotten. There is the enterprising firm of Faran & McLean, looking solemn as the grave, and button-holeing some refractory delegate, telling him how essential it is to the safety of the universe that Douglas should be nominated. They of course don't feel any personal interest in the matter. They are afflicted with principle only. T. Jeff Sherlock, Esq., is looking in upon the crowd, and don't think Douglas can be nominated. He represents the Collector's office, and the virtuous Douglas men, who don't want office, insist that he is nobody because he is in office. And radiant in a full suit of white along comes W. J. Flagg, Esq., legislator—the man who was so bold as to advocate the admission of fresh air into the hall of a deliberative assembly in Ohio. It is clear that he is an innovator, and in these times, when conservatism is so much in demand, be must be held to be dangerous.

Passing along we find a tall portly man in glossy black, with a bad stoop in the shoulders, a new stove-pipe hat retaining in places the original shine, a bright red face out of which look brilliant eyes, carrying in his right hand, as if it were a mace, a huge gold-headed cane—it is Col. Orr, of South Carolina, late Speaker of the House, and now suspected of Douglas inclinations and of a willingness to be either President or Vice President of the United States. He is in the midst of a confidential talk with a burly, piratical looking person in a gray business suit, the sack coat making him look even more squatty than he really is. The features of this individual are a little on the bull-dog order. He does not look like a man of much intellect, but is evidently a marked man—a man of energy and perseverance, of strength and strategy. Ponderous as he is, he moves lightly. Fat as he is, he is restless, and as he smokes his cigar, he consumes it with furious incessant whiffs. The black whiskers are sprinkled lightly with gray. It is Young America, otherwise Geo. Sanders. And, so, so, Mr. Orr, we see how the cat is jumping with you. You would have no objections to be second choice of the Douglas men—not a bit. You would be willing to take the Vice Presidency at the hands of the Douglas Democracy, wouldn't you? And, so, so, you got up a Convention in South Carolina the other day, Mr Orr. The Platform was a little too strongly anti-Douglas to suit you, but that could not be helped. You could not do too much violence to the traditional leading Southern proclivities of South Carolina. You did all you could. Your intentions were toward Douglas, and yourself. If you dared, you would, with your South Carolina delegation, make common cause with the Douglas men. But you dare not do that. And we leave you, Col. Orr, in the care of Geo Sanders.

At the Charleston House we find another atmosphere. Here are the fire-eaters in full force. We miss the prince of them, Yancey of Alabama. He is not a man to talk confidentially in crowds. He don't talk politics with or like the common herd. He may be found in the private parlor of the Alabama delegation. And there is Barksdale, the Congressman of Mississippi, with his hat pulled down over his right eye. He has a way of throwing his head on one side and turning up his chin, and talking in a short sharp way, like a New York B'hoy. He is thick set, broad shouldered and short-legged. His eye is small and fierce. The whole country knows that he wears a wig—for Potter, of Wisconsin, knocked it off once upon a time. But as for a duel, beware of meeting Barksdale with bowie-knives! He knows how to handle the implement and has handled it. The fire eaters are talking about principle. A Douglas man or two have strayed down here, and are trying to explain that Douglas don't really mean any thing by popular sovereignty. "He had to talk that pretty strong to get back to the Senate." The people must be talked to violently about something—might as well say popular sovereignty to them as any thing else. "Douglas would leave it all to the Courts at last. The Courts will fix it all right. Let us drop this immaterial issue and go in for the strongest man—and his name is Stephen A. Douglas." The South listens and commences—"What, and we must throw a bone to the Abolitionists, must we, eh? We must compromise with Abolitionism in order to carry the North—must we? We must take up an unsound man, or lose the battle—must we? No, sir. We have had too much of this. It is time the Democratic party took up sound men, and fought on principle. It is the best policy to fight on principle. Mayor Wood carried New York on principle. Connecticut would have been carried, if it had not been for the taint of Douglasism. Rhode Island victory! There is no such thing. The Seward Republicans and Douglas Democrats in Rhode Island united and beat a John Brown Helperite. That's the way of it. I tell you we can succeed without Douglas. He is the weakest man out. But if he was strongest, I would not give a damn for a victory with him. I want the party destroyed if it is a one-man party. I want defeat if we can't have honest victory. No unfriendly legislation shall exclude our property from the Territories. We must have our property protected."

This is not, by any means, an imaginary conversation. I have heard two to-night that were in substance as I have set down here.

To complete the rounds to-night, we must go over to King street, and look in upon the head-quarters of the Administration Senators established luxuriously there, in a large old-fashioned building, overlooking and entered through an ice-cream garden, which, though this is Sunday evening, is open to the public, and thronged by visitors. The Administration Senators tell us that they are not at all uneasy on the subject of the nomination of Douglas. They say he cannot possibly get more than one hundred and six votes on the first ballot; that his strength will never be as great as it was at Cincinnati after Pierce was withdrawn; that is, they say, "if there is truth in men." But sometimes, and this is one of them, there is not truth in men. Douglas will not, I presume, be nominated, but he will get more than one hundred and six votes.

The Administration Senators tell us Douglas is not to be the nominee—cannot get one-half the votes—nothing like it. If these Senators are speaking the truth, then there are lies enough told at the Mills House every day to sink a ship, if each one only weighed but an ounce. And the Senators produce the figures. Douglas will hardly get a vote from a slave State, unless it may be one or two from each of the States of Maryland and Missouri. New York is dead against him. Neither delegation from that State is for him, and the State must vote as an unit. But will it? Senators say yes. And Pennsylvania? Senators say Douglas cannot certainly get a vote from Pennsylvania. The majority of the delegation is for Breckenridge, and it is the Hunter and Guthrie men who are strongest against State unity. But they will all come in—every man—and the State will be an unit against Douglas. It will all be fixed in the morning. And Senators say also that Massachusetts is against Douglas—dead and united against him—and Maine evenly divided. New Hampshire is for him, and waiting to have him slaughtered, in order to introduce to the Convention the name of Franklin Pierce. Senators are bitter. They are not only against the Presidential aspirations of the Senator of Illinois, but they hate him most cordially, and some of them swear vengeance.

The full-faced gentleman without a vest, sitting on the corner of a chair, and smoking a fragrant cigar in the contemplative style—the gentleman with long brown curling hair, parted in the middle—is Senator Bayard, of Delaware, a distinguished lawyer and a Democratic partisan of long standing. He could do his State some service, by helping her to get rid of slavery, but he is a pro-slavery man. He is a descendant of the illustrious Chevalier Bayard, the knight without fear or reproach. Senator Bayard is a handsome, courtly gentleman, who is personally a goodly man to know.

The heavy, closely-shaven gentleman, with yellow vest, open, that its wearer may have the benefit of the breeze—the gentleman leaning against the railing, in his chair, looking like a business man more than a Senator (if we may be allowed such a distinction), is Jesse D. Bright, who has long been the king caucus of Indiana. Mr. Bright's hatred of Douglas is, perhaps, just now, the strongest passion of his soul. Douglas voted to exclude him from the Senate, and their relations are those of irreconcilable and deadly hate. It is reported that he swears he will stump Indiana, county by county, against Douglas, if he should be nominated.

The rosy gentleman, with the farmer-like aspect, slightly inclined to be just fat enough to be sleek, and whose countenance is so placid that you would not imagine he had ever been crushed by Douglas in debate, or become weak in the knees, and been guilty of wincing at Southern thunder, the gentleman who has just ascended the stairs, and has thrown himself into a perspiration, and who is alternately mopping with his handkerchief and fanning with his hat, is the Hon. William Bigler, of Pennsylvania. Within, seated at a round table, on which books, newspapers and writing material is scattered about, is a gentleman with long, thin white hair, through which the top of his head blushes like the shell of a boiled lobster. The gentleman has also a cherry-red face, the color being that produced by good health, and good living joined to a florid temperament. His features are well cut, and the expression is that of a thoughtful, hard-working, resolute man of the world. He is a New Yorker by birth, but has made a princely fortune at the New Orleans bar. He is not a very eloquent man in the Senate, but his ability is unquestioned; and it is universally known that he is with the present Administration, the power behind the throne greater than the throne itself. Mr. Buchanan is as wax in his fingers. The name of this gentleman is John Slidell. His special mission here is to see that Stephen A. Douglas is not nominated for the Presidency. If I am not much mistaken, he just now manipulated a few of the North-eastern men with such marvelous art, that they will presently find they are exceedingly anxious to defeat the nomination of Douglas, and they will believe that they arrived at the conclusions now coming uppermost in their minds in their own way.

There has been a great deal more drunkenness here to-day than heretofore. Most of the violent spreeing is done by roughs from the Northern Atlantic cities who are at last making their appearance. There have been a number of specimens of drunken rowdyism and imbecility about the hotels. And I hear, as I write, a company of brawlers in the street making night hideous.

LIST OF DELEGATES TO THE NATIONAL DEMOCRATIC CONVENTION.

[From the Secretary's Roll.]

The following, furnished by the Secretary of the Convention to the Charleston newspapers, is the most correct List of Delegates published. The list cannot be absolutely accurate, for the reason that some of the originally accredited delegates never appeared—and after the first day of the Convention, changes were constantly being made:

MAINE.
Thos. Bradbury, Eastport.
George F. Stapley, Portland.
E. Wilder Finley, Newcastle.
Amos M. Roberts, Bangor.
S. R. Lyman, Portland.
Thomas K. Lane, Saco.
S. C. Blanchard, Yarmouth.
Calvin Record, Auburn.
Thomas D. Robinson, Bath.
Henry W. Owen, Bath.
Henry A. Wyman, Snowhegan.
Charles D. Jameson, Bangor.
J. Withrop Jones, Ellsworth.
P. S. J. Talbot, East Machias.
J. Y. McClintock, Belfast.
W. H. Burvill, Belfast.

VERMONT.
John S. Robinson, Bennington.
Jasper Rand, Berkshire.
Henry Keys, Newbury.
E. M. Brown, Woodstock.
Charles G. Eastman, Montpelier.
Pitt W. Hyde, Hydeville.
H. E. Stoughton, Bellows Falls.
Stephen Thomas, West Fairlee.
Lucius Robinson, Newport.
H. B. Smith, Milton.

NEW HAMPSHIRE.
Josiah Minot, Concord.
Daniel Marcy, Portsmouth.
Robert S. Webster, North Barnstead.
George W. Stevens, Dover.
Aaron P. Hughes, Nashua.
Edward W. Harrington, Manchester.
Alpheus F. Snow, Claremont.
Ansel Glover, Alstead.
William Burns, Lancaster.
George A. Bingham, Bath.

MASSACHUSETTS.
Caleb Cushing, Newburyport.
Jas. G. Whitney, Boston.
Oliver Stevens, Boston.
Isaac Davis, Worcester.
Wm. C. N. Swift, New Bedford.
Edward Merrill, New Bedford.
Phineas W. Leland, Fall River.
Alex. Lincoln, Hingham.
Orison Underwood, Milford.

Bradford L Wales, Randolph.
James Riley, Boston.
Isaac H Wright, Boston.
Cornelius Doherty, Boston.
K. S. Chaffee, East Cambridge.
E. G. Williams, Newburyport.
C. G. Clark, Lynn.
F. O. Prince, Winchester.
Geo. Johnson, Bradford.
Benj. F Butler, Lowell.
Walter Fessenden, Townsend.
Henry H Stevens, Dudley.
Geo. W. Gill, Worcester.
C. W Chapin, Springfield.
Josiah Allis, Whately.
D. N. Carpenter, Greenfield.
Charles Huebner, Lee.

CONNECTICUT.

James T Pratt, Rock Hill.
Samuel Arnold, Haddam
Andrew C. Lippitt, New London.
W. D. Bishop, Bridgeport.
A. G. Hasard, Enfield.
M. R. West, Stafford.
E. Aug Russell Middletown.
C. M. Ingersol, New Haven.
Wm. L. Converse, Norwich.
Rufus L. Baker, Windham.
James Gallagher, New Haven.
P. C. Calhoun, Bridgeport.

RHODE ISLAND.

Welcome D. Sayles, Providence.
Charles S Bradley, Providence.
George H. Browne, Providence.
John N. Francis, Providence.
Edward F. Newton, Newport.
Amasa Sprague Providence.
Gideon Bradford Providence.
Jacob Babbit, Bristol.

NEW YORK.

Dean Richmond, Buffalo.
Augustus Schell, New York city.
Isaac V. Fowler, New York city.
Delos DeWolf Oswego.
Wm. H Ludlow, Sayville.
Teunis G. Bergen, Bayridge.
H. McLaughlin, Brooklyn.
Francis H. Spinola, Brooklyn.
John Y Savage, New York city.
Wm. Miner, New York city.
Samuel L M Barlow, New York city.
John Claney, New York city.
Isaiah Rynders, New York city.
Edmund Driggs, Brooklyn.
John Cochrane, New York city.
Auguste B Imont New York city.
Nelson J Waterbury, New York city.
Wm. N. McIntyre, New York city.
Edward Cooper, New York city.
Samuel F. Butterworth, New York city.
Gouverneur Kemble, Cold Springs.
Edwin Crosswell, New York city.
Benjamin F. Edsall, Goshen.
John C. Holley, Monticello.
Wm. F. Russell, Saugerties
Geo. Beach Cairo
Theodore Miller Hudson.
Henry Staats, Red Hook.
David L Seymour, Troy.
Moses Warren, Troy.
Erastus Corning, Albany.
Peter Unger, Albany
John Titcomb, Waterford
Charles R Ingalls, Greenwich.
Lemuel Stetson, Plattsburgh.

Henry A. Tilden, New Lebanon.
James C. Spencer, Ogdensburg.
Lorenzo Carryl, Salisbury.
Alonzo C. Paige, Schenectady.
David Spraker, Canajoharie.
Samuel North, Unadilla
Alexander H. Burhans, Roxbury.
John S.ryker, Rome.
D. P Bissel, Utica.
Henry S. Randall, Cortlandville.
John F Hubbard, jr., Norwich.
Willard Johnson, Fulton.
Sidney T. Fairchild, Cazenovia.
D. C. West Lowville
Allen C. Beach, Watertown.
James P. Haskin Syracuse.
John J. Peck, Syracuse
Elmore P. Ross, Auburn.
John N. Knapp, Auburn.
Wm. W. Wright, Geneva.
Darius A Ogden, Penn Yan.
Henry D. Barto, Trumansburgh.
Charles Hulett, Horseheads.
C. C. B Walker, Corning.
A. J. Abbott, Genesee.
S. B. Jewett, Clarkson.
B. F. Gilkeson, Rochester.
Marshall B Champlain, Cuba.
Henry J. Glowacki, Batavia.
Sanford E Church, Albion.
A. H Eastman, Lockport.
John T. Hudson, Buffalo.
Alpheus Prince, Clarence.
John C. Devereux, Ellicottville.
H. J. Miner, Dunkirk.

NEW JERSEY.

William Wright, Newark.
Benjamin Williamson, Elizabeth.
James W. Wall (absent), Burlington.
John C Rafferty. New Germantown.
Samuel Hanna, Camden.
John L. Sharp, Millville.
George F. Fort, New Egypt.
David Naar, Trenton
Albert R. Speer, New Brunswick.
Joshua Doughty, Somerville.
Robert Hamilton, Newton.
John Husler, Hackensack.
Samuel Westcott, Jersey city.
Jacob Van Arsdale, Newark.

DELAWARE.

John H. Beverley, Smyrna.
William H Ross Seaford.
James A. Bayard, Wilmington.
John B Pennington, Dover.
William G Whitely, Newcastle.
William Saulsbury, Georgetown.

MARYLAND.

John Contee, Buena Vista.
William T. Hamilton, Hagerstown.
Levin Woolford, Princess Ann.
John R Emory, Centreville.
Wm. S Gittings, Baltimore city.
Samuel S Mallit, Elkton.
Carville S Stimsbury, Stemner's Run.
Wm. Byrne, Baltimore city
E L. F. Hardcastle, Royal Oak.
Daniel Field, Federalsburg.
Robert J Brent, Baltimore city.
T. M Lanahan, Baltimore city.
Bradley J Johnson, Frederick city.
John J Morrison, Barton.
Oscar Miles, Viestown.
William D Bowie, Prince George county.

VIRGINIA.

Arthur R. Smith, Portsmouth.
John J Kindred, Jerusalem.
Lewis E. Harvie, Chala.
Wm. F. Thompson, Crimea.
William H. Clark, Halifax Court House.
Walter Coles. Pittsylvania Court House.
Edmund W. Hubard, Curdsville.
Robert H. Glass, Lynchburg.
William L. Early, Madison Court House.
Robert A. Coghill, New Glasgow.
Walter D. Leake. Goochland Court House.
Jas. Hobbs, Manchester.
George Booker. Hampton.
M. W Fisher. Eastville.
Wm. A Buckner, Bowling Green.
Henry T Garnett, Oak Grove.
James Harbour, Brandy Station.
John Seddon, Fredericksburg.
John Blair Hoge. Martinsburg.
O. R. Funsten, White Post.
S. M. Yost, Staunton.
S. H. Moffatt, Harrisonburg.
Daniel H. Ho e. Blacksburg.
James W. Davis, Greenville Court House.
Robert L. Crockett, Wytheville.
William T. Cecil, Tazewell Court House.
Henry Fitzhugh. Kanawha Court House.
John Brannon, Weston.
William G. Brown, Kingwood.
Charles W. Russell, Wheeling.

NORTH CAROLINA.

William W. Avery, Morganton.
William S. Ashe, Wilmington.
Bedford Brown, Locust Hill.
William H. Holden. Raleigh.
William A. Moore, Edenton.
Nicholas M. Long, Weldon.
Robert R. Bridgers, Tarboro'.
Lotte W. Humphrey, Richland.
Walter L. Steele, Rockingham.
James Fulton, Wilmington.
Thomas S Green, Warrenton.
J. W B. Watson, Smithfield.
Robert P. Dick. Greensboro'.
Charles S. Winstead, Roxboro'.
Samuel Hargrave, Lexington.
Hampton B. Hammond, Wadesboro'.
William Landers, Lincolnton.
Columbus Mills, Columbus.
Henry T. Farmer, Flat Rock.

SOUTH CAROLINA.

James Simons, Charleston.
Samuel McGowan. Abbeville Court House.
H. B. Wilson, Georgetown.
R. B. Joylston, Winnsboro'.
J. H Witherspoon. Lancaster Court House.
E. W. Charles, Darlington Court House.
George N. Reynolds, Charleston.
Thomas Y. Simons, Charleston.
James Patterson, Barnwell Court House.
B. H Brown, Barnwell Court House.
Arthur Simpkins. Edgefield Court House.
Lemuel Boozer Lexington Court House.
B. F. Perry, Greenville.
J. P. Reid. Anderson Court House.
John S. Preston. Columbia.
Franklin Gaillard, Columbia.

GEORGIA.

Henry L. Benning, Columbus.
John H Lumpkin. Rome.
Isaiah T Irwin, Washington.
Henry R Jackson. Savannah.
Junius Wingfield Eatonton.
Hiram Warner, Greenville.

Solomon Cohen, Savannah.
James L Seward, Thomasville.
Julian Hartridge. Savannah.
W. B. Gaulden, Huntsville.
W. J. Johnson, Fort Gaines.
John A. Jones. Columbus.
James M. Clark, Lumpkin.
W. M. Slaughter. Albany.
E. L. Stroecker, Macon.
P. Tracy, Macon.
O. C. Gibson, Griffin.
E J. McGehee. Perry.
James J. Diamond Stone Mountain.
J. A. Render, Greenville.
Samuel C. Chandler, Carrollton.
G. J Fain, Calhoun
E. R. Hardin, Dalton.
James Hoge, Atlanta.
Mark Johnston, Cartersville.
William H. Hull, Athens.
George Hillyer, Monroe.
A. A. Franklin Hill, Athens.
Henry P. Thomas, Lawrenceville.
L. H. Brisco, Milledgeville.
Jeff. Lamar, Covington.
J. W. Burney, Monticello.
James Thomas, Sparta.
L. A. Nelms, ———
D. C. Barrow, Lexington.
H. Cleveland, Augusta.
H. R. Casey, Appling.

FLORIDA.

T. J. Eppes, Apalachicola.
John Milton, Marianna.
B. F. Wardlaw, Madison Court House.
C. E. Dyke, Tallahassee.
George L. Bowne, Key West.
James B. Owens, Ocala.

ALABAMA.

F. S. Lyon, Demopolis.
A. B. Meek Mobile.
D. W. Bayne, Hayneville.
W. L. Yancey, Montgomery.
L. A Lander, Talladega.
J. A. Winston, Mobile.
L P. Walker, Huntsville.
H. D. Smith, Graveley Springs
G. G. Griffin. Demopolis
N. H. R. Dawson. Selma.
R. G. Scott, Claiborne.
J W. Porter. Neggsvills.
L. L. Cato, Eufala.
T. J. Burnett, Greenville.
J. R. Breare. Newton.
M. J Bulger, Dadeville.
P. O. Harper. West Point.
J. C. B. Mitchell. Mount Meigs.
W. C. McIver, Tuskeegee.
John Erwin, Greensborough.
W. M. Brooks, Marion.
J. C. Guild, Tuscaloosa.
A. W. Dillard, Livingston.
F G Norman, Tuscumbia.
R. M. Patton, Florence.
W. C. Sherrod Courtland.
R. Chapman, Huntsville.
G. C. Bradley, Huntsville.
T. B. Cooper, Centre.
A. J. Henry. Guntersville.
T J. Bradford. Talladega.
W Garrett, Bradford.
P. G. King, Montevallo.

MISSISSIPPI.

W. S Barry, Columbus.
Charles Clarke, Prentiss.
E. Barksdale, Jackson.

W. S. Wilson, Port Gibson.
James Drane, Bankston.
Beverly Matthews, Columbus.
P. M. Thomson, Houston.
W. H H. Tison Carrollville.
Joseph R. Davis, Canton.
C. E. Hooker, Jackson.
J. T. Sims, Delta.
D. C. Glenn, Mississippi city.
Geo. H. Gordon, Woodville.

ARKANSAS.

J. P. Johnson, Laconia.
T B. Flournoy, Laconia.
N. Burrows, Van Buren.
F. A. Perry, Waverly Post Office.
Jno. J. Stirman, Dardanelle.
Jno. A Jordan, South Bend.
Van H. Manning, Hamburg.
F. W. Hoadley, Little Rock.

KENTUCKY.

G. A. Caldwell, Louisville.
D. P. White, Greensburg.
J. C. Mason, Owingsville.
R. K. Williams, Mayfield.
Wm. Bradley, Madisonville.
G. H. Morrow, Paducah.
Lafayette Green, Falls of Rough.
S. D. Greenfield, Hopkinsville.
G. T Wood, Munfordsville.
J. A. Finn, Franklin.
S. D. Field, Columbia.
John S. Kindrick, Somersett.
R. Spalding, Lebanon.
W B. Read, Hodgesville.
John Dishman, Barbourville.
Colbert Cecil, Piketon.
Wm. Garvin, Louisville.
S. E. Dehaven, LaGrange.
R. M. Johnson, White Sulphur.
J. B. Beck, Lexington.
N. Green, New Liberty.
R. McKee, Louisville.
H. D. Helm, Newport.
R. P. Butler, Carrolton.

TENNESSEE.

Andrew Ewing, Nashville.
John R. Howard, Lebanon.
J. D. C. Atkins, Paris.
Samuel Milligan, Greenville
Wm. Henry Maxwell, Jonesboro'.
John D. Riley, Rogersville.
Thomas M. Lyon, Knoxville.
W. E. B. Jones, Livingston.
George W. Rowles, Cleveland.
William Wallace, Maryville.
David Bunford, Dixon Springs.
James M. Sheid, Manchester.
John McGavock, Franklin.
James M. Avent, Murfreesboro'.
Robert Matthews, Shelbyville.
W. L. McClelland, Lewisburg.
Thomas W Jones, Pulaski.
W. C. Whitthorne, Columbia.
Alfred Robb, Clarksville.
Thomas Menees, Springfield.
Wm. H. Wall, Paris.
James Connor, Ripley.
Wm. H. Carrol, Memphis.
Samuel McClonahan, Jackson.

MISSOURI.

J. B. Henderson, Louisiana.
W. J W. McIlhany, St. Charles.
R. F. Lakeman, Hannibal.
O. A. Shortridge, Bloomington.
John B. Clark, Washington City, D. C.

Austin A. King, Richmond.
George P. Dorris, Platte city.
James Craig, St. Joseph.
Wm. Douglass, Boonville.
N. C. Claiborne, Kansas city.
P. S. Wilkes Springfield.
J. A. Scott, Elk Mills.
C. G. Corwin, Jefferson city.
J. F. Menee. Washington, Franklin county.
A. Hunter, Benton.
John O'Fallon, jr., Sulphur Springs.
John M. Krum, St Louis.
Sam. B. Churchill, St. Louis.

IOWA.

A. C. Dodge, Burlington.
B. M. Samuels, Dubuque.
D. O. Finch, Des Moines.
Wm. H. Merritt, Cedar Rapids.
T. W. Claggett, Keokuk.
J. W. Bosler, Sioux City.
E. H Thayer, Muscatine.
W. H. M. Pusey, Council Bluffs.

WISCONSIN.

John R. Sharpstein, Milwaukee.
Alex. S. Palmer, Geneva.
Alex. F. Pratt, Waukesha.
Wm. A. Barstow, Janesville.
James H. Earnest, Shulsburgh.
Charles Whipple, Eau Claire.
Perry H. Smith, Appleton.
Frederick W. Horn, Cedarburg.
Edward S. Bragg, Fond Du Lac.
John Fitzgerald, Oshkosh.

MINNESOTA.

W. A. Gormans, St. Paul.
George L. Becker, St. Paul.
Henry H Sibly, Mendota.
A. J. Edgerton, Mantorville.
A. M. Fridley, St. Anthony.
J. Travis Rosser, Mankato.
W. W. Phelps, Red Wing.

ILLINOIS.

S. S. Marshall. McLeansboro'.
O. B. Ficklin, Charleston.
W. A. Richardson, Quincy.
R. T. Merrick, Chicago.
Wm M. Jackson, Union.
John D. Platt, Warren.
John B. Turner, Chicago.
A. M. Herrington, Geneva.
Allen Withers, Bloomington.
R. E. Goodell, Joliet.
B. S. Prettyman, Pekin.
R. Holloway, Monmouth.
W. H. Rolleson, Dallas city.
James M. Campbell, Macomb.
Murry McCounell, Jacksonville.
Wm. F. Thornton, Shelbyville.
Aaron Shaw, Lawrenceville.
W. F. Linder, Chicago.
S. A. Buckmaster, Alton.
Z. Casey, Mount Vernon.
W J. Allen, Marion.
W. H. Green, Metropolis.

OHIO.

Geo. W. McCook, Steubenville.
Geo. E. Pugh, Cincinnati.
D. P. Rhodes, Cleveland.
Washington McLean, Cincinnati.
Henry B. Bowman, Cincinnati.
Charles Rule, Cincinnati.
Wesley M. Cameron, Cincinnati.
William T. Forrest, Cincinnati.
A. P. Miller, Hamilton.

George W. Houk, Dayton.
Sabirt Scott, St. Mary's.
Joshua Townsend, Greenville.
James B. Steedman, Toledo.
Wm. Mungen, Findlay.
J. B. Cockerill, West Union.
T. C. Kennedy, Batavia.
Durbin Ward, Lebanon.
W. M. Stark, Xenia.
George Spence, Springfield.
R. E. Runkle, West Liberty.
Edward F. Dickinson, Fremont.
Abner M. Jackson, Bucyrus.
Thomas McNalley, Chilicothe.
Wells A. Hutchins, Portsmouth.
Lot L. Smith, Athens.
E. F. Bingham, McArthur.
Wayne Griswold, Circleville.
Geo. B. Smith, Newark.
Thomas W Bartley, Mansfield.
John Tifft, Norwalk.
J. A. Marchand, Wooster.
J. P. Jeffries, Wooster.
J. G Stewart, Coshocton.
R. H. Nugen, Newcomerstown.
S. R. Hosmer, Zanesville.
W. W. Coues, Cincinnati.
J. S. Way, Woodsfield.
W. Eaton, Morristown.
S. Lahm, Canton.
S. D Harris, jr., Ravenna.
H. B. Payne. Cleveland.
J. W. Gray, Cleveland.
David Tod, Brier Hill.
D. B. Woods, Warren.
Thomas S. Woods, New Lisbon.
B. F. Potts, Carrollton.

INDIANA.

E. M Huntington, Terre Haute.
S. H Buskirk. Bloomington.
Robert Lowry, Goshen
James B Foley, Greensburgh.
John S. Gavitt, Evansville.
Smith Miller, Patoka
J. B Norman, New Albany.
S. K. Wolfe, Corydon.
P. C. Dunning, Bloomington.
H. W. Harrington, Madison.
J. V. Bemusdaffer, Greensburgh.
John Auderegg, Lawrenceburgh.
Lafe Devlin, Cambridge City.
Edmund Johnson, Newcastle.
W. H. Talbot, Indianapolis.
J. M Gregg, Danville.
E. Read, Terre Haute.
H. K. Wilson, Sullivan.
L. B. Stockton, Lafayette.
Isaac C. Ellston. Crawfordsville.
G. Hathaway, Lap rre.
S. A. Hall, Logansport.

P. Hoagland, Fort Wayne.
G. W. Mc'Connell, Angola.
Wm. Garver, Noblesville.
John R. Laffroth, Huntington.

LOUISIANA.

E. LaSere, New Orleans,
E. Lawrence, New Orleans.
F. H Hatch, New Orleans.
A. Talbot, Iberville
R. A. Hunter, Alexandria.
Richard Taylor. St. Charles Parish.
D D. Withers, New Orleans
John Tarlton, Bayou Bueff, St. Mary's Parish.
Charles Jones, Trinity.
B. W. Pearce, Sparta, Bienville Parish.]
A. Mouton, Vermilionville.
James A. McIIatton, Baton Rouge.

TEXAS.

H. R. Runnels, Boston.
E Greer, Marshall.
Thos P. Ochiltree, Marshall.
M. W. Covey, Jefferson.
F. R. Lubbock, Houston.
Guy M Bryan, Galveston.
Josiah F. Crosby, El Paso.
F. S. Stockdale, Port Lavaca.

MICHIGAN.

George V. N. Lothrop, Detroit.
Charles E. Stuart, Kalamazoo.
H. H. Riley, Constantine.
George W. Peck, Lansing.
Benj. Follett, Ypsilanti.
Fidus Livermore. Jackson.
John G. Parkhurst, Coldwater.
Philo Wilson, Canandaigua.
Franklin Muzzy, Niles.
Alex F. Bell, Detroit.
Augustus C Baldwin, Pontiac.
William S. Bancroft, Port Huron.

OREGON.

Lansing Stout, Washington, D. C.
J. R Lamerick, Jacksonville.
Isaac J. Stevens, Washington, D. C.
Justus Steinberger, Washington, D. C.
R. B Metcalfe, Independence, Texas.
A P. Dennison, The Dalles, Oregon.

CALIFORNIA.

J. Bidwell, Chico
G. W. Patrick, Sonora.
Lewis R Bradley. Stockton.
Austin E Smith, San Francisco.
John A Dreibelhis, Shasta.
John S. Dudley, Yreka.
John Rains, Los Angelos.
D. S. Gregory, Monterey.

2

FIRST DAY.

The opening Scenes—The Actors in the First Fight—John Cochrane—William A. Richardson—E. Barksdale—Walker of Alabama—Clark of Missouri—Butler of Massachusetts.

INSTITUTE HALL,
Charleston, S. C., April 23d.

The hour appointed for the meeting of the Convention was at twelve, M. About eleven a delightful shower came up, which was quite welcome, for the country has been suffering excessively from drouth, and the air was full of the hot dust of the streets. Orders were issued that the doors should not be opened until twelve o'clock. That hour has passed. The reporters are at their places, with piles of paper and bunches of pencils sharpened at both ends. A boy is waiting, ready to run to the telegraph office with dispatches. The delegates are pouring in and finding their places. About a dozen ladies occupy seats in the gallery, looking down with critical interest on the seething mass below. One-third of the space in the galleries is allotted to the ladies, and the remaining two-thirds to the outsiders, whose occupation is the manufacture of public opinion. Each delegation has a certain number of tickets for distribution among outsiders. They admit the holders into the gallery. The hall is far more spacious, better ventilated, and better arranged than that in which the Convention was held four years ago. The delegates are in groups all over the floor, talking and gesticulating as in all other conventions. The scene is very much like that in the Hall of the House of Representatives on the opening day of a session of Congress. The men who, by their position upon the Executive committee appointed at Cincinnati, have to initiate proceedings, are Judge Smalley, of Vermont, Chairman, and C. L. Vallandigham, Secretary. Judge Smalley arises and calls the Convention to order. He states the business of the Convention with the utmost simplicity, omitting, as was agreeable to every body, the opportunity afforded of making an "able and eloquent" speech. He calls for the nomination of a President, *pro tem.* Mr. Flournoy of Arkansas was nominated by McCook of Ohio. There was no opposition. A committee was appointed to escort him to the chair. He stated upon assuming the chair that he should exert himself to produce a speedy organization of that body. As an earnest of his intention to proceed to business, he sat down. Thus two opportunities to make speeches were irrevocably lost. Mr. Flournoy is a gentleman at least six feet two inches in height, and would weigh two hundred and thirty pounds. He is a splendid specimen of physical manhood, but is not troubled with too much brain. The next thing in order is a written sermon in the form of a prayer. Some portly, white-headed, red-faced and gold-spectacled parson, from the South, being called upon for a prayer, proceeds to recite one which he has written down and pasted in the cover of a book for the occasion. There are not ten men in the house who can hear what he says—and the fine, old, fat clergyman is pronounced an unmitigated bore. His solemn tone is worse than a stump speech would have been from the rostrum. In case of the speech we might have had a few rabble-rousing sentences. As it is we have only a noise that is in the usual intonation of prayer. A Virginia delegate arises and makes a nomination of temporary secretary.

It already appears that the hall is one in which it will be almost impossible to hear what is said. The street in front of the hall is paved with bowlders (Cincinnati fashion), and the incessant clatter of the wheels is deafening.

Mr. Fisher of Virginia tried to introduce a resolution, and to read before introducing that resolution. It was well understood that this was a resolution respecting the contested seats of New York. John Cochrane rose to a point of order. An Alabamian and a Mississippian pitched in. Fisher of Virginia appealed from the decision of the chair, who had ruled him out of order. The chair was sustained by a roaring aye. Another struggle took place as to which should be appointed first: the committee on Credentials or on Organization. The object of the ultra Southerners was to exclude Illinois and New York from the committee on Credentials and Organization. Richardson of Illinois, and Cochrane of New York, disclaimed any desire to participate in the committee on Credentials. They were not disposed, however, to give up their places in the committee on Organization. In the course of the struggle on this point, it became evident that the weight of the outsiders was for the Douglas delegation from Illinois, and the Cassidy, Richmond, Cagger, John Cochrane and Co. delegation from New York. At last the Convention came to a vote on a proposition that the committees on Credentials and Organization should be simultaneously appointed, the committeemen on Credentials from Illinois and New York not having authority to vote on the contested cases of their own States. The vote was taken by States. The proposition was affirmed, Virginia, Louisiana, Texas, Arkansas, Alabama, Mississippi, and half of California, voting no. Mr. Fisher of Virginia protested in behalf of his State against the record, because the vote of New York, the delegates' seats being contested, had been taken. A resolution was offered by a Mississippian, that the New York and Illinois delegations be requested not to take part in the proceedings until the committee on Credentials had reported, and the contests had been settled. Payne of Ohio moved to lay this resolution on the table. A vote was taken by States on Payne's motion, and it prevailed by a heavy majority. This is a vote which indicates that the Fernando Wood and Cook delegations will have to remain outside the Convention. Richardson of Illinois pronounced the contest in his State, the most frivolous and contemptible ever heard of. The committees were appointed, and the Convention adjourned. The noise of wheels on the streets was so great, that sawdust is to be heaped in front of the hall, to deaden the clamor.

The ultra-South was guilty of a very foolish thing to-day. They made a bitter fight on a question, when there was no possible chance of doing any thing. The Convention was against them six to one, and yet they struggled with as much energy as if they expected to accomplish something wonderful. In this way they lost prestige in the Convention. They threw themselves away without sufficient cause. If they continue this style of performance Douglas will be the nominee at last. I consider his chances augmented by the proceedings to-day. The Ike Cook and Fernando Wood movement was in the preliminary stages utterly overthrown. Several of the scenes of the fight were highly entertaining. Mr. Fisher, of Virginia, was picked out to make the onslaught. He is a slight gentleman, with a thin face and high, bald head, small voice on a high key, and more zeal than discretion. He was about to have a communication read, which every body knew was in reference to the New York contest, when a point of order was raised upon him by John Cochrane, of New York, who is the brains of the Cagger-Cassidy delegation, a man of high order of ability, an accomplished and forcible public speaker, an old bachelor, and a man of the world. He is perfectly at home in a parliamentary fight, and has a splendid voice, which in a noisy convention is a gift, when coupled with brass, of the highest value. Cochrane is a large but not a big man, full in the region of the vest, wears all his beard, which is coarse and sandy, trimmed short, and is bald—a blemish which he attempts to conceal by combing the hair that remains at the sides over the barren region. His countenance is bold, but not amiable, and there are assurances in his complexion that he is what is known as a generous liver. In fact, he looks as though it would require a very strong cup of coffee to bring him into condition in the morning. He is a fair type of the fast man of intellect and culture, of the city of New York, whose ambition is to figure in politics. He is in Congress, as most of our readers know, and can command the ear of the House at any time. His great trouble is his Free Soil Record. He had a very violent attack of Free Soil opinions some years ago. He took Free Soilism like a distemper, and mounted the Buffalo platform. He is well over it now, however, with the exception of a single heresy: that of the Homestead law. He is for giving homesteads to the actual settlers upon the public land. He appeared to much advantage in the Convention to-day, and his sonorous voice, imposing manner and parliamentary tactics told with great force.

Richardson of Illinois made one of his earnest-toned speeches, vindicating the Douglas delegation from Illinois. The Douglas men would not know what to do without him. From appearances, though there are several gentlemen ambitious to lead the Douglas forces in this war, Richardson will overbear them all. He is a large, coarse, powerful man, with a harsh but distinct voice that is heard above the clamor of a Convention, like a fire-bell over the clatter of engines in the street. He evidently felt that there was a critical time to-day, whether there was one or not, and was stalking up and down among the Douglas delegations, his forehead furrowed with heavy wrinkles, his face glowing, his shirt-collar wilted down, his coat-cuffs rolled half-way up to his elbows, a palm-leaf fan in his hand which he used spasmodically; and as he moved about, he pulled the wires here and there, encouraging this man to pitch in and that one to subside. When he spoke he commanded universal attention. And I venture to guess that whenever his broad shoulders, shaggy head and broad-axe nose is seen above the throng, and his voice is heard he will have attention, for he is the strong man of the Northwest, and a representative man, too. I remember well how he bore himself in the crisis of the Cincinnati Convention, when Buchanan having a majority vote, the dispatch from Douglas directed to Richardson was read, withdrawing his name. Richardson's behavior was very manly then. And now, if Douglas should get a majority vote, Richardson will revive the recollection of the scene which I have just mentioned, and demand the same consideration for Douglas that he showed Buchanan. It is likely that Buchanan would have been nominated at any rate, but the Douglas dispatch and Richardson's speech make up a precedent that the Douglasites will be happy to put to the Convention. It is doubtful, however, whether they ever get that far. They will, however, if the South does not behave better than she did to-day.

The spokesman of Mississippi was E. Barksdale, editor of the Mississippian, and brother of the Congressman. He is not so large a man as his brother, but has more brains. He is hardly up to the middle size, but is well put together, wiry, and active as a cat. He has not a good voice for a turbulent crowd, as it is rather sharp and wants body; but he is "game to the backbone," as they say. His face would indicate a man of unusual amiability, if it were not for the sarcasm in his smile, and a mischievous glimmer in his eye. He is, perhaps, the most fierce of the fire-eaters, but did not exhibit any very striking qualities as a tactician to-day.

The most conspicuous of those who resisted the current of the day was Walker of Alabama, a tall, gentlemanly man, with long pale face and high forehead, whose health is feeble, and who so exhausted himself in forcing the chair and the Convention to hear him, that he had not much to say when he had the ear of the Convention. He was determined not to be chocked down. At first he stood upon his chair, and the noise being so great that he could not be heard, he took a position in front of the seats on the vacant space between the Convention and the chair, and finally mounted the Secretary's desk near the platform upon which the chairman sits, and the Convention seeing that he would occupy the time until heard at every hazard, consented to hear him.

Clark of Missouri pushed himself into the fight, and seemed to have a mission to perform, which the Convention could not appreciate. He would have some qualities of a strong speaker if his words had not a way of becoming bungled in his mouth, and coming out in confusion, and in a mutilated condition. I imagine Clark had a notion that he would be able to save the fire-eaters from the blunder they were committing in making hopeless fight. But he was incapable of curbing them. Mr. Clark is the man who introduced the Helper book resolution into the House in December last, and to whom Helper sent a copy of his affectionate production, bound in Russia. A little old dapper, comical fellow from Pennsylvania, tried several times to " put in his jaw " when it was evident he had nothing to say, and would be incompetent to say any thing if he had occasion to do so. It may be improper to print profane language, but the desire which possesses me to give the spirit of this Convention, induces me to say that several heartless wretches said to the little old dapper gentleman : " G— d——

you, sit down "—and that such questions were put to him as, "What the hell do you want to talk for?"

All persons who attended the Cincinnati Convention, will remember the bald-headed and rampant Butler of Massachusetts. He is here. He springs to his feet with wonderful quickness, and rips out, "Mr. Chairman," in a tone like the sound of a file on a cross-cut saw, and with a gesture as if he proposed to stab the presiding officer, if he did not devote his attention instantly to "the gentleman from Massachusetts."

Butler was one of the Free Soil Democracy of Massachusetts, who elected, by a coalition with ultras, the Hon. Charles Sumner to the U. S. Senate. He, like John Cochrane, has repented. He is pro-slavery as possible, and the little, brown moustache under his sharp, crooked nose, would curl with wrath if he should be reminded of his record. He admits that he had a Free-soil attack—a sort of political measels—but considers himself all the better for having recovered from it.

Yancey of Alabama, the leader of the ultras, was evidently aware that his friends were doing a foolish thing to-day. He took no part in the squabble, but it is understood that he has a vast amount of ammunition for a bombardment of the Douglas castle, ready for use when the decks are cleared for action, and the occasion when it will be worth while to make a fight, shall have arrived.

The first vote taken by States was on a proposition submitted by Mr. Cessna of Pennsylvania, looking to the simultaneous appointment of the committees on Credentials and Organization, and providing that "in determining the controversy in regard to the disputed seats from the State of Illinois, the member of the committee on Credentials from that State shall not be permitted to vote thereon. And in determining the controversy from the State of New York, the member of the committee from that State shall not be permitted to vote thereon."

The vote stood:

States.	Yeas.	Nays.	States.	Yeas.	Nays.
Maine	8	0	Indiana	13	0
New Hampshire	5	0	Illinois	11	0
Vermont	5	0	Ohio	23	0
Massachusetts	13	0	Mississippi	0	7
Rhode Island	4	0	Texas	0	4
Connecticut	6	0	Florida	3	0
New Jersey	7	0	Tennessee	12	0
Pennsylvania	27	0	Kentucky	12	0
Delaware	3	0	Wisconsin	5	0
Maryland	8	0	Iowa	4	0
New York	35	0	Michigan	6	0
Virginia	0	15	Arkansas	0	4
North Carolina	10	0	California	2	2
South Carolina	8	0	Oregon	3	0
Georgia	10	0	Minnesota	4	0
Alabama	0	9			
Louisiana	0	6		256	47
Missouri	9	0			

And thus extreme Southernism (Cotton Stateism) first placed itself on the record of the Convention.

The committees appointed were as follows:
Committee on Credentials.—C. D. Jameson, Maine; A. P. Hughes, New Hampshire; Stephen Thomas, Vermont; Oliver Stephens, Massachusetts; George H. Brown, Rhode Island; James Gallagher, Connecticut; Delos De Wolfe, New York; A. R. Speer, New Jersey; H. M. North, Pennsylvania; Wm. G. Whiteley, Delaware; W. S. Gittings, Maryland; E. W. Hubbard, Virginia; R. R. Bridges, North Carolina; B. F. Perry, South Carolina; J. Hartridge, Georgia; W. M. Brooks, Alabama; W. S. Barry, Mississippi; F. H. Hatch, Louisiana; James B. Stedman, Ohio; G. T. Wood, Kentucky; W. H. Carroll, Tennessee; S. A. Hall, Indiana; W. J. Allen, Illinois; John M. Krum, Missouri; Van H. Manning, Arkansas; Benjamin Follett, Michigan; C. E. Dyke, Florida; E. Grier, Texas; D. O. Finch, Iowa; P. H. Smith, Wisconsin; John S. Dudley, California; H. H. Sibley, Minnesota; Lansing Stout, Oregon.
Committee on Organization.—W. H. Burrill, Maine; R. S. Webster, New Hampshire; H. E. Stoughton, Vermont; C. W. Chapin, Massachusetts; John N. Francis, Rhode Island; A. C. Lippett, Connecticut; S. F. Fairchild, New York; Robert Hamilton, New Jersey; J. Cessna, Pennsylvania; J. B. Pennington, Delaware; John R. Emory, Maryland; John Brannon, Virginia; W. A. Mole, North Carolina; B. H. Wilson, South Carolina; J. H. Lumpkin, Georgia; A. B. Meek, Alabama; Charles Clark, Mississippi; T. J. Eppes, Florida; Emile LaSere, Louisiana; F. R. Lubbock, Texas; John J. Stirman, Arkansas; S. D. Churchill, Missouri; T. M. Jones, Tennessee; C. Cecil, Kentucky; George W. Houk, Ohio; S. K. Wolf, Indiana; A. M. Harrington, Illinois; A. C. Baldwin, Michigan; E. S. Bragg, Wisconsin; E. H. Thayer, Iowa; J. T. Rosser, Minnesota; G. W. Patrick, California; John K. Lamerick, Oregon.

SECOND DAY.

MORNING SESSION.

INSTITUTE HALL, April 24th.

There is an impression prevalent this morning that the Convention is destined to explode in a grand row. The best informed and most dispassionate men are unable to see how such a termination of this party congress can be avoided. The Southern delegates last night, in caucus assembled, resolved to stand by the Jeff. Davis resolutions. There is tumult and war in prospect. The first thing in order after calling the Convention to order, was the report of the committee on Permanent Organization, made by Mr. Cessna of Pennsylvania, its chairman, as follows:

FOR PRESIDENT:
Hon. CALEB CUSHING, of Mass.

FOR VICE-PRESIDENTS AND SECRETARIES.

Maine.
Vice-President—Thomas D. Robinson.
Secretary—C. Record.

New Hampshire.
Vice-President—Daniel Marcy.
Secretary—George A. Bingham.

Vermont.
Vice-President—Jasper Rand.
Secretary—P. W. Hyde.

Massachusetts.
Vice-President—Isaac Davis.
Secretary—B. F. Watson.

Rhode Island.
Vice-President—Gideon Bradford.
Secretary—Amasa Sprague.

Connecticut.
Vice-President—Samuel Arnold.
Secretary—M. R. West.

New Jersey.
Vice-President—Wm. Wright.
Secretary—John C. Rafferty.

New York.
Vice-President—Erastus Corning.
Secretary—Edward Cooper.

Pennsylvania.
Vice-President—Thomas Cunningham.
Secretary—Franklin Vansant.

Delaware.
Vice-President—W. H. Ross.
Secretary—John H. Buley.

Maryland.
Vice-President—W. P. Bowie.
Secretary—E. L. F. Hardcastle.

Virginia.
Vice-President—O. R. Funston.
Secretary—Robert H. Glass.

North Carolina.
Vice-President—Bedford Brown.
Secretary—L. W. Humphrey.

South Carolina.
Vice-President—B. H. Brown.
Secretary—Franklin Gaillard.

Georgia.
Vice-President—James Thomas.
Secretary—J. J. Dimond.

Alabama.
Vice-President—R. G. Scott.
Secretary—N. H. R. Dawson.

Mississippi.
Vice-President—James Drane.
Secretary—W. H. H. Tyson.

Louisiana.
Vice-President—R. Taylor.
Secretary—Charles Jones.

Ohio.
Vice-President—David Todd.
Secretary—W. M. Stark.

Kentucky.
Vice-President—B. Spalding.
Secretary—Robet McKee.

Tennessee.
Vice-President—J. O. C. Atkins.
Secretary—John R. Howard.

Indiana.
Vice-President—Isaac C. Elston.
Secretary—Lafayette Devlin.

Illinois.
Vice-President—Z. Casey.
Secretary—R. E. Goodell.

Arkansas.
Vice-President—Francis A. Terry.
Secretary—F. W. Hoadley.

Michigan.
Vice-President—H. H. Riley.
Secretary—John G. Parkhurst.

Florida.
Vice-President—B. F. Wardlaw.
Secretary—C. E. Dyke.

Texas.
Vice-President—H. R. Runnels.
Secretary—Thomas P. Ochiltree.

Missouri.
Vice-President—Abraham Hunter.
Secretary—J. T. Meuse.

Iowa.
Vice-President—T. W. Claggett.
Secretary—J. W. Bosler.

Wisconsin.
Vice-President—Frederick W. Horn.
Secretary—A. F. Pratt.

California.
Vice-President—J. A. Dreibelbis.
Secretary—John S. Dudley.

Minnesota.
Vice-President—W. W. Phelps.
Secretary—G. T. Rosser.

Oregon.
Vice-President—A. P. Denison.
Secretary—R. P. Metcalf.

The committee further recommended that the rules and regulations adopted by the National Democratic Conventions of 1852 and 1856 be adopted by this Convention for its government, with this additional rule:

"That in any State which has not provided or directed by its State Convention how its vote may be given, the Convention will recognize the right of each delegate to cast his individual vote."

This was a Douglas dodge, to allow minorities in Pennsylvania and other States, in which the anti-Douglas men were in the majority, to vote for the Little Giant. The war at once raged along the whole line.

Richardson of Illinois defended the report of the committee, as follows:

Mr. Richardson, of Illinois. "If I propose to go into an inquiry of what was done by the committee, it might be proper to say that the proposition now submitted was acted upon in a fuller meeting, as I am told, than that of last night, and adopted unanimously. I do not propose to discuss with the gentleman from Mississippi the subject as to the action of the committee. I propose to place it upon the basis of its own merits. Where a State Convention has met and instructed its delegation as a unit, and they have accepted the condition, they are bound by it. Wherever they give no such instruction, wherever they have refused in State delegation to give such instruction, it is proper to place the right of the delegate upon the broad and distinct ground of right. But where they have entered into an organization, and are pledged, they are not at liberty to overrun the expressed wishes and will of their constituents. But I propose to place the question of individuality upon the broad ground of right, and right alone. [Applause.] I say upon that ground the report of the committee ought to be adopted."

Texas, Mississippi, Illinois and Pennsylvania were heard on this subject. Randall of Pennsylvania made a speech, in which he said he would not go for any candidate who was not acceptable to a majority of the South. He also hinted that Douglas was the weakest man whose name was before the Convention. Richardson, of Illinois, said it might be interesting to inquire how long the gentleman had been a member of the Democratic party. The fight was understood to be a fair and square one between the Douglas and anti-Douglasites. It was thrust into the Convention before its premanent organization, because Flournoy, the chairman, was favorable to the Douglasites. The chair, however, blundered, and twisted, and twisted, and got his precedents tied into several hard knots. Richardson held the floor, though about twenty points of order were raised upon him. He was, however, allowed to proceed. He made a speech which was not called for, and which was injurious to the Douglas faction. He referred, in the midst of his heat, to Mr. Randall as one of the recruits of yesterday, and to himself as an old soldier in the cause. He wanted the raw recruits to tarry awhile at Jericho, until their beards were grown, before they instructed him, an old soldier. Mr. Randall was highly excited, and offered Richardson his card, indicating that he would hold him personally responsible. At this demonstration there was hissing about the hall. The war proceeded. Wright, of Pennsylvania, made a long speech. The chair finally decided that the question on the adoption of the report was divisible, and put the question as to the adoption of so much of the report as related to the organization exclusively. That part of the report was then adopted, and the permanent officers installed. This decision of the chair was really a sort of blunder. Mr. Flournoy being anxious to get out of the chair, allowed himself to defeat the purposes of his friends.

Before leaving the chair Mr. Flournoy uncorked a speech—the memorable passages of which were references to "eternal icebergs and everlasting frosts"—and the following gigantic effort on the Mississippi:

"The great father of waters, the river which commences at its source in the mountains, in springs and streams so small, that a hunter would scarcely widen his steps to cross them. But, running on, it mingles with other streams; yet so shallow that the mother duck can scarcely swim her fallow young in its waters. Then rolling onward, it mingles with yet other streams, until, at last, it forms the great Mississippi River—so deep and so vast that all the navies of the world could ride in safety upon its waters."

Mr. Flournoy introduced Mr. Cushing, who was received with warm applause, though the Douglas men dislike him intensely. They would not needlessly offend him, as they have to do the best they can with him. While they may have the bulk of the Convention, they have not a majority of the States, and were consequently defeated in committee.

The interest to hear the speech of Mr. Cushing was intense. Outsiders had been admitted until all the galleries and spaces not covered by chairs on the floor were densely filled. When Mr. Cushing was introduced he seemed for the moment slightly nervous, and in a heat. He was dressed in a short, brown, sack coat, grey pants, and black satin vest. Considering the amount of intellectual labor he has performed, he seems in a remarkably fine state of preservation. He is partially bald, but not at all gray. Such hair as he possesses has the gloss of youth and bear's grease. He uses a plain eye-glass, suspended about his neck by a black ribbon. His hands are brown as a laborer's. He evidently preserves himself by out-door exercise. His head is round and lofty; the forehead high and full; nose straight and sharp; lips thin and expressive of intellectual consciousness and pluck, and his face shows very few wrinkles. His voice is clear, musical, and powerful; every syllable of his speech was heard in every part of the house. The Convention is fortunate in having a presiding officer so accomplished.

The following is Mr. Cushing's speech, as officially reported:

"*Gentlemen of the Convention:* I respectfully tender to you the most earnest expression of profound gratitude for the honor which you have this day done me in appointing me to preside over your deliberations. It is, however, a responsible duty imposed, much more than a high honor conferred. In the discharge of that duty, in the direction of business and of debate, in the preservation of order, it shall be my constant endeavor faithfully and impartially to officiate here as your minister, and not humbly to reflect your will. In a great deliberative assembly like this, it is not the presiding officer in whom the strength resides. It is not *his* strength, but *yours*—your intelligence, your sense of order, your instinct of self-respect. I rely, gentlemen, confidently upon you, not upon myself, for the prompt and parliamentary dispatch of the business of this Convention.

"Gentlemen, you have come here from the green hills of the Eastern States—from the rich States of the imperial centre—from the sun-lighted plains of the South—from the fertile States of the mighty basin of the Mississippi—from the golden shores of the distant Oregon and California—[loud cheers]—you have come hither in the exercise of the highest functions of a free people, to participate, to aid in the selection of the future rulers of the Republic. You do this as the representatives of the Democratic party—of that great party of the Union, whose proud mission it has been, whose proud mission it is, to maintain the public liberties—to reconcile popular freedom with constituted order—to maintain the sacred, reserved rights of the sovereign States—[loud and long-continued applause]—to stand, in a word, the perpetual sentinels on the outposts of the Constitution. [Cries of "that's the talk," and loud cheers.] Ours, gentlemen, is the motto inscribed on that scrool in the hands of the monumental statute of the great statesman of South Carolina, "Truth, Justice, and the Constitution." [Loud cheers.] Opposed to us are those who labor to overthrow the Constitution, under the false and insidious pretense of supporting it; those who are aiming to produce in this country a permanent sectional conspiracy—a traitorous sectional conspiracy of one half the States of the Union against the other half; those who, impelled by the stupid and half insane spirit of faction and fanaticism, would hurry our land on to revolution and to civil war; those, the branded enemies of the Constitution, it is the part —the high and noble part of the Democratic party of the Union to withstand; to strike down and to conquer! Aye! that is our part, and we will do it. In the name of our dear country, with the help of God, we will do it. [Loud cheers.] Aye, we *will* do it, for, gentlemen, we will not distrust *ourselves;* we will not despair of the genius of our country; we will continue to repose with undoubting faith in the good Providence of Almighty God. [Loud applause.]

"Gentlemen, I will not longer detain you from the important business of the Convention. Allow me a few moments for the purpose of completing the arrangements with the elected officers of the Convention, and then the chair will call upon you for such motions and propositions as may be in order before the Convention." [Applause.]

After the speech, some time was occupied in arranging the duties of the various clerks, so as to proceed with system and order, to business. Cushing had the good sense, while this was going on, to give the Convention a recess.

The business first in order was the test struggle on the proposed amendment of the rules which had been incorporated into the report of the committee on Permanent Organization, but which had been gotten rid of for a time by the division of the question.

A motion was made to strike out from the report of the committee on Organization the original rule, and the vote was called by States, resulting as follows:

States.	Yeas.	Nays.	States.	Yeas.	Nays.
Maine	0	8	Mississippi	7	0
New Hampshire	0	5	Texas	4	0
Vermont	0	5	Arkansas	4	3½
Massachusetts	0	5½	Missouri	2	7
Rhode Island	0	4	Tennessee	0	12
Connecticut	0	6	Kentucky	0	12
New York	0	35	Ohio	0	23
New Jersey	0	7	Indiana	0	13
Pennsylvania	14	10½	Illinois	0	11
Delaware	1½	1½	Michigan	0	6
Maryland	3½	4½	Wisconsin	0	5
Virginia	15	—	Iowa	0	4
North Carolina	7	3	Minnesota	0	4
South Carolina	8	0	California	2½	1½
Georgia	10	0	Oregon	3	0
Florida	6	0			
Alabama	9	0		101	198
Louisiana	6	0			

This vote is tolerably near a correct representation of the strength of Mr. Douglas, in the last analysis of the Convention, by the final struggle. The nays, those opposed to striking out the interpolation, are not all for Douglas now, by any means. Many of them are against him, so far as to have some other first choice. But they may, under the pressure that will come, be brought to vote for him. And we may add to them the vote of South Carolina. It is too soon yet for the delegation from that State to show its hand. To avoid scandal, it voted with the South, but it is of the Softs of South Carolina.

The conclusions which I draw from this vote are very sturdily disputed here by the anti-Douglas men. And the New Yorkers and Kentuckians say they meant no such thing as I say. The first choice of Kentucky is Mr. Guthrie, and her second, Breckenridge,—but a majority of her delegates would acquiesce in the nomination of Douglas, and might, under pretext of saving the nation, vote for him in an extremity, to give him a two-thirds vote. And John Cochrane will lead the New Yorkers into the Douglas camp, the moment he can do so with the greatest eclat, and make sure of giving him the nomination. Then John will expect the grateful recognition of Mr. Douglas if he should become President. Douglas might, of course, afford to give the English mission for the vote of New York in this Convention, and enough besides of Federal fatness to buy thirty politicians of easy virtue.

Poor Lafe Develin of Indiana gave one shriek for freedom to-day. He is hedged about by his colleagues, and iron-bound by the instructions of the State Convention of Indiana, that her delegation should vote there as an unit. Lafe has insisted that he would not be bound by State instructions, but I believe that in an "unguarded moment" he voted in the Indiana Convention for the unity of the Charleston delegation. Lafe's zeal cooled, when Buchanan appointed the grandfather of the English bill U. S. Marshal of Indiana. But to-day he could not stand it, and shrieked loudly that he was authorized to cast two votes from Indiana. But he was put down. He fell in his tracks, as it were, and Freedom shrieked when Lafayette Develin fell. A portion of the Tennessee delegation squirmed at the vote thrown as above.

Nearly half the delegation were determined to vote the other way, but the majority ruled.

There are a large number of gentlemen here from Kentucky, working for John C. Breckenridge. Among them are Senator Powell, Gov. Magoffin, Burnet (Congressman), Preston, Minister to Spain, and others of distinction. But the Kentucky delegation stands firm for old Ironsides, that is to say, James Guthrie.

The following committee was reported to-day:

Committee on Resolutions and Platform—Maine, A. M. Roberts; New Hampshire, Wm. Beven; Vermont, E. M. Brown; Massachusetts, B. F. Butler; Rhode Island, C. S. Bradley; Connecticut, A. G. Hazard; New York, Ed. Cogswell; New Jersey, Benj. Williamson; Pennsylvania, A. B. Wright; Delaware, J. A. Bayard; Maryland, B. S. Johnson; Virginia, J. Barbour; North Carolina, W. W. Avery; South Carolina, J. S. Preston; Georgia, J. Wingfield; Florida, J. B. Owens; Alabama, John Erwin; Louisiana, H. A. Hunter; Mississippi, E. Barksdale; Texas, F. S. Stockdale; Arkansas, N. B. Burrow; Missouri, ———; Tennessee, Sam. Milligan; Kentucky, R. K. Williams; Ohio, H. B. Payne; Indiana, P. C. Dunning; Illinois, O. B. Ficklin; Michigan, G. V. N. Lothrop; Wisconsin, A. S. Palmer; Iowa, B. M. Samuels; Minnesota, J. M. Cavanaugh; California, Austin E. Smith; Oregon, James J. Stevens.

COMMENTARY ON SECOND DAY'S PROCEEDINGS.

CHARLESTON, S. C., April 24th (at night).

The advantages gained by the Douglas men in the Convention to-day were important, and will, in my judgment, certainly result in Mr. Douglas receiving a majority of the votes in the Convention. Then the struggle to give him two-thirds will be tremendous, and in spite of the bitter opposition of the ultra South, and of the Administration, President, Cabinet, and Senators, he may get two-thirds, and it is my present impression that he will. The friends of Douglas have not only the strongest compact body of delegates, but have thus far displayed the best tactics. The South has been not only divided in counsel but deficient in judgment. The current has run steadily for Douglas from the first. It was apparent several days ago, that the outside pressure was for him. Every Southern man of any force, who is for Douglas, though in a small minority at home, and repudiated by the Conventions, has been summoned here to manufacture public opinion. This has been done calculatingly and systematically, and has its effect. There are men here from every Southern State, working directly or indirectly for Douglas. The first gain of the Douglasites was in the action of Judge Smalley, in admitting the Cagger, Cassidy, Richmond, and Cochrane New York delegation, and the Douglas Illinois delegation to seats, and excluding Fernando Wood, Ike Cook, and their followers.

The next gain was in the confirmation of this action of the Executive committee, by the Convention yesterday, which was not so important in itself, as in the weakness of the ultra South exposed by it. The great gain to-day was in passing a rule allowing single delegates in

States not instructed to vote as an unit, to vote as they please. This will add about twenty-five votes to the Douglas strength—and will give the current which is running toward his nomination greater impetuosity and more formidable power. There is a great deal in this current, in a Convention in which, as in this, the mere politicians largely predominate. There are many eager to make themselves conspicuous in the eyes of the man upon whom they look as the next President. He has offices within his gift, foreign missions—and all that. You know how it is—you know how it was in the Cincinnati Convention.

There are several Southern States whose delegations are "unsound." Even the Alabama delegation contains two Douglas men. They have to vote with the rest, but their presence is influential. The ultras of South Carolina, standing upon their dignity, did not go into the Convention for the nomination of delegates to the National Convention. Their virtue was superior to the blandishments of a National caucus. The consequence is, Mr. Orr, whose position I detailed you in another letter, comes here with the vote of the State in his hand—and I am now convinced that Douglas can get it whenever it would give him the nomination. The New Yorkers, of both factions—and Fernando Wood has no chance—are purchasable. Some of the delegates are government officers, but the last sands of this administration are running out, and its displeasure is no longer feared. The eyes of Federal gold worshipers are turned to the coming man, and when Douglas can be nominated by the vote of New York, he will get it. And so of other States. But there will be a rupture. There is a portion of the South, as represented here, that cannot and will not submit to Douglas on a platform that tolerates the notion of "Popular Sovereignty." A great battle is to be fought on the platform. It is, I believe, as I write, being fought in the committee on Resolutions. There are radical and inextinguishable feuds in the Democratic party, and they must come out here and now.

THIRD DAY.

INSTITUTE HALL,
Charleston, S. C., April 25th.

There was much noise and confusion about town last night. The Southern men kept up their spirits by aid of a band of music, and speeches by the leaders of the fire-eaters. The speakers were very severe on the "bobtailed pony from Illinois. Fernando Wood was serenaded, and made an able and adroit response, which was entirely acceptable to the South. He was looking forward to an explosion of the Convention, and his nomination as Vice-President by the Southern leaders. It is the general impression this morning, as I have just informed you by telegraphic dispatch, that there will be an explosion of the Convention—that it is indeed inevitable, and that the Convention is only held together now by endeavors of the various factions, which are irreconcilably hostile, to make a record suitable for their ulterior purposes.

The hall is very much crowded. Those who have tickets, send them out after they get in, and others come in. In this way every body who understands the trick, and nearly every body does, gets in. So there is an infernal crowd. Fortunately the atmosphere is much cooler than heretofore. The ladies have become anxious on the subject of the Convention. Their gallery is as full as possible, and still crowds of them are besieging the stairways.

The Convention was opened with prayer, which is presumed to have been very solemn and fervent, but nobody heard it.

The first thing in order was to inquire whether there was any committee ready to report. There being none, the unfinished business of yesterday was taken up. This was in relation to the adoption of a rule that, in debate, no delegate should speak more than once, nor more than fifteen minutes.

Proceedings were interrupted by a gallant gentleman from Missouri, who proposed to relieve the ladies who were "hanging on the stairways." The Convention invited the ladies to come in and take seats in the chairs under the galleries.

The immoderately anxious Douglas men wanted the fifteen minute rule adopted. They were too anxious to put down the screws, however, and were defeated. The vote was 121 for the fifteen minute rule, and 182 against. Now, according to the rules adopted—being those of the House of Representatives—the hour rule is in force.

The vote as taken by States stands as follows—not a test for or against Douglas—but a test of prudence:

States.	Yeas.	Nays.	States.	Yeas.	Nays.
Maine	8	0	Mississippi	0	7
New Hampshire	0	5	Texas	0	4
Vermont	0	5	Arkansas	0	4
Massachusetts	0	13	Missouri	9	0
Rhode Island	0	4	Tennessee	12	0
Connecticut	1	5	Kentucky	11	1
New York	0	35	Ohio	0	23
New Jersey	7	0	Indiana	13	0
Pennsylvania	27	0	Illinois	11	0
Delaware	3	0	Michigan	6	0
Maryland	0	8	Wisconsin	5	0
Virginia	0	15	Iowa	4	0
North Carolina	0	10	Minnesota	0	4
South Carolina	0	8	California	4	0
Georgia	0	10	Oregon	0	3
Florida	0	3			
Alabama	0	9		121	182
Louisiana	0	6			

It is a general remark that the Convention has narrowly escaped doing a very foolish thing. It would have been unsafe to have choked down debate into fifteen minute speeches. It would not do to bottle up wrath so intense. It is now hoped that the South's fire will pale in long speeches, and become ineffectual in the course of their hour harangues. A debate followed, on the propriety of gag laws. It was said, on behalf of the South, that eloquence must be resorted to. The State of Alabama must not be gagged. Her eloquence must be allowed to flow. Lowry of Indiana thought it a very equivalent compliment to the delegates, to suppose that much talk would move any of them from their convictions. As for eloquence, on such occasions, it was too prone to degenerate into invective.

It was contended by a delegate from Delaware, that the hour rule, under the operation of the previous question, would be the most horrible of gags. After a free interchange of views, the fifteen minute rule was adopted, with this proviso, that the rule should not be applied in discussions on the platform. The speakers will each be allowed an hour to ventilate the Territorial question. This is about the best thing that could be done. A conversation sprung up between Walker of Missouri, and Cochrane, pending a motion to open the galleries to the public. Walker informed the ladies that Mr. Cochrane was a bachelor. The information was received with immense approbation. Cochrane acknowledged his desperate condition, and expressed his willingness to enter into the marriage relation. Walker said that it was apparent that the reason why Cochrane had not married was because he could not. He moved to lay the New York bachelor on the table. The Chair tolerated this nonsense for some time, but at last interposed, and summarily shut down upon it. Mr. Vallandigham made an explanation of the action of the Executive committee regarding the issue of tickets, which was satisfactory. The Convention then refused to throw open the doors to the miscellaneous public.

There was now no business before the Convention, the committee on Credentials not being able to report—the Convention adjourned to four o'clock, when the New York fight will come off. It will be warm, and loud and long. A considerable majority of the Convention will be in favor of excluding the Fernando Wood and Ike Cook delegations.

The Convention is most fortunate in having so excellent a presiding officer as Caleb Cushing. Mr. Cushing's head is wonderfully clear, and his knowledge of parliamentary law—and the rules of the House of Representatives—perfect. All his statements of the questions that are before the house, are distinct and downright, and no one thinks, as yet, of taking an appeal from his decisions. This will help the Convention materially in its great tribulation.

More intense interest than has yet prevailed is felt in the forthcoming New York fight. This will consume the afternoon session, and to-morrow we will have the platform fight, and I do not see how it will be possible to prevent a disruption of the Convention. The South makes it a point of honor that the platform shall not be one capable of a double construction, but shall be one which cannot be fairly interpreted to mean any thing short of "sound Southern doctrine," that is, the protection of slave property in the Territories, and the unequivocal repudiation of the Douglas doctrine of squatter, or popular sovereignty. The Northern delegates don't care much about the honor of the matter. It is of the most grave consequence to them, involving, as I have before said, for them, the issues of life and death. Their political existence depends absolutely upon their ability to construe the platform adopted here to mean "popular sovereignty," in other words, upon such a form of words in the platform, as will allow them to declare, in the North, that the officially expressed Democratic doctrine is that the people of the Territories may, while in their territorial condition, abolish or exclude slavery. They cannot, dare not yield the opportunity for pressing this pretext. The South will not allow it. Here, then, is the "irrepressible conflict" —a conflict between enduring forces. You may with propriety use, respecting it, language as strong as that of Mr. Seward in his Rochester speech. The Douglas Democracy, you know, only want the pretext to use before the people. They are willing to acquiesce in the decision of the Supreme Court, knowing beforehand that the decision would be against them. The South stands upon what they believe to be principle, and they cannot in honor, as they say, allow the Northern branch of the party to yield so far to the Abolition pressure, as to take refuge from it under a false and fraudulent pretense.

The preponderant faction of the Northern Democracy say the Southern doctrine of protection of slave property in the Territories is "inadmissible"—that is the word—and I believe they have, when the pinch comes, a majority of the Convention. The South says a platform with two faces is no longer tolerable. And the South has in this position a majority of the States. There is a majority in the committee on Platform in favor of amending the Cincinnati Platform so as to repudiate its Northern interpretation. The States of Pennsylvania, Oregon and California, as here represented, are with the South in this matter. The inevitable consequence is, there will be two reports from the committee on Platform. The majority report, favored by a minority of the Convention—and the minority report, favored by the majority. Upon the adoption of the Cincinnati Platform, with its "popular sovereignty heresy" understood to be attached, and constituting its vitality, the South must withdraw. At least half a dozen States will certainly go, and how many more, and how many fragments of others, it is impossible to say. Then the majority Convention will nominate Douglas. The South will be sustained in its secession by the whole power of the Administration, and by the Southern Senators, who would be murdered, politically, by the nomination of Douglas in a full Convention, upon a platform on which it would be possible for him to stand.

When it was determined yesterday, as it was by an overwhelming vote, to adopt a platform before nominating a candidate, it appeared that there was no hope remaining of the unity of the Convention. Both factions voted to have the platform first. The only possible way to keep the Convention together from the start, was for the Douglas men to withdraw his name; and then the South, with another man, would have been willing to mitigate the asperities of the slave code platform. The disruption of this Convention insures the nomination of Seward at Chicago—but not his election. Southern secession here, would give Douglas strength in some of the Northern States. There would be no possibility of his election, however, for he would certainly lose several Southern States. He might, and the chances are that he would, carry Northern States enough to defeat the election of Seward. Thus the election would be thrown into Congress—and eventually into the Senate. This is beyond question the game of the Southern men, and it looks as if the chances were that it would win. These are not only my opinions and speculations here to-day, but they are such as are current among those who are candid with themselves and frank in giving expression to their views.

AFTERNOON SESSION.

After some immaterial controversy,

Judge Krum of Missouri, chairman of the committee on Credentials, presented the following report and resolutions, upon which the committee had agreed, and he claimed for it the attention of the Convention:

MAJORITY REPORT.

To the National Democratic Convention:

MR. PRESIDENT :—Your committee on Credentials, immediately after their appointment, entered upon the discharge of the duties assigned them, and carefully examined the credentials of the several delegates to this Convention.

Your committee find that all the States of the Union, except the States of Massachusetts, Maryland, Illinois and New York are represented in this Convention by delegates duly elected in the several States by State or District organizations of the Democratic party, and your committee append to this report, as a part thereof, full lists of the delegates so selected.

Your committee further report that there were contesting claimants to the seats held by the delegations in the following cases, viz :
In the Fifth Congressional District of Massachusetts.
In the Fourth Congressional District of Maryland.
In the State of Illinois, and—
In the State of New York.

The contestants in these several cases had a full and impartial hearing before your committee, and, after a full consideration of their respective claims, your committee are of opinion that the sitting delegates in these Districts and States are justly entitled to their respective seats.

All of which is respectfully submitted,
JOHN M. KRUM, Chairman.

Resolved, That the sitting delegates to this Convention from the State of Illinois, of whom Col. W. A. Richardson is chairman, are entitled to their respective seats.

Resolved, That Cornelius Doherty and K. S. Chappee, delegates representing the Fifth Congressional District of Massachusetts, are entitled to their respective seats.

Resolved, That F. M. Landham and Robert J. Brent, delegates representing the Fourth Congressional District of Maryland, are entitled to their respective seats.

Resolved, That the delegates to this Convention from the State of New York, of which Dean Richmond is chairman, are entitled as such to seats therein.

Adopted.

Mr. Brooks, of Alabama, presented the following Minority Report and Resolutions:

MINORITY REPORT.

To the Honorable President of the National Democratic Convention:

The undersigned, members of the committee on Credentials, under an imperious sense of duty, are constrained to dissent from the report of the majority of this committee, and respectfully recommend that the two delegations from the State of New York be authorized to select each thirty-five delegates, and that the seventy Delegates thus selected be admitted to this Convention as the delegates of the New York Democracy, and that they be allowed two hours to report their selection—the two delegates to vote separately, each to be entitled to

seventeen votes, the remaining vote of said State to be cast alternately by the two delegations, the sitting members casting it the first time.
(Signed) WILLIAM M. BROOKS,
Delegate from Alabama.
JOHN S. DUDLEY,
Delegate from California.
E. GREEN,
Delegate from Texas.
VAN H. MANNING,
Delegate from Arkansas.
JULIAN HARTRIDGE,
Delegate from Georgia.
W. S. BARRY,
of Mississippi.

Mr. Brooks of Alabama offered the following resolution:

Resolved, That the two delegations from New York be authorized to select each thirty-five delegates, and that the seventy Delegates thus selected, be admitted to this Convention as delegates from the New York Democracy, and that they be allowed two hours to report their selection. The two delegations to vote separately, each to be entitled to seventeen votes, the remaining vote to be cast alternately by the two delegations—the sitting members to cast it the first time.

A discussion followed in which New York politics were well ventilated.

Then the several resolutions reported by the majority were adopted, down to the resolution on the New York case.

The question then being on the amendment of Mr. Brooks of Alabama, the State of Alabama called for the vote by States, and the State of Mississippi seconded the call.

The amendment was lost by the following vote:

States.	Yeas.	Nays.	States.	Yeas.	Nays.
Maine	0	8	Mississippi	7	0
New Hampshire	0	5	Texas	4	0
Vermont	0	5	Arkansas	3	1
Massachusetts	0	13	Missouri	1	8
Rhode Island	0	4	Tennessee	9	3
Connecticut	0	6	Kentucky	0	12
New York	0	0	Ohio	0	23
New Jersey	0	7	Indiana	0	13
Pennsylvania	0	27	Illinois	0	11
Delaware	0	3	Michigan	0	6
Maryland	0	8	Wisconsin	0	5
Virginia	3½	10	Iowa	0	4
North Carolina	5	4	Minnesota	0	4
South Carolina	0	8	California	3½	½
Georgia	10	0	Oregon	0	3
Florida	0	3			
Alabama	9	0		55	210½
Louisiana	0	6			

The question then recurring on the adoption of the resolution of the majority, the same was adopted by a large majority.

The entire report of the committee was then adopted.

Mr. North of Pennsylvania moved to reconsider the motion to adopt the report, and to lay that motion on the table. Agreed to.

Mr. North of Pennsylvania then moved that the rejected claimants for seats in this Convention be invited to take honorary seats on this floor. [Cries of "No!" "No!" "No!"]

Mr. Lawrence of Louisiana. The gentlemen whose claims have been rejected will not accept such an offer.

A Voice. Then let them stay out.

The Illinois contest was not alluded to in debate. The Cook delegation were kicked out without a dissenting voice. This must be very pleasant to Mr. Buchanan, whose postmaster at Chicago, and especial pet, Mr. Cook is. Poor Cook swears profusely and piteously, and that is the extent of his capacity.

The death of the chairman of the Vermont delegation, Hon John S. Robinson, was then announced and resolutions of respect passed.

The credential controversy being closed, the contest comes on the platform, and then—the disruption! An explosion is certain to take place, and the only question is as to the extent of the Southern secession. The air is full of rumors, and there is general concurrence in the proposition that it will be impossible for the unity of the Convention to be preserved up to the commencement of the balloting for candidates. I am informed by a delegate from one of the border Southern States, that his delegation will not withdraw when the Southern platform is rejected, and the Northern one with two interpretations is adopted, but will withdraw when Douglas is nominated on the equivocal platform, an event which is certain to follow the secession of the Gulf States, which will take place after the platform fight.

CHARLESTON, S. C., April 25th (at night).

The Convention is now ready for the great business upon which it has come together—that of constructing a platform and nominating a candidate. The committee on Platform is now in session, and in agony no doubt, with the various ambiguous resolutions before it. The case is very simple. There is, to begin with, an irreconcilable difference in the doctrines respecting slavery in the Territories between the Northern and Southern wings of the Democratic party. The platform must be drawn with elaborate ambiguity, and capable of two constructions, or the party must be divided.

It is only certain just now, that the understanding this morning that there would be a disruption of the Convention, caused a panic, and that a disposition to compromise and be ambiguous prevails.

I hear it asserted on that which seems reliable authority, that Mr. Richardson of Illinois has authority to withdraw the name of Douglas, and will withdraw it, if there is any thing about the protection of slavery in the Territories in the platform.

The party must take refuge under false pretenses of doctrine, or go in pieces. The question is: Will the South yield the point of honor, which they have been insisting upon, so far as to allow the platform to be made ambiguous? If they will, the Douglas men are so confident in their ability to nominate Douglas, and in the potency of their war-whoop, that they will probably allow the Cincinnati Platform to be amended by the addition of something equivalent in the estimation of the South to the affirmation of the Dred Scott decision doctrine, with the interpretation put upon the decision by Judge Black, in his pamphlet controversy with Douglas.

Douglas men are asserting warmly at the Mills House that they never will yield an inch—never, never. And they want a little Southern sensation on the platform. They want about forty Southern delegates to go out, for that would insure the nomination of Douglas, and help him in the North. Their fear is, that the secession will be uncomfortably large. A slight secession of merely the "shred of Gulf States" would be a help; and a great secession, carrying with it the weight of the South, would be ruinous. To-morrow is understood to be the crisis of the Convention. We hear hourly that a crisis involving the fate of the country is at hand.

The more I see of this city the more I am impressed with its singular beauties. The most charming spot it contains is the Battery—which is in fact a park situated at the extreme end of the peninsula upon which the city is built. On one side is the harbor, the islands, the shores of the bay, the forts and shipping. On the other is a street of stately edifices, splendid private residences, surrounded by trees.

In the pleasant evenings, the people of leisure congregate here; hundreds of carriages and buggies, full of ladies and gentlemen, whirl along the drives—loving couples, and nurses with babies in their arms or in hand-carriages, and leading or directing groups of children, throng every promenade. At times it seems the whole town must have turned out for a grand reunion, and the sea-breeze comes up with health on its wings. During the session of the Convention there has been a band of music from Boston, used principally in serenading great men at a late hour, and bringing out speeches ("unpremeditated," of course, though the speakers are usually notified beforehand), which has made the battery especially delicious of evenings, by discoursing there the most exquisite music. About dusk the streets leading to the battery are full of people returning from visits to it. The sidewalks are lined as if some street public assemblage, political or religious, had just been dissolved.

The delegates that took precaution to have contracts with the hotel keepers, have found themselves badly sold. The North-western delegates are taxed at least fifty dollars each extra, in consequence of their contracts. The Kentucky delegation made a contract with the proprietor of the Charleston Hotel for parlors and bed-rooms, capable of accommodating fifty persons, agreeing to pay two hundred and fifty dollars per day, from the fifteenth of April to the end of the Convention. Only twenty persons appeared, and the poor fellows came together and appointed a deputation to wait on the hotel-keeper. He agreed to allow the expiration of the contract ten days from its commencement, and then to board them at the rate of two dollars per day.

The twenty gentlemen thereupon shelled out one hundred and twenty-five dollars each, and had their contract canceled. Most of them were men who had plenty of money, but they travailed and groaned in spirit, confessing, however, that they had only themselves to blame.

There are accommodations here for three times the number of persons present.

FOURTH DAY.

INSTITUTE HALL,
Charleston, S. C., April 26th.

The committee on Platform is again in session, and doing its best to make a platform. It adjourned at a late hour last night, without having accomplished the objects of its sessions. A member of the committee informed me that there would in all probability be three reports—an ultra-Southern—a Popular Sovereignty—and a "safe middle ground report," according to the exceedingly moderate and conservative views of our illustrious Administration.

The rumors are this morning, that the endeavors to patch up matters will fail entirely. The cohesive power of public plunder, when that plunder is worth one hundred million dollars per year, is tremendous, but the ferment of factions here is such that this power may be overcome. The Convention has to choose between subterfuge and disruption.

It is, for the present, the policy of the Douglas men not to excite controversy. They feel so confident of their strength in the Convention, that they are exceedingly anxious to preserve its unity, that they may use it. If they could induce thirty or forty ultra-Southern votes to go out, they might nominate Douglas. They do not provoke discussion. Many speeches are made at night, at the principal hotels, all extreme Southern in character. If a man should undertake to make such a Democratic speech here as is heard from every stump of the North, favoring the exclusion of slavery from the Territories by the people thereof, he would be hooted down as an Abolitionist, and possibly mobbed as an incendiary. Several gentlemen were called out at the Mills House last night. Among them was Burnett, member of Congress from Kentucky, who made a fire-eating speech, violently opposing all concessions of principle, all subterfuges, all equivocations, all doubtful candidates. The speech was a blow at Douglas, and the reply of his friends who were in the crowd was, "Never mind, when we get to voting we beat them like hell." O. Jennings Wise made a speech, glorifying the State conservatism of South Carolina, and the memory of the immortal Calhoun, who is referred to here as if he were the patron Saint of the Democracy.

Fernando Wood was called out and made a speech, pledging himself in advance to the platform and candidate of the Convention. Wood, though excluded from the Convention, has made a strongly favorable impression here. He is one of the first favorites of the "South Cari-lee-nee-ans," as they all style themselves. There were several scenes of uproar in front of the hotel. One poor fellow, piteously drunk, made a running speech for half an hour, during which the crowd roared at him, calling him all sorts of names, telling him to "go to bed," etc., etc. As the Convention assembles there are a dozen rumors about the platform, flying. One that there is wonderful harmony—another that there is intense antagonism. The ladies crowd in in greater numbers than ever. "South Caroleena" beauty is well represented. Many of the ladies have fine features but most of them bad complexions. They are splendid in eyes and hair, with fine profiles and bright countenances, but not excellent forms. The ladies are a great feature of the Convention. The delegates are desperately gallant.

There is a general understanding this morning that the crisis has arrived at last. The Convention must speedily become indivisible, or it must separate, and there are many here who sincerely belive that the fate of the country turns on this point.

The prayer this morning has the advantage of being heard in the hall. And it is probably as able and fervent as was ever "delivered to a Boston audience." Harmony was especially prayed for, as it is especially needed about these times. The Reverend gentleman said:

"Oh, come, Heavenly Father, and with Thy spirit guide and over-rule the deliberations of those now present. Grant unto them that, in harmony and peace, and with a patriotic desire for the preservation of all that is sacred in the institutions of the country, they may come to a true and wise conclusion in their counsels. And not unto us, not unto us; but unto Thee shall be the honor and the glory."

The Convention is flooded with resolutions. Mr. Fitzhugh of Virginia introduces the following:

Resolved, That the rendition of fugitive slaves and other property by one State to another is a right secured by the laws of nations, recognized by the Colonies and the mother country previous to the Declaration of Independence, by the Courts of Great Britain and by the Supreme Court of the United States, and by the law and Courts of all civilized nations, and *a fortiori* is the duty of the States of this Confederacy under the Constitution and laws.

Resolved, That the refusal of the Governors of the several States to deliver up fugitives from justice and fugitive slaves, is an open and palpable violation of the above natural and international law and the Constitution and laws of the United States, constituting official perjury by such Governors as have evaded or refused to perform this duty, and if persevered in must lead to the severance of the Union.

Mr. Hughes of Pennsylvania:

Resolved, That while recognizing the doctrine that the General Government has no power to create in, or exclude from, by legislation, any species of property in any State or Territory, yet we maintain that it is the duty of that Government to provide the Courts with ample process and ministerial officers for the protection and enforcement of any existing right, or the correction of any wrong, over which said Government, under the Constitution, has jurisdiction.

Mr. Browne of Pennsylvania moved the following:

Resolved, That the citizens of the several States when emigrating into a Federal Territory, retain the right to slave and other property which they take with them, until there is some prohibition by lawful authority; and that, as declared by the Supreme Court, Congress cannot interfere with such right in a Territory, nor can a Territorial Legislature do so, until authorized by the adoption of a State Constitution; and that the attempted exercise of such a function by a Territorial Legislature is unconstitutional, and dangerous to the peace of the Union.

Mr. Walker of Alabama:

Resolved, That it is the duty of the Federal Government, in all its departments within their constitutional sphere, to afford adeqate protection and equal advantage to all descriptions of property recognized as such by the laws of any of the

States as well within the Territories as upon the high-seas, and every place subject to its exclusive power of legislation.

Mr. Wall of Tennesee offered the following resolutions, being the Platform advocated by that State:

Be it Resolved, That we hereby reaffirm the principles announced in the Platform of the Democratic party, adopted in Convention at Cincinnati, in June, 1856, and that we hold them to be a true exposition of our doctrines on the subjects embraced.

Resolved, That the views expressed by the Supreme Court of the United States in the decision of the case of "Dred Scott," are, in our opinion, a true and clear exposition of the powers reposed in Congress upon the subject of the Territories of the United States, and the rights guarantied to the residents in the Territories.

Resolved, That the States of the Confederacy are equals in political rights; each State has the right to settle for itself all questions of internal policy; the right to have or not to have slavery, is one of the prerogatives of self-government—the States did not surrender this right in the Federal Constitution, and Tennessee will not now do so.

Resolved, That the Federal Government has no power to interfere with slavery in the States, nor to introduce or exclude it from the Territories, and no duty to perform in relation thereto, but to protect the rights of the owner from wrong and to restore fugitives from labor; these duties it cannot withhold without a violation of the Constitution.

Resolved, That the organization of the Republican party upon strictly *sectional* principles, and its hostility to the institution of slavery, which is recognized by the Constitution, and which is inseparably connected with the social and industrial pursuits of the Southern States of the Confederacy, is war upon the principles of the Constitution and upon the rights of the States.

Resolved, That the late treasonable invasion of Virginia by an organized band of Republicans, was the necessary result of the doctrines, teachings and principles of that party; was the beginning of the "*irrepressible conflict*" of Mr. Seward; was a blow aimed at the institution of slavery by an effort to excite a servile insurrection; was war upon the South, and as such, it is the duty of the South to prepare to maintain its rights under the Constitution.

Resolved, That if this war upon the Constitutional rights of the South is persisted in, it must soon cease to be a war of words. If the Republican party would prevent a *conflict of arms,* let them stand by the Constitution and fulfill its obligations—we ask nothing more, we will submit to nothing less.

Mr. Wolfe of Indiana moved the following:

Resolved, That the Federal Government has no power to interfere with slavery in the States, nor to introduce or exclude it from the Territories, and no duty to perform in relation thereto, but to faithfully enforce the Fugitive Slave law, and all the decisions of the Supreme Court of the United States in regard to all the rights of the people of every State and Territory under the Constitution of the United States.

Mr. Glenn of Mississippi presented the following:

1. A citizen of any State in the Union may immigrate to the Territories with his property, whether it consists of slaves or any other subject of personal ownership.

2. So long as the Territorial condition exists the relation of master and slave is not to be disturbed by Federal or Territorial legislation; and if so disturbed the Federal Government must furnish ample protection therefor.

3. Whenever a Territory shall be entitled to admission into the Union as a State the inhabitants may, in forming their Constitution, decide for themselves whether it shall authorize or exclude slavery.

Mr. Horn of Wisconsin offered the following:

Resolved, That the letter of President Buchanan accepting the nomination at Cincinnati, where he explains the Cincinnati Platform in relation to the power of a Territorial Legislature on the subject of slavery is eminently sound, and is hereby referred to the committee on Resolutions for their consideration.

Mr. Mouton of Louisiana offered the following:

Resolved, That the Territories of the United States belong to the several States as their common property, and not to the individual citizens thereof—that the Federal Constitution recognizes property in slaves, and as such the owner thereof is entitled to carry his slaves into any Territory of the United States and hold them as property. And in case the people of the Territories by inaction, unfriendly legislation or otherwise, should endanger the tenure of such property or discriminate against it by withholding that protection given to this species of property in the Territories, it is the duty of the General Government to interpose, by an active exertion of its Constitutional powers to secure the rights of slaveholders.

Mr. Greenfield of Kentucky offered the following:

Resolved, That it is the duty of the National Government to provide, by law, for paying for such fugitives from labor as, by the illegal interposition of State authorities, the owners thereof may be prevented from receiving under the Fugitive Slave law.

Mr. Bidwell of California moved the following:

Resolved, That our States and Territories on the Pacific, and the Territories of the Great Basin, and of both slopes of the Rocky Mountains, demand the early construction of a railroad to connect them with the internal navigation and railway system of the Atlantic States; and that on the ground of postal communication, protection of Territories and States, and of military defense, the General Government has accepted authority under the Constitution.

Mr. Craig of Missouri offered the following:

Resolved, That the Democratic party are in favor of granting such constitutional aid as will insure the speedy construction of a railroad connecting the Atlantic and Pacific States.

Mr. Stout of Oregon offered the following:

Resolved, That to preserve the Union, the equality of States must be maintained, and every branch of the Federal Government should exercise all their Constitutional powers for the protection of persons and property.

Mr. McConnell of Illinois offered the following:

Resolved, That the Federal Government has no power to interfere with slavery in the States, or to introduce it or exclude it from the Territories, and has no duty to perform in relation thereto, except to secure the rights of the owner by a return of the fugitive slave, as provided by the Constitution.

Mr. Seward of Georgia presented the following:

Resolved, That the Constitution of the United States extends to the several States, and to every citizen, the full protection of persons and property in all the States and Territories, and that those rights, as declared and determined by the Courts, under the Constitution, are to be respected and maintained by the Government of the United States; and that James Guthrie of Kentucky be the nominee of the Democratic party for President of the United States, on this platform.

Mr. Cessna of Pennsylvania offered the following:

Resolved, That the convictions of the Democratic party of the country remain unshaken in the wisdom and justice of an adequate protection of iron, coal, wool, and the other great staples of our country, based upon the necessities of a reasonable revenue system of the General Government; and approving of the views of President Buchanan upon the subject of specific duties, we earnestly desire our Representatives in Congress to produce such modifications of the existing laws as the unwise legislation of the Republican party in 1857 renders absolutely necessary to the prosperity of the great interests of the country.

Capt. Rynders wanted protection extended over Monongahela whiskey.
All these resolutions were referred to the committee on Platform.
Resolutions became ridiculous, and on motion of Mr. Pugh, it was voted that they should in future be referred without reading.
This was throwing the mantle over the nakedness of the party. Mr. Pugh is a good boy.
The committee on Resolutions being still in travail, almost hopeless, the Convention adjourned until 4 P. M., having no business before it.
The evening session amounted to nothing. There was much talk of "the crisis"—and the Convention adjourned in a hopeless mood.
There is but one course for it to pursue and be honest—that is, divide. They cannot agree, and every man in the Convention knows they cannot. Cool-headed men here are impressed that the chances in the next campaign are with the Chicago nominee. This thing is in a hopeless jumble. The South has driven the Northern Democracy to the wall, and now insists upon protection of slavery in the Territories. In other words, insists upon the political execution of every Northern Democrat, and the total destruction of the Democratic party. The Northern Democracy here are smitten with great terrors, and are willing to do almost any thing for harmony, but bow their necks to the knife of their political opponents. They are unwilling to submit themselves to assassination or to commit suicide. And the South will not yield a jot of its position as master of the party, nor abate its devotion to constitutional abstractions and the propagandism of slavery. It is perfectly clear, glaringly apparent here, seen in every face, heard in every voice, and pervades the city like an atmosphere, that the doctrine of the Democratic party must be that of exerting all powers of the Federal Government for the extension of slavery, and the increase of the political power of the master class of the Southern section. The record of this Convention will prove this fact to a demonstration. The word is just now that the committee will agree upon a platform which will be adopted. But the most sagacious of the politicians are uneasy. The sessions of the committee on Resolutions are protracted and exciting. Their labor of splitting hairs is enormous. And they know they must bring in a subterfuge, or throw a bomb-shell.

FIFTH DAY.

INSTITUTE HALL,
Charleston, S. C., April 27th.

The crisis which was to have arrived yesterday, was postponed by the failure of the committee on Platform to report The committee, when the Convention came together this morning, was still unprepared.

The reports were not made until half-past eleven o'clock, when Mr. Avery of North Carolina presented the following from a majority of the committee on Resolutions:

MAJORITY REPORT.

Resolved, That the platform adopted at Cincinnati be affirmed, with the following resolutions:
1. *Resolved*, That the Democracy of the United States hold these cardinal principles on the subject of slavery in the Territories: First, That Congress has no power to abolish slavery in the Territories. Second, That the Territorial Legislature has no power to abolish slavery in any Territory, nor to prohibit the introduction of slaves therein, nor any power to exclude slavery therefrom, nor any right to destroy or impair the right of property in slaves by any legislation whatever.
2. *Resolved*, That the enactments of State Legislatures to defeat the faithful execution of the Fugitive Slave law are hostile in character, subversive of the Constitution, and revolutionary in their effect.
3. *Resolved*, That it is the duty of the Federal Government to protect, when necessary, the rights of persons and property on the high-seas, in the Territories, or wherever else its constitutional authority extends.
4. *Resolved*, That the Democracy of the nation recognize it as the imperative duty of this Government to protect the naturalized citizen in all his rights, whether at home or in foreign lands, to the same extent as its native-born citizens.
5. *Resolved*, That the National Democracy earnestly recomend the acquisition of the Island of Cuba, at the earliest practicable period.

Whereas, that one of the greatest necessities of the age, in a political, commercial, postal and military point of view, is a speedy communication between the Pacific and Atlantic coasts: Therefore, be it

Resolved, That the National Democratic party do hereby pledge themselves to use every means in their power to secure the passage of some bill for the construction of a Pacific Railroad, from the western line of the Mississippi River to the Pacific Ocean, at the earliest practicable moment.

Mr. Avery was instructed, as chairman of the committee, to report this Platform. He was further instructed to say that entire unanimity did not prevail on a portion of the resolutions.

The first and third resolutions in relation to slavery in the Territories, and the duty of the General Government to protect the right of person and property, were adopted by a bare majority of the committee. The second resolution, in relation to the Fugitive Slave law, and the fourth resolution, in relation to naturalized citizens, were adopted unanimously, and the fifth resolution, in relation to the acquisition of Cuba, was adopted without a division. The last resolution of the series, in reference to the Pacific Railroad, was adopted by a majority vote.

Mr. Payne of Ohio submitted the

MINORITY REPORT.

The undersigned, a minority of the committee on Resolutions, regretting their inability to concur with the report of the majority of your committee, feel con-

strained to submit the following as their report, and recommend its adoption as a substitute for the report of the majority.
Respectfully submitted,
AMOS ROBERTS, delegate from Maine.
W. BURNS, delegate from New Hampshire.
E. M. BROWN, delegate from Vermont.
C. S. BRADLEY, delegate from Rhode Island.
A. G. HAZZARD, delegate from Connecticut.
BENJ. WILLIAMSON, delegate from New Jersey.
H. B. PAYNE, delegate from Ohio.
P. C. DUNNING, delegate from Indiana.
O. B. FICKLIN, delegate from Illinois.
G. V. N. LOTHROP, delegate from Michigan.
A. S. PALMER, delegate from Wisconsin.
BEN. M. SAMUEL, delegate from Iowa.
JAS. M. CAVANAUGH, delegate from Minnesota.
EDWIN CROSWELL, delegate from New York.
H. B. WRIGHT, delegate from Pennsylvania.

The name of Mr. Croswell was followed by the note that he signed the report in accordance with the wishes of his delegation, and agreed with the resolutions as far as they went. The resolutions of the minority, which he would read, contained one or two resolutions similar to those of the majority; but as they hoped their report would be the platform of the party, they had thought it best to embody these in that report. The resolutions are as follows:

1. *Resolved*, That we, the Democracy of the Union, in Convention assembled, hereby declare our affirmance of the resolutions unanimously adopted and declared as a platform of principles by the Democratic Convention at Cincinnati in the year 1856, believing that Democratic principles are unchangeable in their nature when applied to the same subject-matters; and we recommend, as the only further resolutions, the following:

2. *Resolved*, That all questions in regard to the rights of property in States or Territories arising under the Constitution of the United States are judicial in their character, and the Democratic party is pledged to abide by and faithfully carry out such determination of these questions as has been or may be made by the Supreme Court of the United States.

3. *Resolved*, That it is the duty of the United States to afford ample and complete protection to all its citizens, whether at home or abroad, and whether native or foreign-born.

4. *Resolved*, That one of the necessities of the age, in a military, commercial and postal point of view, is speedy communication between the Atlantic and Pacific States; and the Democratic party pledge such Constitutional Government aid as will insure the construction of a Railroad to the Pacific coast, at the earliest practicable period.

5. *Resolved*, That the Democratic party are in favor of the acquisition of the Island of Cuba, on such terms as shall be honorable to ourselves and just to Spain.

6. *Resolved*, That the enactments of State Legislatures to defeat the faithful execution of the Fugitive Slave law, are hostile in character, subversive of the Constitution, and revolutionary in their effect.

Mr. B. F. Butler of Massachusetts presented the following minority report, signed by himself as a substitute for the amendment proposed by the gentleman from Ohio:

Resolved, That we, the Democracy of the Union, in Convention assembled, hereby declare our affirmance of the Democratic Resolutions unanimously adopted and declared as a Platform of Principles at Cincinnati, in the year 1856, without addition or alteration, believing that Democratic principles are unchangeable in their nature, when applied to the same subject-matter, and we recommend as the only farther resolution, the following:

Resolved, That it is the duty of the United States to extend its protection alike over all its citizens, whether native or naturalized.

A minority of your committee have agreed to report the above as the sole resolutions upon the subject of the principles of the party.

In behalf of a minority of the committee,

B. F. BUTLER.

Mr. Cochrane of New York gave notice that as soon as one of the amendments was out of the way he would offer the following:

Resolved, That the several States of this Union are, under the Constitution, equal, and that the people thereof are entitled to the free and undisturbed possession and enjoyment of their rights of person and property in the common Territories, and that any attempt by Congress or a Territorial Legislature to annul, abridge or discriminate against any such equality or rights would be unwise in policy and repugnant to the Constitution; and that it is the duty of the Federal Government, whenever such rights are violated, to afford the necessary, proper and constitutional remedies for such violations.

Resolved, That the Platform of Principles adopted by the Convention held in Cincinnati, in 1856, and the foregoing resolutions, are hereby declared to be the Platform of the Democratic party.

A dreary discussion followed. Mr. Avery spoke first, going over the usual ground traversed by Southern gentlemen of second-rate abilities in dismissing the slavery question.

Mr. Clark of Missouri interrupted him in the course of his remarks, saying he was one of the majority who had indorsed the platform. The gentleman had alluded to his State as one that stood by the report. He wanted to announce to the Convention that he did not approve wholly of the report, and would not vote for the first resolution in the report. He had signed the report only in order to enable the committee to report.

Mr. Avery did not make much headway.

Mr. Payne of Ohio defended the minority report. He made a vigorous speech, deeply earnest, and strongly fortified his position by extracts from the speeches of Southern gentlemen. He said of the action of the Platform committee:

He deemed it due to say, by way of testimony for all his colleagues on the committee, that they had, for three days, soberly, earnestly and solemnly discussed the issues that now divide the Democratic party.

It is not a personal victory they seek to achieve, but every gentleman had, he believed, felt in his conscience and in his heart, that upon the result of the deliberation of the Convention, in all human probability, depended the fate of the Democratic party and the destiny of the Union, and they would have been no patriots if they had brought into their deliberations any but an earnest desire to adjust the differences that exist in the party. It was with that purpose and that feeling that he took a seat in the Convention and on the committee; and if he knew his own heart, there is no personal sacrifice he would not make, short of his honor, to rekindle the spirit of harmony that prevailed in former days in the Democratic party of the Union. But there existed a difference between the members of the committee. After a protracted discussion they had been unable to agree, and it was the most painful act of his political life when he found himself compelled to dissent from the majority of the committee in their final action.

In conclusion, he asked the South:

Are you for a very abstraction going to yield the chance of success? Is there any disposition to rob you of your political influence on the part of your Northern brethren?

We say we *will* abide by the decision of the Courts. The Dred Scott decision having been rendered since the Cincinnati Platform was adopted, renders this proper. We will take that decision, and abide by it like loyal, steadfast, true-hearted men. Is not that enough?

He would appeal to the South to put no weights upon the North—to let them run this race unfettered and unhampered. If the appeal is answered, the North will do her duty in the struggle. Should the platform of the majority be adopted, he would go home and do his best; but hopeless of success. But he would ask, in that case, that his gallant Southern friends who desire to spend their summer farther North, would visit the State of Ohio, and join in the battle on the Western Reserve.

Gen. Butler of Massachusetts proceeded to dissect both platforms, and did it with an incisive ferocity that was refreshing to behold. The Cincinnati Platform had had two interpretations placed upon it, eh! So had the Bible and the Constitution of the United States. Gentlemen could not construct a platform that would not have a double interpretation.

The "rights of persons and property on the high-seas" to the protection of the Federal Government, were asserted by Gen. Butler to be capable of a construction, showing it to assert the duty of Government to protect the African slave-trade. The General was assured that the South did not mean that, but the construction could not be got rid of. It would adhere, and would, if it were adopted, do the Northern Democracy incalculable mischief. Gen. Butler was right in this. The resolution asserts the duty of Government to protect slavery in the Territories no more clearly than its duty to protect the slave-trade on the high-seas, and such, doubtless, was the intention of the writer of the resolutions.

Mr. Butler waded into the platform presented by Mr. Payne of Ohio. He said the Cincinnati Platform contained a resolution on the annexation of Cuba, much more delicately, diplomatically and properly expressed, than that in Mr. Payne's report. He was not in favor of the Pacific Railroad. This doctrine of internal improvements by Government, was a new thing for the Democratic party. It was not according to his style of democracy. The first part of the resolution in the minority report—that clause in reference to slavery in the Territories, asserting the question of property to be a judicial question, was a mere truism when considered in the sense in which it was meant. The second part of that resolution was very dangerous. It pledged the Democratic party to all the decisions the Supreme Court might make. Was this the doctrine of Old Hickory? Why, it would be enough to make the bones of old Jackson rattle in his coffin, to have such a resolution as that entertained by a Democratic Convention. Suppose the

Democratic party should be divided, by some foolish differences arising here, and Wm. H. Seward should become next President of the United States.

The judges of the Supreme Court were old men, and some of them would soon die. Seward proposed, at any rate, to reorganize the Supreme Court. Was the South ready to indorse in advance all the decisions of the Supreme Court, when it might become Black Republican, when Seward might have the manufacture of it? There were shouts of "No, no."

The Convention adjourned when Gen. Butler concluded his speech, taking a recess until four o'clock. [There were hundreds of ladies in the hall without umbrellas in hand or carriages at command, and during the morning session the rain commenced falling heavily. The long drouth was over at last. The people in the hall were in a bad condition, but the city and the country need the rain badly.

Many of the ladies contrived to do without their dinners and spent the recess in their gallery. The poor creatures, with their new dresses and loves of bonnets, were in sore tribulation. The atmosphere of the hall was already damp and chilly,—and their fine feathers are drooping.

The doctrinal position of the Democracy as displayed in the debate to-day, is pitiable enough. It is indeed ridiculous and absurd for this body of delegates to be pretending to try to agree on a platform, when the whole country, themselves included, know well their disagreements are radical and absolute.

AFTERNOON SESSION.

The first thing after the Convention was called to order in the afternoon, was a speech from Mr. Barksdale, editor of the Mississippian, which was a clear, well-expressed, shrewd, and keen ultra-Southern speech, demanding the protection of slavery in the Territories, and insisting upon adhering to principle rather than consulting expediency.

Mr. Barksdale is, I presume, a more forcible writer than speaker. The speech which he made to-day will read better than it sounded. He is a disciple of Jefferson Davis. His personal appearance is much in his favor; but he is full of fire and prone to fly off the handle. Some expressions of his countenance are very amiable; but there is a dangerous glitter in his eye, and his thin, white lips are, when in repose, shut like the jaws of a steel clasp.

Mr. King of Missouri, an old Tom Benton Democrat, who has only recently repented of associations with Frank Blair, B. Gratz Brown and Co., followed. He made an ultra-Douglas speech, indorsing the Northern Democracy in the most unqualified manner. He told the South that their demand for the protection of slavery in the Territories would, if persisted in, result in a Black Republican Congress, which would give them such protection as wolves gave lambs.

Mr. King is an elderly gentleman, who impresses all who hear him that he is thoroughly sincere. He was put forward by the Douglasites as a Southerner to answer Barksdale, and his effort was warmly applauded by the Northern faction of the party. He stated in commendation of Northern Democrats that they were always willing to assist in returning fugitive slaves. Wherever a Southerner, when hunting his peculiar property gone astray, could find a sound Democrat, he was certain of sympathy and assistance. He lamented the injustice done by the South to Northern Democrats, and deplored the hard political fate of those in the North who stood up for the South, and fought the battles of her rights. He appealed to the South not to drive the Northern Democracy to the wall, and alienate them, and thereby secure the election of Seward to the Presidency.

Mr. Yancey of Alabama rose to reply and received a perfect ovation. The hall for several minutes rang with applause. It appeared at once that the outside pressure was with the fire-eaters.

Mr. Yancey is a very mild and gentlemanly man, always wearing a genuinely good-humored smile, and looking as if nothing in the world could disturb the equanimity of his spirits. He commenced by saying that no time could be more appropriate for an Alabamian to be heard, than after the strange and unnatural speech they had just heard from a son of the South (Mr. King). Mr. Yancey asked for more time than was allowed by the rules of the Convention, and by common consent was allowed an additional half hour. He filled up his time (an hour and a half) with great effect. There was no question after he had been upon the platform a few minutes, that he was a man of remarkable gifts of intellect and captivating powers as a speaker. He reviewed the differences on the slavery question of the Democracy. He charged that the defeats of the Democracy in the North were to be traced to the pandering by the party in the free States to anti-slavery sentiments; they had not come up to the high ground which must be taken on the subject, in order to defend the South—namely, that slavery was right. He reviewed the Kansas question, and detected enormity in the action of Stephen A. Douglas and his followers, in refusing to admit Kansas into the Union as a slave State under the Lecompton Constitution, and sorrowed over the fact that only three constitutional Democrats were to be found in the Northern States to vote against the admission of Kansas under the Wyandotte Constitution. He traced the history of Northern aggression and Southern concession as he understood it. He spoke of the deep distrust the South had begun to entertain of the Northern Democracy, and urged the propriety of the demand of the South, that the Democratic party should now take clear and high ground upon a constitutional basis. He pronounced false all charges that the State of Alabama, himself or his colleagues, were in favor of a dissolution of the Union *per se*. But he told the Democracy of the North that they must, in taking high constitutional ground, go before the people of the North and tell them of the inevitable dissolution of the Union if constitutional principles did not prevail at the ballot-boxes. He spoke of the Democratic indorsement which the majority platform had received, saying that not one State which had voted against it, in committee, could be certainly relied upon to cast Democratic electoral votes, while every State that had supported that platform, with but one exception (Maryland) could, upon that platform, be counted absolutely certain in the electoral college for the Democratic candidate. He spoke directly to Southern men and appealed to them to present a united front in favor of a platform that recognized their rights and guaranteed their honor. He said defeat upon principle was better than a mere victory gained by presenting ambiguous issues and cheating the people. He referred to the defeat of the Democratic party when it made a fight on principles against coon-skins and log cabins in 1840, and called attention to the overwhelming tide on which they rode again into power—the tide of the "second sober thought of the people." The Southerners in the hall were thoroughly warmed up by his speech, and applauded with rapturous enthusiasm. Several of his points were received with outbursts of applause that rung around the hall as if his hearers had been made to shout and stamp by the simultaneous action of electricity. One of his most effective points was in relation to the Dred Scott decision and the plea made by Douglas and others that almost all of it was mere *obiter dicta*. This plea was disrespectful to the venerable man, who, clothed in the supreme ermine, had made an exposition of constitutional law, which had rolled in silvery cadence from the dark forests of the North to the glittering waters of the Gulf.

He distinctly admitted that the South did ask of the Northern Democracy an advanced step in vindication of Southern rights; and Mr. Yancey's hour and a half closed while he was in the midst of a series of lofty periods, and Mr. Pugh of Ohio sprung to his feet. The speech of Mr Yancey had been the speech of the Convention. Some time before it was concluded the day had expired, and the gas had been lit about the hall. The scene was very brilliant and impressive. The crowded hall, the flashing lights, the deep solicitude felt in every word, the importance of the issues pending, all combined to make up a spectacle of extraordinary interest, and something of splendor.

Mr. Pugh took the platform in a condition of considerable warmth. There was an effort made to adjourn, but the crowd was eager for the fray, and insisted that Pugh should go on. He did so, thanking God that a bold and honest man from the South had at last spoken, and told the whole truth of the demands of the South. It was now before the Convention and the country, that the South did demand an advanced step from the Democratic party. Mr. Pugh read the resolutions of the Alabama Convention four years ago, reported by Mr. Yancey, showing that the delegation of Alabama demanded of the Democracy assembled at Charleston, more than they required of the Democracy at Cincinnati, four years ago. His point was weakened, however, by the fact that he did not read all of the Alabama resolutions until forced to do so by the peremptory demands of Yancey and Judge Meek. Mr. Pugh said that his political life was almost over, and so far as he was personally concerned, he did not regret it. He then traced the downfall of the Northern Democracy, and the causes of that fall, charging the South with it. And now the Northern Democracy were taunted by the South with weakness. And here, it seemed, the Northern Democracy. because they were in the minority, were thrust back and told in effect they must put their hands on their mouths, and their mouths in the dust. "Gentlemen of the South," said Mr. Pugh, "you mistake us—you mistake us—we will not do it." Mr. Pugh was interrupted my motions to adjourn, and the Convention took a recess of one hour.

At half-past nine o'clock in the evening, the Convention again assembled, and Mr. Pugh took the platform, in the face of a magnificent audience, and spoke with intense energy and animation, in his best style.

His first point was against the exercise of doubtful constitutional powers; and he insisted that the Southern demand for peculiar protection of their peculiar property in the Territories, had no warrant in the Constitution.

Mr. Pugh's effort is conceded to have been bold and adroit. It had not the silvery music, the grace and polish, that distinguished the oration of Mr. Yancey, but it was keen, shrewd and telling.

A Washington reporter, who has heard all Mr. Pugh's Senate speeches, says this effort was far superior to the best of them.

He spoke of the sacrifice of the Northern Democrats of their political lives, battling for the doctrine of the South, now scornfully repudiated; and pointed out among the delegates, men who had been Senators and Representatives, and who had fallen in the fight. In conclusion, he stated the Democracy, who were prepared to stand by the old faith, would be sorry to part with their Southern friends, but if the gentlemen from the South could only stay on the terms proposed, they must go. The Democracy of the North-west would make itself heard and felt. The Northern Democrats were not children under the pupilage of the South, and to be told to stand here and there, and moved at the beck and bidding of the South. The hall was still, as it was understood that Pugh was the spokesman of Douglas, and that the fate of the Democratic party was in issue.

[When Mr. Pugh concluded, Mr. John Cochrane pressed a motion to have a place assigned for his amendment to the majority report.

After some discussion, it was ruled out of order.

Mr. Bishop of Connecticut now said he thought nothing new could be said of the dissentions of the Democratic party, if the Convention remained in session and debated all summer. All these questions had been discussed time and again, and the minds of gentlemen made up, he therefore demanded the previous question.

In an instant the house was in an uproar—a hundred delegates upon the floor, and upon chairs, screaming like panthers, and gesticulating like monkeys. The President, for the first time, completely lost control over the Convention; not a word was audible. The reporters climbed upon their tables, the delegates mounted the chairs, the people in the galleries stretched their necks and hung over the balustrade, and literally, as was said of a scene in the House of Representatives, "you would see the Speaker's hammer going, but could not hear it." The chair singled out a red-haired member from Missouri, who was standing on a front seat, and shaking his gory locks, and trying to shriek louder and louder, and to look more terrible than any body else, and recognized him as moving to adjourn. The chair probably thought it the part of prudence to see that the Convention adjourned, for voting on the platform in the midst of such a tornado, and at that hour (it was after ten o'clock), would be certain to blow up the Convention.

Still the Convention roared and raged, and the chairman, seeing it was not worth while to try to put it down by vehement efforts, looked quietly at it; and after he had recognized the Mississippian, remained quiescent.

The first voice that rose above the din was that of some frightened delegate, crying aloud "like some strong swimmer in his agony," emitting a "bubbling groan," that the application of the gag would be disastrous to the party. The poor fellow thought the party was about to bust and the thing die—so he shrieked for the salvation of the Democratic party. Presently the chairman managed to take the reins in his hands, and with great equanimity, firmness and calmness of manner, stated that there was no occasion for so much agitation and discomposure. A crowd gathered about Bishop, and some seemed to menace him. The delegates gathered in groups and grappled with each other, and surged about like waves of the sea..

The chair recognized the motion of adjournment, and a vote by States was called for, and an adjournment carried by a small majority—yeas, 158½; nays, 143. The following is the vote:

States.	Yeas.	Nays.	States.	Yeas.	Nays.
Maine	8	0	Mississippi	7	0
New Hampshire	0	5	Texas	4	0
Vermont	0	5	Arkansas	4	0
Massachusetts	7	5½	Missouri	3	6
Rhode Island	0	4	Tennessee	12	0
Connecticut	1	5	Kentucky	12	0
New York	0	35	Ohio	0	23
New Jersey	7	0	Indiana	0	13
Pennsylvania	8	19	Illinois	5	6
Delaware	3	0	Michigan	0	6
Maryland	8	0	Wisconsin	0	5
Virginia	15	0	Iowa	0	4
North Carolina	10	0	Minnesota	1½	2½
South Carolina	8	0	California	4	0
Georgia	10	0	Oregon	3	0
Florida	3	0			
Alabama	9	0		158½	143
Louisiana	6	0			

The Convention separated in a bad humor. There was a call on the Southerners to remain and consult. It was a cold, rainy night, but there was intense heat about the hotels. Men stalked about with dripping umbrellas, and consulted eagerly and anxiously. Every body said that there would necessarily be an explosion in the morning. During the evening, as it was known that "the crisis" could not much longer be put off, dispatches were flying between Washington and Charleston. The Southern members of Congress were telling the delegates from their States that they must go out with Alabama. Toombs telegraphed to the Georgians that they must not stay after Alabama went out. Gartell did the same thing. The South Carolinians also sent dispatches, saying that the Palmetto delegates must not be outstripped in the race of zeal for Southern rights and independence.

SIXTH DAY.

CHARLESTON, *Saturday*, April 28th.

The first thing was a pathetic appeal from Bigler of Pennsylvania. Bigler in his wisdom, considered the occasion critical. He feared the union of the Democratic party could not be maintained. He was in favor of the union of the Democracy for the sake of the union of the States; of course the union of the States would go up, the moment the Democratic party went down.

He moved that the majority and minority reports be recommitted to the Convention, with instructions to report in an hour the following resolutions:

Resolved, That the platform adopted by the Democratic party at Cincinnati be affirmed, with the following explanatory resolutions:

Resolved, That the government of a Territory, organized by an act of Congress, is provisional and temporary, and, during its existence, all citizens of the United States have an equal right to settle in the Territory, without their rights either of person or property, being destroyed or impaired by Congressional or Territorial legislation.

Resolved, That the Democratic party stands pledged to the doctrine that it is the duty of the Government to maintain all the constitutional rights of property of whatever kind, in the Territories, and to enforce all the decisions of the Supreme Court in reference thereto.

Resolved, That it is the duty of the United States to afford ample and complete protection to all its citizens, whether at home or abroad, and whether native or foreign.

Resolved, That one of the necessities of the age, in a military, commercial and postal point of view, is speedy communication between the Atlantic and Pacific States; and the Democratic party pledge such constitutional government aid as will insure the construction of a railroad to the Pacific coast at the earliest practical period.

Resolved, That the Democratic party are in favor of the acquisition of the Island of Cuba, on such terms as shall be honorable to ourselves and just to Spain.

Resolved, That the enactments of State Legislatures to defeat the faithful execution of the Fugitive Slave law, are hostile in character, subversive of the Constitution, and revolutionary in their effect.

The question was divided, and a vote was taken upon the first branch of the motion of Mr. Bigler to commit the resolutions offered by the committee on Resolutions, with the amendments, back to the committee.

Alabama demanded that the vote be by States.

The question was taken, and it was decided in the affirmative. Yeas, 152; nays, 151, as follows:

States.	Yeas.	Nays.	States.	Yeas.	Nays.
Maine	3	5	Maryland	5½	2½
New Hampshire	0	5	Virginia	14	1
Vermont	0	5	North Carolina	10	0
Massachusetts	8	5	South Carolina	8	0
Rhode Island	0	4	Georgia	10	0
Connecticut	1½	4½	Florida	3	0
New York	0	35	Alabama	9	0
New Jersey	4	3	Louisiana	6	0
Pennsylvania	16	11	Mississippi	7	0
Delaware	3	0	Texas	4	0

States.	Yeas.	Nays.	States.	Yeas.	Nays
Arkansas	4	0	Wisconsin	0	5
Missouri	5	4	Iowa	0	4
Tennessee	11	1	Minnesota	1	3
Kentucky	12	0	California	4	0
Ohio	0	23	Oregon	3	0
Indiana	0	13			
Illinois	0	11		152	151
Michigan	0	6			

So the proposed platforms were recommitted.

The effect of the vote to recommit was to dampen the ardor of the Douglas men very much.

Mr. Bigler's motion instructing the committee, was laid on the table by a vote of 242 to 56½, when the State of Georgia was called. As this vote was being taken a minority of her delegation, Douglasites, made a struggle to assert their right to vote as they individually pleased. The Georgia delegation had been *requested* to vote as a unit. The rule adopted by the Convention provided that the individual delegates should cast their votes as they pleased, when it was not provided or directed by the State how they should cast their votes.

The President reviewed the facts of the case as brought to the knowledge of the Convention, and held that the words of the rule, which, allowed any delegate to cast his individual vote, except where the State he represented had *provided* or directed how the vote of the delegation should be cast, covered, in his judgment, the resolution that it had been agreed upon by both parties, had been adopted by the Georgia State Convention. The word *"provided,"* in the rule was evidently meant to cover something more than *"directions,"* as both words had been used. The request of a State should certainly be liberally construed, and he thought it was a *provision* as to how the vote of the State should be cast. He, therefore, resolved to receive the vote of the State of Georgia, through the chairman of the delegation, as a unit.

Senator Salisbury was exceedingly anxious to talk of the perilous condition of the Democratic party.

A Delegate from Florida rose to the question of privilege. He was anxious to get along harmoniously and with order. As there were a certain number of gentlemen who seemed bound to make the Convention look at their faces, by hopping up every minute to some question or other, he would suggest that their daguerreotypes be taken and handed round, then there would be no occasion for them to thus annoy and trouble the Convention.

The Convention adjourned until four o'clock, to give the committee time to report.

AFTERNOON SESSION.

On reassembling there was the same old trouble. Three reports very slightly modified from those originally reported.

Mr. Avery of North Carolina. Mr. President, I beg leave, on behalf of the committee on Resolutions, to make a report, and I will take occasion to avail myself of the opportunity, before reading it, to make a single remark.

These resolutions meet the approbation of a majority of the States represented upon that committee. I will state further, that the committee understood that this report embodies in substance the Bayard resolutions, and in substance the resolutions of the gentleman from Pennsylvania (Mr. Bigler), and in substance the resolutions offered by the gentleman from New York (Mr. Cochrane), being modified in such shape as the committee think will meet the approbation of the Covention. [Applause.]

Resolved, That the platform adopted by the Democratic party at Cincinnati be affirmed, with the following explanatory resolutions:

First, That the government of a Territory organized by an act of Congress, is provisional and temporary; and, during its existence, all citizens of the United States have an equal right to settle with their property in the Territory without their rights, either of person or property, being destroyed or impaired by Congressional or Territorial legislation.

Second, That it is the duty of the Federal Government, in all its departments, to protect, when necessary, the rights of persons and property in the Territories, and wherever else its constitutional authority extends.

Third, That when the settlers in a Territory having an adequate population to form a State Constitution, the right of sovereignty commences, and, being consummated by admission into the Union, they stand on an equal footing with the people of other States; and the State thus organized ought to be admitted into the Federal Union, whether its constitution prohibits or recognizes the institution of slavery.

Fourth, That the Democratic party are in favor of the acquisition of the Island of Cuba, on such terms as shall be honorable to ourselves and just to Spain, at the earliest practicable moment.

Fifth, That the enactments of State Legislatures to defeat the faithful execucution of the Fugitive Slave law, are hostile in character, subversive of the Constitution, and revolutionary in their effect.

Sixth, That the Democracy of the United States recognize it as the imperative duty of this Government to protect the naturalized citizen in all his rights, whether at home or in foreign lands, to the same extent as its native-born citizens.

Whereas, one of the greatest necessities of the age, in a political, commercial, postal and military point of view, is a speedy communication between the Pacific and Atlantic coasts: Therefore, be it

Resolved, That the Democratic party do hereby pledge themselves to use every means in their power to secure the passage of some bill, to the extent of the constitutional authority of Congress, for the construction of a Pacific Railroad, from the Mississippi River to the Pacific Ocean, at the earliest practicable moment.

Mr. Avery remarked:

It is proper, Mr. President, that I should state that the Bayard resolutions have been amended, first by inserting in the first resolution, after the word "settle," the words "with their property;" by inserting in the second resolution, after the words "Federal Government," the words "in all its departments;" after the word "protect," the words "when necessary;" by striking out in the same resolution the words "on the high-seas," as they seem to have led to some misapprehension in regard to the views entertained by the committee in asserting that amendment. In the resolution relating to a postal and military road to California, the words "to the extent of a constitutional authority of Congress" are inserted after the word "bill."

I would further state that the second resolution is amended in this particular: As originally drafted, it read, "the rights of persons and property on the high-seas, in the Territories, or wherever else its constitutional authority extends." The committee have stricken out the words "high-seas," and after the word "Territory," they have stricken out the word "or," so that the resolution now reads:

"That it is the duty of the Federal Government, in all its departments, to.protect, when necessary, the rights of persons and property in the Territories, and wherever else its constitutional authority extends."

Mr. Butler of Massachusetts. I desire to say that I have a report to offer from the minority of the committee, which I am instructed to present, and to move its submission as an amendment, for the report of the gentleman from Iowa (Mr. Samuels), who represents the larger minority of the committee.

I have also the happiness to state that I have an addition to my thirty-two companions of yesterday. At such time as it will suit the pleasure of the Convention I will offer my amendment, which is the Cincinnati Platform, pure and undefiled. [Applause.]

Mr. Samuels of Iowa. I am instructed by the minority committee on resolutions to offer the following report. It is identical with the report that was presented by the minority committee yesterday, with the exception that the second resolution of the minority report of yesterday has been stricken out, and the following has been substituted. I will read the resolution which has been substituted. [Voices—"Read them all."]

I will read them all, then. The resolutions are as follows:

1. *Resolved*, That we, the Democracy of the Union, in Convention assembled, hereby declare our affirmance of the resolutions unanimously adopted and declared as a platform of principles by the Democratic Convention at Cincinnati in the year 1856, believing that Democratic principles are unchangeable in their nature when applied to the same subject-matters; and we recommend, as the only further resolutions, the following:

Inasmuch as differences of opinion exist in the Democratic party as to the nature and extent of the powers of a Territorial Legislature, and as to the powers and duties of Congress, under the Constitution of the United States, over the institution of slavery within the Territories;

2. *Resolved*, That the Democratic party will abide by the decisions of the Supreme Court of the United States on the questions of constitutional law.

3. *Resolved*, That it is the duty of the United States to afford ample and complete protection to all its citizens, whether at home or abroad, and whether native or foreign.

4. *Resolved*, That one of the necessities of the age, in a military, commercial and postal point of view, is speedy communication between the Atlantic and Pacific States; and the Democratic party pledge such constitutional Government aid as will insure the construction of a Railroad to the Pacific coast, at the earliest practicable period.

5. *Resolved*, That the Democratic party are in favor of the acquisition of the Island of Cuba, on such terms as shall be honorable to ourselves and just to Spain.

6. *Resolved*, That the enactments of State Legislatures to defeat the faithful execution of the Fugitive Slave law, are hostile in character, subversive of the Constitution, and revolutionary in their effect.

Mr. Avery made a speech in which he told the Northern delegates a great deal about the concessions of the South—and urged them to recollect that the slaves who now grow cotton in Alabama, Mississippi and Georgia are the children of slaves who were formerly slaves in their own States.

Mr. Samuels filled up an hour with a pompous stump speech advocating the minority report.

Mr. Butler of Massachusetts rehearsed his speech of the previous day in favor of that singulaly luminous proposition, the Cincinnati Platform, pure and simple. As to the two interpretations on the Cincinnati Platform, he stated that there were already two interpretations upon each of the reports before the Convention. There would always be two interpretations.

Gov. Stephens of Oregon made a speech in favor of the majority report.

Mr. Brent of Maryland made a speech for the minority report. The debate was dreadfully dull and intolerably long—one dull fellow after another takes the floor and bores the immense and impatient audience for an hour. It becomes apparent that there is a determination not to allow a vote on the resolutions.

Now, the majority report is at least tolerably honest. You can tell what it means. There can be no dispute, however, but the minority report is a miserable and cowardly evasion. The favorite phrase of our North-western gentry—one that they have abided by through all their troubles—is that " Democratic principles are unchangeable in their nature, when applied to the same subject-matters." They then proceed to indorse the Cincinnati Platform, knowing it to be an exposed cheat—that the Administration elected upon it, has not construed it as it was interpreted before the people. They want to "cheat and to be cheated." The next thing is an indorsement for time and eternity of the Supreme Court. Both platform reports were in favor of the exercise of constitutional power (which means none at all) for the construction of the Pacific Railroad. Both were in favor of Cuba on terms " honorable to ourselves and just to Spain" (which means, that Cuba is to be grabbed whenever an opportunity affords). Both were opposed to unfriendly legislation in the Northern States, and both in favor of doing wonderful things for the foreign-born citizen at home and abroad.

After the debate had gone on several hours, being more wretched in substance and unentertaining in manner than an ordinary wrangle in the House of Representatives, the previous question was demanded. This was done by a trick. Mr. Claiborne, delegate from Missouri, wanted to explain the position of that State. Cushing had the floor farmed out, and expected to make a speech himself. He sent a messenger, to inquire whether the Missourian proposed to move the previous question. The messenger saw the wrong man, and was deceived, and in turn deceived Cushing, who thus lost the opportunity for which he was aching, to speak on the platform.

And now ensued a parliamentary struggle, exceedingly exciting and interesting. The Douglas men were intensely anxious to finish up the week's work in good style by adopting their platform. The opponents of Douglas were resolved that the vote should not be taken on the platform. The Douglasites were resolute, in the majority, and good tacticians. But the South fell back upon its old tactics in Congress—that of filibustering to save time. They heaped up motions to adjourn, and motions to lay the whole matter upon the table, and rose to privileged motions and personal explanations. The Chair ruled steadily, but carefully, in favor of the filibusters. He was in a tight place, too, and felt it. He became nervous and fidgety, and threatened to leave the chair and abandon the Convention; and the Convention positively seemed alarmed and disheartened at the idea of Caleb leaving it to devour itself. Caleb said, it was impossible for him to maintain a contest of physical endurance with six hundred gentlemen. He said: "The Chair will entertain no motion, until the Convention is restored to order, and when that is done, the Chair desires to make another suggestion to the Convention. The Chair has already stated, that it is physically impossible for him to go on with the business of the Convention, so long as one-half of the members are upon their feet and engaged in clamor of one sort or another. The Chair begs leave to repeat that he knows but one remedy for such disorder, and that is, for your presiding officer to leave the chair. He, of course, would deeply regret that painful necessity, but it would be a less evil than that this incessant confusion and disorder, presenting such a spectacle to the people of South Carolina, should continue to prevail in this most honorable body of so many respectable gentlemen of the highest standing in the community, engaged in debate and deliberation upon the dearest interests of the country." [Applause.]

There was a Mississippian, Jackson, who was particularly prominent in putting motions. He had a good voice, and was standing in his chair and roaring all the time. Now, Caleb saw in him an opportunity of making a scape-goat. He (Caleb) had been holding the helm hard down against the Douglas parliamentarians, and now, taking a virtuous spasm, he told Jackson in a tone most unphilosophically indignant, that he could not tolerate him on his feet incessantly putting an endless series of motions.

Mr. Walker of Alabama wanted the unanimous consent of the Convention to hear the Hon. Caleb Cushing on the resolutions, but was hooted down.

A gentleman from Tennessee, who had made many efforts to get the floor, finally obtained a hearing, when the motion he wished to put was not in order, and took advantage of his opportunity to introduce himself formally to "the distinguished President of this Convention." Cushing was puzzled for a moment, and was then guilty of an awkward bow, and a very thin artificial smile.

During the parliamentary squabble two votes by States were taken on motions to adjourn. The first was as follows:

States.	Yeas.	Nays.	States.	Yeas.	Nays.
Maine	0	8	Connecticut	0	6
New Hampshire	0	5	New York	0	35
Vermont	0	5	New Jersey	7	0
Massachusetts	5	7½	Pennsylvania	13	11
Rhode Island	0	4	Delaware	3	0

States.	Yeas.	Nays.	States.	Yeas.	Nays.
Maryland	5½	2½	Kentucky	7½	1½
Virginia	14	1	Ohio	0	23
North Carolina	10	0	Indiana	0	13
South Carolina	0	8	Illinois	0	11
Georgia	10	0	Michigan	0	6
Florida	3	0	Wisconsin	0	5
Alabama	9	0	Iowa	0	4
Louisiana	6	0	Minnesota	0	4
Mississippi	7	0	California	4	0
Texas	4	0	Oregon	3	0
Arkansas	4	0			
Missouri	0	9		139	109
Tennessee	12	0			

It is believed that the column of nays in this vote represents the utmost strength of Mr. Douglas; and there are some votes in it that he cannot get. It is now thought that the South is in such a condition, that it would be absolute suicide for the South Carolina delegates to vote for him, however great the emergency. There are also in this vote two votes from Pennsylvania that he cannot get for the nomination. And there will be one vote from Minnesota against him for the nomination. There are also five of the nine Missouri votes forever against him. It will be perceived, too, that the Douglas men screwed out of the Southern States their last half votes—one vote and a half from Kentucky, and one vote from Virginia. There are, however, one or two votes from Tennessee, that we find in the column of yeas above, that are for Douglas. On the whole, a close analysis of this vote shows that Douglas will get a majority vote, but cannot get a two-thirds vote, unless the expected Southern secession should draw off thirty or forty votes. Then the Douglas men would use their numerical superiority to construe the rules so, as to allow two-thirds of the votes present to nominate.

The fight on adjournment was at last a drawn battle. The main question was ordered, and the Convention adjourned at 11 o'clock P. M.

It will be necessary on Monday morning to proceed to vote on the platform.

CHARLESTON, April 29th.

This, the "day of rest," is the most busy day of the session among the politicians. The vote on the platform must come off in the morning. The question on the platform of principles to-day, is which side has the most money and can make the biggest promises to obtain the floating vote. The uncertain men here, as in the late contest for the Speakership of the House, have the decision of the question. If the majority platform should be adopted, Douglas is dead without further ceremony. The Douglas stock is falling. Several of his delegations are shaky; men can be picked from all the delegations for him that are at heart against him, and that will be happy to lead a stampede. These gentlemen are very busy to-day, and were in a flutter yesterday. There is a feeling of distrust in the delegations of Ohio, Indiana, and even Illinois. Those who are for Douglas through thick and thin, now and forever, are becoming disgusted and alarmed at the coldness of some of their colleagues. They are also in trepidation about the South. Every imaginable effort will be made to-day by the deadly enemies of Douglas to keep the South in the Convention. If Alabama and company will stay in, after the minority platform is adopted, Douglas cannot receive the nomination. There are, at least, one hundred and thirty votes immovably against him. He can get more than that number, but there are not that many anxious about him. The New York vote will be cast as an unit for him, and yet there are more than one-third of the delegation hotly opposed to him. The Douglas men have become so solicitous on the subject of the going out of the ultra-South, that the ultras are rather disposed to stay inside and disappoint them. Yesterday, for instance, an Ohioan asked a Louisianian in a very solemn way, how many of them would be likely to go. "Oh, never mind," said Louisiana, "we won't go out until we are ready. You are too damn keen for us to go." I am inclined to believe, from the information that comes to me from various sources, that ten times the number of offices in existence under the Government, have been promised by Douglas & Co., in case he should become President. I am told of one delegate from a Southern State who has been three times approached, and asked whether he would not like a foreign mission, and could not be reconciled to Douglas. Foreign missions, collectorships, indeed, all offices within the gift of the President, are the currency here.

I do not know but I will have to take back a statement made in this correspondence, that the preponderance of brains in the Convention was, or would be, with the South. If the South has the greatest weight and brilliancy of brains in the Convention, the fact has not appeared very definitely, up to this time.

The tactics of the Douglas men have been much better than those of their opponents. No Southern speech upon the floor has been remarkable for power, except that of the Hon. Wm. L. Yancey; and there have been a considerable number of displays of the worst sort of Southern blatherskiteism, and some notable instances of Southern ill-manners. The Douglas men came here with a regular programme, with a powerful mass of instructed delegates, and an enthusiastic corps of outsiders. The South, and the Administration forces, came without a candidate, a programme, or even a conceit of a policy. They have rested secure in the idea of their strength. The force of the zeal and impudence of the Douglas men amazes and confounds, while it exasperates, them. And now they find themselves face to face, with a pressing danger that Douglas will overwhelm them. They did not know the tremendous efforts the Little Giant was capable of putting forth. It is very evident here to-night, that with the Federal Government, and the dominant men of the section of the greatest strength of the Democratic party against him, he is, in generalship, more than a match for them all. He inspired his followers, who gathered around him in Washington, as they passed on their way to this place, with the wildest enthusiasm, and the most resolute determination to nominate him at all hazards, together with confidence in their ability to do so. And now, in spite of the South's prestige, in spite of the Administration's hate, nothing stands between him and a triumphant nomination but the *two-thirds rule;* and it is not certain that even that will avail. It would be unwise to under-estimate the man who is competent to such a performance as this. From the beginning of the struggle here, his enemies have been swimming against the tide. Slidell and all the rest, have been, as it were, but taking up arms against a sea of troubles, and they have not made much progress toward ending them. The South has not yet produced upon the floor in the rough-and-tumble fights of the Convention, a champion who could cope with the rude giant Richardson, while it required very acute ruling, by that most clear-headed sophist Caleb Cushing, at one time, to prevent Stuart of Michigan (the Democratic Senator who stood with Douglas and Broderick against Lecompton) from ending the platform fight disastrously for the Administration, by a parliamentary *coup d'etat*. I am not unwilling to admire, as all the world does, a bold game played with enormous force and splendid impudence for an imperial stake, like as this Douglas game for the Presidency. That there is infinite rottenness and corruption under it, there is abundant evidence. This is not confined to the Douglas side, however. It is a part of the caucus system. The revenues of King Caucus are bribes.

The crowd here has thinned out rapidly within the last three days. Every train goes away full—and two steamers, one for New York and another for Philadelphia, left to-day, bearing off at least two hundred outsiders. The halls of the hotels are not obstructed, nor the bar-rooms crowded as they were two weeks since. Scores of faces that became familiar in the early days of the Convention, have departed. The outside pressure from both sections melts away day by day. The stages rattle away from the hotels, loaded down with trunks, and filled with passengers. The purses of the bar-room orators and ward politicians of the North were becoming collapsed, and as this is just now a bad place to borrow money, they took flight while they had enough to see them safe home. And the Southern men are talking constantly about their "cotton." They are nearly as much interested with cotton talk, as with the logic to which they are greatly devoted, concerning the "protection of slave property in the Territories." They are also solicitous as to how their "boys" and "girls" are getting along—and Southern mails will not bring them letters at satisfactory speed.

A great calamity has come upon the Ohio delegation. Their private whiskey, of which they laid in a supply supposed to be equal to all emergencies, the nomination of Douglas included, gave out this morning. They attribute their good health which they have enjoyed to this article. The Kentucky whiskey, too, is nearly all gone. The barrel in which it is contained, and which occupies an honorable position, and receives much attention, in their parlor, gives forth, when consulted as to its condition, a dismal tone of emptiness.

The weather has been wonderfully changeable during my residence in this city. It was sultry and prostrating for a time. The sun shone with such power that there seemed, when walking on the sunny sides of the streets, to be danger of sunstroke. We had some days like those scorching ones of June in Southern Ohio. But for three days past there has been a cold rain and blustering wind, and good fires have been good things during the first part of this day. The rain fell fast, and the wind carried a chill to the bones. About noon, all the clouds were blown over into the Atlantic. The sky was stripped in an hour of the whole mass of bleak and drifting clouds, and the sun shone with reviving warmth, while the wind was not chilly, but merely cool enough to be refreshing. The planters were at the breakfast table this morning gossiping about the frost. This evening they are comforting themselves with visions of growing cotton—and wondering how will the " boys " have it set by this time.

One of our Northern delegates, a gentleman whose name or State I shall not mention, strolling down a side street the other day, saw a sign, "Slaves for sale." He walked in, and was asked, in effect, whether he meant business. He promptly replied that he wanted to buy a nice woman, and they told him they could sell him a very fine seamstress. He concluded to look at her, and she turned out to be a clever mulatto girl, well dressed, and, like a great many of her race, sporting considerable jewelry, ear-drops, finger-rings, etc. Her qualities as a seamstress were dwelt upon, and our friend was told that as it was him, he might have her cheap—price only $1500. He concluded to think of it, and look further before purchasing.

SEVENTH DAY.

CHARLESTON, S. C., *Monday*, April 30th.

The Convention came together this morning with a curious mingling of despair of accomplishing any thing, and hope that something will turn up, hope as illogical as those everlasting anticipations of Mr. Micawber.

I am not stating the case over-strongly, when I say there is a general consciousness that the Convention is making so bad a record, that its deliberations are becoming of little importance, so impossible will it be to defend any conclusion likely to be reached, before the country. The Democratic party has here furnished to its enemies the ammunition that will enable them to annihilate the preposterous pretensions which it has for some years put forth. The scenes around me are those of the dissolution of the Democratic organization.

The North-western delegates are disheartened. They see that it will hardly be worth while to nominate Douglas, as it will be impossible for him to drag through the coming campaign so cumbrous a mass of antagonisms as have been presented here.

I have several times this morning heard the remark, "The President will be nominated at Chicago." It is my own opinion, however, that there will be as irreconcilable adverse interests and sentiments developed in the Republican party at Chicago as have obtruded themselves here.

The hall is more densely crowded this morning than ever before. A great many strangers have gone home—and there are but feeble swarms buzzing about the hotels, compared with those who were crushing each other and roaring a week ago. But the South Carolinians have become interested, and the doors being opened to them this morning, they have rushed in and filled vacancies. The Convention, so far as outsiders are concerned, "wears a Southern aspect." The delegates are all here, or vacancies supplied; but the manufacturers of public opinion, satisfied with their exertions, are making their way Northward.

The vote first in order was on Butler's amendment, that is, the Cincinnati Platform. During the call of the roll of the States, a row broke out in the New Jersey delegation, as to whether the delegates had been instructed to vote as an unit. This was important, as it would determine on which side three votes should be cast. The chair decided that the recommendation of the New Jersey Convention, that the delegates should vote as an unit, was equivalent to a provision to that effect; and the rules required that delegates should vote as had been provided. The decision of the chair was appealed from. A motion was made to lay the appeal upon the table. A vote by States was demanded. The appeal was not laid upon the table; vote 145 to 150. The vote was then taken directly whether the chair should be sustained. The chair was overruled by a vote of 145 to 151. The roll being called through on the Butler resolution, the vote stood for the Cincinnati Platform, without the dotting of an i, or the crossing of a t, but with a resolution about the protection of foreign-born citizens, 105 ayes, 198 noes, as follows:

YEAS—Maine 3, Massachusetts 8, Connecticut $2\frac{1}{2}$, New Jersey 5, Pennsylvania $16\frac{1}{2}$, Delaware 3, Maryland $5\frac{1}{2}$, Virginia $12\frac{1}{2}$, North Carolina 10, Georgia 10, Missouri $4\frac{1}{2}$, Tennessee 11, Kentucky 9, Minnesota $1\frac{1}{2}$, Oregon 3—105.

NAYS—Maine 5, New Hampshire 5, Vermont 5, Massachusetts 5, Rhode Island 4, Connecticut $3\frac{1}{2}$, New York 35, New Jersey 2, Pennsylvania $10\frac{1}{2}$, Maryland $2\frac{1}{2}$, Virginia $2\frac{1}{2}$, South Carolina 8, Florida 3, Alabama 9, Louisiana 6, Mississippi 7, Texas 4, Arkansas 4, Missouri $4\frac{1}{2}$, Tennessee 1, Kentucky 3, Ohio 23, Indiana 13, Illinois 11, Michigan 6, Wisconsin 5, Minnesota $2\frac{1}{2}$, Iowa 4, California 4—198.

Just before this vote was declared, an old gentlemen declared on the floor that the gentleman in the galleries were spitting upon those below. This was styled a "privileged question." The gentlemen in the gallery were respectfully requested not to use the heads of gentlemen below them for spittoons, and not to wear their hats in the presence of the uncovered Convention.

And now came the tug of war—the crucial test—on the adoption of the minority, or Douglas-Popular Sovereignty-Supreme Court-ambiguous, report. When this report was read, Butler of Massachusetts moved to lay the whole subject on the table, and proceed to ballot for President. This was overruled, and the vote was taken direct on the minority platform. While this was pending a Marylander renewed Butler's motion, and an Alabamian seconded it by mistake. Discovering his mistake, he said, "Mr. President, I don't second the motion of that man down yonder." The Marylander was indignant, and jumping up, displayed a neat-fitting pair of light kid gloves, and the round face of a young man. He gave his name, and said he would be very glad to know the name and address of the delegate who talked of "that man down yonder." A great hearty, good-natured gentleman—a two hundred and twenty pounder—with as honest a face as you would find in a day, loomed up from his chair, and said, "I intended no disrespect to the gentleman from Maryland—but my name is Tom Cooper, of Alabama." The house thundered applause, and the Marylander looked as if he had fished for a seal and caught a rhinoceros. He gave his address, and said if Tom Cooper would call upon him him, they would take a drink together.

Flournoy of Arkansas had a personal explanation, and said he was for Popular Sovereignty.

The States were then called on the motion to adopt the minority resolutions in lieu of the majority report, and they were adopted by the following vote:

YEAS—Maine 8, New Hampshire 5, Vermont 5, Massachusetts 7, Rhode Island 4, Connecticut 6, New York 35, New Jersey 5, Pennsylvania 12, Maryland 3½, Virginia 1, Missouri 4, Tennessee 1, Kentucky 2¼, Ohio 23, Indiana 13, Illinois 11, Michigan 6, Wisconsin 5, Iowa 4, Minnesota 4—165.

NAYS—Massachusetts 6, New Jersey 2, Pennsylvania 15, Delaware —, Maryland 4½, Virginia 14, North Carolina 10, South Carolina 8, Georgia 10, Florida 3, Alabama 9, Louisiana 6, Mississippi 7, Texas 4, Arkansas 4, Missouri 5, Tennessee 11, Kentucky 9½, Michigan 10, California 4, Oregon 3—138.

There was one more straight vote required to clinch the thing,—that was a majority vote on the platform as amended by the substitution of the minority report. Mr. Butler moved for a division of the proposition, and moved for as much of it as indorsed the Cincinnati Platform simply. the chair ruled that each substantive and intelligible proposition (?) could be taken separately. The crisis was now, after long postponement, at hand. In calling the vote on the reaffirmation of the Cincinnati Platform, a delegate from Mississippi arose, his face livid with excitement, and said that Mississippi, believing the Cincinnati Platform to be a miserable swindle on one side of the house or the other, voted no. Arkansas followed—and the cotton States generally came into line under the lead of Mississippi. Under Mr. Butler's motion and the ruling of the chair, there was a vote on the first resolution of the series, thus:

1. *Resolved*, That we, the Democracy of the Union, in Convention assembled, hereby declare our affirmance of the resolutions unanimously adopted and declared as a Platform of Principles by the Democratic Convention at Cincinnati, in the year 1856, believing that Democratic principles are unchangeable in their nature, when applied to the same subject-matters.

It was carried as follows:

YEAS—Maine 8, New Hampshire 5, Veamont 5, Massachuesetts 13, Rhode Island 4, Connecticut 6, New York 35; New Jersey 7, Pennsylvania 27, Delaware 2, Maryland 5, Virginia 14, North Carolina 10, Missouri 7¼, Tennessee 10¼, Kentucky 12, Ohio 23, Indiana 13, Illinois 11, Michigan 6, Wisconsin 5, Iowa 4, Minnesota 4, California ¼ —237½.

NAYS—Delaware 1, Maryland 3, Virginia 1, South Carolina 8,

Georgia 10, Florida 3, Alabama 9, Louisiana 6, Mississippi 7, Texas 4, Arkansas 4, Missouri 1½, Tennessee 1, California 3½, Oregon 3—65.

Mr. Driggs of New York said the Convention having adopted the Cincinnati Platform, he moved to lay all the resolutions on the table. The motion to lay on the table was lost.

YEAS—Massachusetts 8½, Connecticut 2, New Jersey 5, Pennsylvania 16½, Delaware 2, Virginia 11, North Carolina 9, South Carolina 8, Tennessee, 10¾, Kentucky 7½, Minnesota 1—81.

NAYS—Maine 8, New Hampshire 6, Vermont 5, Massachusetts 4¾, Rhode Island 4, Connecticut 4, New York 35, New Jersey 2, Pennsylvania 10¾, Delaware 1, Maryland 8, Virginia 4, North Carolina 1, Georgia 10, Florida 3, Louisiana 6, Arkansas 1, Missouri 9, Tennessee 1½, Kentucky 4½, Ohio 23, Indiana 13, Illinois 11, Michigan 6, Wisconsin 5, Iowa 4, Minnesota 3, California 4, Oregon 3—188.

During the call, Mr. Walker of Alabama withdrew the vote of his State.

Mississippi withdrew her vote.

Arkansas withdrew three of her votes.

The cry goes forth from one delegate after another, "in these solemn moments"—that the party must stick together, for the country will be ruined if it does not. If the party remains united, on whatever false and hypocritical platform, or pretense, the country is safe. If the party blows up, the country is doomed, of course.

It is said that the South can't stay in the Convention if the Cincinnati swindle, and an indorsement of a court decision variously interpreted, is thrust upon the country as the Democratic platform. The South thought yesterday they could stay in the Convention, after the ambiguous platform was put forth, for the sake of defeating Douglas. But to-day, they have slept upon it and become hotter, and are up to the explosive point.

Mr. Gittings of Maryland insisted on talking out of order. He accused the chair of ruling him out of order because he came from a slaveholding State. As the President was somewhat peremptory with him, he said:

"Only one word, sir. I want to be heard. The only time I ever remember to have seen our worthy chairman before was in 1840, when he made one of the most violent Whig speeches I ever heard." [Cheers, hisses and laughter.]

Mr. Ewing of Tennessee called for a separate vote on the following preamble and resolution:

Inasmuch as differences of opinion exist in the Democratic party as to the nature and extent of the powers of a Territorial Legislature, and as to the powers and duties of Congress, under the Constitution of the United States, over the institution of slavery within the Territories;
Resolved, That the Democratic party will abide by the decisions of the Supreme Court of the United States on the questions of constitutional law.

Mr. Stuart of Michigan said, if the gentleman did not want the resolution, we of the North did not.

Hon. Bedford Brown of North Carolina warned his Northern friends not to adopt this preamble and resolution. It swept off every barrier of the Constitution, and would destroy the Democratic party and the country. [Great applause.]

Mr. Richardson wanted to speak, but Mr. Hooker of Mississippi persisted in raising a point of order on him. John Cochrane said there might be peace-offerings coming.

Amidst a babel of noise and confusion the vote was taken according to the call of Mr. Ewing.

The roll call was constantly interrupted by questions and explanations.

The Northern States first voted affirmatively, but finding the South refused to vote, changed their votes to the negative, amidst cries of "What's the dodge now?" "That's a back down!" and the like.

The vote was announced, and the preamble and resolutions were rejected.

It was rejected by the following vote:

YEAS—New Hampshire 1, Rhode Island 4, Pennsylvania 8, Missouri 4, Kentucky 4—21.

NAYS—Maine 8, New Hampshire 4, Vermont 5, Massachusetts 13, Connecticut 6, New York 35, New Jersey 7, Pennsylvania 19, Delaware 2, Maryland 8, Virginia 15, North Carolina 10, South Carolina 8, Missouri 5, Tennessee 12, Kentucky 8, Ohio 23, Indiana 13, Illinois 11, Michigan 6, Wisconsin 5, Iowa 4, Minnesota 4, California 4, Oregon 3—238.

A division was called on all the remaining resolutions, and they were severally adopted; that relating to the rights of naturalized citizens receiving a unanimous vote, even in this divided Convention. The resolutions adopted, in addition to the Cincinnati Platform, are as follows:

3. *Resolved*, That it is the duty of the United States to afford ample and complete protection to all its citizens, whether at home or abroad, and whether native or foreign.

4. *Resolved*, That one of the necessities of the age, in a military, commercial and postal point of view, is speedy communication between the Atlantic and Pacific States; and the Democratic party pledge such constitutional Government aid as will insure the construction of a Railroad to the Pacific coast, at the earliest practicable period.

5. *Resolved*, That the Democratic party are in favor of the acquisition of the Island of Cuba, on such terms as shall be honorable to ourselves and just to Spain.

6. *Resolved*, That the enactments of State Legislatures to defeat the faithful execution of the Fugitive Slave law, are hostile in character, subversive of the Constitution, and revolutionary in their effect.

Mr. Stuart of Michigan now procured the floor, and made a very irritating speech, exceedingly ill-timed, unless he intended to drive out the Gulf States, and he has been accused of entertaining such purpose.

Writing, some days afterward, of this scene, I said of the part Mr. Stuart performed:

So, as soon as the platform was adopted, he took the stand upon a motion to reconsider, made for the purpose of injecting a speech into the proceedings at that stage, and proceeded in the most offensive way to claw at the old sore of the party, already full of fever. If his object was to produce irritation, he succeeded admirably. The explosion followed fast upon his incendiary shaking of fire-brands in the party powder-house. But there was more powder in the explosion than Stuart calculated upon. Instead of merely blowing off a fragment or two, and producing the long-coveted reaction in the North, one half of the South—the very citadel and heart of Democracy—was blown away; and the other half prevented from following, only by that which was in effect a real reconsideration of the platform, the last thing which Stuart wanted.

After Stuart's speech, Mr. Walker of Alabama read the protest of that State against the proceedings of the Convention, and formally withdrew from it.

Mr. Barry did the same thing for Mississippi. Mr. Mouton did the same for Louisiana; Gen. Simmons for South Carolina; Mr. Milton for Florida; Mr. Bryan of Texas, and Mr. Burrows of Arkansas. The speeches which give the spirit of this exciting period better than any others, were those of Mr. Mouton of Louisiana, and Mr. Glenn of Mississippi, the latter making decidedly the speech of the occasion.

SPEECH OF MR. MOUTON.

Mr. Mouton of Louisiana. I have but a short communication to make to this Convention. I do not do so in my individual name. I am instructed by the delegates of Louisiana, whom I represent, to say that they will not participate any more in the proceedings of this Convention. Heretofore we have been in the habit of saying, that the Democracy of the country were harmonious; but can we say so to-day with any truth? Are we not divided, and divided in such a manner that we can never be again united and reconciliated, because we are divided upon principle? Can we adopt this platform voted for by the majority of the Convention? Can we go home to our constituents, and put one construction upon it, and the Northern Democrats another? No. I think I speak the sentiment of my State when I say, she never will place a double construction upon a platform.

If we are to fight the Black Republicans, let us do it with a bold front, and together. Let us take the same arms—let us sustain the same regiment. We say that the Douglas principles, adopted to-day by the majority, can never be the principles of the South. And let me say, at the same time, that I should have suggested the propriety of dispensing with all these votes, and have come at once to the conclusion we have now reached.

Mr. M. then argued on the principles of the two platforms, and declared his conviction that the only way to meet and to check Black Republican aggression was to adopt the doctrine of protection by Congress to the property of Southern citizens in all the Territories of the Union.

SPEECH OF MR. GLENN.

Mr. Glenn of Mississippi arose. He said: For the first time, for the only time, for the last time, and in the name of the State he had the honor in part to represent, he desired to say a few words. He held in his hand the solemn act of the Mississippi delegation upon this floor. It was not a hasty act, not conceived in passion or carried out from mere caprice or disappointment. It was the firm resolve of the great body they represented, which was expressed in the Convention who sent them here, and that resolve that people, we, their representatives, will maintain at all times and at all costs. They came not to dictate, and since their arrival, the intercourse has been courteous with their brethren from other State Conventions, as far as personality was concerned. But that was not all. They claimed the exercise of the principles upon which the party must stand. He did not ask them to adopt a platform opposed to their conscientious principles. He claimed to come as an equal member of the common Confederacy, with the simple desire of an acknowledgment of their equal rights within that Confederacy. What was the construction of the platform of 1856? You of the North said it meant one thing; we of the South another. Either you were right or we wrong. They ask which was right and which wrong. The North had maintained their position, but, while doing so, they did not acknowledge the rights of the South. Turn back to one of their leading men, once representing a sovereign State in the Union, who then voted that Congress had the constitutional power to pass the Wilmot proviso, or to exclude, and now, when the Supreme Court has said it is in that power, he comes forward and says that Congress is impotent to protect slave power.

The speaker then referred to the gentleman from Ohio, who, a few days since, said if a Territorial Legislature should misuse its powers or abuse them, Congress can wipe it out altogether. They would part with their lives before they would acknowledge the principles for which they contend. We say go your way, and we will go ours. The South leaves not like Hagar in the wilderness; but he would tell them that in less than sixty days they would find a united South, standing shoulder to shoulder.

Senator Bayard of Delaware now announced his withdrawal from the Convention, and Senator Saulsbury of the same State, stated that he did not know what to do.

Mr. Merrick of Illinois made a little speech. He said:

"A Southern man by birth—it is but three years since I parted from that Southern soil—and upon the tide of emigration sought my fortunes in the great North-west. Coming back here, and hoping to join in fraternal concord and mutual love with my Southern brethren of the Democratic party, I find, sir, star after star madly shooting from the great Democratic galaxy. Why is it, and what is to come of it? Does it presage that, hereafter, star after star will shoot from the galaxy of the Republic, and the American Union become a fragment, and a parcel of sectional republics?"

Points of order were raised.

Mr. Russell of Virginia made a speech for that State. He said:

"Hitherto the career of Virginia has been side by side with all her sister States, North, South, East and West, and beneath a banner on which every State has its star, as members of one common and united constellation; but it must be known to this assembly that if indeed the hour shall ever come when the North and South must separate, the destiny of Virginia is with the South. [Loud cheers.] She will then have to

say to the South, 'where thou goest I will go; thy people shall be my people, and thy God shall be my God.' [Great cheering.]
"But, sir, she will pause before the determines that that event is inevitable. Virginia stands in the midst of her sister States, in garments red with the blood of her children slain in the first outbreak of the 'irrepressible conflict.' But, sir, not when her children fell at midnight beneath the weapon of the assassin, was her heart penetrated with so profound a grief as that which will wring it when she is obliged to choose between a separate destiny with the South and her common destiny with the entire Republic."

In conclusion, he stated Virginia wanted an opportunity for consultation, and the Convention adjourned.

[So great is the interest felt in this day's proceedings, that I recapitulate to some extent, by inserting the descriptive letter below:]

SCENES OF THE DAY DESCRIBED—HOW THE DISRUPTION HAPPENED.

CHARLESTON, S. C., *Monday night*, April 30.

It was asserted, early in the sitting of the Convention, that it would be impossible for the South to submit to Mr. Douglas as the nominee upon a platform on which it would be possible for him to stand. The Douglas men at first laughed this to scorn. Presently they saw such indications of earnestness, that they paused and considered the matter, and became much more tolerant, and seemed willing to acquiesce in any sort of a platform, provided the South would allow the nomination of Douglas. The determination of the New York contest, and the adoption of a rule allowing individual delegates from uninstructed States to vote as they pleased, gave the friends of Mr. Douglas a majority in the Convention. They proceeded to use that majority, for the purpose of making sure of their game. They joined the ultra-Southern States in demanding the test fight upon the platform. It became apparent the moment the platform was taken into consideration that there were differences it would be impossible for honest men to accommodate. The Douglas men begged for a chance for ambiguity. They craved and clamored for a false pretense. They begged to be allowed to cheat, and for the privilege of being cheated. They were particularly anxious for success. They were not so particular about principle. The South would stand fast for the great principle of constitutional rights as she understood it; and by her more ultra-representatives declared, that if by the bare numerical majority of votes, the Southern Platform was rejected, and the Squatter Sovereignty Platform, or some dishonorable equivocation protruded, she would withdraw from the Convention. By this time the Douglas men had discovered, that whereas they had just about a majority, it would be impossible for them to obtain a two thirds vote in a full Convention. They were willing, therefore, that a few ultra-Southern States might go out, and allow them to nominate their man. All at once they became very cheerful on the subject of a disruption of the Convention. They could go North and get two votes (electoral) for their nominee, for every Southern vote that would leave the Convention. Their game then was, to have three or four States, at most, go out. They wanted a little eruption, but not a great one. On Friday last it appeared that if the majority insisted upon its ambiguous platform, there would be a tremendous explosion. Even the Kentucky delegation had informally determined, only two of the delegates dissenting, that if the exigency arose, that Alabama & Co. must go out, Kentucky must go along. Douglas men were alarmed at the prospect, and Bigler's resolution to recommit the platform to the committee, was carried against the Douglas forces, by a vote of 151 to 152. So the fight went over until Saturday.

The committee succeeded in modifying the reports, but not in changing their essential character. Saturday was spent in the most tedious and tasteless, flat, stale, and unprofitable debate that it has ever been my misfortune to listen to. It was worse than when the House of Representatives resolves itself into a debating society, and fifth-rate members draw on each other and the people to the dismay of the galleries, reams of foolscap filled with essays on the slavery question. After the flood of twaddle was stopped by the call for the previous question, the parlimentary fight was interesting, and made amends for the painful hours spent in listening to the drivel of inconsequential debate. The South filibustered to prevent a vote on the platform that night. The North was resolved to have a vote. After some hours spent in skirmishing, as I have elsewhere described, the matter was compromised by disposing of the preliminary points, and agreeing to come to a fair vote this morning. Yesterday there was a report current that the South, discovering the total impossibility of the nomination of Douglas while the Convention remained consolidated, his full strength having been shown, and amounting to a bare majority, would find some excuse for staying in the Convention even after the adoption of the minority report, and would slaughter Douglas under the two-thirds rule. The most talkative and rabid of the Douglas men swore that if this was done, they would repeal the two-thirds rule, and let the Convention explode if it wanted so to do. Last night it was reported, and I was told by Southern men it was so, that the only State that would go out was Alabama. There was no possibility of preventing Yancey & Co. from going out, but the rest of them would stay in and slaughter Douglas. The partisans of the Little Giant looked blue at this. There were other reports afloat that were somewhat exciting. The rabid Douglasites were alarmed at signs of discontent and shakiness in several of the Northwestern delegations. They said it had been discovered there was a parcel of delegates to whom it would not do to trust the secrets of the Douglas party. Those fellows were leaky, and whenever the Convention adjourned they were found together buzzing and busy as green flies. It was known that Slidell & Co. were willing to buy all such fellows, and there was alarm in the camp of Douglas on the platform question. They were afraid the majority report would be adopted at last. There were threats that if this was the case some of the North-western States would bolt. These threats were seriously made, too. And the Northwestern men had no hesitation in saying that they could not and would not fight upon such a platform. They would go home and fold their hands, and let those who believed in using all the powers of the Federal Government for the protection of slavery against the people of a Territory, do the work. This morning, however, it became apparent that the Douglas majority was firm, and the South desperate. It was not long before every observer saw that the long-looked for explosion was at hand. The South would not stay in the Convention, even to defeat Douglas, if the double-shuffle platform were adopted.

I shall not now trace all the twistings and turnings of the fight. Let it be sufficient to say that, in the first place, the Cincinnati Platform by itself was voted down.

The minority resolutions were then carried as a substitute for the majority resolutions, by a vote of 165 to 138—this 138 is the solid anti-Douglas strength. Now the question came on the *adoption* of the substituted report—the definite, irrevocable vote of the Convention upon the Douglas Platform, was divided into its substantive propositions. The resolution reaffirming the Cincinnati Platform, believing Democratic principles to be unchangeable in their nature, was first voted upon, and it was carried by 237½ to 65. There was a motion now made to lay all the rest of the report upon the table. This would have been simply the adoption of the Cincinnati Platform, and it was defeated, 81 to 188. While this vote was being taken, Alabama, Mississippi and Arkansas withdrew their votes. Now the question arose upon the adoption of the Squatter Sovereignty part of the platform—that part wherein it is stated that, "inasmuch as differences of opinion exist in the Democratic party," it will abide by the Supreme Court. The Hon. Bedford Brown now saw the crisis. The political tornado was about to burst. The barometer indicated a sudden storm. Mr. Brown did not know it was too late to save the party, and the country attached thereto, and he made an appeal to gentlemen, as piteous, as solemn, as agonizingly earnest, as ever a man offered up for his life, that the Convention should not pass that resolution, and thereby disrupt and destroy the Democratic party. He called upon gentlemen to pause upon the brink of the tremendous precipice upon which they stood, and to look into the gulf before they took the leap.

Mr. Yancey caught my eye at this "solemn moment," as various gentlemen in the Convention insisted upon calling it, and he was smiling as a bridegroom. He had evidently made up his mind. He was not perplexed by saucy doubts and fears.

Mr. Stuart of Michigan wished to speak, but was put down by loud cries of "Order."

Mr. William A. Richardson of Illinois wished to speak. As the crisis had arrived, and as Richardson is a great man for a crisis, and had withdrawn Douglas from the Cincinnati Convention, it was hoped that he had something to say which would relieve the party from its misery. There were cries of "Hear Richardson." A thrill of excitement passed around the hall, and every body leaned forward or stood up to see and hear the right-hand man of the Little Giant on the crisis. Richardson commenced with his usual hoarseness and solemnity, when Judge Meek of Alabama, a gentleman six feet eight inches in height, with a splendid voice, arose and made a point of order against Stuart of Michigan, who still seemed, by standing in his place, to claim the floor.

Judge Meek's point of order caused another sensation. Presently the Judge's point of order was ruled not well taken, and silence was obtained, when John Cochrane of New York jumped up and called " Mis-*ter*—*Presi*-DENT !" and proceeded to urge that Richardson might be heard. He believed Richardson was about to bring "peace-offerings." Every body knew there could not be any peace-offerings but the dead body of Douglas, and it was thought that would be a singular time to make an offering of the corpse of the Little Giant. The great crowds in the galleries heaved like big waves. They thought something prodigious was about to occur. But no sooner had Richardson opened his mouth and commenced to speak of the delegation from Illinois, and its intention in appearing there, than Mr. Hooper of Mississippi objected peremptorily, and insisted and persisted in calling Richardson to order; and by insisting upon his point of order, when ninety-nine out of every hundred persons were willing and anxious to hear Richardson, would not let him be heard. This was considered an act of discourtesy toward Mr. R. of the most flagrant character. A Southern gentleman explained it to me this evening, by saying that the South was at that moment in a delicate position, and did not want any traps sprung. He also excused the seeming discourtesy, by speaking of Richardson's discourteous behavior toward Randall of Pennsylvania. And now ensued a most extraordinary scene. Instead of proceeding to put their explanatory resolution upon the Cincinnati Platform, stating that there were differences of opinion in the Democratic party, and referring to the Courts for doctrine, the Douglasites were suddenly discovered in full retreat.

The object of Richardson, in attempting to gain the floor, was then at once seen. He had desired to say, that Illinois and the North-west in general, had not been anxious to have any thing but the Cincinnati Platform, and would be content with that, if the others would. This was to have been his peace-offering—his olive-branch. As the Douglas men did not understand the movement, several delegations stood firm, and voted roundly for the adoption of the explanatory resolution, according to the original programme. Most of the States passed the point, however, and consulted. New York retired from the hall to consult. It took some minutes for the new tactics of Richardson to get circulation, and in the mean time, as one delegation after another understood the point, the votes of States were counted, and finally, with a general rush, the only resolution having the slightest significance in the minority report, was stricken out. The Douglas army had retreated behind the position of Gen. Butler of Massachusetts. By a flank movement, they had placed themselves upon the Cincinnati Platform, pure and simple.

Those who had no insight into things, thought at this moment that the dead point of danger was safely passed. The fact was (if we may change the figure somewhat materially from those hitherto used), the ship had struck the rock, and just as the passengers thought they were floating safely into deep water, the vessel was actually sinking. It was ominous that, from this time, Georgia, Florida, Alabama, Louisiana, Mississippi, Texas and Arkansas, declined to vote.

The Convention now proceeded, as if in earnest, to take the vote by States, on the several propositions tacked to the tail of the explanatory resolution, from which this had been severed. These propositions were about protecting foreigners, and building a Pacific Railroad, and acquiring Cuba "on terms honorable to ourselves and just to Spain," etc.; and the vote was unanimous in all cases excepting that regarding the Pacific Railroad, and nearly so in that case—the Gulf States still refusing to vote. There were several attempts during the reading of the poor clap-trap resolutions (the substance of all of which was in the Cincinnati Platform already) to get up a show of enthusiasm. The failures in each case were extremely dreary. The Convention was under the frown of King Cotton, and his displeasure was upon it like a blight or deadly nightshade. And now the platform was constructed as it stands, the most uncouth, disjointed, illogical, confused, cowardly and contemptible thing in the history of platforms, mean and cowardly as they have been from the beginning. Mr. Stuart of Michigan moved a reconsideration of the vote, and proceeded to speak upon it. He was evidently laboring under the impression that he was full of a very powerful speech. When he undertook to find it, however, he discovered his mistake, and soon got into the old rut about the gallant and glorious North-west, and how wonderfully the Northern Democracy had stood up for the South, and had fought, bled and died for the South—and he seemed to reproach the South with inconsistency, and with having demanded of the Northern Democracy more than they could bear. He stated that Mr. Yancey had admitted that the South had asked new guarantees of Southern safety from the Northern Democracy. Yancey corrected him. He had not made such admission. He had simply contended for the Southern construction of the Cincinnati Platform, and repudiated ambiguity. Stuart was getting into hot water at every plunge, and his fine round bald head glowed like the full moon, as he was making matters worse. Stuart is one of the best parliamentarians in the country, and a man of fine intellect, and he would, in spite of the thinness of his hair, be a handsome man, if it were not for his nose, which is wretchedly broken down, and gives him a P. R. sort of appearance.

Senator Saulsbury of Delaware was greatly concerned. He still hoped to save the Democratic party. He still hoped to prevent the dire combustion and ruin from breaking forth and consuming the precious old party—legacy from our fathers, and so forth. Mr. Saulsbury rushed in to save the country—that is, he stood upright in his chair. He is a very well-looking man—fine, intellectual face, brilliant eyes, and a vast assortment of black hair. He had forgotten his hair, and in the confusion and excitement of the moment it hung all over his forehead and into his eyes. He made an appeal to the patriotism of Stuart to desist, as he was manifestly stirring the waters of bitterness. Three or four gentlemen were anxious to reply to Mr. Stuart. Randall of Pennsylvania wished to do something grand, gloomy, and peculiar, in showing up the fallacy of the statement that the Northern Democracy had ever been committed to Squatter Sovereignty.

Mr. Randall is a short, stout old gentleman with a round and wrinkled sort of head, while his features habitually express the most fierce discontent. Stuart finally retired from the platform, having done a very inflammatory thing, and being tolerably well informed of the fact. And now commenced the regular stampede. Alabama led the Southern column. Mr. Walker of that State, a tall, slender, pale gentleman, able in controversy and graceful in movement, called the attention of the house to a communication from the State of Alabama, which he proposed to read from the clerk's desk. There was a shudder of excitement, an universal stir over the house, and then for the first time during the day, profound stillness. Mr. W. proceeded to give the reasons which had influenced Alabama to retire from the Convention at that point. They were, first, the instructions of the Alabama Convention; second, the conviction the delegation felt that it was its duty to retire, as justice had not been done the South. When he concluded, which he did by stating that there could not thereafter be any representation from the State of Alabama in that Convention, the delegation left their seats and made their way to various points, where they took position as spectators. Mississippi went next, with less formality but more vim. Her declarations of the manner in which the Northern Democracy had been found wanting, and of her purposes, were exceedingly explicit. The Northern Democracy had been found anxious to dodge the issues before the country. That would never do for Mississippi. She cast her fortunes with those of her sister State, Alabama. Mr. Glenn of Mississippi mounted a chair, and facing the Ohio delegation, which sat directly behind Mississippi, made one of the most impassioned and thrilling twenty-minute speeches to which I have ever listened. It was evident that every word was from his deepest convictions. He was pale as ashes, and his eyes rolled and glared, as he told the gentlemen from Ohio how far they were from doing their duty now, and how kindly he felt toward them, and how they would have to take position yet upon the high ground of the South, or it would be all in vain that they would attempt to arrest the march of Black Republicanism. For the present, they must go their ways, and the South must go her ways. He declared, too, with piercing emphasis, that in less than sixty days there would be an United South; and at this declaration there was the most enthusiastic shouting yet heard in the Convention. The South Carolinians cheered loud and long, and the tempest of applause made the circuit of the galleries and the floor several times before it subsided. There was a large number of ladies present, and they favored the secessionists with their sweetest smiles, and with nods and glances of approval, a delighted fluttering of fans and parasols, and even occasional clapping of hands.

The Alabamians and Mississippians were standing in the aisles and getting away from their seats, and as the spokesman of Mississippi concluded what he had to say, Alexander Mouton of Louisiana, and Col. Simmons of South Carolina—the Louisianian a thick-set, gray-haired gentleman, with French manners and accent; and the Carolinian a tall gentleman, of commanding presence—were claiming the floor, each to give warning that his State was going. The Louisianian took precedence, and made a plain, blunt speech, charging upon the Northern Douglasites a disposition to shirk and to dodge under ambiguities which would be dishonorable.

He dwelt upon the platform which had been adopted in terms of withering contempt, and said "that was not the way to fight the Black Republicans." He made a very decided impression, and called down rapturous applause from the swarming galleries. As he spoke he was facing the Ohio delegation, and within a few feet of them, and seemed to be addressing his remarks particularly to them. "Gov." Payne turned his head over upon his left shoulder, and once or twice made a sorrowful effort to laugh, that would have brought tears to the eyes of a tender-hearted and sympathizing friend, it was so hopeless and forlorn.

Colonel Simmons of South Carolina now spoke for that State in a quiet, dignified manner, and presented the reasons for the withdrawal of the State to the Convention. The secession of South Carolina drew down another tempest of approbation. All the delegates from that State (sixteen) had put their names to the paper with the exception of three. Several of them, nearly all perhaps, did not like to do it, but it would be political perdition in South Carolina to those who, professing to represent her, should fail to join in a secession movement. Florida was the next to go, and then Arkansas. In the delegation of the latter State there had been a dispute, but the majority were for going out. And so they did, each delegation forbidding unauthorized persons to fill their places. Merritt of Illinois now obtained the floor, and proceeded to make an appeal. He wanted to try the effect of eloquence upon the secessionists. He was becoming very red in the face, and was almost launching away into the empyrean, when he was cut short by several delegates, who did not want to hear eloquence, and the chairman of the Georgia delegation said Georgia wished to retire, to consult. Leave was granted—and now Virginia, through her spokesman, wanted time for consultation also. Georgia and Virginia expressed the deepest sympathy for their Southern brethren. Their destiny was with the South forever. The Southern feeling ran high, and it seemed that public opinion was about to enforce, as the test of loyalty to the South, secession from the Convention. A large number of gentlemen in the hall looked absolutely frightened. They considered themselves looking upon a spectacle of prodigious significance, and some were muttering with white lips that the hour of revolution was at hand. And there were Neros about, too, who thought the whole matter an extensive joke, and insisted upon calling attention to the ridiculous points.

In the course of the disruption, notice was given that all who sympathized with the movement should meet at St. Andrew's Hall at seven o'clock in the evening.

When the Convention adjourned, the people stood in groups on the corners, and even in the middle of the streets. The outside pressure was for the seceders, and Southern feeling runs high. It is now believed that nearly the whole South will go out, and that there may be an attempt made to organize two "National Democratic" parties. I presume this will be done. The Douglas men are swearing vengeance to-night not loud but deep, and the North-western States say they will nominate him if they have to do it themselves.

THE NIGHT AFTER THE DISRUPTION.

CHARLESTON, S. C., *Tuesday*, May 1st.

Last night, after completing a letter giving an account of the explosion of the Convention, I walked in the direction of the Southern mass meeting.

The night was beautiful with moonlight, which silvered the live oaks along Meeting street, and made the plastered fronts of the old houses gleam like marble. The hour was eleven, and a stranger, unacquainted with the condition of affairs, would not have been long in discovering that there was something extraordinary afloat. People hurried by, looking excited and solicitous. There were still groups about the corners, and the conversations were full of animation. Presently I heard a band of music and the shouts of a multitude. Hurrying past the Mills House and Magnolia Hall, where the Douglasites had congregated in the days of their glory, but which now looked dark and deserted, I soon came upon a street full of people in front of the Court House, and heard a thousand throats call for "Yancey!" "Yancey!" I was just too late to hear Lamar of Mississippi, one of the best speakers in the South. He had concluded a speech of an hour and a half, in which he had analyzed the record of Douglas on Squatter Sovereignty, and with contemptuous fury spurned the pretension that Douglas had been consistent. He followed Douglas in all his turnings and doublings remorselessly as the hounds follow the fox, and when he had snapped him at last in the fanged jaws of his logic and fact, he worried him without mercy.

Mr. Yancey appeared, and was proud and happy to see the South taking so proud a position in favor of her constitutional rights. He spoke of the seceding delegates as about to form the "Constitutional Democratic Convention," and the delegates who remained, as composing the "Rump Convention." He said this Rump Convention would speedily be in fact a Sectional Convention, and would represent only a faction of the Free Soil sentiment of the North. He said the South must come up as a unit, and vindicate its constitutional rights. Every ultra sentiment was applauded with mad enthusiasm. Yancey said that, perhaps, even now, the pen of the historian was nibbed to write the story of a new Revolution. At this, some one of the crowd cried "three cheers for the Independent Southern Republic." They were given with a will.

Yancey closed by saying he would reserve his powers for such service as he might be able to render the South in the Constitutional Democratic Convention which would meet in St. Andrew's Hall. After Yancey, Mr. Hooker of Mississippi spoke, and made a flaming fire-eating harangue. When he concluded, the music and crowd proceeded to the Mercury office, and called out Mr. Rhett, the editor. Thence it moved to the head-quarters of the Louisiana Convention, and heard a couple of speeches, which were received with enthusiasm. The next move was to the Mills House, where Fernando Wood was called out, and that silver-tongued and smiling gentleman made a "Constitutional" speech.

There was a Fourth of July feeling in Charleston last night,—a jubilee. There was no mistaking the public sentiment of the city. It was overwhelmingly and enthusiastically in favor of the seceders. In all her history Charleston had never enjoyed herself so hugely. The Douglas men look badly this morning, as though they had been troubled during the night with bad dreams. Some of them are as jolly as Mark Tapleys, and deserve that "credit for being jolly" under adverse circumstances, which distinguished that philosopher. The disruption is too serious for them. They would have been happy if a couple of Gulf States had gone out and left them with the rest, and the votes to nominate Douglas, and all the prestige of regularity. But they see now that their party is rent as Keitt was going to rend the Union, "from turret to foundation-stone."

The Douglasites find themselves in the position of a semi-Free Soil, sectional party, and the poor fellows take it hard. The bitter cup which they have so often pressed upon the Republicans is now thrust upon them. They are denominated by the ultra-South sectionalists, and are accused of cleaving unto heresies as bad as Sewardism,—of being Frank Blair Republicans at heart. They are told, too, that they have no principles, but are devoted unto death to a man and the spoils.

EIGHTH DAY.

Convention opened with a solemn prayer for harmony. Gen. Cushing looked troubled, but some one had covered his desk with flowers, and he regaled himself by thrusting his pale nose into the red roses.

Business commenced ominously.

Mr. Benning of Georgia announced the result of the consultation of that State. It was the adoption, by a majority of the delegation, of the following resolution:

Resolved, That upon the opening of the Convention this morning our chairman be requested to state to the President that the Georgia delegation, after mature deliberation, have felt it to be their duty, under existing circumstances, not to participate further in the deliberations of the Convention, and that, therefore, the delegation withdraw.

Twenty-six out of thirty-four Georgia delegates then retired from the hall.

A majority of the Arkansas delegation announced their deliberate determination formally to retire; and retired.

The Virginia, Kentucky, North Carolina and Maryland delegations retired to consult.

Solomon Cohen of Savannah, Ga., who remained in the Convention, made a speech ultra-Southern in tone. But he could not then leave the Convention, until the last straw had broken the camel's back. He was with the seceders in sentiment, and they were earnest in action, and would be united. The South would stand together. The substance of his speech was a warning to the Douglasites not to put Douglas in nomination and make the breach irreconcilable.

He said: "I charge my Northern friends—and I yet love to call them so—be not deceived. The feelings which have prompted me to remain in this Convention, are, I trust, high and holy. I am prepared to stay here in the hope—and I trust in God it may not prove a fruitless one—that the spirit of our ancestors, that the spirit of brotherly love, that the spirit of concord and patriotism, which hovered over those who framed the Constitution of the country, may hover over and rest amongst and upon us. Be not deceived, I repeat, for in heart and in principle I am with those who have retired from the Convention. Yet I have deemed it my duty to remain among you, and to mingle in your deliberations, with the hope that the cup of conciliation may not be drained to the dregs.

"You have perhaps supposed that the South are not in earnest. You have perhaps cause for the supposition, in the fact that a portion of the delegation remain here in this Convention, that Georgia is not a unit upon this question. Gentlemen, I have been engaged in many controversies in two States, in which my lot has been cast in different periods of my life; and the only question that has ever divided the people of the South, as far as I have seen, is simply the question of time.

"I will stay here until the last feather be placed upon the back of the camel—I will stay until crushed and broken in spirit, humiliated by feeling and knowing that I have no longer a voice in the counsels of the Democracy of the Union—feeling that the Southern States are as a mere cipher in your estimation—that all her rights are trampled under foot; and I say here that I shall then be found shoulder to shoulder with him who is foremost in this contest."

All of which was understood to mean—never, never nominate Douglas, or all things dire will happen.

Maj. Flournoy then begged to be indulged in one remark. He was opposed to giving up the ship. The following is one of his paragraphs:

"Mr. President, I am a Southern man. Yes, sir, I have been reared amidst the institution. All I have is the product of slave labor. I believe the institution a patriarchal one, and beneficial alike to master and slave. The bread which supports my own wife and tender babe, is the product of slave labor. I trust then that, like Cæsar's wife, I am 'above suspicion.'"

Mr. Gaulden, the slave-trader of Savannah, gave his reasons for remaining in the Convention:

He was a slavery-extension, slave-trade man. He believed the institution to be right, socially, politically, morally and religiously. He believed that, if the institution of slavery were to be abolished, civilization would go back two hundred years. The prohibition of the slave-trade had put an end to all hope of extending the area of slavery at the present time. There was but one remedy at present for the evils the South complained of, and that was, to reopen the African slave-trade. [Cheers and loud laughter.] In this he looked to the Northern Democracy to aid them. [Renewed laughter and cheers.]

He told his fellow-Democrats that the African slave-trade man is the

Union man—the true Christian man. He told them that the slave-trade of Virginia was more inhuman, more unchristian, in every point of view, than the African slave-trade; for the African slave-trader goes to a heathen land, and brings the savage here, and Christianizes and moralizes him, and sends him down to posterity a happy man. [Cheers and loud laughter.]

Mr. Reed of Indiana. I am with you. I favor it.

Mr. Gaulden. Good. Then he would put him down for one. He declared that the Virginia slave-trader, who tore a slave family asunder from those ties which cluster around civilization, whether it be the slave or the free man, was far more open to rebuke than the man who brought the African from a land where he has no ties of country or family around him.

He desired not to be discourteous to Virginia; but, with all deference to the State, he believed they were influenced more than they ought to be by the almighty dollar. He had himself purchased some slaves in Virginia, and had to pay from one thousand to twelve hundred dollars, while he could buy a better nigger in Africa for fifty dollars. [Loud laughter and great applause.] Now, if any of his friends from the North would go down to his plantation in Georgia—it was not far from here, and he hoped many of them would—he would show them negroes he had purchased in Virginia, in Georgia, in Alabama, in Louisiana, and he would also show them the native African, the noblest Roman of them all. [Shouts of laughter and applause repeated round after round.]

The applause and laughter on the floor, during this gentleman's speech, were overpowering. He was in deadly earnest, and talked with no little force of expression. He is a tall, hatchet-faced man, with brown complexion, high nose, great eyes, thin, straggling, black beard and black hair. His personal appearance is much like that of Edgerton, M. C., of Ohio.

Mr. McCook of Ohio moved the adoption of the following resolution:

Resolved, That this Convention will proceed at 2 P. M. of this day, by a call of the States, to nominate a candidate for President, and immediately thereafter, to nominate a candidate for the Vice-Presidency of the United States.

Mr. Rafferty of New Jersey, on the part of his delegation, presented a protest against the vote of the house, overruling the decision of the chair, on the controversy respecting the casting of the vote of that State.

The condition of affairs here and now—Charleston, May 1st, twelve o'clock—is as follows: The seceding Southerners are just calling their Constitutional Democratic Convention to order, at St. Andrew's Hall. A row is in progress in this hall among the California delegates. At this moment, three of them are at sword's points, bickering as to what shall be done and who shall speak the voice of the State. John Cochrane of New York is anxious to make a speech. Mr. McCook of Ohio wants to force a motion to come to a ballot for a candidate for the Presidency at two o'clock. Half a dozen Southern delegations are out consulting, trying to find where they are to go.

One of the Californians obtains full possession of the floor, and proceeds to pour hot shot into the Popular Sovereignty camp. He charged those who had supported the minority platform, with truckling to Black Republicanism. A Connecticut delegate (Gallagher) springs up, white with rage, and black hair flying in his eyes, and raises a question of order, that the gentleman from California has no right to slander the Democracy of Connecticut. He made the point of order, too, that the Californian had no business to stand up and, as with a lash, to belather the men of the North.

California has great happiness in finding that the cap fits the gentleman from Connecticut. He proceeds to say that the South has been maltreated in the confederacy, and says that if the aggressions of the North continue, and the Union should be dissolved, the Pacific States have, thank God, the domain upon which to build up a splendid empire of their own. He concludes by grossly insulting a gentleman from Missouri. This Californian seems eager to vary the exercises by a fight. He looks and talks as if nothing would agree with his stomach so well as a bowie-knife encounter. The insulted Missourian proceeds to make a speech. He would not sit in a Convention where his motives were called in question. The chair had not heard the insult, or he would have called the Californian to order. Missouri proceeded to give forth a doleful sound about the disrupted Democracy. His lamentations were grievous as those of Jeremiah, but nôt so eloquent or poetic. A tall, black-bearded, ferocious looking Californian gets up, and makes the most amiable speech ever heard, rebuking, in the mildest and kindest terms, his ill-mannered and insolent colleague. McCook of Ohio jumps up and wants to press a vote on the Presidency. John Cochrane wants to speak; but objections are raised, and John can't speak. Seward of Georgia wants to explain his position. After a while, he obtains unanimous consent to go on, and proceeds to tell what he thought of the understanding between the North and South in the Kansas and Nebraska fight—all of which he saw, and part of which he was, as a member of Congress from the State of Georgia. As this letter closes, Seward is making a strong popular sovereignty speech, which is oil upon the feverish wounds of the poor Northern Democrats. He is going home to Georgia to state the case to the people of that State. And now a North Carolinian gets up and encourages the Douglasites, by telling them he is not going out.

Mr. Richardson of Illinois tried to speak comfortably to the people.

Mr. Perry of South Carolina, one of the fragments that remained, rose to speak, and was greeted by a storm of hisses from the galleries. Mr. Perry begged the North, making the appeal in the most earnest and pathetic manner, simply to give up the point of controversy. He assured the Northerners that they were wrong, and should give up for the sake of harmony. The Charleston Courier reports him as saying: He deeply regretted the schisms that had been going on. He represented, with his friend, Col. Boozer, only one vote, and if the South all retired, it would be folly for them to remain; so he besought the Convention to give some boon to the South. So far as any practical good could be accomplished, it was a mere abstraction; no issue could arise under it, for no slaveholder would go into Territories unfit for slave labor, when it was sure to become a free State upon entering the Union. He begged the North to consider these things, and to do all in its power to heal the unhappy differences that had arisen.

Mr. Howard of Tennessee had been instructed to ask of the Convention the recognition of Congressional protection. The gentleman from Illinois (Mr. Richardson) said that his honor and manhood forbid him from retreating from his position. Was his honor, was his manhood, only dependent upon a disregard of constitutional rights? He read, on the part of Tennessee and her sister State of Kentucky, which stood between the two extremes of the country, the following resolution, which he believed would reunite the North and the South, and was the ultimatum of the South:

Resolved, That all the citizens of the United States have an equal right to settle, with their property, in the Territories of the United States, and that, under the decisions of the Supreme Court of the United States, which we recognize as a correct exposition of the Constitution of the United States, neither their rights of person nor property can be destroyed or impaired by Congressional or Territorial legislation.

He also presented a resolution, declaring that on the ballot for President and Vice-President, no person should be declared to be nominated who did not receive two-thirds of all the votes the full Convention was entitled to cast.

Mr. Richardson of Illinois took the floor, when the chair reminded him that the debate was not in order.

Mr. Russell of Virginia said the delegation of that State believed, so far as the platform is concerned, the resolution read by the gentleman from Tennessee formed a reasonable basis for a union of the North and South. It affirms the decision in the Supreme Court, in the Dred Scott case, and goes no further. So far as the second resolution was concerned, relating to the selection of a candidate for the Presidency, they believed that if the selection of a candidate was made, national in its character, the South would support them, no matter what the action of delegates might be. It might be suspected that the resolution was aimed at one particular candidate. It was not so. Virginia only desired to receive the nationality of the nomination. The South would only be represented negatively in the choice, for her absent votes could not be counted in the affirmative for any candidate. They believed, too, that the true interpretation of the rule would require the votes of two-thirds of the representation to nominate, and not two thirds of those present, alone. Unless the resolution he offered should be adopted, he was not instructed to cast the vote of Virginia on any question at present in this Convention.

Mr. Howard of Tennessee disclaimed, any intention in his remarks to be threatening.

Mr. Caldwell of Kentucky said: When the delegation had retired for consultation, and had declared that the adoption of the resolution read by the gentleman from Tennessee, would be acceptable to Kentucky, and would, they believe, bring back those who had left the Convention, the Kentucky delegation had also taken action on the two-thirds rule, and had decided that the proper construction of the two-thirds rule was, that it required two-thirds of the vote of the Electoral College to elect.

A motion was made to adjourn, and upon it the vote was taken by States.

When Georgia was called, Mr. Cohen, of that State, said ten delegates remained, and they claimed to have power to cast the vote of the State. The chair decided that the minority had no right to cast the vote of the State.

Mr. Holden of Tennessee appealed from the decision of the chair. He said: Whom the Gods would destroy they first make mad. The decision of the chair is most suicidal and destructive. It destroyed the rights of the State.

The decision of the chair was sustained—148 ayes to 100 nays.

The previous question on the motion of Mr. Howard was seconded. The motion to adjourn, on which the vote by States had been called, was lost—92 ayes to 158 nays. Convention, after skirmishing, adjourned until 5 o'clock P. M.

AFTERNOON SESSION.

Mr. Howard rose to a privileged question, and moved to take up his resolution. The chair said it was not a privileged question.

Mr. Howard. Then I will state it as a privileged question.

Mr. Russell of Virginia wished to state that the decision which the chair makes on this question now, will decide whether Virginia will longer partake in the proceedings of the Convention.

Mr. Howard said the time fixed by Mr. McCook's resolution to ballot for a candidate for President had long since passed, and that the resolution was not, therefore, in order. The chair decided that the time named in the resolution would not affect its passage.

The question, shall the main question be now put, was then put, and the motion carried by the following vote:

States.	Yeas.	Nays.	States.	Yeas.	Nays.
Maine	5	3	Mississippi	0	0
New Hampshire	5	0	Texas	0	0
Vermont	5	0	Arkansas	1	0
Massachusetts	6	7	Missouri	4½	4½
Rhode Island	4	0	Tennessee	1	11
Connecticut	3½	2½	Kentucky	0	12
New York	35	0	Ohio	23	0
New Jersey	7	0	Indiana	13	0
Pennsylvania	9½	16¼	Illinois	11	0
Delaware	0	2	Michigan	6	0
Maryland	3	5	Wisconsin	5	0
Virginia	0	15	Iowa	4	0
North Carolina	0	10	Minnesota	2½	1½
South Carolina	0	0	California	0	4
Georgia	0	0	Oregon	0	3
Florida	0	0			
Alabama	0	0		149	102
Louisiana	0	0			

Mr. Ludlow, before the vote of New York was cast, inquired of the chair if he understood that the question of privilege on the meaning and effect of the two-thirds rule, would be decided before the question was put on the resolution.

The President. It will be so decided.

The proposition of Mr. Howard, declaring that the President would not declare any candidate elected who did not receive two-thirds of the vote of the Electoral College, was then brought forward as a question of privilege.

Mr. Howard said he would use no argument to enforce this on the committee, but would leave it at once to a decision of the chair.

The chair is of opinion that this proposition of the State of Tennessee, involving the question as to how the chair will decide the vote on the election of the candidate for the Presidency, is in order.

Mr. Richardson. On that, I appeal from the decision of the chair, and call the vote by States.

After some discussion, Mr. Richardson withdrew his appeal, and moved to lay the resolution of the gentleman from Tennessee (Mr. Howard) on the table.

The vote was taken by States, and the motion to lay on the table lost:

States.	Yeas.	Nays.	States.	Yeas.	Nays.
Maine	5	3	Mississippi	0	0
New Hampshire	5	0	Texas	0	0
Vermont	5	0	Arkansas	0	1
Massachusetts	4½	8½	Missouri	4½	4½
Rhode Island	4	0	Tennessee	1	11
Connecticut	3½	2½	Kentucky	0	12
New York	0	35	Ohio	23	0
New Jersey	1½	5½	Indiana	13	0
Pennsylvania	10	16½	Illinois	11	0
Delaware	0	2	Michigan	6	0
Maryland	2	6	Wisconsin	5	0
Virginia	0	15	Iowa	4	0
North Carolina	0	10	Minnesota	2½	1½
South Carolina	0	0	California	0	4
Georgia	0	0	Oregon	0	3
Florida	0	0			
Alabama	0	0		111½	141
Louisiana	0	0			

The question then being on Mr. Howard's resolution, Mr. Stuart of Michigan raised the point of order that the effect of the resolution was to change the rule of the Convention, and must lie over. He read the rule, which was that "*two-thirds of the votes given*" should be necessary to nominate. He declared language could not be more explicit.

Mr. Howard said a case in point had arisen in 1844, when the New York delegates were excluded from the Convention. The decision then was that it required two-thirds of the electoral vote to elect.

The President said the rule of the Convention of 1852 was in substance as the gentleman had stated. It was true a rigid construction of the rule would seem to be that it alluded to the votes cast on the ballot in this Convention. But the words are, "Two-thirds of the votes given in this Convention."

The gentleman further argues the inconvenience that would arise from the voluntary absence of one-third of the Convention, so as to prevent a nomination. This Convention has no legal authority—its authority is only of a moral character.

The gentleman had remarked on the inconvenience that might be experienced by a Convention assuming that a third of the delegates should withdraw and prevent a nomination; but it would be a still greater inconvenience should a small minority of a Convention be enabled to force a nomination on the people of the United States. The nomination of a Convention is only a recommendation to the people of the country, but in the judgment of the chair, the consideration of convenience and inconvenience would, if taken into the question at all, require that the act of the Convention should be the act of all the States of the Union.

The chair is not of opinion that the words of the rule apply to the votes cast for the candidate, but to the votes that are cast here, in this Convention, or two-thirds of all the votes to be cast by the Convention. So the chair is of opinion that the resolution of Mr. Howard of Tennessee contemplates *no* change or modification of the rules of the house. Another reason is, that it is not competent for the chair to construe a rule, when it is proposed by a vote of the house to decide its construction. The effect of the resolution of the gentleman from Tennessee, if adopted, will be to direct the President that in the votes to be cast under his inspection, he shall make only such a decision as to the nomination as the resolution dictates. The resolution of the gentleman from Tennessee is, therefore, in order.

Mr. Stuart of Michigan trusted that it was not necessary for him to disclaim any discourtesy to the chair, when he appealed from this decision, and he would only say that the construction of the chair, that the words "the votes given here" were meant to apply to all the votes cast by the Convention, could never receive the sanction of logic.

Several delegations having asked leave to retire for consultation, desired that the chair would state, before they retired, the exact position of the question.

There was intense excitement and great confusion in the hall.

The chair explained that the question was upon the appeal from the decision, that the resolution of Mr. Howard did not change the rules, and was, therefore, in order.

The vote was announced as follows:

States.	Yeas.	Nays.	States.	Yeas.	Nays.
Maine	3	5	Mississippi	0	0
New Hampshire	1	4	Texas	0	0
Vermont	0	5	Arkansas	0	0
Massachusetts	5½	3½	Missouri	4½	4½
Rhode Island	0	4	Tennessee	11	1
Connecticut	2½	3	Kentucky	11½	½
New York	35	0	Ohio	0	23
New Jersey	5½	1½	Indiana	0	13
Pennsylvania	17½	9½	Illinois	0	11
Delaware	2	0	Michigan	0	6
Maryland	6	2	Wisconsin	0	5
Virginia	15	0	Iowa	0	4
North Carolina	10	0	Minnesota	1	2¼
South Carolina	1	0	California	4	0
Georgia	0	0	Oregon	3	0
Florida	0	0			
Alabama	0	0		144	108
Louisiana	0	0			

Mr. Stuart moved to amend the resolution by adding: And that every person who casts a vote binds himself hereby to vote for the candidate nominated.

Mr. Howard. I ask by what right the gentleman makes himself a keeper of the consciences of his peers.

Mr. Butler of Massachusetts raised the point of order that the amendment was not germane to the original resolution. He moved the previous question.

Mr. Russell of Virginia said that if Virginia remained in a Convention, her honor bound her to abide by its decisions. [Applause.]

After further discussion, the chair decided that the amendment of Mr. Stuart was not germane to the original resolution, and hence, was not in order.

The previous question was then ordered, and the vote being called by States, Mr. Howard's resolution was adopted by the following vote:

States.	Yeas.	Nays.	States.	Yeas.	Nays.
Maine	3	5	Mississippi	0	0
New Hampshire	0	5	Texas	0	0
Vermont	0	5	Arkansas	0	1
Massachusetts	8½	4½	Missouri	2½	2½
Rhode Island	0	4	Tennessee	11	1
Connecticut	2½	3½	Kentucky	11	1
New York	35	0	Ohio	0	23
New Jersey	5½	1½	Indiana	0	13
Pennsylvania	17⅞	9½	Illinois	0	11
Delaware	2	0	Michigan	0	6
Maryland	6	2	Wisconsin	0	5
Virginia	15	0	Iowa	0	4
North Carolina	10	0	Minnesota	1½	2½
South Carolina	1	0	California	4	0
Georgia	0	0	Oregon	3	0
Florida	0	0			
Alabama	0	0		141	112
Louisiana	0	0			

Mr. Bigler moved to reconsider the vote and that the motion be laid on the table. The vote of New York was decisive on this question. Balloting for a candidate for the office of President of the United States was now in order. Mr. King of Missouri nominated Stephen A. Douglas. Mr. Caldwell of Kentucky nominated "the favorite son and incorruptible statesman of Kentucky," James Guthrie. Mr. Patrick of California nominated Daniel S. Dickinson. Mr. Russell of Virginia nominated R. M. T. Hunter. Mr. Ewing of Tennessee nominated Andrew Johnson. Mr. Stevens of Oregon nominated Joe Lane.

After the vote of New York had decided that it was impossible to nominate Douglas, she proceeded, the roll of States being called, to vote for him as demurely as if she meant it.

The first ballot for the nomination of a candidate for the Presidency, was taken about dusk, amid the most profound silence. When the name of Douglas was put in nomination, a feeble yelp went up from the North-western delegations. It was not hearty and strong, but thin and spiritless. There was no hopefulness in it, but something of defiance. It was as much as to say, "Well, if we can't nominate him, you cannot nominate any body else."

The spokesmen of the North-western delegations tried to make their votes for Douglas impressive, but it was a failure. They said so many votes for "Stephen A. Douglas, of Illinois," but it would not do. They were overhung now by a cloud of South Carolinians in the galleries, and the cold steel of the new construction of the two-thirds rule had pierced their vitals. The North-western delegations, commencing with Ohio, had always, until now, produced something of an effect, voting in solid column, according to the direction on the Douglas programme. But McCook of Ohio failed to give any rotundity to the vote, "twenty-three votes for Stephen A. Douglas." Gavit of Indiana ripped out the vote of that State, and glared round with the air of an assassin. He looked as if he would cut any man's throat who had any thing to say against that. Richardson of Illinois looked as if at a funeral, and gave the vote of Illinois in a voice like the sound of clods on a coffin. The following is the

FIRST BALLOT.

STATES.	Douglas.	Guthrie.	Dickinson.	Hunter.	Johnson.	Lane.	Davis.	Toucey.	Pierce.
Maine............................	5	3	..	.	..	..	..	..	..
New Hampshire.................	5	..	..	..	..	..	..	..	..
Vermont.........................	5	..	..	..	..	..	..	..	..
Massachusetts..................	5½	..	..	6	..	..	1½	..	..
Rhode Island....................	4	..	..	..	..	..	..	..	..
Connecticut.....................	3½	..	..	..	..	..	..	2½	..
New York........................	35	..	..	..	..	..	..	..	..
New Jersey......................	..	7	..	..	..	..	..	..	..
Pennsylvania....................	9	9	2	3	..	3	..	..	1
Delaware........................	..	..	..	2	..	..	..	..	..
Maryland........................	2	..	1	5	..	..	..	..	..
Virginia.........................	..	..	..	15	..	..	..	..	..
North Carolina..................	1	..	..	9	..	..	..	..	..
South Carolina..................	..	..	..	1	..	..	..	..	..
Georgia.........................	..	..	..	..	..	..	..	..	..
Florida..........................	..	..	..	..	..	..	..	..	..
Alabama........................	..	..	..	..	..	..	..	..	..
Louisiana.......................	..	..	..	..	..	..	..	..	..
Mississippi.....................	..	..	..	..	..	..	..	..	..
Texas...........................	..	..	..	..	..	..	..	..	..
Arkansas........................	..	..	..	1	..	..	..	..	..
Missouri........................	4½	4½	..	..	..	..	..	..	..
Tennessee.......................	..	..	..	..	12	..	..	..	..
Kentucky........................	..	12	..	..	..	..	..	..	..
Ohio.............................	23	..	..	..	..	..	..	..	..
Indiana..........................	13	..	..	..	..	..	..	..	..
Illinois..........................	11	..	..	..	..	..	..	..	..
Michigan........................	6	..	..	..	..	..	..	..	..
Wisconsin.......................	5	..	..	..	..	..	..	..	..
Iowa.............................	4	..	..	..	..	..	..	..	..
Minnesota.......................	4	..	..	..	..	..	..	..	..
California.......................	..	..	4	..	..	..	..	..	..
Oregon..........................	..	..	..	..	..	3	..	..	..
Total...........................	145½	35½	7	42	12	6	1½	2½	1

SECOND BALLOT.
Douglas 147
Hunter 41½
Guthrie 36½
Johnson 12
Dickinson 6½
Lane 6
Toucey 2½
Davis 1

THIRD BALLOT.
Douglas 148½
Guthrie 42
Hunter 36
Johnson 12
Dickinson 6½
Lane 6
Davis 1

FOURTH BALLOT.
Douglas 149
Hunter 41½
Guthrie 37½
Johnson 12
Lane 6
Dickinson 5
Davis 1

FIFTH BALLOT.
Douglas 149½
Hunter 41
Guthrie 37½
Johnson 12
Lane 6
Dickinson 5
Davis 1

SIXTH BALLOT.
Douglas 149½
Guthrie 39½
Hunter 36
Johnson 12
Lane 7
Dickinson 3
Davis 1

SEVENTH BALLOT.
Douglas 150½
Hunter 41
Guthrie 38½
Johnson 11
Lane 6
Dickinson 4
Davis 1

EIGHTH BALLOT.
Douglas 150½
Hunter 40½
Guthrie 38½
Johnson 11
Lane 6
Dickinson 4½
Davis 1

NINTH BALLOT.
Douglas 150½
Guthrie 41½
Hunter 33½
Johnson 12
Lane 6
Davis 1½
Dickinson 1

While the roll was being called, Mr. Edgerton of Minnesota desired to have his vote recorded for Johnson of Tennessee.

The question was, whether, before the Convention adjourned, Douglas would get a majority of the Electoral College. He crawled up, half a vote at a time, until, on the ninth ballot, he reached the figure 152; but before the vote was declared, the column of the North-west was broken. Gorman denied Edgerton's right to change his vote—chair recognized Edgerton's right to vote as he pleased.

TENTH BALLOT.
Douglas 150½
Guthrie 39½
Hunter 39
Johnson 12
Lane 5½
Dickinson 4
Davis 1½

ELEVENTH BALLOT.
Douglas 150½
Guthrie 39½
Hunter 38
Johnson 12
Lane 6½
Dickinson 4
Davis 1½

TWELFTH BALLOT.
Douglas 150½
Guthrie 39½
Hunter 38
Johnson 12
Lane 6½
Dickinson 4
Davis 1½

On motion of Mr. Richardson of Illinois, the Convention then adjourned.

The Douglas men were very despondent after this day's experience. The delegates generally are dispirited, worried out by the long wrangle, and disgusted. It is the prevalent impression that the Democratic party has been done for. Even if it should be possible to patch up a superficial reconciliation, and nominate with a whole Convention, the nomination would be worthless. I hear it stated here a hundred times a day, by the most orthodox Democrats and rampant Southerners, "William H. Seward will be next President of the United States." And I have heard this remark several times from South Carolinians: "I'll be damned if I don't believe Senator Seward would make a good President." The fact is, there is a large class to whom the idea of Douglas is absolutely more offensive than Seward.

Our North-western friends will go home with hatred of the Democratic party, as it has appeared here, rankling in their hearts. As Douglas will not be the nominee, they will wish to see the nominee defeated. Some of them say, openly and earnestly, they will go home and join the Black Republicans. I never heard Abolitionists talk more uncharitably and rancorously of the people of the South, than the Douglas men here. Our North-western friends use language about the South, her institutions, and particularly her politicians, that is not fit for publication, and my scruples in that respect are not remarkably tender. A good many of them will eventually become the most intolerant Republican partisans. Their exasperation and bitterness toward the South, that has insisted upon such a gross repudiation of the only ground upon which they could stand in the North, can hardly be described. Many of them would not lift a finger to prevent the election of Seward to the Presidency. They say they do not care a d—n where the South goes, or what becomes of her. They say "she may go out of the Convention into hell," for all they care. I know it will be asserted that this is a highly-colored statement—but it certainly is not; on the other hand, it is mild. There will be no fight in the North-west worth thinking about. The Douglas men will permit the election to go by default. No matter what this Convention does after this date, the Chicago Convention has all the cards in its hands to win the next Presidency and the spoils of the Federal Government.

This is a "fixed fact," as the honorable President of this Convention once said. By the way, the Douglas men are desperately bitter on Caleb Cushing. They call him all manner of hard names.

People are fast leaving the town. Mr. Douglas's outside pressure has melted away. The Charleston disunionists now gloat over the pitiful and disgraceful wrangling that occupies the attention of the Convention.

NINTH DAY.

MORNING SESSION.

CHARLESTON, May 2, 1860

Prior to the opening of the proceedings to-day, the Boston Brass Band, accompanying the Boston delegation, appeared in the gallery and played several national airs, and at the close of which, Mr. Flournoy of Arkansas proposed three cheers for the Union, which were given.

The roll of States was called for the thirteenth ballot (202 votes being necessary to a choice), which resulted as follows:

THIRTEENTH BALLOT.
Douglas 149½
Guthrie 39½
Lane 20
Hunter 28½
Johnson 12
Dickinson 1
Davis 1½

FOURTEENTH BALLOT.
Douglas 150
Guthrie 41
Dickinson .... ½
Hunter 27
Johnson 12
Lane 20½
Davis 1

FIFTEENTH BALLOT.
Douglas 150
Guthrie 41½
Dickinson .... ½
Hunter 26½
Johnson 12
Lane 20½
Davis 1

SIXTEENTH BALLOT.
Douglas 150
Guthrie 42
Dickinson .... ½
Hunter 26
Johnson 12
Lane 20½
Davis 1

SEVENTEENTH BALLOT.
Douglas 150
Guthrie 42
Dickinson .... ½
Hunter 26
Johnson 12
Lane 20½
Davis 1

EIGHTEENTH BALLOT.
Douglas 150
Guthrie 41½
Dickinson 1

Hunter 26
Johnson 12
Lane 20½
Davis 1

NINETEENTH BALLOT.
Douglas 150
Guthrie 41½
Dickinson 1
Hunter 26
Johnson 12
Lane 20½
Davis 1

TWENTIETH BALLOT.
Douglas 150
Guthrie 42
Dickinson .... ½
Hunter 26
Johnson 12
Lane 20½
Davis 1

TWENTY-FIRST BALLOT.
Douglas 150½
Guthrie 41½
Dickinson .... ½
Hunter 26
Johnson 12
Lane 20½
Davis 1

TWENTY-SECOND BALLOT.
Douglas 150½
Guthrie 41½
Dickinson .... ½
Hunter 26
Johnson 12
Lane 20½
Davis 1

TWENTY-THIRD BALLOT.
Douglas 152½
Guthrie 41½
Dickinson .... ½
Hunter 25
Johnson 12
Lane 19½
Davis 1

Before the twenty-third ballot was declared, there was trouble in the Virginia delegation. One of the votes was cast for Mr. Douglas by the delegates of one of the districts. The chairman of the State delegation was opposed to this, and produced the instructions. Gov. Todd of Ohio (temporarily in the chair), ruled that the Virginia vote could be cast for Douglas, in spite of the majority of the delegation. This vote gave Douglas on this ballot a majority of the Electoral College vote, and his friends were greatly inspirited. If Cushing had been in the chair, the fractious Virginians would have been ruled under. Cushing rushed in, out of breath, just after the vote was declared, and took his position with some discomposure—an extraordinary thing for him.

TWENTY-FOURTH BALLOT.
Douglas........................ 151½
Guthrie........................ 41½
Dickinson...................... 1½
Hunter......................... 25
Johnson........................ 12
Lane........................... 19½
Davis.......................... 1

TWENTY-FIFTH BALLOT.
Douglas........................ 151½
Guthrie........................ 41
Dickinson...................... 1½
Hunter......................... 35
Johnson........................ 12
Lane........................... 9½
Davis.......................... 1

In this ballot North Carolina changed her ten votes from Lane to Hunter.

TWENTY-SIXTH BALLOT.
Douglas........................ 151½
Guthrie........................ 41½
Dickinson...................... 12
Hunter......................... 25
Johnson........................ 12
Lane........................... 9
Davis.......................... 1

When North Carolina was called on this ballot, Mr. Brown of North Carolina said: "North Carolina casts her ten votes for that incorruptible statesman and pure patriot, Daniel S. Dickinson of New York." [Applause.]

TWENTY-SEVENTH BALLOT.
Douglas........................ 151½
Guthrie........................ 42½
Dickinson...................... 12
Hunter......................... 25
Johnson........................ 12
Lane........................... 8
Davis.......................... 1

TWENTY-EIGHTH BALLOT.
Douglas........................ 151½
Guthrie........................ 42
Dickinson...................... 12½
Hunter......................... 25
Johnson........................ 12
Lane........................... 8
Davis.......................... 1

TWENTY-NINTH BALLOT.
Douglas........................ 151½
Guthrie........................ 42

Adjourned until 5 o'clock.

Dickinson...................... 13
Hunter......................... 25
Johnson........................ 12
Lane........................... 7½
Davis.......................... 1

THIRTIETH BALLOT.
Douglas........................ 151½
Guthrie........................ 45
Dickinson...................... 13
Hunter......................... 25
Johnson........................ 11
Lane........................... 5½
Davis.......................... 1

THIRTY-FIRST BALLOT.
Douglas........................ 151½
Guthrie........................ 47½
Dickinson...................... 3
Hunter......................... 32½
Johnson........................ 11
Lane........................... 5½
Davis.......................... 1

On this ballot North Carolina cast her vote between Hunter and Guthrie.

THIRTY-SECOND BALLOT.
Douglas........................ 152½
Guthrie........................ 47½
Dickinson...................... 3
Hunter......................... 22½
Johnson........................ 11
Lane........................... 14½
Davis.......................... 1

North Carolina in this ballot cast one vote for Douglas again, giving him a majority of the entire electoral vote.

THIRTY-THIRD BALLOT.
Douglas........................ 152½
Guthrie........................ 47½
Dickinson...................... 3
Hunter......................... 22½
Johnson........................ 11
Lane........................... 14½
Davis.......................... 1

THIRTY-FOURTH BALLOT.
Douglas........................ 152½
Guthrie........................ 47½
Dickinson...................... 5
Hunter......................... 22½
Johnson........................ 11
Lane........................... 12½
Davis.......................... 1

AFTERNOON SESSION.

THIRTY-FIFTH BALLOT.	
Douglas..................152	Hunter....................22
Guthrie...................47½	Johnson...................12
Dickinson.................4½	Lane......................13
	Davis.....................1

Mr. Gittings of Baltimore moved to adjourn to that city on the first Monday in July. Withdrew his motion.

THIRTY-SIXTH BALLOT.	
Douglas..................151½	Hunter....................22
Guthrie...................48	Johnson...................12
Dickinson.................4½	Lane......................13
	Davis.....................1

The vote of Arkansas having been cast for John C. Breckenridge in this ballot,

Mr. Beck of Kentucky asked that the vote might be withdrawn. On the part of Mr. Breckenridge, he desired to say, that it was not the desire of that gentleman that his name should be used in opposition to the distinguished gentlemen now in nomination. The vote was withdrawn.

When the vote was announced,

Mr. Ewing of Tennessee said that the Tennessee delegation had presented a name for the nomination—Mr. Johnson. They now desired to withdraw that name, and to express the hope that a nomination might be made. Their vote on the next ballot was cast 10½ for Guthrie, 1 for Douglas, and ½ for Johnson.

THIRTY-SEVENTH BALLOT.	
Douglas..................151½	Dickinson.................5
Guthrie...................64½	Hunter....................16
Dickinson.................5½	Lane......................13
Hunter....................16	

FORTY-SECOND BALLOT.

Johnson...................1½	Douglas..................151½
Lane......................12½	Guthrie...................66½
Davis.....................1	Dickinson.................5
	Hunter....................16
THIRTY-EIGHTH BALLOT.	Lane......................13
Douglas..................151½	

FORTY-THIRD BALLOT.

Guthrie...................66	
Dickinson.................5½	Douglas..................151½
Hunter....................16	Guthrie...................65½
Lane......................13	Dickinson.................5
	Hunter....................16
THIRTY-NINTH BALLOT.	Lane......................13
Douglas..................151½	Davis.....................1
Guthrie...................66½	

FORTY-FOURTH BALLOT.

Dickinson.................5½	
Hunter....................16	Douglas..................151½
Lane......................12½	Guthrie...................65½
	Dickinson.................5
FORTIETH BALLOT.	Hunter....................16
Douglas..................151½	Lane......................13
Guthrie...................66½	Davis.....................1
Dickinson.................5½	

FORTY-FIFTH BALLOT.

Hunter....................16	
Lane......................12½	Douglas..................151½
	Guthrie...................65½
FORTY-FIRST BALLOT.	Dickinson.................5
Douglas..................151½	Hunter....................16
Guthrie...................66½	Lane......................13
	Davis.....................1

FORTY-SIXTH BALLOT.
Douglas 151½
Guthrie 65¼
Dickinson 5
Hunter 16
Lane 13
Davis 1

FORTY-SEVENTH BALLOT.
Douglas 151½
Guthrie 65½
Dickinson 5
Hunter 16
Lane 13
Davis 1

FORTY-EIGHTH BALLOT.
Douglas 151½
Guthrie 65½
Dickinson 5
Hunter 16
Lane 13
Davis 1

FORTY-NINTH BALLOT.
Douglas 151½
Guthrie 59½
Dickinson 4
Hunter 16
Lane 14
Davis 1

FIFTIETH BALLOT.
Douglas 151½
Guthrie 65¼
Dickinson 4
Hunter 16
Lane 14
Davis 1

FIFTY-FIRST BALLOT.
Douglas 151½
Guthrie 65½
Dickinson 4
Hunter 16
Lane 14
Davis 1

FIFTY-SECOND BALLOT.
Douglas 151½
Guthrie 65¼
Dickinson 4
Hunter 16
Lane 14
Davis 1

FIFTY-THIRD BALLOT.
Douglas 151½
Guthrie 65½
Dickinson 4
Hunter 16
Lane 14
Davis 1

FIFTY-FOURTH BALLOT.
Douglas 151½
Guthrie 61
Dickinson 16
Hunter 20½
Lane 14
Davis 1

FIFTY-FIFTH BALLOT.
Douglas 151½
Guthrie 65½
Dickinson 14
Hunter 16
Lane 14
Davis 1

Mr. Gittings said it was no use voting this way like a machine. He moved that it was inexpedient to nominate a candidate. There were cries that his motion was out of order. He said: I want to see if you'll come up and face the music. I mean to vote against it myself, but I want to find out what you're going to do. If you'll nominate Douglas we can elect him, by G—d! [Laughter and cheers.]

The President. The motion is not in order.

Mr. Gittings. No, of course not; that's the way we are prevented getting a vote on it.

FIFTY-SIXTH BALLOT.
Douglas 151½
Guthrie 65½
Dickinson 4
Hunter 16
Lane 14
Davis 1

FIFTY-SEVENTH BALLOT.
Douglas 151½
Guthrie 65½
Dickinson 4
Hunter 16
Lane 14
Davis 1

Mr. Gittings moved to adjourn till the 1st Monday in June. Laid on the table. Adjourned.

Mr. Douglas's friends were quite nervous after getting a majority vote.

The leaders were quite fidgety. Stuart of Michigan, Richardson of Illinois, McCook of Ohio, and others, had their heads together at intervals, and were evidently proposing to do something desperate. Just before the Convention adjourned, Stuart sought the floor and clearly obtained it, but Mr. Cushing with stony face looked over his shoulder and saw "the gentleman from North Carolina, Mr. Ashe," who made the motion to adjourn until five o'clock, which was carried, by declaration of the chair, though there was a strong negative vote.

The New York vote is ready to be cast for the Tennessee conciliatory resolution, which is readily a mild but unmistakable slave code resolution. It would deaden Douglas. The spectators have become tired of the Convention. The galleries are no longer crowded, and it is hardly worth while to keep up the ceremony of presenting tickets. The ladies' gallery is very thin, and the poor creatures look down into the hall, vainly seeking objects of interest.

The South Carolina delegates who remained after the secession have withdrawn. They were loudly hissed every time they voted, and the expressions of public disapprobation were so strong that they have succumbed.

Developments of some sort are expected and insisted upon. The outsiders are becoming as impatient as the insiders. The whole arrangement is pretty nearly beyond endurance. There is little hope of reaching any conclusion this or even next week. It is very clear that the Douglas men have strength enough to prevent nomination whether they have or have not to nominate. His friends are obstinate and are becoming more embittered every hour. There are some who hope he will cut the Gordian knot here by a summary telegraphic despatch peremptorily withdrawing his name. But his friends say he promised them in Washington a fortnight since, when all contingencies were being considered and his counsel was taken, that he would not repeat the Cincinnati despatch under any contingency. There are serious propositions made to adjourn, to meet in New York or Baltimore in June. This would seem, however, to be a mere hopeless attempt at evasion of the present interminable difficulty. The only substantive thing, thus far, that has been done here is the disruption of the party.

TENTH DAY.

THE CLOSING SCENE.

CHARLESTON, S. C., May 3d.

The Convention—or rather that which is left of the Convention, the "Rump" as Yancey calls it—meets this morning with the understanding that it is to adjourn to meet in Baltimore early in June. The North-western delegates are said to be in favor of Baltimore, on the third Monday in June. This is in sheer desperation. The Douglas men expect to have "soft" Conventions held in the cotton States, which will send up to the Convention two representatives favorable to the Little Giant. They are against a "new deal" in the Northern States, and holding what they have, will grab what they can. There will be two Conventions, the Squatter Sovereignty one at Baltimore, and the Constitutional one, which will assemble at the call of the cotton States.

The Convention opens with prayer. Mr. Russell of Virginia obtained the floor, to make an explanation relative to the position of the delegation of his State, on the resolution offered by Mr. Howard of Tennessee, which had been printed erroneously in the papers. The Mercury, of this morning, contained an article denouncing the resolution as no better than squatter sovereignty. The editor had been under a misapprehension as to the strength of the resolution; the resolution asserted that the right of property in slaves in the Territories could not be destroyed or impaired by Congress or a Territorial Legislature. The editor of the Mercury had omitted the words, "or impaired." Mr. Russell of Virginia stated that it had been ascertained that there was strength enough in the Convention to pass this resolution whenever it came up. This is known to be a fact.

The language of Mr. Russell was:

All the Southern States, he believed, had agreed on this, and he understood the State of New York had given her assent to its adoption. He now offered the following:

Resolved, That when this Convention adjourns to-day, it adjourn to reassemble at Baltimore, Md., on Monday, the 18th day of June, and that it be respectfully recommended to the Democratic party of the several States to make provision for supplying all vacancies in their respective delegations to this Convention when it shall reassemble. [Applause.]

[A dispute has arisen about the wording of this resolution—a pamphlet copy of the proceedings at Charleston having been published in Washington, in which the resolution reads:

Resolved, That when this Convention adjourns to day, it adjourn to meet in Baltimore on the 18th day of June, in order to afford the States that are not now represented an opportunity to fill up their delegations.

Senator Mason of Virginia considered this matter of sufficient importance to address a card to the Washington Constitution concerning it. Mr. Mason quotes the two forms of the resolution, and says of that first above, which I take from the file of the Charleston Courier:

The above is a copy taken by me from the resolution in Mr. Russell's possession, which he brought with him from Charleston.

The marked difference between the two will strike the reader at once. As printed in the pamphlet, it is addressed only to "States that are not now represented," imputing that there were States, in the judgment of the Convention, not *then* represented in the Convention; thus seeming to imply that the seats of the delegations of those States who had withdrawn were *then* vacant.

In the resolution really presented and adopted, a recommendation is addressed "to the Democratic party of the several States to make provision for supplying all vacancies in their respective delegations when it shall reassemble."]

The rules were quickly suspended to allow Mr. Russell's resolution to be considered.

Then there was an amendment made to strike out Baltimore and insert Philadelphia. There was moved an amendment to the amendment, to strike out Philadelphia and insert New York. Pending these amendments there were several very funny scenes, which would have been exciting, if the Convention had not become an inconsequential mob.

Randall of Pennsylvania several times jumped up with his gnarled gray head and comically severe expression, and attempted to put something before the house with which he was swollen. Several malicious fellows, to tease the old man, raised points of order upon him. The old gentleman would get out of his place, close up to the chair, to put a motion, and some rascal would raise the point upon him, that he was out of his place. Cushing would look down upon him with a queer pucker at the corners of his mouth—the smile of a lion looking kindly upon a sheep—and would slaughter him by sustaining the point of order and sending him back to his place. At last the old gentleman mounted a chair in his place and screamed at the chair, and was recognized. The Convention was in great good humor with him, and gave him a vociferous round of applause. The old gentleman moved to substitute for the various motions before the house, that the Convention meet on the fourth of July, in Independence Hall. He thought a meeting at that holy time and place, would do them all a great deal of good.

The country would have been saved at once, but the motion was out of order.

Mr. Montgomery of Pennsylvania was desperately anxious to address the chair, and when the chair recognized somebody else, he was indignant, and declared his voice (which is a roarer) too weak, and his form (which is a whopper) too small, for the one to be seen or the other to be heard by the chair. The chair arose in indignation and struck the table three violent blows with his hammer, which he would evidently have been happy to bestow upon the head of Montgomery. He then stated the case to Montgomery in the most explicit terms.

The question on substituting New York for Baltimore, was lost by a *viva voce* vote The question on substituting Philadelphia for Baltimore, was lost by the following vote:

YEAS—Maine 3, Massachusetts 10½, Connecticut 1, New Jersey 7, Pennsylvania 26½, Delaware 2, North Carolina 4, Missouri 4, Tennessee 10½, Kentucky 11½, Minnesota 1¾, California 1—88½.

NAYS—Maine 5, New Hampshire 5, Vermont 5, Massachusetts 2½, Rhode Island 4, Connecticut 5, New York 35, Maryland 8, Virginia 15, North Carolina 6, Arkansas 1, Missouri 5, Tennessee 1½, Kentucky ½, Ohio 23, Indiana 13, Illinois 11, Michigan 6, Wisconsin 5, Iowa 4, Minnesota 2¼, California 3, Oregon 3—166.

The original resolution was then carried by the following vote:

YEAS—Maine 5, New Hampshire 5, Vermont 5, Massachusetts 10, Rhode Island 4, Connecticut 6, New York 35, New Jersey 2, Pennsylvania 23½, Maryland 5, Virginia 14¼, Arkansas 1, Missouri 6, Tennessee 7, Ohio 23, Indiana 13, Illinois 11, Michigan 6, Wisconsin 5, Iowa 4, Minnesota 4, California 3—195.

NAYS—Maine 3, Connecticut 3. New Jersey 5, Pennsylvania 3, Maryland 3, Virginia ½, North Carolina 14, Missouri 3, Tennessee 5, Kentucky 12—55.

The President. The chair, before putting the final motion to adjourn, requests for a few moments the attention of the Convention.

Order being restored, the President said:

"*Gentlemen of the Convention:*—Allow me, before putting the question of adjournment, to address to you a parting word.

"I desire, first, to say, and, in saying it, to bear testimony to your constituents and to the people of the United States that, considering the numerousness of the assembly, the important interests involved in its deliberations, and the emotions thus naturally awakened in your bosoms; considering all this, I say your sessions have been distinguished by order, by freedom from personalities, by decorum and by observance of parliamentary method and law. In the competition for the floor, in the zeal of gentlemen to promote their respective opinions by motions or objections to motions in the lassitude of protracted sittings, occasions have occurred of apparent, but only apparent, confusion. But there has been no real confusion, no deliberate violation of order. I am better able than any other person to speak knowingly on this point, and to speak impartially, and I say it with pride and pleasure, as a thing especially proper for me to say from the chair.

"I desire further to say for and in behalf of myself, that I also *know*, by the knowledge of my own heart and conscience, that in the midst of circumstances always arduous, and in some respects of peculiar embarrassment, it has been my steady purpose and constant endeavor to discharge impartially the duties of the chair. If, in the execution of these duties, it shall have happened to me to address any gentleman abruptly, or not to have duly recognized him, I beg pardon of him and of the Convention.

"Finally, permit me to remind you, gentlemen, that not merely the fortunes of the great Constitutional party which you represent, but the fortunes of the Constitution also, are at stake on the acts of this Convention. During the period now of eighty-four years, we, the States of this Union, have been associated together in one form or another, for objects of domestic order and foreign security. We have traversed side by side the wars of the Revolution, and other and later wars. Through peace and war, through sunshine and storm, we have held our way manfully on, until we have come to be the Great Republic. Shall we cease to be such? I will not believe it: I will not believe that the noble work of our fathers is to be shattered into fragments; this great Republic to be but a name, a history of a mighty people once existing, but existing no longer save as a shadowy memory, or as a monumental ruin by the side of the pathway of time! I fondly trust that we shall continue to march on forever—the hope of nations, as well in the Old World as in the New—like the bright orbs of the firmament, which roll on without rest, because bound for eternity; without haste, because predestined for eternity; so may it be with this glorious Confederation of States.

"I pray you, therefore, gentlemen, in your return to your constituents and to the bosoms of your families, to take with you as your guiding thought the sentiment of the Constitution and the Union. And with this, I cordially bid you farewell, until the prescribed reassembling of the Convention."

The address was received with loud applause, and at its close the President declared that the Convention stood adjourned until the 18th of June, then to meet at 12 o'clock, noon, in the city of Baltimore.

The final fall of the hammer was the signal for a general stampede, and the delegates rushed from the hall.

The moment before the Convention assumed a nebulous appearance, a Baltimorean had something very sweet to say of the hospitalities of the Monumental City. The loss of interest in the proceedings of this Convention will strikingly appear from the fact, that while there are seats in the ladies' gallery for at least four hundred, and that at times they had not only filled them, but appeared on the floor by scores, there were but seven ladies in the hall when the adjournment took place.

Public opinion has for some days been divided as to the abilities of Mr. Cushing as a presiding officer. He is accused of being too elaborate, and too formal, and incapable of despatching business. But it should be remembered that during a great part of the time here, his object has not been to despatch business, but to procrastinate. Certainly there has been admirable success in this. It must, however, be said of Mr. Cushing as a presiding officer, that he is a little too fond of making a speech in deciding a point of order, and that he gives too many reasons for a ruling, especially where it is tolerably clear that he is not strictly impartial.

CHARLESTON, S. C., May 3d (evening).

The adjournment of the Convention has been followed by an outrageous eagerness to get home. Yesterday the Northern delegates generally professed the most amazing capacities for endurance. They were ready to stay here any length of time. There was nothing either in their families or their business to call them home. They were prepared to brave yellow fever or any other form of pestilence. They were ready to defy the plague, though it might be as malignant as tradition says it was in other countries. To-day, the Convention adjourned at a few minutes after eleven, and there was a little more than an hour left before the principal Northern and North-eastern trains took their departure. The rush to the hotels, and the calls for baggage and bills, the hurried cramming of carpet-bags, valises and trunks, the headlong races up and plunges down stairs, the yelling after coaches, the shaking hands and taking "parting drinks," made up a scene that was somewhat amazing to the leisurely people of Charleston. Some of those who were yesterday loudest in their professions of willingness to spend the summer months here, made the most reckless despatch in getting out of town.

Douglas men think they have done it up beautifully, in adjourning, and calling for new representations for the cotton States. But the path before them is by no means clear, as yet. The vote of New York is the pivot on which things turn, and it is uncertain as the wind at a street-crossing.

THE CONSTITUTIONAL DEMOCRATIC CONVENTION.

FIRST DAY.

CHARLESTON, S. C., May 1st.

The seceding delegations met, in the first place, the evening after the disruption of the National Convention, at St. Andrew's Hall, where the names of Secretaries were reported—Mayor Wood and his New York delegation also registering their names, upon the invitation of Mr. Yancey.

Pursuant to call, the seceding delegates met at Military Hall, Tuesday, May 1st, at 12 M. John S. Preston, of S. C., called the meeting to order.

The following number of delegates were found to be enrolled:

From Delaware, 2; Virginia, 1; South Carolina, 14; Georgia, 2; Florida, 6; Alabama, 21; Mississippi, 14; Texas, 10; Arkansas, 4; Missouri, 3; New York, 41.

Other delegates proceeded to enroll their names.

Mayor Wood & Co. withdrew, because "the New York delegation were not in the attitude of being members of the Convention which sat in Institute Hall."

The following gentlemen were elected officers of the Convention:

FOR PRESIDENT.

JAMES A. BAYARD, of Delaware.

FOR VICE-PRESIDENTS.

James Simons, South Carolina.
I. T. Irwin, Georgia.
Robert G. Scott, Alabama.
James Drane, Mississippi.
Emile LaSere, Louisiana.
John Milton, Florida.
John A. Jordon, Arkansas.
H. R. Runnels, Texas.
William G. Whiteley, Delaware.
M. W. Fisher, Virginia.

FOR SECRETARIES—Thomas P. Ochiltree, of Texas; Franklin Gaillard, of South Carolina; N. H. R. Dawson, of Alabama; F. W. Hoadley, of Arkansas; D. D. Withers, of Louisiana; W. H. H. Tison, of Mississippi.

Mr. Bayard, in taking the chair, made a lengthy speech.

A committee on Resolutions was appointed as follows:

Delaware, W. G. Whiteley; South Carolina, A. A. Allemong; Georgia, Henry R. Jackson; Florida, Charles E. Dyke; Alabama, John

Ervin; Mississippi, Ethan Barksdale; Louisiana, Robert A. Hunter; Arkansas, W. E. Burrows; Texas, Fletcher S. Stockdale.

Mr. Yancey offered the following, to be referred to the committee on Resolutions:

Resolved, That desiring to base its action entirely upon the Constitution, this meeting style itself the Constitutional Democracy.

Resolved, That the platform adopted by the Democratic party at Cincinnati be affirmed, with the following explanatory resolutions:

[Those of the majority report of the other Convention.]
Adjourned.

SECOND DAY.

CHARLESTON, S. C., May 2d.

Convention met in the theatre. The seats in the dress circle were occupied by a brilliant array of beauty and fashion. The family circle and galleries were filled with spectators, citizens and strangers. The pit had been reserved for the delegates.

In correcting the journal, Mr. Walker of Alabama moved to correct by striking out the word "seceding" before delegations, and inserting the word "retiring," so as to make it read retiring delegates.

Mr. Winston suggested the word "withdraw." The word "retiring" was adopted.

Mr. Burrows, from the committee on Resolutions, reported a series of resolutions, the material ones of which were:

Resolved, That the platform adopted by the Democratic party at Cincinnati, be affirmed, with the following explanatory resolutions:

First. That the government of a Territory organized by an act of Congress, is provisional and temporary; and during its existence, all citizens of the United States have an equal right to settle with their property in the Territory, without their rights either of person or property being destroyed or impaired by Congressional or Territorial legislation.

Second. That it is the duty of the Federal Government, in all its departments, to protect, when necessary, the rights of persons and property in the Territories, and wherever else its constitutional authority extends.

Third. That when the settlers in a Territory having an adequate population, form a State Constitution in pursuance of law, the right of Sovereignty commences, and, being consummated by admission into the Union, they stand on an equal footing with the people of other States; and the State thus organized ought to be admitted into the Federal Union, whether its constitution prohibits or recognizes the institution of slavery.

Mr. Yancey said: I think, sir, that the Convention is prepared to act now on the platform. That is all, I believe, that it is proposed to act on until another contingency arises, to wit, the nomination of a candidate by the National Democratic Convention in session, the rump Democracy or rump Democrats, when it may be our privilege to indorse the nominee, or our duty to proceed to make a nomination according to the will of this body.

Mr. Jackson of Mississippi was not in favor of stopping with the adoption of a platform. He said: This is no time to pause for further reflection. But I am not prepared to pause simply upon a platform of principle. To pause at all is, in my judgment, a symptom of weakness. We have met the Democracy now in session. We have left it upon principle, and upon principle alone will I ever return to it. [Applause.] Boldly, Mr. Chairman, boldly have we taken our position, and it is a position of positions. Are we to be tempted back into that organization by the nomination of any man. [Cries of "No! never!"]

Mr. Yancey argued that that was simply a meeting of delegates retired from another Convention. He said further: We may be called Disunion Democrats. We are not disunionists. We have put nothing upon the record to justify the assertion; yet it will be easy to attach to the name the weight of the disunion movement.

After a long discussion, the platform was unanimously adopted. A discussion then ensued on the propriety of proceeding to nominate candidates. The time was spent in speeches, however.

THIRD DAY

CHARLESTON, S. C., May 3d.

After some discussion, the motion of Mr. Jackson, that the Convention proceed to nominate candidates, was withdrawn.

Next a discussion sprung up about an address to the people of the United States. There were several propositions of this nature. Judge Meek, in stating the facts as to the strength of the different branches of the Democracy in Alabama, said:

"They [alluding to the delegates of the other Convention, which had just adjourned] had then adjourned to meet at Baltimore at a future day. They had thus, to use a popular phrase, clinched their action, and now they called upon the South to send new delegates to the adjourned Convention. Alabama would never be represented in a Convention so formed, founded on a Squatter Sovereignty Platform. The vote in the Convention that elected the present delegation to Charleston, stood four hundred and ninety-nine to twelve, and that was the strength of the Douglas Squatter Sovereignty doctrine in Alabama. Indeed, out of this twelve, seven were in fact opposed to the doctrine of Squatter Sovereignty. Now, what the present Convention had really desired, was to have put forward a great historic name, that would have commanded confidence and respect all over the Union—he alluded to Jefferson Davis of Mississippi. They had also, he might say, contemplated putting in connection with that name the name of the honored gentleman who now presided over their deliberations, and thus have secured a ticket *sans peur, sans réproche*. But any definite action now was deemed inexpedient."

It was decided, finally, not to address the country. Mr. Yancey disclaimed disunionism *per se*. Mr. Jackson of Georgia offered a resolution, calling for a Convention at Washington City on the second Monday in June. Adjourned.

EVENING SESSION.

President Bayard made a speech, retiring from the Convention. He made a strong speech for the Union.

Judge Meek replied to Bayard. He said: "The gentleman said they had come here to save the Union. They had not—they had come here to save the Constitution." [Applause.]

The following resolution was adopted, and the Convention adjourned:

Resolved, That the Democratic party of the United States who are in favor of the platform of principle recommended by a majority of States in the Charleston Convention, be invited to send delegates to a Convention to be held in Richmond, on the second Monday in June next; and that the basis of representation be the same as that upon which the States have been represented in the Charleston Convention.

APPEARANCE OF THE SECEDERS' CONVENTION IN SESSION.

CHARLESTON, S. C., May 3d.

After the adjournment of the National Democratic Convention, I looked in upon the Seceders in their theatre. The dress circle was densely crowded by ladies. You see at once the patriotism of the Carolina ladies exemplified. There were not more than a dozen of them to witness the proceedings of the Rump Convention this morning, and here they were smiling upon the "constitutional" champions of the South by hundreds. I do not think I had seen the Carolina beauties. There were actually plenty of beautiful women in the theatre this morning, and it has been a customary remark during the sessions of the Convention at Institute Hall, that female beauty was a scarce article in the Carolinas, so far as appeared. But though the women were beautiful, they had not the peach-bloom cheeks and May-cherry lips of the Ohio girls—no, not by any means. Well, the principal feature of the Convention was the ladies. The "performance," while I was present, was fair. In fact, it looked very like a play, the actors having not only occupied the stage, but taken possession of the parquette. The latter was occupied by the delegates, and no impartial spectator could have said, that the representatives of the cotton States there assembled were other than a noble set of men. The chevalier Senator Bayard occupied the chair, and sat near the footlights—a courtly gentleman, whose romantic ancestry and name, as well as his long curls, and fine features, and distinguished air, were admirably adapted to concentrate the gaze of the ladies. The stage scene which was on, was that of the Borgia Palace. Those who have seen the play, will of course remember the "bloods" on a spree, one of whom struck off the B, leaving ORGIA, whereupon there was an unnecessary (as always occurred to me) amount of amusement and alarm concerning the freak, and immoderate offense taken at it. Well, in this play the B was already off—the deed had been done. As I first looked at the stage, two gigantic policemen —Irishmen, of course—with blue frock-coats and brass buttons, and large stars on their breasts, and maces eighteen inches long in their hands, stalked behind the President and Secretaries and Reporters, and mysteriously passed beyond a side scene.

They seemed to be the heavy villains, procured by the designing scoundrel to carry off the virgin in the case, who was in love with somebody else.

The real play was going on in the pit. Mr. Burrows of Arkansas, a black-haired, black-eyed, swarthy, hook-nosed, portly gentleman, had the floor, and was making some very general and very extreme proposition. His idea—and it was not a novel one—of being a bold and original man—is to be as ultra as possible—to out-Herod all the Herods of his party. The fundamental article of his faith, just now, is that Squatter Sovereignty is a great deal worse than the rankest sort of Abolitionism—that Douglas is ever so much more dangerous to the South than Seward, and that the Douglas men are a very bad type of Abolitionists.

Judge Meek of Alabama was next on the floor. The Judge is a gentleman whose height is variously estimated between six feet four and six feet eight inches. He is a lofty specimen, at any rate, and a very powerful public speaker. I do not mean powerful in the "able and eloquent" sense in which it has been used in Kentucky. It is remarkable, that in the speeches of the extreme Southern men in this Convention, we have not had any of that peculiar eloquence which we are accustomed to call "Kentucky," because, I suppose, it is a bad imitation of the style of Henry Clay.

WASHINGTON, D. C., May 7th.

The evening after the adjournment of the Convention, Charleston was herself again. But she had not been so dreadfully disturbed as she had anticipated. I was told by gentlemen of the city that they had several times seen greater crowds about the hotels during racing week. The Charlestonians were rather inclined to say, as the contemporary of Noah remarked of the deluge—not much of a shower after all.

We left Charleston for Washington at eleven o'clock of the night of the last day of the Convention. The train was an enormous one for a Southern road, but would have been a trifling affair up North. There were many "distinguished" passengers—there being about an equal number of United States Senators and keepers of Faro tables, the latter wearing decidedly the most costly apparel, having made the most money during their sojourn in the Palmetto City; one gambling house realized twenty-four thousand dollars clear profits, I am told. The moon was up and the night beautiful, but there was nothing to see from the windows of the car but swamps and pine forests; but it was the ground made classic by Marion, which was some comfort. The principal features in the journey to me were pine-trees along the road, and six changes of cars.

PRESIDENTIAL CANDIDATES IN THE SENATE—DOUGLAS, SEWARD AND DAVIS.

WASHINGTON, D. C., May 8th.

*   *   *   *   *   *   *

And here, coming from the cloak room on the Democratic side, is a queer little man, canine head and duck legs—every body knows the

Little Giant—he looks conscious of being looked at ; and he is pointed
out by a hundred hands, as he makes pretentious strides of about
eighteen inches each toward his chair. Two or three of his admirers in
the gallery are disposed to applaud, but you hear merely the rattle of a
single boot heel. He shakes hands with Clingman of North Carolina,
and chuckles with him over something that seems to be highly relished
on both sides. The Little Giant wears his black hair long, but it is
getting thin, and is not the great tangled mass we saw on his neck a
few years ago. And, O Little Giant! it grows gray rapidly. Now he
proceeds to twist himself down in his chair as far as possible, and places
his feet in his desk; and thus his admirers in the gallery look upon the
prodigious little man, squirming flat on his back. He don't feel very
elastic this morning, that is evident. His mouth is closed up as if he
was trying to bite a pin in two. He is not "all brain," as Senator
Brown says. He requires a large vest—and large as he is about the
chest, his waist is becoming still more extensive. But he *has* an immense
head—in height, and breadth and depth—in indications of solidity and
force, you cannot find its equal in Washington. There is power under
that massive brow, and resolution in that grim mouth; no doubt at all
of that. After he has fairly stretched himself and rolled over in his
chair, like the trained lion in his cage, he becomes fidgety, and clasps
and unclasps his stumpy hands, drums with his white fingers on the
arms of his chair, rubs his nose, places his hands affectionately on
Clingman's knee, and seems at a loss for occupation.

And now an individual appears on the other side of the House, who
at first sight seems to be rather a comical person. He has the most
singular head in all the assortment before you. It rises above the ears
like a dome, and looks not unlike a straw stack in shape and color.
His nose—a high, sharp beak—strikes out below the strawy hair that
thatches the dome. Can you imagine a jay-bird with a sparrow-hawk's
bill—the high tuft of feathers towering above the eyes—the keen hook
below? There is a quaintness in that high head and high, sharp nose.
You are anxious about the forehead. You are sure that must be a
man of talent, and he must have a forehead. But to save you,
you cannot tell which is hair and which is forehead. All is of
the same parchment hue. You seem once in a while to catch a
glimpse of a lofty mountain range of ideality, etc., according to
the maps of the phrenologists. And then you are not sure but it is
hair. This tall and peaked and pallid head is perched upon a body
that is active and restless. It moves about with school-boy elasticity.
It walks with a slashing swagger. It strikes off with a rollicking gait
from one point to another, and is in and out of the chamber by turns.
There is an oddity in the dress in harmony with the general queerness
of the thing. The pantaloons have a dingy oaken appearance. You
would not be surprised to see breeches of that color in Oregon, but in
the Senate-chamber they are without a parallel. And did you ever see
so much tail to a frock-coat in your life? Hardly. There is certainly
a grotesque amount of coat tail. Now after making the round of the
Republican side of the chamber about twice in ten minutes he offers
from the chair (next the main aisle and most remote from the Vice-

President's) a petition, in a hoarse croaking voice ; and when the Vice-President recognizes "The Senator from New York," there is a stir in the galleries and a general stare at the gentleman with the top-knot and beak and voice. He sits down, takes a pinch of snuff, and presently you hear a vociferous sneezing, and the high-headed, straw-thatched gentleman is engaged upon his beak with a yellow silk handkerchief. And you remember that Seward takes snuff, and has ruined his voice by the nasty habit. In the Republican corner of the Senate-chamber is a familiar face and form—you recognize the portly person and massive intellectual developments, the thin frizzly hair and oval brow of Salmon P. Chase. Next him is Gov. Dennison. Seward comes up to them and seems to be guilty of some good thing, for they laugh violently but quietly, and Seward rubs his oaken breeches with his hands and then gives his nose a tremendous tweak with the yellow handkerchief. He is wonderfully affable. He acts as though he would kiss a strange baby. Ah, he is a candidate for the Presidency.

The crowd has filled the galleries of the Senate-chamber, expecting to hear Jeff. Davis's speech; and there are expectations that Douglas will reply. The hands of the Senate clock approach the points indicating the hour of one, and the people are weary of the monotonous reading of bills and petitions by title, and the presentations of the miscellany of deliberative bodies in audible tones. Ah! here he comes. The crowd in the galleries give a buzz of relief, and every body tells his right hand man—"here he comes—that's Jeff. Davis." And can it be possible that he proposes to make a speech? You are surprised to see him walking. Why, that is the face of a corpse, the form of a skeleton, Look at the haggard, sunken, weary eye—the thin white wrinkled lips clasped close upon the teeth in anguish. That is the mouth of a brave but impatient sufferer. See the ghastly white, hollow, bitterly puckered cheek, the high, sharp, cheek bone, the pale brow full of fine wrinkles, the grizzly hair, prematurely gray; and see the thin, bloodless, bony, nervous hands! He deposits his documents upon his desk, and sinks into his chair as if incapable of rising. In a few minutes the Vice-President gives his desk a blow with his ivory hammer, calls for profound order, and states "that the Senator from Mississippi" has the floor. Davis rises with a smile. His speech was closely reasoned, and his words were well chosen. Once in a while he pleased his hearers by a happy period; but it was painfully evident that he was ill.

THE BALTIMORE NATIONAL CONSTITUTIONAL UNION CONVENTION.

LIST OF DELEGATES.

[From the Secretary's Roll.]

PENNSYLVANIA.

Senatorial Delegates—Hon. Joseph R. Ingersoll, Gen. Abraham Markley.
Alternates—Col. H. M. Fuller, Alfred Howell.
Congressional Districts—E. P. Molyneau, Charles D. Freeman, Wm. S. Elder, E. Harper Jeffries, Wm. H. Slingluff, Capt Frank Smith, M. Mundy, Jno. A. Banks, H. K. Killian, Henry Keller, Merritt Abbott, Col. Joseph Paxton, J. W. Martein, Edw. Shippen, E. C. Pechin, J. D. Bayne, John A. Ettinger, Thomas Hayney, —— Patten, F. W. Grayson, J. K. McDonald, Joseph H. Irwin, Gen. Wm. Shall, A. S. Redstreake, John H. Hicks.
Alternates—Sam'l M. Lee, F. S. Altemus, John Slemer, John Bell Robinson, John S. Littell, T. W. Woodward, Wm. Graeff, H. C. Fondersmith, C. C. Lathrop, Wm. H. Pierce, Wm. Hillman, C. H. Breisler, Robert M. McClure, E. P. Borden, Col. W. Lee, Chas. Chadwick.

NEW YORK.

At Large—Washington Hunt, Erastus Brooks, B. David Noxen, Jonas C. Hearts.
Alternates—George A. Halsey, John S. Van Rensalier.
Districts—Alfred Doolon, Thos. R. Webb, J. DePeyster Ogden, Charles Beck, Horace H. Day, A. M. Bininger, Frederick A. Tallmadge, Clark Peck, Daniel R. St. John, Peter Cantine, A. K. Chandler, George B. Warren, James Kydd, Clarence Buck, James L. Smith, Orville Page, Charles B. Freeman, Edwin J. Brown, A. W. Northrup, Aaron Mitchell, Newton B. Lord, R. F. Stevens, Frederick C. Wagner, Jacob P. Faurotte, Chas. Coryell, Sam'l J. Wilkin, D. W. Tomlinson, Erastus S. Mack, G. A. Scroggs, Jas. W. Gerard, Harle Haikes.
Alternates—John P. Dodge, Alfred Watkins, Jonas Bartlett, William J. Bunce, Harrison Hall, Wm. H. Falconer, Wm. T. Jennings, John C. Ham, Fenlon Harbrouck, O. B Wheeler, William Duer, Silas Swain, Rufus Ripley, W. D. Murphy, Wm. Burling, John Leveridge, Louis Lillie, Abel Smith, Harvey Smith, Jon. Munn, W. M. Conkey, Daniel L. Couch, Alfred Wolkya, A. G. Mynck, Daniel S. Baker, Anson Spenser, S. L. Huggins, H. H. Goff, M. F. Robertson, John H. White, John F. Morton, L. L. Platt.

TENNESSEE.

W. G. Brownlow, Bailey Peyton, John S. Brien, G. A. Henry, W, Brazleton, Robert Craighead, John J. Craig, N. S. Brown, Edw. H. Ewing, J. W. Richardson, A. J. Donelson, W. Homar, O. P. Temple, C. F. Trigg, R. Brabson, Joseph Pickett, Wm. Hickerson, S. H. Combs, Jordan Stokes, R. S. Northcott, A. S. Colzar, Henry Cooper, L. J. Polk, J. C. Brown, W. P. Kendrick, Jos. C. Starke, J. H. Callender, Clay Roberts, Joseph Barbien, J. M. Parker, T. A. R. Nelson, H. Maynard, Wm. Stokes, Robt. Hatton, Jas. M. Quarles, Wm. Etheridge, P. W. Maxcey.

ILLINOIS.

Gen. John Wilson, Chairman; Geo. V. Byrd, Josiah Snow, John T. Stuart. Alfred Dutch, D. J. Snow, Alternate: Eliphalet Wood; D. W. Ford, Alternate.

INDIANA.

John J. Hayden, R. W. Thompson, James Montgomery, Lewis Howe, J. M. Havron, Dennis Gregg, A. H. Davidson, C. W. Prather, W. K. Edwards, John P. Early, J. M. Smith, J. W. Dawson, J. A. Bridgland, Thos. B. Long, H. M. Gram, Jas. L. Bradley.

MISSOURI.

Delegates—Sol. Smith, William F. Switzler, Edward M. Samuel, John P. Bruce, Matthew H. Moore, Thos. A. Harris, John Scott, Joseph B. Terry, Adolphus Masser.
Alternates—J. T. Clements, J. E. Barron, R. H. Porter, J. R. Hammond, J. B. Williams.

VIRGINIA.

District Delegates—Samuel Watts, Travis H. Epes, Wm. Martin, Edward D. Christian, Wm. L. Goggin, Marmaduke Johnson, Geo. T. Yerby, E. T. Tayloe, Robert E. Scott, N. B. Meade, A. H. H. Stuart, James Witherow, Wm. J. Dickinson, George W. Summers, Waitman T. Willey.
Alternates—Thomas L. Pretlow, Daniel Lyon, George Towns, W. W. Henry, Alex. Rives, Peyton G. Coleman, Robert Saunders, George W. Lewis, Henry W. Thomas, Wm. Andrews, Chas. H. Lewis, Wm. Copeland, Isaac J Leftwich, Arthur J. Boreman, James S. Wheat.

OHIO.

Senatorial Delegates—Gov. Allen Trimble, Hon. John Scott Harrison.
Congressional Districts—N. G. Pendleton, Gilbert Kennedy, J. R. Nelson, A. J. Thorp, N. McBeth, Dr. J. Way, Jos. N. Snyder, M. J. N. Glover, H. T. Barnes, C. L Garro, Jas. H Laws, J. T. Hyatt, Joel Funk, R. R. Seymour, R. H. Geary, Jas. H. Emminger, J. M. Bushfield, Amos Glover.

MISSISSIPPI.

Hon. Wm. L. Sharkey, Hon. J. W. C. Watson, Col. J. M. Patridge, E. F. McGehee, Hick Bell, R. H. Rivers, T. B. Mosely, J. K. Yerger, Joseph Regan, W. H. Vasser, A. S. Mitchell.

MASSACHUSETTS.

Delegates—Hon. Jos. Grinnell, Col. James W. Leva, Hon. Marshall R. Wilder, Hon. S. L. Crocker, Leverett Salstonstall, Hon. Geo S. Hillard, Benj. L. Allen, Col. Winthrop Faulkner, Jonathan Johnson, Wm. B. May, Hon. Luther V. Bell, Hon. Abel S. Lewis, Henry White.
Alternates—Franklin Weston, N. F. Safford, J. L. Baker, Hon. D. Warren.

CONNECTICUT.

Delegates at Large—Hon. Jno. A. Rockwell, Hon. Austin Baldwin.
Alternates—E. M. Shelton, F. H. Whitmore.
Districts—Hezekiah Huntingdon, Hon. Ezra Clarke, jr., H. C. Miles, C. R. Alsopp, C. A. Lewis, Henry Burr, C. H. Leeds, D. W. Pierce, S. H. White, Wait M. Hawley, Walter H. Bacon, Lyman W. Cole, F. F Loomis, Hon. J. Dunham, R. E. Hitchcock, B. A. Hawley.

MAINE.

S. R. Hanson, Jos. R. Brozier, Phineas Barnes, Samuel Taylor, Geo. E. B. Jackson, Sam'l P. Shaw, Geo. C. Getchell, Daniel L. Choate.

NEW JERSEY.

Senatorial Delegates— Hon. Jos. F. Randolph, Hon. Jas. Bishop.
Alternates—Dr. Chas. G. McChesney, Elisha Day.
Delegates—Jesse E. Peyton, Col. J. W. Allen, Hon. Peter J. Clark, Samuel G. A. Van Lain, James A. Williamson.
Alternates—Geo. M. Robertson, Jacob Herbert, Hon. Abraham V. Schenck, A. W. Coulter, Peter S. Duryea.

VERMONT.

At Large—John Wheeler.
Alternates— R. McKinley Ormsby, E. J. Phelps, A. Stebbins.
Congressional Districts— J. M. Knox, M. Cottrill, Daniel Tilden.
Alternates— Ab. Brown, Andrew Tracey, —— Jewitt.

ARKANSAS.

C. C. Danly, Q. K. Underwood, Jno. Bradley.
Alternate—J. B. Keatts.

GEORGIA.

R. A. T. Ridley, Hon. Joshua Hill, Hon. Thomas Hardeman, jr., H Hopkins, J. A. L. Lee, James M. Calhoun, George W. Adair, J. R. Parrott, Thomas W. Walker, Isaiah Fairview, Z. H. Clark, Williard Boynton.

DELAWARE.

William Temple, Jos. P. Comegys, Jas. R. Loffland, Chas. Cullen, Wm. Elegood, Laban L. Lyons, J. M. Barr, H. P. Blandy, Geo. W. Karsner.
Alternates—A. Stockley, Thomas Wallace, John M. Denning, Manlove Hays, Wm. Loffland, Wm. Wilson, L. G. Gooch, Dr. J. F. Wilson, Reese G. Wolf, Henry F. Fookes.

KENTUCKY.

State at Large—Leslie Coombs, Laban T. Moore, Gibson Mallory, James S. Jackson.
Districts — J. D. M. Goodwin, Benjamin Derry, F. M. Bristow, S. G. Suddarth, B. B. Thompson, C. F. Burnham, John Barbee, J. K. Goodloe, Wm. R. Duncan, John W. Finnell.
Alternates—Thos. A. Duke, S. G. Rhea, Blanton Duncan, A. H. Sneed, G. W. Foreman, D. A. Sayre, W. C. Whittaker, S. F. Gano, J. J. Miller, Samuel Davis.

ALABAMA.

N. W. Shelly, Philip Morgan, J. Q. Dure.

NORTH CAROLINA.

State at Large—Hon. John M. Morehead, Hon. Richard S. Donnell, Hon. Nathaniel Bayden.
Districts—David A. Barnes, D. D. Ferebie, E. W. Jones, Richard H. Smith, Jos. B. Cherry, W. H. Clark, John H. Haughton, W. Foy, Walter Dunn, Thomas Sparrow, E. C. Yellowby, Daniel L. Russell, E. J. Hale, Giles Leitch, A. N. Waddell, John G. Blue, R. McNair, Hon. R. B. Gilliam, Wm. H. Harrison, Hon. E. G. Reade, John Manning, John M. Cloud, R. W. Wharton, Hon. J. M. Leach, T. C. Ham, Thos. S. Ashe, Rufus Barringer, S. H. Walkup, Todd R. Caldwell, Wm. M. Shipp, A. S. Merrimon.

TEXAS.

A. Banning Norton, A. M. Gentry, B. H. Epperson, —— Evans.

FIRST DAY.

BALTIMORE, May 9th.

The hotels were filled up last night by the delegates and outsiders in attendance upon this Convention. There were crowds of good looking gentlemen, talking of the prospect of redeeming the country. The candidates under consideration are Botts of Virginia, Houston of Texas, Bell of Tennessee, Crittenden of Kentucky, Everett of Massachusetts, and McLean of Ohio. The chances seem to be in favor of John Bell. There is a disposition to use Mr. Everett as candidate for the Vice-

Presidency. The delegates seem to be in high spirits, and to be confident of their ability to make at least a powerful diversion. The general foolishness of the two great parties has given the third party unusual animation.

The "American" element appears at once upon entering the hall, which is an old church, with galleries on three sides. The galleries are festooned with tri-colored drapery. There is a full-length painting of Washington, surmounted by an American Eagle, and two great flags of our country, behind the President's chair. The south wall, above and below the galleries, is covered with an assortment of star-spangled banners. The general appearance is patriotic as the Times office, on Washington's birth-day—as described on one occasion, four days in advance.

As the delegates pressed in, the galleries were on the look-out for lions, and applauded in the old style of the "spreads," whenever a "distinguished" gentleman could be made out. Crittenden had quite an ovation.

When the hour arrived for calling the Convention to order, Mr. Crittenden advanced upon the platform and took the chair. There was a vociferous outburst of applause. Some one called for "Three cheers for John J. Crittenden." They were given as only the "spreads" can give them. "Three more" were called for and given; and then "three more," wild and shrill, hats and handkerchiefs waving, and great delight appearing in every countenance. Crittenden bowed until he was tired, and then took his seat. When the noise subsided, we had a prayer, a very fair pious political speech. It was written out and read from manuscript. The difficulty with it was as to whom it was addressed—to the Lord or the Convention. It was very eloquent and well delivered.

Mr. Crittenden, as chairman of the National Constitutional Union Convention, called the Convention to order. A speech was expected from him, but he only said:

"It has been made my duty, gentlemen, as chairman of the Executive committee of the Constitutional party, to perform the honored task of calling this Convention to order, and I will discharge the duty with as much brevity as I can. I hesitated, and was a little diffident about the propriety of my occupying your attention for a single moment on thus calling to order this Convention. You are, in yourselves, the great body that represents the party of the whole country. I will, therefore, only perform the duty without an unnecessary word.

"I would recommend, in the first place, the appointment of a temporary chairman; and I nominate, in accordance with an arrangement which I understood had to some degree been made before, Washington Hunt, former Governor of the State of New York, as your temporary chairman." [Applause.]

Mr. Hunt was unanimously elected temporary chairman. Mr. Hunt made a very fair speech, embodying many good sentiments, and glittering with the usual generalities about peace, concord, fraternity, love, good will, no North, no South, etc. He referred to the disruption of the Democratic party, wrecked on the mysteries of territorial sovereignty.

The Convention insisted on applauding nearly every sentence, and several times refused to let him finish a sentence. It was worse than the applause given by an Irish audience at an Archbishop's lecture. The Americans must never laugh at the Irish for their irrepresssble disposition to applaud. As the committee on Permanent Officers was being appointed, nearly every name received a round of applause. During the first hour and a half of the session, I presume at least one hundred rounds of applause were were given, and the more the "spreads" applauded, the greater became their zeal. I have stated, in letters from Charleston, I believe, that the Douglas men were the most noisy fellows in the world, in proportion to their dimensions. I take it back. The "Plugs" can beat them at their own game.

The committee on Permanent Officers, consisting of one from each State, was constituted as follows:

Alabama—N. W. Shelley.
Arkansas—C. C. Danley.
Connecticut—Hon. John A. Rockwell.
California—
Delaware—Wm. Temple.
Florida—
Georgia—J. S. Fannin.
Indiana—John G. Heydon.
Illinois—John Wilson.
Iowa—
Kentucky—John W. Finnell.
Louisiana—
Maine—C. B. Jackson.
Massachusetts—L. V. Bell.
Michigan—
Minnesota—T. J. Barrett.
Maryland—Thomas Swann.

Mississippi—John K. Yerger.
Missouri—Sol Smith.
New Hampshire—
New York—B. Davis Noxon.
New Jersey—J. W. Allen.
North Carolina—Nathaniel Boyden.
Ohio—Allen Trimble.
Oregon—
Pennsylvania—Joseph Paxton.
Rhode Island—
South Carolina—
Texas—
Tennessee—A. J. Donelson.
Vermont—John Wheeler.
Virginia—Wm. L. Goggin.
Wisconsin—

No delegates appearing from the States of California, Florida, Iowa, Louisiana, Michigan, New Hampshire, Oregon, Rhode Island, South Carolina and Wisconsin.

Several of the Southern States are very strongly represented here. Virginia and Tennessee have exceedingly able delegations on the floor.

A great portion of the delegates are of the "eminently respectable" class of gentlemen—and most of them are somewhat stale in politics.

The Convention took a recess until four o'clock in the afternoon, when A. J. Donelson, from the committee on Organization, reported the following names for permanent officers of the Convention:

PRESIDENT.

WASHINGTON HUNT, of New York.

VICE-PRESIDENTS.

S. R. Jackson, Maine.
R. M. Ormsley, Vermont.
Marshall P. Wilder, Massachusetts.
Austin Baldwin, Connecticut.
Frederick A. Tallmadge, New York.
Peter J. Clark, New Jersey.
Jos. R. Ingersoll, Pennsylvania.
Dennis Claude, Maryland.
Alex. H. H. Stuart, Virginia.
Robert B. Gillian, North Carolina.

James Calhoun, Georgia.
J. J. Dew, Alabama.
Richard W. Thompson, Indiana.
David A. Sayer, Kentucky.
Edward F. McGehee, Mississippi.
Q. K. Underwood, Arkansas.
Gustavus Henry, Tennessee.
J. Scott Harrison. Ohio.
Jos. P. Comegys, Delaware.

SECRETARIES—S. C. Long, Maryland ; A. Payton, New Jersey : Ezra Clark, Connecticut ; —— Snow, Illinois ; L. Saltonstall, Massachusetts ; John W. Lynn, Massachusetts ; Samuel Davis, Kentucky ; J. P. Early, Indiana ; Adolphus Musser, Maine ; Richard Bell, Mississippi ; John H. Callender, Tennessee.

The report was unanimously adopted. Mr. Hunt made another speech, and several other gentlemen followed "ably and eloquently." Mr. Coombs of Kentucky, the subject of platforms being introduced, made a hit as follows :

So deeply have I been impressed with the necessity of a platform to a great political party, that I have taken upon myself the labor of preparing three [laughter], one for the harmonious Democracy, who have lately agreed together so beautifully at Charleston [laughter] ; one for the "irrepressible conflict" gentlemen, who are about to assemble at Chicago, and another for the National Unionists now before and around me. [Laughter]. And as all are brief and perfectly intelligible, I shall take the liberty here to repeat them.

First, for the harmonious Democracy ; the Virginia and Kentucky resolutions of 1798-9 [laughter], without preamble or comment, followed by two upon the slave question, one in favor of excluding slavery from the Territories of the United States, and the other in favor of forcing it into them [applause] ; both to be adopted unanimously by the Convention under the previous question, and no questions asked afterward. [Laughter].

For the "irrepressible conflict" philanthropists about to assemble at Chicago, I suggest the blue laws of Connecticut [laughter]; with a slight modification upon two points ; first in reference to the right of a man to kiss his wife on Sunday, and the second in reference to burning witches, providing that the young wife shall have the privilege to be kissed and the old witches to be burned. [Great applause.]

In reference to this Convention I have provided a still shorter platform—The Constitution of the United States as it is ["Good ! good ! " and applause] ; the Constitution as it is, and the Union under it now and forever. [Great applause.] I will not speak in reference to the first at large, but I venture to say that it will be as intelligible hereafter to the wide-spread Democracy, as it has been heretofore ; and being thus intelligible, I venture to stake all I am worth—not very much—that not one in five hundred have read those resolutions, and not one in five hundred who have read them understand them.

In reference ot our platform—the Constitution as it is—the Legislative, Judicial and Executive departments, each in its separate department supreme. I think that will be platform enough for the Union party to stand upon [applause]—the Congress of the United States to enact the laws, the Judicial department to interpret, and the Executive to have them executed.

This is all we want ; that is all we need. Were I an assemblage of Christians about to establish a creed for Christians, do you think I would take dipping or sprinkling? I would take the Bible as it is, leaving all to construe it, they being responsible for its construction. [Immense applause, and three cheers for Mr. Coombs, the Convention rising in their places.]

Erastus Brooks said:
Sir, we misjudge the people of the country, if any of us suppose that they are not heart-sick and head-sick of what are called, technically, party platforms. We know it; what we have seen at Charleston is but illustrating the fable of Saturn, for they literally devoured their own progeny. [Applause]. What we see elsewhere in regard to the great Republican party is equally true—they are composed in one State of various classes of men; a conservative class in favor of the Fugitive Slave law and the Constitution of the United States, and that class addresses themselves to the commercial community and to the manufacturing community. There is another class of men who follow in the wake of these, leaving the city and going into the rural districts, and there they preach as the great architect of that party preached at Cleveland, for a higher law than the Constitution of the United States.

A committee on Resolutions and Business was constituted as follows:

Alabama—A. F. Alexander.
Arkansas—M. S. Kennard.
Connecticut—Austin Baldwin.
Delaware—Chas. F. Cullen.
Georgia—Hon. Joshua Hill.
Indiana—Hon. R. W. Thompson.
Illinois—John Wilson.
Kentucky—C. F. Burnham.
Maine—George E. B. Jackson.
Massachusetts—Abial S. Lewis.
Minnesota—T. J. Barrett.
Maryland—George A. Pearrie.
Mississippi—John W. C. Watson.
Missouri—Thomas A. Harris.
New York—Hon. Erastus Brooks.
New Jersey—Joseph F. Randolph.
North Carolina—Richard S. Donald.
Ohio—N. G. Pendleton.
Pennsylvania—Hon. Jos. R. Ingersoll.
Texas—A. B. Norton.
Tennessee—Hon. Bailie Peyton.
Vermont—John Wheeler.
Virginia—Robert E. Scott.

SPIRIT OF THE FIRST DAY'S PROCEEDINGS.

BALTIMORE May 9th (at night).

The Convention organized in this city to-day does not furnish a very animating theme. Not that it was not animated in itself. There were the same furious demonstrations of enthusiasm that we had occasion to remark in the Fillmore performances in 1856. A hundred of the Fillmore men would make more noise than three times as many Democrats or ten times the number of Republicans. There is too much unanimity here, however, to be interesting. Every body is eminently respectable, intensely virtuous, devotedly patriotic, and fully resolved to save the country. They propose to accomplish that political salvation so devoutly to be wished, by ignoring all the rugged issues of the day. The expression against platforms was universal and enthusiastic. Instead of proceeding to make a platform, the worthies here in Convention assembled all fell to abusing platforms. There was probably as much discretion as virtue in this, for the delegates would find it impossible to agree on an expression of principles formally laid down, and the intention is, to make the canvass simply upon an assumption that this body represents the "Conservative American Constitutional Union element." What this element proposes to do, can be stated in one way in the South and another way in the North, and thus our excellent friends will have all the advantages of an ambiguous platform, and will not encounter any of the disabilities attendant upon a written standard of orthodoxy. Mayor Swann stated that, when John J. Crittenden took the stand, he saw platform enough for him, and the "plugs" who were in the galleries, cheered him tremendously. I have heard a great deal of virtuous twaddle in public speeches within a few weeks, but the essence of the article was uncorked to-day. Erastus Brooks gave his idea of a platform. It was the Constitution and laws. The Constitution as interpreted by the constituted authorities—the highest judicial authorities—and the enforcement of the laws. Now, Erastus is the editor of the New York Express, and therefore a great man. He was consequently applauded throughout with even unusual vigor. He is in favor of the nomination of Gen. Sam. Houston, a rather good old soul, as we all know, but the most shallow of the shallow politicians who have been engaged for some years in attending to the affairs of our beloved country. He probably has a very brilliant understanding of that Constitution and law which is to be the platform. His appreciation of and respect for the constituted authorities was exemplified in his recent proposition to invade Mexico. While speeches were being made, the chair announced that the delegation from Texas was at the door. [Tremendous applause.] The chair directed the door-keeper to admit the delegation from Texas. [Tremendous applause.] The delegation from Texas was admitted. [More tremendous applause.] The delegation, headed by a man with a beard half a yard long, who was dressed in home-spun and bore a great buck-horn-handle cane, made its way to a front seat, amid "tremendous applause." An officious delegate said that the long-haired man had agreed at one time not to have his hair cut until Henry Clay was elected President. [Still more tremendous applause.]

During both sessions of the Convention this day, every speech was received in this "tremendous" style. The moment a speaker would say *Constitution; law; Union; American; conservative element; glorious victory; our fathers; our flag; our country;* or any thing of the sort, he had to pause for some time, until the general rapture would discharge itself by stamping, clapping hands, rattling canes, etc., etc. I have likened the enthusiasm to that of an Irish audience at an archbishop's lecture. It was so, with some additional peculiarities of extravagance. The noise and confusion of applause became a disgusting bore to all but the patriotic "plugs."

If I had not known otherwise, I should have thought sometimes that the incessant rage of approbation was factious; but the "plugs" by whom the galleries were loaded, meant only to emit their pent-up ecstasy. So vivid were their perceptions of patriotic sentiments, that they could not in dozens of cases await the conclusion of a sentence, before shouting and stamping like Yahoos on a spree. When a speaker would put off something about the Constitution and laws of our beloved country, he would be obliged to suspend his remarks, until the tempest of approbation subsided. And if he should, in order to make himself intelligible, so far as he might, commence the broken sentence over again, ten to one, when he arrived at the patriotic point, where the fracture commenced, the storm would break out again, with redoubled fury. As a matter of necessity, a committee to report business was constituted

It was necessary to present some business to the Convention. About every other committee man's name was received with outrageous yells of admiration from the galleries, and stamping so desperate that the mortar rattled down, and there were apprehensions that the galleries themselves might tumble under the weight of rampant patriotism heaped into them.

It is presumed that a nomination will take place to-morrow, and that several cheers will go up, and that a determination to elect the nominee and save our sweet country, will be expressed by a large number of "able and eloquent" gentlemen, who will cause the skies to be rent with roars of American enthusiasm.

The turn out of delegates is larger than was expected. I believe there are really as many people in attendance here, as there were at Charleston. The hotels are full, and the narrow Baltimorean sidewalks can hardly contain the groups of exuberant and vociferous patriots. John Bell stock was high to-day, and is tolerably well high up yet, but there are many who are anxious to avail themselves of the battle of San Jacinto. The persuasion that presses John Bell is, that he is strong in the North. But nearly every body ought to know, that he could not carry a single Northern State. The pressure for Houston is upon the presumption that he is powerful in the South. I am very seriously told that he could sweep every State in the South with perfect ease, and New York also, thereby securing his election in the Electoral College. And, I am further informed, that if by some unforeseen accident or most illogical turn of affairs, he should not be triumphantly elected according to the first form made and provided by the Constitution, and the election should be thrown into Congress, the Republicans there would prevent the election of an ultra-Southern man by the Senate, by joining in the House with the men who have taken the Constitution, Union, and salvation of the country into special consideration; and by elevating their champion to the Presidency, give the nation another lease of life. I have been obliged to say to some of our Constitution-loving friends, that I did not think the nominee of this Convention, even with the naked Constitution for a platform, would be certain to carry the State of Ohio. I have gone so far as to indicate an apprehension that the chances were, the electoral vote of the State would be thrown for somebody else.

SECOND DAY.

BALTIMORE, May 8th.

When the President of the Convention, Washington Hunt, Esq., appeared upon the platform this morning he was received with the usual joyous cries and stamping. The Convention being called to order, we had a fervent prayer for the Union. The minister did not, like his brethren in some cases at Charleston, pray directly for the triumph of the ticket that might be put forward. The Union being prayed for, however, it was inferred that as this body had the confederacy in charge, the petition for the preservation of the Union included an invocation for the success of the Convention's nominees before the people.

The old church used by the Convention is very much crowded this morning. The ladies' gallery is well filled; but there is hardly a fair representation of that female loveliness, for which this city has a just celebrity.

There are many distinguished men on the floor, but they are mostly "venerable men," who have come down to us from a former generation of politicians, and whose retirement from the busy scenes of public life have been rather involuntary than otherwise, and whose disgust at political trickery may perhaps in part be attributed to the failure of the populace to appreciate their abilities and virtues.

The Hon. Jos. R. Ingersoll made the report of the Business committee. He said of the committeemen:

They met with entire cordiality; they proceeded with entire good feeling, and they terminated their proceedings with great unanimity, and I may say with patriotism. [Applause.] I would not venture to present as an example at all to a great and highly respectable body like this the feeling and the courteous deportment of the gentlemen with whom I had the pleasure to sit as chairman last evening; but I would say that a more entirely respectable set of men—in manner, appearance, and in result—I never saw. [Applause.]

THE PLATFORM.

Whereas, experience has demonstrated that platforms adopted by the partisan Conventions of the country have had the effect to mislead and deceive the people, and at the same time to widen the political divisions of the country, by the creation and encouragement of geographical and sectional parties; therefore

Resolved, That it is both the part of patriotism and of duty to recognize no political principles, other than

THE CONSTITUTION OF THE COUNTRY,
THE UNION OF THE STATES, AND
THE ENFORCEMENT OF THE LAWS;
(Loud and prolonged cheering.)

and that, as the representatives of the Constitutional Union men of the country in National Convention assembled, we here pledge ourselves to maintain, protect, and defend, separately and unitedly, those great principles of public liberty and national safety, against all enemies, at home and abroad, believing that thereby peace may once more be restored to the country, and the just rights of the people, and of the States re-established, and the Government again placed in that condition of justice, fraternity and equality, which, under the example and constitution of our fathers, has solemnly bound every citizen of the United States to maintain, "a more perfect union, establish justice, insure domestic tranquillity, provide for the common defense, promote the general welfare, and secure the blessings of liberty to ourselves and our posterity." [Prolonged cheers.]

Mr. Ingersoll in making this report was cheered when he took the stand, cheered when he opened his mouth, given nine cheers when he said the committee had with entire unanimity and surprising enthusiasm agreed that there should be no formal platform. When the declaration of principles was read, there was more cheering. The opening proceedings were, in fact, a long yell, partially subsiding at intervals, so that a few remarks could be interpolated. The declaration of principles was passed unanimously, with a proper amount of the article of enthusiam. But the perfect harmony which had thus far prevailed, was now disturbed. There was a distressingly earnest and dreadfully protracted discussion, on the report as to the process of business, which was prescribed in the following resolutions :

Resolved, That each State shall be entitled to the same number of votes in this Convention as its electoral vote, and that each delegation shall, for itself, determine the manner in which its vote shall be cast.

Resolved, That in balloting for President and Vice-President, ballots shall be taken until the candidate nominated shall receive a majority of all the votes cast; that the candidate for President shall first be balloted for and selected, and then the candidate for Vice-President.

There was an impression somewhere that there was a disposition in the various States to coerce the minorities, and out of this the trouble grew.

The Convention got itself into a very uncomfortable condition of confusion, and about twenty resolutions were heaped upon each other. The "gallant and gifted Goggin," of Virginia, at last offered a resolution, which brought the Convention out of tribulation and the rapids of controversy into calm and deep water.

It was as follows :

Resolved, That the chairman of each delegation shall cast the vote of his State for each delegate, in such way as he may be instructed by the delegate entitled to vote, and when there is not a full representation from any State, then the majority of such delegation shall decide how the vote of the district unrepresented shall be cast ; and where there be two delegates who cannot agree, each of said delegates shall be entitled to one-half a vote.

This was adopted.

At half-past eleven, the nomination of a candidate for the Presidency was in order. Some time was spent by the various State delegations, in preparing their votes, and there was no little sensation in the hall. The Maryland delegation being unable to get the proper construction of the Goggin resolution through its head without a surgical operation, retired for consultation, and to have the necessary operation performed. A delegate from Minnesota had a delicacy. He was the only man from that State, and had not been appointed a delegate. He was a substitute, consequently he did not feel like representing the State. The voice of the Convention overcame his modesty. The names most loudly cheered as the balloting proceeded were those of John Bell and Edward Everett. Everett received a long and loud clamor, and the ladies waved their handkerchiefs. When the vote of Texas was called for, her hairy delegate got up and mentioned the battle of San Jacinto, and tried to give peculiar emphasis to the SAM part of Houston's name. But it did not take wonderfully.

The first ballot resulted as follows :

FIRST BALLOT.

States.	Everett.	Houston.	Bell.	Crittenden.	Goggin.	Graham.	McLean.	Botts.	Sharkey.	Rives.
Alabama	9									
Arkansas		3	1							
Connecticut		2½	2½	1						
Delaware			3							
Florida						3				
Georgia							10			
Indiana							13			
Illinois			5½					5½		
Kentucky				12						
Maine			8							
Massachusetts	13									
Maryland		½	7½							
Mississippi									7	
Missouri				9						
New York		28	4	1		2				
New Jersey	2	1	2				2			
North Carolina							10			
Ohio	1	5	11				4	2		
Oregon		9						2		
Pennsylvania		7½	17½				2			
Texas		4								
Tennessee			12							
Vermont				5						
Virginia								2		13
Total	25	57	68½	28	3	22	21	9½	7	13

The President announced the result as follows:

Whole number of votes cast 254
Necessary to a choice 128
Of which John Bell of Tennessee received 68½
Sam. Houston of Texas 57
John J. Crittenden 28
Edward Everett 25
Wm. A. Graham 22
John McLean 21
Wm. C. Rives 13
John M. Botts 9½
Wm. L. Sharkey 7
Wm. L. Goggin 3

As the second ballot was being taken it became apparent that the friends of John Bell were in the ascendant.

As the vote of New York was being taken, Jas. W. Garrard, of that State, gave his political biography. He stated that he had been in the habit of standing up in favor of the South. He was a Northern man with Northern principles. Northern conservative principles were the same as Southern conservative principles. He mentioned that he had several times talked like a prophet. He had something to say of Washington, the American Eagle, the Washington monument, the Battle monument, and striking upon expediency, availability, etc., wound up with a screech for Sam. Houston, appealing in behalf of the Dutch and Irish of New York. He declared that what was wanted was a Southern Democrat to sweep up the votes.

Pendleton of Ohio declared that Ohio wanted a Southern Whig. This expression was received with an uproar of approbation, as it was understood to be a stroke for John Bell. So it was Southern Whig against Southern Democrat.

Houston's long-haired friend from Texas, made a wild speech for him. He (long hair) was an old friend of Henry Clay—loved, admired, revered him, and followed him through his days of adversity. But Sam. Houston was the man.

It was now clear, however, that the flood was for John Bell.

When the State of Virginia was called, Mr. Summers of Virginia stated that the delegation asked to be allowed a few moments for consultation, before announcing her vote.

The excitement was intense throughout the Convention, as upon the vote which Virginia might give, would depend the nomination of Hon. John Bell of Tennessee upon this ballot, as he then lacked but three votes of a majority of all the electoral votes represented in the Convention.

The ballot, as it then stood, was as follows:

SECOND BALLOT.

States.	Bell.	Houston.	Graham.	Everett.	Botts.	Sharkey.	Crittenden.	McLean.
Alabama	9							
Arkansas		4						
Connecticut	3½	2½						
Delaware	3							
Florida	3							
Georgia		3½	6½					
Kentucky	4	6			1½		½	
Indiana	12				1			
Illinois		5½				5½		
Maine	8							
Massachusetts	12	1						
Maryland	7½	½						
Mississippi						7		
Missouri		1	1	6				
New York	4	29	1					
New Jersey	5				1		1	
North Carolina			10					
Ohio	18	5						
Pennsylvania	19	7						1
Texas		4						
Tennessee	12							
Vermont	5							
Virginia								
Total	125	68	18½	9½	5½	8½	0	1

Mr. Summers, on the part of the Virginia delegation, announced that he had been instructed to announce that they cast 13 votes for John Bell of Tennessee, and 2 votes for John Minor Botts.

This gave Bell a majority, and there was a great clamor of applause, a tearing roar of cheers, a violent stamping—Bedlam broken loose.

The Convention now went through the formality of changing votes, so as to make the nomination unanimous. As State after State changed its vote, there were the usual demonstrations of delight, by which this Convention has been distinguished above all other caucuses ever heard of.

Leslie Coombs, in changing the vote of Kentucky, paid a high compliment to Gen. Sam. Houston, and went over to Bell. Coombs said since the death of Clay, he had not been in active political life; but since the tocsin of disunion had been sounded North and South, he had thought it his duty to come up out of his political grave, and join the throng of the living, and enter into the campaign for the Union.

There was a great deal said of the great Bell that was to toll the knell of the Democratic party. Several gentlemen were quite captivated by their ability to pun on the name of the "favorite son of Tennessee," and a delegate from Pennsylvania proposed to furnish the bell-metal necessary for the enormous National Bell which was to be sounded over the Union. And so on for quantity.

While New York was changing her vote, there was a crash somewhere, and it suddenly occurred to every body that the galleries, which were enormously loaded, were giving way. There was a tremendous rush of terrified men for the doors and windows. By great efforts of those who were too far from the windows to get out, and those who were in a position, and cool enough to see that there was no danger, the panic was subdued. When it was discovered that there was no peril, the crowd stared at each other, with white faces, and laughed.

The changing of votes was so tedious, that it became an almost insufferable bore. It was over with at last, however. Erastus Brooks moved to make the nomination unanimous, and the chairman put the question whether that should be done. Thereupon there was a yell that was called unanimous. Then the chairman arose to perform the proudest duty of his life. It was almost too big for him. But he struggled with it and triumphed, and he proclaimed that John Bell was the unanimous choice of that Convention.

Major G. A. Henry, of Tennessee, grandson of Patrick Henry, responded in behalf of his State. He spoke in glowing terms of John Bell, whose whole record he declared to be sound. No sectional sentiment ever soiled the paper on which his speeches were written.

He proceeded to make a Union speech. It would not do to allow the Union to be dissolved. He, for one, could not stand by and permit it. The revolutionary blood in his veins forbade him to be passive on such an occasion. A voice here cried out—"A grandson of Patrick Henry!" There was at once a sensation. Three cheers and three more were given, and Washington Hunt sprang up, his eyes streaming tears, and grasped his hand. Mr. Henry is a tall, well-formed gentleman, with fine pleasant face, bald head, and fringe of silvery white hair about the ears. The old man had really inherited some of the powers as an orator of his illustrious ancestor, and made the speech of the Convention.

"We are Union people; shall we throw this Union away? How can we avoid the responsibility of standing up to defend it? With what face could we meet the wondering nations, if by strife and hate and blinded councils, and the blasted sway of demagogues accursed, we throw away the richest heritage that God ever gave to man, blot out our fair escutcheon to all coming time, deliver down our names to be accursed, teach despots that freedom is but a dream, quench its fair light wherever it may dawn, and bid the lovers of mankind despair? If such must be our country's early doom; if all her pride, her power, her cherished hopes, our stripes, our stars, our heritage of glory, and the bright names we have taught our children to revere—if all must end in this, never let free man meet free man again, and greet him with length of years.

"'An early tomb,
Wherein to escape the hiss and scorn
Of all mankind, were sure a better doom.'

"Tear down your flag; burn your Capitol; dismiss your navy; disband your army; let our commerce rot; overturn all your monuments, here in Baltimore and everywhere else; give to the flames the once loved record of our father's deeds; scatter the sacred dust of Washington ['Never,' 'never,'], teach your boys to forget his name, and never let the pilgrim's foot tread the consecrated groves of Mount Vernon. Can we surrender all these bright and glorious hopes? If we can, then we of the Union party are the most recreant of all mankind, and the curses of all time will cling upon us like the shirt of Nessus."

His description of the return of delegates from Charleston was rich. He said:

"As I was coming on here, the other day, I saw some of the delegates returning from Charleston, and I declare to you that I never saw a more broken down and desponding set. [Laughter.] They were tired, sleepy, and disheartened; and I must say without any figure of speech, they were 'unwashed.' [Renewed laughter and applause.] I said to them, 'Gentlemen, what upon earth is the matter with you now? What has happened to you?' 'Oh!' says one man, 'our national Democracy is broken up, and the lamentations of the whole world, I reckon, will attend it.' 'Oh! yes,' said I, 'I shed oceans of tears over the result.' [Laughter.] They looked to me like the broken columns of Napoleon's army when they returned discomfited from Moscow.

"Here and there I caught one and asked him what occurred down there. 'Why,' said one, 'I have not slept a wink for four nights.' [Laughter.] I said to one, who I thought treated me a little scurvily about it, 'Why, perhaps a little good brandy would cheer you up.' 'No,' said he, 'even burnt brandy wouldn't save me now.' [Renewed laughter.] Gentlemen, upon my honor, I expect every one of them to die soon, and in every paper I read I look to see the death of some of the Charleston members."

The old man was in good earnest, and his effort was immensely acceptable. In truth, I have seldom heard a speech better calculated to arouse popular feeling. When he closed he was given about twenty-five cheers, and the Convention being in the humor for talk rather than business, the Hon. W. L. Sharkey of Mississippi was called upon for a speech, at the conclusion of which the Convention took a recess.

Upon reassembling, there was an eagerness on the part of nearly all the delegations to put forward for nomination for the second place on the ticket, the name of the Hon. Edward Everett. Only one other name was proposed. Col. Finnell of Kentucky nominated the chairman of the Convention, Washington Hunt, who declined to allow the use of his name, in a speech entirely too long and rather awkward. After about twenty speeches, which filled up three hours, and such stamping and shouting as was absolutely deafening, the nomination of Everett was made by acclamation.

The speech of this part of the performance was made by the Hon. Geo. S. Hillard, one of the editors of the Boston Courier. Mr. Hillard's effort was exceedingly graceful, and well worded, and the ladies honored him by throwing bouquets upon the platform. He responded by telling them that unfortunately the ladies of Massachusetts were Republicans almost to a man.

The following is the passage of his speech:

"Now, gentlemen of the Convention, you have this day done a good and glorious work. It will send a thrill of joy and hope all over the land. I know well the feeling which will be awakened in New England. It would be felt there like the breeze from the sea after a day of exhausted heat; like as a man at the poles who is languishing after the protracted darkness of an arctic winter feels, when he sees the first ruddy spark which tells him that the spring and summer is coming, so shall we at the North welcome the intelligence of this Convention. [Applause.] As the greater part of creation waiteth for the manifestation of the Son of God, so all over the land will the true and patriotic citizens of America rise up and call you blessed. As you go home you will be received with applause, with the waving of handkerchiefs, the clapping of hands, and eyes sparkling with joy and triumph. As the English poet has said upon a great occasion—

"'Men met each other with erected look ;
The steps were highest which they took ;
Friends to congratulate their friends made haste,
And long inveterate foes saluted as they passed.'

When we go back to Massachusetts, and to New England, all over our hills and valleys which are but just beginning to feel the genial touch of spring, what a thrill of joy and exultation will ring along our cities, our towns, our villages, our solitary farm-houses, which nestle in the hollows of the hills! It will be so every where. [Applause.] 'How beautiful on the mountains are the feet of those who bring tidings of peace.' How beautiful, beautiful upon the mountains, are the feet of those who reconcile sectional discord; that bring together the North and the South and the West, and bind them together in the unity of the spirit of the land of peace!" [Cries of "Good," "good," and applause.]

On motion of Mr. Lathrop of Pennsylvania, the following persons were constituted a National Central Executive Union committee:

Anthony Kennedy, of Maryland.
A. R. Boteler, of Virginia.
Joshua Hill, of Georgia.
John A. Campbell, of North Carolina.
Robert Mallory, of Kentucky.
Thos. A. R. Nelson, of Tennessee.
Henry M. Fuller, of Pennsylvania.
J. B. St. John, of New York.
R. W. Thompson, of Indiana.
John Wilson, of Illinois.
James Bishop, of New Jersey.
John A. Rockwell, of Connecticut.
Marshal P. Wilder, of Massachusetts.
William Temple, of Delaware.

Several gentlemen spoke of Mr. Everett as the "Ladies' candidate," and the ladies were especially called upon to persuade their husbands and sweethearts to vote for him. They were frequently informed that they must remember how assiduously he had labored for them in the Mount Vernon business; while the rest of mankind were informed that while engaged in that business he had become wonderfully imbued with the spirit of Washington.

Among the glowing compliments paid Mr. Everett was the following, by Mr. Watson of Mississippi:

"I have made the remark again and again, that Edward Everett was at this moment better known throughout the length and breadth of this land than any other living being at this good hour. [Applause.]

"I have been told that every man was familiar with his name. I say that not only every man, but every lady is familiar with his name; and not only every lady, but every child is familiar with his name; and every school-boy has recited his glowing eloquence again and again. You may take his record up from first to last, and see his patriotism in his antecedents. His ability is matchless, and above all, his virtue is fearless in every sense of the word. [Applause.] That man has studied the character of Washington, and in his studying, he has drawn in an inspiration that has so purified and elevated his patriotism that it is enough of itself to save the Union, were there no other embodiment of patriotism within our limits." [Applause.]

It was remarkable, and I shall not say it was not a refreshing fact, that the Covention avoided altogether the discussion of the slavery question. It was only referred to by indirection. Hon. Neil S. Brown of Tennessee thanked God that he had at last found a Convention in which the "nigger" was not the sole subject of consideration. Not a word was said from first to last about the question of slavery in the Territories, or the execution of the Fugitive Slave law, and old John Brown was only referred to a couple of times.

And there was nothing said of Americanism—not a word. The Hon. Erastus Brooks declared that the Convention was of a new party, a party only six months old, and that all old party affiliations were submerged. The whole talk was of the Constitution, the Union and the laws, of harmony, fraternity, compromise, conciliation, peace, good will, common glory, national brotherhood, preservation of the confederacy. And of all these things it seemed to be understood the Convention had a monopoly. The Constitution, the Union, and peace between the sections would appear from the record of proceedings to be in the exclusive care of, and the peculiar institutions of, the no-party and no-platform gentlemen here assembled.

The Convention adjourned in high spirits.

At night a ratification meeting was held in Monument square. An extraordinarily large and elaborate stage was erected. There was a platform for the speakers and musicians. Upon each flank of this was a tower near thirty feet in height, each tower bearing a flag-staff from which the celebrated flag of our country streamed. In front of one of the towers was a likeness of Washington, and Clay adorned the other. On one tower appeared the name of John Bell, on the other that of Edward Everett. An arch spanned the platform, inscribed, "*The Union, the Constitution, and the Enforcement of the Laws.*" Circling above the inscription were the coats of arms of the States. The centre of the arch was intended for the American Eagle. But a suitable bird could not be procured to perch in that exalted place, and a few small flags were substituted. The whole thing was decorated by lamps, and presented an exceedingly brilliant appearance. I imagine that nothing more complete in design, or elaborate in execution, was ever in the United States constructed to serve a similar purpose.

THE CHICAGO CONVENTION.

CHICAGO, **May 15.**

Leaving Baltimore in a flood we found the West afflicted with a drouth. At one end of the journey, there was a torrent tearing down every ravine; at the other there was a fog of dust all along the road.

The incidents of the trip were a land-slide on the Pennsylvania Central, and the unpleasantness of being behind time to the extent of six hours on the Pittsburgh, Fort Wayne and Chicago. The detention was occasioned by the fact of the train consisting of thirteen cars full of "irrepressibles." I regret to say that most of the company were "unsound," and rather disposed to boast of that fact.

The difference between the country passed over between Baltimore and Chicago, and that between Louisville and Baltimore, by way of Charleston, is greatly in favor of the former. I have not had any disposition to speak in disparaging terms of the Southern country, but it is the plain truth that the country visible along the road from Baltimore to Harrisburg alone, is worth more by far than all that can be seen from Charleston to the Potomac. In the South few attempts have been made to cultivate any lands other than those most favorably situated, and most rich. But in Pennsylvania, free labor has made not only the valleys bloom, but the hill-tops are radiant with clover and wheat. And there are many other things that rush upon the sight in the North as contrasted with the South, that testify to the paramount glory of free labor.

And while pursuing the path of perfect candor in all these matters, it becomes necessary to say that the quantity of whiskey and other ardent beverages consumed on the train in which I reached this city, was much greater than on any train that within my knowledge entered Charleston during Convention times. The number of private bottles on our train last night was something surprising. A portion of the Republicans are distressed by what they see and hear of the disposition to use ardent spirits which appears in members of their supposed to be painfully virtuous party. And our Western Reserve was thrown into prayers and perspiration last night by some New Yorkers, who were singing songs not found in hymn-books. Others are glad to have the co-operation of Capt. Whiskey, and hail the fact of the enlistment of that distinguished partisan as an evidence that the Republicans are imbibing the spirit as well as the substance of the old Democratic party. I do not wish, however, to convey the impression that drunkenness prevails here to an extent very unusual in National Conventions, for that would be doing an injustice. I do not feel competent to state the precise proportions of those who are drunk, and those who are sober. There are a large number of both classes;—and the drunken are of course the most demonstrative, and according to the principle of the numerical force of the black sheep in a flock, are most multitudinous.

The crowd is this evening becoming prodigious. The Tremont House is so crammed that it is with much difficulty people get about in it from one room to another. Near fifteen hundred people will sleep in it to-night. The principal lions in this house are Horace Greeley and Frank P. Blair, Sen. The way Greeley is stared at as he shuffles about, looking as innocent as ever, is itself a sight. Whenever he appears there is a crowd gaping at him, and if he stops to talk a minute with some one who wishes to consult him as the oracle, the crowd becomes dense as possible, and there is the most eager desire to hear the words of wisdom that are supposed to fall on such occasions.

The curiosity of the town—next to the "wigwam"—is a bowie-knife seven feet long, weighing over forty pounds. It bears on one side the inscription, "*Presented to John F. Potter by the Republicans of Missouri.*" On the other side is this motto, "*Will always keep a 'Pryor' engagement.*" This curiosity is gaped at almost as much as Greeley, and it is a strange and dreadful looking concern. It is to be formally presented to Potter at Washington, by a committee from Missouri.

The city of Chicago is attending to this Convention in magnificent style. It is a great place for large hotels, and all have their capacity for accommodation tested. The great feature is the *Wigwam*, erected within the past month, expressly for the use of the Convention, by the Republicans of Chicago, at a cost of seven thousand dollars. It is a small edition of the New York Crystal Palace, built of boards, and will hold ten thousand persons comfortably—and is admirable for its accoustic excellence. An ordinary voice can be heard through the whole structure with ease.

The political news is the utter failure of the Ohio delegation to come to any agreement, and the loss of influence by that State.

CHICAGO, May 16th.

This is the morning of the first day of the Convention. The crowd is prodigious. The hotel keepers say there are more people here now than during the National Fair last year, and then it was estimated that thirty thousand strangers were in the city. This figure was probably too high, but there are, beyond doubt, more than twenty-five thousand persons here in attendance upon the Convention. This is a great place for hotels, and the multitude is fortunately distributed through them all over the town. There are only a few points where the jam is painfully close. One of those places is the Tremont House, where about fifteen hundred persons are stowed away, and which is the focus of political excitement.

As in the case of all other Conventions, the amount of idle talking that is done, is amazing. Men gather in little groups, and with their arms about each other, and chatter and whisper as if the fate of the country depended upon their immediate delivery of the mighty political secrets with which their imaginations are big. There are a thousand rumors afloat, and things of incalculable moment are communicated to you confidentially, at intervals of five minutes. There are now at least a thousand men packed together in the halls of the Tremont House, crushing each other's ribs, tramping each other's toes, and titillating each other with the gossip of the day; and the probability is, not one is possessed of a single political fact not known to the whole, which is of the slightest consequence to any human being.

The current of the universal twaddle this morning is, that "Old Abe" will be the nominee.

The Bates movement, the McLean movement, the Cameron movement, the Banks movement, are all nowhere. They have gone down like lead in the mighty waters. "Old Abe" and "Old Ben" are in the field against Seward. Abe and Ben are representatives of the conservatism, the respectability, the availability, and all that sort of thing.

The out-and-out friends of Mr. Chase here are very much embittered against the Wade movement. They are mistaken about it in some particulars. While this movement has certainly been used to slaughter Mr. Chase, it was not, in my judgment, originated with any such purpose

The room mates, the pleasure of whose society I have the pleasure of enjoying, were in magnificent condition last night. They were "glorious,"—"o'er all the ills of life victorious," and, to use the expression which is here in every body's mouth every minute, they were irrepressible until a late hour. And this morning I was aroused by a vehement debate among them, and rubbing my eyes, discovered that they were sitting up in bed playing cards to see who should pay for gin cock-tails all around, the cock-tails being an indispensable preliminary to breakfast.

The badges of different candidates are making their appearance, and a good many of the dunces of the occasion go about duly labeled. I saw an old man this morning with a wood-cut of Edward Bates pasted outside his hat. The Seward men have badges of silk with his likeness and name, and some wag pinned one of them to Horace Greeley's back yesterday, and he created even an unusual sensation as he hitched about with the Seward mark upon him.

The hour for the meeting of the Convention approaches, and the agitation of the city is exceedingly great. Vast as the wigwam is, not one-fifth of those who would be glad to get inside can be accommodated.

FIRST DAY.

OFFICIAL ROLL OF THE CONVENTION.

The following is the Official Roll of the delegates admitted to seats in the Convention:

PRESIDENT.

Hon. GEO. ASHMUN, of Massachusetts.

VICE-PRESIDENTS.

California—A. A. Sargent.
Connecticut—C. F. Cleveland.
Delaware—John C. Clark.
Iowa—H. P. Scholte.
Illinois—David Davis.
Indiana—John Beard.
Kentucky—W. D. Gallagher.
Maine—Samuel F. Hersey.
Maryland—Wm. L. Marshall.
Massachusetts—Ensign H. Kellogg.
Michigan—Thomas White Ferry.
Minnesota—Aaron Goodrich.
Missouri—Henry T. Blow.
New York—Wm. Curtis Noyes.
New Jersey—E. Y. Rogers.
New Hampshire—Wm Halle.
Ohio—Geo. D. Burgess.
Oregon—Joel Burlingame.
Pennsylvania—Thad. Stevens.
Rhode Island—Rowland G. Hazard.
Texas—Wm. T. Chandler.
Vermont—Wm. Hebard.
Virginia—R. Crawford.
Wisconsin—Hans Crocker.
Nebraska—A. S. Paddock.
Kansas—W. W. Ross
District of Columbia—Geo. Harrington.

SECRETARIES.

California—D. J. Staples.
Connecticut—H H. Starkweather.
Delaware—B J. Hopkins.
Iowa—William B. Allison.
Illinois—O. L. Davis.
Indiana—Daniel D Pratt.
Kentucky—Stephen J. Howes.
Maine—C. A. Wing.
Maryland—William E. Coale.
Massachusetts—Charles O Rogers.
Michigan—W. S. Stoughton.
Minnesota—D. A. Secombe.
Missouri—J. K. Kidd.
New York—Geo. W. Curtis.
New Jersey—Edward Brettle.

New Hampshire—Nathan Hubbard.
Ohio—N. J. Beebe.
Oregon—Eli Thayer.
Pennsylvania—J. B. Serrill.
Rhode Island—R. R. Hazard, jr.
Texas—Dunbar Henderson.
Vermont—John W. Stewart.
Wisconsin—L. F. Frisby.
Kansas—John A. Martin.
Nebraska—H. P. Hitchcock.

DELEGATES.

MAINE—EIGHT VOTES.

At Large.

George F. Talbot, Machias.
William H. McCrillis, Bangor.
John L. Stevens, Augusta.
Rensellaer Cram, Portland.

Districts.

1 Mark F. Wentworth, Kittery.
  Leonard Andrews, Biddeford.
2 Charles J. Gilman, Brunswick.
  Seward Dill, Phillips.
3 Nathan G. Hichborn, Stockton.
  George W. Lawrence, Warren.
4 C. A Wing, Winthrop.
  J. S. Baker, Bath.
5 Samuel F. Hersey, Bangor.
  Going Hathorn, Pittsfield.
6 John West, Franklin.
  Washington Long, Fort Fairfield.

NEW HAMPSHIRE—FIVE VOTES.

At Large.

Hon. Edward H. Rollins.
Hon. Aaron H. Cragin.
Hon. William Haile.
Hon. Amos Tuck.

Delegates

1 Nathaniel Hubbard.
  George Matthewson.
2 B. F. Martin.
  F H. Morgan.
3 Jacob Benton.
  Jacob C. Bean.

VERMONT—FIVE VOTES.

At Large.

E. N. Briggs, Brandon.
Peter T. Washburn, Woodstock.
E. D. Mason, Richmond.
E. C. Redington, St. Johnsbury.

Districts.

1 John W. Stewart, Middlebury.
 E. B. Burton, Manchester.
2 Hugh H. Henry, Chester.
 Wm. Hebord, Chelsea.
3 Wm. Clapp, St. Albans.
 E. B. Sawyer, Hyde Park.

MASSACHUSETTS—THIRTEEN VOTES.

At Large.

John A. Andrew, Boston.
Ensign H. Kellogg, Pittsfield.
George S. Boutwell, Groton.
Linus B. Comins, Boston.

Districts.

1 Joseph M. Day, Barnstable.
 Jonathan Bourne, jr., New Bedford.
2 Robert T. Davis, Fall River.
 Seth Webb, jr., Scituate.
3 Edward L. Pierce, Milton.
 William Claflin, Newton.
4 Charles O. Rogers, Boston.
 Josiah Dunham, Boston.
5 Samuel Hooper, Boston.
 George William McLellan, Cambridge.
6 Timothy Davis, Gloucester.
 Eben F. Stone, Newburyport.
7 George Cogswell, Bradford.
 Timothy Winn, Woburn.
8 Theodore H. Sweetser, Lowell.
 John S. Keyes, Concord.
9 John D. Baldwin, Worcester.
 Edward B. Bigelow, Grafton.
10 John Wells, Chicopee.
 Erastus Hopkins, Northampton.
11 John H. Coffin, Great Barrington.
 Matthew D. Field, Southwick.

RHODE ISLAND—FOUR VOTES.

At Large.

James F. Simmons, U. S. Senate.
Nathaniel B. Durfee, Tiverton.
Benedict Lapham, Centreville.
W. H. S. Bayley, Bristol.

Districts.

1 Benjamin T. Eames, Providence.
 Rowland R. Hazard, jr., Newport.
2 Rowland G. Hazard, Peacedale.
 Simon Henry Greene, Phenix.

CONNECTICUT—SIX VOTES.

At Large.

Gideon Welles, Hartford.
Elenzer K. Foster, New Haven.
Chauncey F. Cleveland, Hampton.
Alexander H. Holley, Salisbury.

Districts.

1 Samuel Q. Porter, Unionville P. O.
 Leverett E. Pease, Somers.
2 Stephen W. Kellogg, Waterbury.
 Arthur B Calef. Middletown.
3 David Gallup, Plainfield.
 Henry H. Starkweather, Norwich.
4 Edgar S. Tweedy, Danbury.
 George H. Noble, New Milford.

NEW YORK—THIRTY-FIVE VOTES.

At Large.

William M. Evarts, New York.
Preston King, Ogdensburgh.
John L. Schoolcraft, Albany.
Henry R. Selden, Rochester.

Districts.

1 George W. Curtis, New York.
 Robert L. Meeks, Jamaica, L. I.
2 James S. T. Stranahan, Brooklyn.
 Henry A. Kent, Brooklyn.
3 John A. Kennedy, New York.
 John A. King, Jamaica.
4 Owen W. Brennan, New York.
 Robert T. Haws, New York.
5 Thomas Murphy, New York.
 Charles M. Briggs, Williamsburg.
6 Joseph C. Pinckney, New York.
 Marshall B. Blake, do
7 Daniel D. Conover, do
 John Keyser, do
8 Wm. Curtis Noyes, do
 James W. Nye, do
9 Edmund J. Porter, New Rochelle.
 John G. Miller, Carmel.
10 Ambrose S. Murray, Goshen.
 C. V R. Luddington, Monticello.
11 Peter Crispell, jr.
 Henry Green.
12 Albert Van Kleeck, Poughkeepsie.
 John T. Hogeboom, Ghent.
13 Jonathan W. Freeman.
 Gideon Reynolds, Troy.
14 H. H. Van Dyck, Albany.
 Henry A. Brigham, West Troy.
15 Edward Dodd, Argyle.
 Jas. W. Schenck, Glensfalls.
16 Orlando Kellogg.
 Wm. Hedding.
17 John H Wooster, Newport.
 A. B. James, Ogdensburgh.
18 Henry Churchill, Gloversville.
 Thomas R. Horton, Fultonville.
19 Horatio N. Buckley, Delhi.
 Samuel J. Cooke.
20 Palmer V. Kellogg, Utica.
 Henry H. Fish, Utica.
21 Giles W. Hotchkiss, Binghamton.
 Benj. S. Rexford, Norwich.
22 Samuel F. Case, Fulton.
 Robt. Stewart, Chittenango.
23 Isaac H. Fiske, Watertown.
 Hiram Porter, Louisville.
24 Vivus W. Smith, Syracuse.
 D. C. Greenfield, Baldwinsville.
25 Alex B. Williams, Lyons.
 Theodore M. Pomeroy, Auburn.
26 Obadiah B. Latham, Seneca Falls.
 Charles C. Shepard, Penn Yan.
27 Wm. W. Shepard, Waverly.
 Geo. W. Schuyler, Ithaca.
28 Wm. Scott, Geneseo.
 Stephen T. Hayt, Corning.
29 D. D. S. Browne, Rochester.
 Alexander Babcock, Rochester.
30 Joshua H. Darling, Warsaw.
 John H. Kimberly, Batavia.
31 Wm. Keep, Lockport.
 Noah Davis, jr., Albion.
32 Alexander W. Harvey, Buffalo.
 Joseph Candee, do
33 Alonzo Kent, Ellicottville.
 Dolos E. Sill, do

NEW JERSEY—SEVEN VOTES.

At Large.

James T. Sherman, Trenton.
Thomas H. Dudley, Camden.

Edward Y. Rogers, Rahway.
Ephraim Marsh. Jersey City.
F. T. Frelinghuysen, Newark.
Jonathan Cook. Trenton.
Dudley S. Gregory, Jersey City.
John J. Blair, Blairtown.

Districts.

1 Providence Ludlam, Bridgeton.
  Robert K. Matlock, Woodbury.
  Edward Brettle, Camden.
  Jonathan D. Ingham, Salem.
2 Archibald R. Pharo, Tuckerton.
  Stephen B. Smith, Pennington.
  Anzi C. McLean, Freehold.
  Bernard Connolly, do
3 A. P. Bethonde, Washington.
  A. N. Voorhees, Clinton.
  Wm. D. Waterman, Janesville.
  Moses F. Webb, New Brunswick.
4 Henry M. Low, Paterson.
  Wm. O. Lathrop, Boonton.
  Thomas Cumming, Hackensack.
  Henry B. Crosby, Paterson.
5 Hugh H. Bowne, Rahway.
  H. N. Congar, Newark.
  Marcus L. Ward, Newark.
  Denning Duer, Weehawken.

PENNSYLVANIA—TWENTY-SEVEN VOTES.

At Large.

David Wilmot, Towanda.
Samuel A. Purviance, Pittsburgh.
Thaddeus Stevens, Lancaster.
John H. Ewing, Washington.
Henry D. Moore, Philadelphia.
Andrew H. Reeder, Easton.
Titian J. Coffee, Pittsburgh.
Morrow B. Lowry, Erie.

Districts.

1 John M. Butler, Philadelphia.
  Elias Ward,   do
  J. Money,   do
  Wm. Elliott,   do
2 Geo. A. Coffee,   do
  Richard Ellis,   do
  Francis Blackburn,   do
  John M. Pomroy,   do
3 Wm. D. Mann,   do
  James M'Manus,   do
  Benj. H. Brown,   do
  George Read,   do
4 A. C. Roberts,   do
  Wm. H. Kern,   do
  Wm. D. Kelly,   do
  M. S. Buckley, Richmond.
5 James Hooven, Norristown.
  Dr. C. M. Jackson, Philadelphia.
  William B. Thomas, Philadelphia.
  George W. Pumroy, Philadelphia.
6 John M. Broomal, Chester.
  Washington Townsend, West Chester.
  Joseph J. Lewis, West Chester.
  Jacob S. Serrill, Darby.
7 Caleb N. Taylor, Bristol.
  Joseph Young, Allen Town.
  George Beisel, Allen Town.
  Henry J. Saeger, Allen Town.
8 Isaac Eckert, Redding.
  David E. Stout, Redding.
  J. Knabb, Redding.
  J. Bowman Bell, Redding.
9 O. J. Dickey, Lancaster.
  C. S. Kauffman, Columbia.
  Samuel Evoch, Columbia.
  Jos. D. Pownall, Christiana.
10 G. Dawson Coleman, Lebanon.
   Levi Kline, Lebanon.

Jos Casey, Harrisburg.
Wm. Cameron. Louisburg.
11 Robert M. Palmer, Pottsville.
   Jacob G. Frick, Pottsville.
   S. A. Bergstresser, Elysburg
   Wm. C Lawson, Milton.
12 W. W. Ketcham, Wilkesbarre.
   P. M. Osterbout. Junkhannock.
   Frank Stewart, Berwick.
   Davis Alton, Carbondale.
13 Chas. Albright, Mauch Chunk.
   Wm. Davis, Stroudsburg.
   W. H. Armstrong, Easton.
   Sam'l E. Dimmick, Houesdale.
14 H. W. Tracy, Standing Stone.
   Hon Wm. Jessup, Montrose.
   F. E. Smith, Tioga Point.
   Dr. Abel Humphreys, Tioga Point.
15 Wm. Butler, Lewiston
   B. Rush Peterkin. Lockhaven.
   Lindsay Mehalley, Seaverry.
   G B. Overton, Coudersport.
16 Kirk Haines, Millerstown.
   W. B. Irvin. Mechanicsburg.
   Alex. J. Frey York.
   Jacob S. Haldeman, New Cumberland.
17 Wm. M'Clellan. Chambersburg.
   D. MCaunaghy, Gettysburg.
   John J. Patterson. Academia.
   Francis Jordan Bedford.
18 A. A. Barker, Elensburg.
   S. M. Green, Bailey's Forge.
   L. W. Hall, Altoona.
   Wm. H. Koons, Somerset.
19 W. M. Stewart, Indiana.
   Darwin E Phelps, Kittaning.
   Addison Leech, Leechburg.
   D. W. Shryok, Greensburg.
20 Andrew Stewart, Uniontown.
   Smith Fuller, Uniontown.
   Alex. Murdoch, Washington.
   Wm. E. Gapen, Waynesburg.
21 Wm. H. Mersh. Pittsburgh.
   Col. James A. Ekin Elizabeth.
   John F. Dravo McKeesport.
   J. J. Siebeneck, Pittsburgh.
22 D. N. White, Sewickley.
   Stephen H. Guyer. Alleghany City.
   John N. Purviance Butler county.
   W. L. Graham. Butler county.
23 L. L. McGuffin, New Castle.
   David Craig New Castle.
   Wm. G. Brown, Mercer.
   John Allison, New Brighton.
24 Henry Souther Ridgway.
   S. P. Johnston, Warren.
   Jas. S. Meyers, Franklin.
   D. C. Gillaspie, Brooklyn.
25 B. B. Vincent, Erie.
   Thomas J. Devore, Erie.
   J. C. Hayes, Meadville.
   S. Newton Pettis, Meadville.

DELAWARE—THREE VOTES.

Nathaniel B. Smithers, Dover.
John C. Clark. Delaware City.
Benjamin G. Hopkins, Vernon.
Lewes Thompson, Pleasant Hill.
Joshua T. Heald, Wilmington.
Alfred Short, Milford.

MARYLAND—EIGHT VOTES.

At Large.

Francis P. Blair, Washington, D. C.
Wm. L. Marshall, Baltimore.

Districts.

1 James Bryan, Cambridge.
2 James Jeffery, Churcville.

Wm. P. Ewing, Flkton.
3 Francis S Corkran, Baltimore.
James F. Wagner. Baltimore.
4 Wm. E. Coale, Baltimore.
5 Chas. Lee Armour, Frederick.
6 Montgomery Blair. Washington, D. C.
D. S. Oram, Church Creek.

Isaac Steese, Massillon.
19 Robt. F. Paine, Cleveland.
R. Hitchcock, Painesville.
20 Joshua R Giddings, Jefferson.
Milton Sutliffe, Warren.
21 Samuel Stokely, Steubenville.
D. Arter, Carrollton.

VIRGINIA—FIFTEEN VOTES.
At Large.
Alfred Caldwell, Wheeling.
F. M Norton.   do
W. W. Gitt, Montgomery Co. Court House.
J. C. Underwood, Clark Co.   do

KENTUCKY—TWELVE VOTES.
At Large.
Geo. D Blakey, Russellville.
A. A. Burton, Lancaster
Wm. D. Gallagher, Pewee Valley.
Charles Liendley, Newport.

Districts.
1 Jacob Hornbrook, Wheeling.
 J G. Jacob, Wellsburgh.
 Joseph Applegate. Wellsburgh.
2 A. G. Robinson, Wheeling.
 R. Crawford,   do
3 Thos. Horobrook,   do
 J. M. Pumphrey.   do
4 R. H. Gray, Lynchburg.
 F. D. Norton, Wheeling.
5 John Underwood, Prince William Court H.
 J. B. Brown. Alexandria.
6 W. J. Blackwood, Clark Co, Court House.
 J. T. Freeman, Hancock Court House.
7 A. W. Campbell, Wheeling.
 D. W. Roberts, Morgantown.
8 W. E. Stevenson, Parkersburg.
 S. M. Peterson,   do
 S. H. Woodward, Wheeling.
9 James Wilson,   do

Districts.
1 Abner Williams, Covington.
 H. G. Otis. Louisville.
2 Fred. Frische. Louisville.
 E. H Harrison, McKee.
3 Joseph Glazebrook, Glasgow.
 Jos. W. Calvert, Bowling Green.
4 John J. Hawes, Louisville.
5 H. D Hawes, Louisville.
 Lewis M. Dembitz, Louisville.
6 Curtis Knight, Kingston.
 Joseph Rawlings, White Hall.
7 A. H Merriaether, Louisville.
 Henry D. Hawes, Louisville.
8 H. B Broaddus, Ashland.
 L. Marston, Millersburg.
9 Edgar Needham, Louisville.
 J. S Davis,
10 Jas. R. Whittemore, Newport.
 Hamilton Cummings, Covington.

OHIO—TWENTY-THREE VOTES
At Large.
Hon. D. K. Cartter, Cleveland.
Hon. V B. Horton, Pomeroy.
Hon Thomas Spooner, Redding.
Hon. Conrad Broadbeck, Dayton.

INDIANA—THIRTEEN VOTES.
At Large.
William T. Ott, New Albany.
Daniel D. Pratt, Logansport.
Caleb B. Smith, Indianapolis.
P. A. Hackelman, Rushville.

Districts.
1 Benj. Eggleston, Cincinnati.
 Fred. Hassaureck,   do
2 R M. Corwine,   do
 Joseph H. Barrett,   do
3 Wm Becket, Hamilton.
 P. P Lowe. Dayton.
4 G. D. Burgess, Troy.
 John E. Cummings. Sidney.
5 David Taylor. Defiance.
 E. Graham, Perryburg.
6 John M Barrere. New Market.
 Reeder W Clarke. Batavia.
7 Hon. Thos. Corwin, Lebanon.
 A. Hivling. Xenia.
8 W. H. West, Bellefontaine.
 Levi Geiger. Urbana.
9 Earl Bill. Tiffin.
 D. W. Swigart, Bucyrus.
10 J V. Robinson, jr., Portsmouth.
 Milton L Clark, Chillicothe.
11 N. H Van Vorhees, Athens.
 A. C. Sands, Zelaski.
12 Willard Warner, Newark.
 Jonathan Renick, Circleville.
13 John J. Gurley, Mt Gilead.
 P. N. Schuyler. Norwalk.
14 James Monroe, Oberlin.
 G. U. Haro, Wooster.
15 Hon. Columbus Delano, Ml. Vernon
 R. K. Enos, Millersburg.
16 Daniel Applegate Zanesville.
 Caleb A. Williams, Chesterfield.
17 C. J. Allbright, Cambridge.
 Wm. Wallace. Martin's Ferry
18 H. Y. Beebe, Ravenna.

Districts.
1 James C. Veatch, Rockport.
 C. M. Allen, Vincennes.
2 Thos. C. Slaughter, Corydon.
 J. H. Butler. Salem
3 John R. Cravens, Madison.
 A. C Vorbies. Bedford.
4 Geo. Holland, Brookville.
 J. L. Yater. Versailles.
5 Miles Murphy, Newcastle.
 Walter March, Muncie.
6 S. P. Oyler, Franklin.
 John S. Bobbs, Indianapolis.
7 Geo. K. Steele, Rockville.
 D. C. Donobue, Green Castle.
8 John Beard, Crawfordsville.
 J. N. Simms, Frankfort.
9 Chas. H. Test, Mudges Station.
 D. H. Hopkins, Crown Point.
10 Geo. Moon, Warsaw.
 Geo. Emmerson, Angola.
11 Wm. W. Connor, Noblesville.
 John M. Wallace, Marion.

MICHIGAN—SIX VOTES.
At Large.
Austin Blair, Jackson.
Walton W. Murphy, Jonesville.
Thos White Ferry, Grand Haven.
J. J. St. Clair, Marquette.

Districts.
1 J. G. Peterson, Detroit.
 Alex. D. Crane, Dexter.
2 Jesse G Beeson, Dowagiac.
 William L. Stoughton, Sturgis.

3 Francis Quinn, Niles.
Erastus Hussey, Battle Creek.
4 D. C. Buckland, Pontiac.
Michael T. C. Plessner, Saginaw City.

ILLINOIS—ELEVEN VOTES.

At Large.

N. B. Judd, Chicago.
Gustavus Koerner, Belleville.
David Davis, Bloomington.
O. H. Browning, Quincy.

Districts.

1 Jason Marsh, Rockford.
Solon Cummings, Grand de Tour.
2 George Schneider, Chicago.
George T. Smith Fulton.
3 B. C. Cook, Ottawa.
O. L. Davis, Danville.
4 Henry Grove, Peoria.
E. W. Hazard, Galesburg.
5 Wm. Ross, Pittsfield.
James S. Erwin, Mt. Sterling.
6 S. T. Logan Springfield.
N. M. Knapp, Winchester.
7 Thos. A Marshall, Charleston.
Wm. P. Dole, Paris.
8 F. S. Rutherford, Alton.
D. K. Green, Salem.
9 James C. Sloo, Shawneetown.
D. L. Phillips, Anna.

WISCONSIN—FIVE VOTES.

At Large.

Carl Schurz, Milwaukee.
Hans Crocker, Milwaukee.
T. B. Stoddard, La Crosse.
John P. McGregor, Milwaukee.

Districts.

1 H. L. Raun, Whitewater.
C. C. Sholes, Kenosha.
2 M S. Gibson, Hudson.
J. R Bennett, Janesville.
3 Elisha Morrow, Green Bay.
L. F. Frisbey, West Bend.

MINNESOTA—FOUR VOTES.

At Large.

John W. North, Northfield.
D. A. Secombe, St. Anthony.
Stephen Miller, St. Cloud.
S. P. Jones, Rochester.

Districts.

1 A. H. Wagener, New Ulm.
Aaron Goodrich, St. Paul.
2 John McCusick, Stillwater.
Simeon Smith, Chatfield.

IOWA—EIGHT VOTES.

At Large.

Wm. Penn Clark, Iowa City.
L. C Noble, West Union.
John A. Kasson, Des Moines.
Henry O'Conner, Muscatine.
J. F. Wilson, Fairfield.
J. W. Rankin, Keokuk.
M. L. McPherson, Wintersett.
C. F. Clarkson, Metropolis.
N. J Rusch, Davenport.
H. P. Scholte, Pella.
John Johns, Fort Dodge.

Districts.

1 Alvin Saunders, Mount Pleasant.
J. C. Walker, Fort Madison.

2 Jos. Caldwell, Ottumwa.
M. Baker, Congdon.
3 Benj. Rector, Sidney.
Geo. A Hawley, Leon.
4 H. M. Hoxie, Des Moines.
Jacob Butler, Muscatine.
5 Thos. Seeley, Guthrie Centre.
C. C. Nourse, Des Moines.
6 Wm. M. Stone, Knoxville.
J. B. Grinnell, Grinnell.
7 Wm. A. Warren, Bellevue.
John W Thompson, Davenport.
8 John Shane, Vinton.
Wm. Smyth, Marion.
9 Wm. B. Allison, Dubuque.
A. F Brown, Cedar Falls.
10 Reuben Noble, McGregor.
E. G Bowdoin, Rockford.
11 W. P. Hepburn, Marshalltown.
J. J. Brown, Eldora.

MISSOURI—NINE VOTES.

At Large.

Francis P. Blair, jr., St. Louis.
B. Gratz Brown, St. Louis.
F. Muench, Marthasville.
J. O. Sitton, Hermann.

Districts.

1 P. L. Foy, St. Louis.
C. L. Bernays, St. Louis.
2 A Krekle, St Charles.
A. Hammer, St. Louis.
3 N. T. Doane, Trenton.
Asa S. Jones, St. Louis.
4 H. B. Branch, St. Joseph.
G. W. H. Landon, St. Joseph.
5 Jas. B. Gardenhire, Jefferson City.
B. Bruns Jefferson City.
6 J. K. Kidd, Linn.
J. M. Richardson, Springfield.
7 Jas. Lindsay, Ironton.
Thos. Fletcher, DeSoto.

CALIFORNIA—FOUR VOTES.

At Large.

F. P. Tracy, San Francisco.
A. A. Sargent, Nevada.
D. W. Cheeseman, Orville.
J. C. Hinckley, Shasta.
Chas. Watrous, San Francisco.
Sam. Bell, Mariposa.
D. J. Staples, Staples' Branch.
J. R. McDonald, Haywards.

OREGON—FIVE VOTES.

Joel Burlingame, Scio, Oregon.
Horace Greeley, New York City.
Henry Buckingham, Salem, Oregon.
Eli Thayer, House Rep's, Washington, D. C
Frank Johnson, Oregon City.

TEXAS—SIX VOTES.

At Large.

D. C. Henderson, Austin.
G. A. Fitch, Austin.
James P. Scott, San Antonio.
A. A. Shaw, Little Elm.

Districts.

1 Gilbert Moyers, Ga veston.
2 M. S. C. Chandler, Galveston.

KANSAS.

A. C. Wilder, Leavenworth.
John A. Martin, Atchison.

Wm. A. Phillips, Lawrence.
W W R ss, Topeka.
A. G. Proctor, Emporia.
John P. Hatterschiedt, Leavenworth.

NEBRASKA—SIX VOTES.
O W Irish, Nebraska City.
S. W. Elbert, Plattsmouth
E. D. Webster, Omaha.

John R. Meredith, Omaha.
A S Paddock, Fort Calhoun.
P. W. Witchcock, Omaha.

DISTRICT OF COLUMBIA.
Geo. Harrington, Washington.
Joseph Gerhardt, Washington.
G. A. Hall, Washington.
J. A. Wyso, Washington.

The Hon. Edward D. Morgan of New York, Chairman of the National Republican Executive Committee, called the Convention to order, and read the call under which it had been summoned. He concluded by nominating the Hon. David Wilmot for temporary President. Mr. Wilmot, upon taking the chair, made a very positive anti-slavery speech. A committee on Permanent Organization was constituted as follows:

Maine—Leonard Andrews.
Vermont—Hugh L. Henry.
New Hampshire—Aaron H. Cragin.
Massachusetts—Linus B. Comins.
Connecticut—Arthur B. Calef.
Rhode Island—Simeon H. Greene.
New York—Henry H. Van Dyck.
New Jersey—Ephraim Marsh.
Pennsylvania—T. J. Coffey.
Delaware—Joshua T. Heil.
Maryland—James Jeffries.
Virginia—Edward M. Norton.
Ohio—V. B. Horton.
Indiana—P. A. Hackleman.

Illinois—William Ross.
Michigan—Walter W. Murphy.
Wisconsin—John P. McGregor.
Iowa—James F. Wilson.
Minnesota—Simeon Smith.
Missouri—Allen Hammer.
Kansas—A. C. Wilder.
California—Samuel Bell.
Oregon—Grant Johnson.
Kentucky—Allen J Bristow.
Texas—M. S. C. Chandler.
Nebraska—O. H. Irish.
District of Columbia—Geo. A. Hall.

A delegate from Kentucky—Mr. President, I would suggest that the names of all the States be called. [Applause.]

The Chair—Tennessee, Arkansas, Mississippi [great laughter], Louisiana, Alabama [laughter and hissing], Georgia, South Carolina [laughter], North Carolina. [Feeble hisses and much laughter.] I believe that includes the names of all the States.

The committee on Credentials was made up as follows:

Maine—Rensseller Cram.
New Hampshire—Jacob Benton.
Vermont—Edward C. Redington.
Massachusetts—Timothy Davis.
Connecticut—E. K. Foster.
Rhode Island—Benedict Lapham.
New York—Palmer V. Kellogg.
New Jersey—Moses M. Webb.
Pennsylvania—J. N. Purviance.
Delaware—Lewes Thompson.
Maryland—Wm. E. Cole.
Virginia—Jacob Hornbrook.
Kentucky—Charles Hendley.
Ohio—Samuel Stokeley.

Indiana—John E. Cravens.
Illinois—Stephen T. Logan.
Michigan—Francis Quinn.
Wisconsin—H. L. Rann.
Iowa—C. F. Clarkson.
Minnesota—John McGinisick.
Missouri—James B. Gardenhire.
Kansas—Wm. A. Phillips.
Nebraska—John R. Meredith.
California—Chas. Watrous.
Oregon—Joel Burlingame.
Texas—D. C. Henderson.
District of Columbia—James A. White.

When the roll was called on this committee, three names were received with great applause—Greeley of "Oregon," Carl Schurz, and Francis P. Blair, Sen. Greeley had the greatest ovation, and though there is an impression to the contrary, those who know him well, know that nobody is more fond of the breath of popular favor than the philosophic Horace.

The committee on Business was constituted as follows:

Maine—John L. Stephens.
New Hampshire—B. F. Martin.
Vermont—Edwin D. Mason.
Massachusetts—Saml. Hooper.
Connecticut—Geo. H. Noble.
Rhode Island—Nath. B. Durfee.
New York—A. B. James.
New Jersey—H. N. Congar.
Pennsylvania—Wm. D. Kelly.
Delaware—John C. Clark.
Maryland—Wm. P. Ewing.
Virginia—John G. Jenks.
Ohio—R. M. Corwine.
Kentucky—Louis M. Dembitz.

Indiana—Walter Marks.
Michigan—Austin Blair.
Illinois—Thos. A. Marshall.
Wisconsin—Elisha Morrow.
Minnesota—S. P. Jones.
Iowa—Reuben Noble.
Missouri—S. G. Letcher.
California—J. C. Hinckley.
Oregon—Eli Thayer.
Kansas—A. G. Proctor.
Nebraska—Samuel W. Elbert.
District of Columbia—Jos. Gerhardt.
Texas—G. Moyers.

The Convention had proceeded thus far with its business, when a communication, inviting the Convention to take an excursion on the lake, was received and accepted, and then indefinitely debated, much time being frittered away. The question as to whether it would be proper to constitute the committee on Platform, before a permanent organization was effected, was also discussed. Convention adjourned until 5 P. M.

Upon reassembling, the report of the committee on Permanent Organization was in order and made. The Hon. Geo. Ashmun, the presiding officer, was escorted to his chair by Preston King and Carl Schurz, the one short and round as a barrel and fat as butter, the other tall and slender. The contrast was a curious one, and so palpable that the whole multitude saw it, and gave a tremendous cheer. Mr. Ashmun was speedily discovered to be an excellent presiding officer. His clear, full-toned voice was one refreshing to hear amid the clamors of a Convention. He is cool, clear-headed and executive, and will despatch business. He is a treasure to the Convention, and will lessen and shorten its labors. His speech was very good for the occasion, delivered with just warmth enough. He was animated, and yet his emotions did not get the better of him. In conclusion he referred, as if it were an undoubted fact, to the "brotherly kindness" he had everywhere seen displayed. He had not heard a harsh word or unkind expression pass between delegates. Now, the gentleman must have kept very close, or his hearing is deplorably impaired. He certainly could not stay long among the Seward men at the Richmond House, without hearing unkind and profane expressions used respecting brother delegates of conservative notions. He would very frequently hear brother Greeley, for example, who is hated intensely by them, called a "d—d old ass." Indeed, that is a very mild specimen of the forms of expression used. Mr. Ashmun was, however, as nearly correct in his statement of the case, as Caleb Cushing was at Charleston in adjourning the Convention, in praising it for unexampled decorum. It is worthy of remark, that he had nothing directly to say of the "nigger." The Hon. David Wilmot had attended to that department sufficiently.

9

A gavel was presented in behalf of the mechanics of Chicago, by Mr. Judd, to the presiding officer. It was made of the oak of the flag-ship of Com. Perry, the Lawrence—"Don't give up the ship."
Mr. Judd said:
There is a motto, too, adopted by that mechanic, which should be a motto for every Republican of this Convention—the motto borne upon the flag of the gallant Lawrence, "Don't give up the ship." [Great applause.] Mr. President, in presenting this to you, in addition to the motto furnished by the mechanic who manufactured this, as an evidence of his warmth and zeal in the Republican cause, I would recommend to this Convention to believe that the person who will be nominated here, can, when the election is over in November, send a despatch to Washington in the language of the gallant Perry, "We have met the enemy, and they are ours." [Terrific cheering.]

The committee on Resolutions was appointed:

Maine—George F. Talbott.
New Hampshire—Amos Tuck.
Vermont—Ebenezer M. Briggs.
Massachusetts—George S. Boutwell.
Rhode Island—Benjamin T. Eames.
Connecticut—S. W. Kellogg.
New York—H. R. Selden.
New Jersey—Thos. H. Dudley.
Pennsylvania—William Jessup.
Delaware—N. B. Smith.
Maryland—F. P. Blair.
Virginia—Alfred Caldwell.
Ohio—Joseph H. Barrett.
Kentucky—George D. Blakey.
Indiana—Wm. T. Otto.
Michigan—Austin Blair.
Illinois—Gustavus Koerner.
Wisconsin—Carl Schurz.
Minnesota—Stephen Miller.
Iowa—J. A. Kasson.
Missouri—Chas. L. Bernays.
California—F. P. Tracy.
Oregon—Horace Greeley.
Texas—H. A. Shaw.
D. of Columbia—G. A. Hall.
Nebraska—A. Sidney Gardner.
Kansas—John P. Hatterschiedt.

The Convention adjourned without transacting any further business.
The question on which every thing turns is whether Seward can be nominated. His individuality is the pivot here, just as that of Douglas was at Charleston.
Horace Greeley and Eli Thayer have agreed upon the following resolution, which Greeley is at work to make one of the planks in the platform:

Resolved, That holding of liberty to be the natural birthright of every human being, we maintain that slavery can only exist where it has been previously established by laws constitutionally enacted; and we are inflexibly opposed to its establishment in the Territories by legislative, executive, or judicial intervention.

The first part of this resolution is Greeley's, the latter part Thayer's. It is the nearest right of any platform resolution anywhere adopted or proposed, being nearest to real popular sovereignty, and Greeley thinks he can carry it through the Platform committee. It is called the Oregon Platform.

The scenes when the doors of that part of the Wigwam set apart for the masculine public in general, are opened, are highly exciting and

* Mr. Greeley did not accomplish his purpose regarding this resolution. But it will be found, upon examination of the Republican Platform, that it does not assert the duty of Congress to intervene in the Territories to exclude Slavery.

amusing. This afternoon the rush for places was tremendous. Three doors about twenty feet wide each, were simultaneously thrown open, and three torrents of men roared in, rushing headlong for front positions. The standing room, holding four thousand five hundred persons, was packed in about five minutes. The galleries, where only gentlemen accompanied by ladies are admitted, and which contains nearly three thousand persons, was already full. There was a great deal of fun, and some curious performances, in filling the galleries. Ladies to accompany gentlemen were in demand—school-girls were found on the street, and given a quarter each to see a gentleman safe in. Other girls, those of undoubted character (no doubt on the subject whatever), were much sought after as escorts. One of them being asked to take a gentleman to the gallery, and offered half a dollar for so doing, excused herself by saying she had already taken two men in at each of the three doors, and was afraid of arrest if she carried the enterprise any further. An Irish woman passing with a bundle of clothes under her arm was levied upon by an "irrepressible," and seeing him safely into the seats reserved for ladies and accompanying gentlemen, retired with her fee and bundle. Another "irrepressible" sought out an Indian woman who was selling moccasins, and attempted to escort her in. This was a little too severe however. He was informed that she was no lady—and the point was argued with considerable vehemence. It was finally determined that a squaw was not a lady. The young Republican protested indignantly against the policeman's decision, claiming equal rights for all womankind.

The Republicans have all divided into two classes, the "irrepressibles" and the "conservatives."

The favorite word in the Convention is "solemn." Every thing is solemn. In Charleston the favorite was "crisis." Here there is something every ten minutes found to be solemn. In Charleston there was a *crisis* nearly as often. I observed as many as twenty-three in one day.

A new ticket is talked of here to-night, and an informal meeting held in this house since I have been writing this letter, has given it an impetus. It is "Lincoln and Hickman." This is now the ticket as against Seward and Cash. Clay.

The Ohio delegation continues so divided as to be without influence. If united it would have a formidable influence, and might throw the casting votes between candidates, holding the balance of power between the East and the West.

SECOND DAY.

REPUBLICAN WIGWAM,
Chicago, May 17, 1860.

Masses of people poured into town last night and this morning, expecting the nomination to be made to-day, and desiring to be present. All adjectives might be fairly exhausted in describing the crowd. It is mighty and overwhelming; it can only be numbered by tens of thousands. The press about the hotels this morning was crushing. Two thousand persons took breakfast at the Tremont House.

Many of the delegates kept up the excitement nearly all night. At two o'clock this morning part of the Missouri delegation were singing songs in their parlor. There were still a crowd of fellows caucusing—and the glasses were still clinking in the bar rooms—and far down the street a brass band was making the night musical.

The Seward men made a demonstration this morning in the form of a procession. The scene at the Richmond House as they formed and marched away after their band of music—the band in splendid uniform and the Sewardites wearing badges—was exceedingly animating and somewhat picturesque. The band was giving, with a vast volume of melody, "*O isn't he a darling?*"—the procession was four abreast, filing away in a cloud of dust—and one of their orators, mounted upon a door-step, with hat and cane in his hands, was haranguing them as a captain might address his soldiers marching to battle. The Seward procession was heedless of the dust as regular soldiers, and strode on with gay elasticity and jaunty bearing.

As they passed the Tremont House where the many masses of the opponents of "Old Irrepressible" were congregated, they gave three throat-tearing cheers for Seward. It will be a clear case if he is not nominated, that the failure cannot be charged to his friends. Few men have had friends who would cleave unto them as the Sewardites to their great man here.

The Pennsylvanians declare, if Seward were nominated, they would be immediately ruined. They could do nothing. The majority against them would be counted by tens of thousands. New Jerseyites say the same thing. The Indianians are of the same opinion. They look heart-broken at the suggestion that Seward has the inside track, and throw up their hands in despair. They say Lane will be beaten, the Legislature pass utterly into the hands of the Democracy, and the two Republican Senators hoped for be heard of no more. Illinois agonizes at the mention of the name of Seward, and says he is to them the sting of political death. His nomination would kill off Trumbull, and give the Legislature into the hands of Democrats, to make the next Congressional apportionment. Amid all these cries of distress, the Sewardites are true as steel to their champion, and they will cling to "Old Irrepressible," as they call him, until the last gun is fired and the big bell rings.

The crowd in the Wigwam this morning is more dense than ever. The thing was full yesterday, but it is crammed to-day.

The following communication was read:

"*To the Honorable President of the National Republican Convention:*

"Sir—Can you not arrange to send out some effective speaker, to entertain twenty thousand Republicans and their wives, outside the building?"

There were many expressions of a desire to proceed at once to business. But the moment the committee on Rules reported, it was seen that there was to be an "irrepressible conflict" raging through the day, about preliminary matters. The majority reported that a majority of the votes of the whole Electoral College of the Union, should be required to nominate candidates for President and Vice-President. The minority report was that a majority of the votes in the Convention only, should be required to nominate.

The fourth rule as reported by the majority, was a follows:

RULE 4. 304 votes, being a majority of the whole number of votes when all the States of the Union are represented in this Convention, according to the rates of representation presented in Rule 2, shall be required to nominate the candidates of this Convention for the offices of President and Vice-President.

The Convention was proceeding into battle on this subject, when Cartter of Ohio suggested that they were about to undertake the serious business without the report of the committee on Credentials. War then took place about credentials. The anti-Seward men were anxious to put out Virginia and Texas, particularly Texas, fearing that those States would decide the contest in favor of Seward. A great deal of speech-making followed. David Wilmot made an attack on delegations from slave States that had no constituencies. A Marylander replied to him with great force, sneering at the Pennsylvanians as too cowardly to bear the Republican banner, and so docile as to sneak under the flag of a People's Party. "First blood for the delegate from Maryland." The name of the young man who drew it was Armour. I have seldom heard so plump a speech. Every sentence was a blow "straight from the shoulder," and when he left the floor the author of the Wilmot Proviso had gone to grass and come to grief. The next thing was a speech from Dr. Blakesly of Kentucky, who mentioned that Kentucky had voted for Wilmot for Vice-President in 1856, in the Philadelphia Convention. He inquired whether he could be forgiven for that *sin*? Cries of "Yes," and he sat down. "First knock-down blow for old Kentucky." There was at last a vote on the recommitment of the report of the committee on Credentials. The following was the vote:

States.	Yeas.	Nays.	States.	Yeas.	Nays.
Maine	3	13	Ohio	46	0
New Hampshire	9	1	Indiana	26	0
Vermont	9	1	Missouri	4	14
Massachusetts	13	9	Michigan	0	12
Rhode Island	8	0	Illinois	22	0
Connecticut	10	2	Wisconsin	0	10
New York	1	69	Iowa	8	0
New Jersey	0	14	California	4	2
Pennsylvania	53¼	½	Minnesota	0	8
Maryland	4	6	Oregon	0	5
Delaware	1	5			
Virginia	30	0		275½	172½
Kentucky	24	0			

This was not a test vote, but it worried the Seward men exceedingly, as it looked to the exclusion of the delegates from Texas.

The debate preceding was really entertaining and full of fire. There has not been in any previous Republican Convention sharp-shooting so keen, and sarcasm so bitter and incisive. The Convention is very like the old Democratic article. We only occasionally hear the sentimental twang, the puritanic intonation that indicates the ancient and savory article of anti-slaveryism. The truth is the Republican party is rapidly becoming Democratized in its style of operations.

The Convention took a recess.

Upon reassembling, the committee on Credentials reported, through its chairman, that it found gentlemen entitled to seats in the following States, and each State to the following number of delegates:

States	No. of Delegates.	No. of Elect'l votes.	States.	No. of Delegates.	No. of Elect'l votes.
Maine	16	8	Indiana	26	13
New Hampshire	10	5	Missouri	18	9
Vermont	10	5	Michigan	12	6
Massachusetts	26	13	Illinois	22	11
Rhode Island	8	4	Wisconsin	10	5
Connecticut	12	6	Iowa	8	4
New York	70	35	California	8	4
New Jersey	14	7	Minnesota	8	4
Pennsylvania	54	27	Oregon	5	3
Maryland	11	8	*Territories.*		
Delaware	6	3	Kansas	6	
Virginia	23	15	Nebraska	6	
Kentucky	23	12	District of Columbia	2	
Ohio	46	23			

[Cries of "Texas," "Texas."] The chairman, Mr. Benton of New Hampshire, said: The committee have considered the question in regard to the representation from the State of Texas; they have given to the examination all that care which they were able to, and which the time from the adjournment of the Convention this forenoon would allow, and they have instructed me almost unanimously, with a solitary vote as an exception, to report that Texas be allowed six votes in this Convention. [Tremendous applause and cries of "Good," "good."] It was proved before the committee that the Convention which elected the delegates from Texas—resident delegates who are here in attendance, was a mass Convention; that it was called upon a petition signed by some three hundred of the legal voters of Texas. [Applause.] That that call was published in some two of the German papers published in the State; that written notices and advertisements were posted up in various parts of Texas, where there is any number of people in favor of the principles of the Republican party, and the committee were almost unanimously of the opinion that these delegates, elected under these circumstances, were fairly entitled to act as the representatives of the Republican party of the State of Texas. [Prolonged applause.]

The question being on the adoption of the report, it was adopted unanimously amid great cheering.

The report of the committee on Rules was taken up, and after interesting speeches made on both sides, the fourth rule of the majority report was amended by substituting the minority report, which was that a simple majority should nominate—the following was the vote on the substitution:

States.	Yeas.	Nays.	States.	Yeas.	Nays.
Maine	16	0	Missouri	0	18
New Hampshire	10	0	Michigan	12	0
Vermont	10	0	Illinois	7	0
Massachusetts	22	3	Texas	6	0
Rhode Island	4	4	Wisconsin	10	0
Connecticut	8	4	Iowa	5	3
New York	70	0	California	8	0
New Jersey	12	1	Minnesota	8	0
Pennsylvania	33½	20½	Oregon	3	1
Maryland	5	6	*Territories.*		
Delaware	6	0	Kansas	6	0
Virginia	13	8	Nebraska	6	0
Kentucky	10	9	District of Columbia	2	0
Ohio	32	9			
Indiana	25	1		358½	94½

The platform was now reported. The platform was received with immense enthusiasm. Several sections, at the demand of the audience, were read twice. Pennsylvania went into spasms of joy over the "Tariff Plank," her whole delegation rising and swinging hats and canes.

Mr. Cartter—Mr. Chairman: That report is so eminently unquestionable from beginning to end, and so eloquently carries through with it its own vindication, that I do not believe the Convention will desire discussion upon it, and I therefore call the previous question upon it. [Applause, and mingled cries of "Good, good," and "No, no."]

Mr. Giddings—I arise, sir, solemnly to appeal to my friend. [Great confusion; cries of "Withdraw the previous question." A voice—"Nobody wants to speak, but we don't want to be choked off," etc.]

Mr. Cartter—I insist upon the previous question.

Mr. Giddings—I arise, and I believe I have the right, with the leave of my colleague, to offer a short amendment before the previous question is called.

Mr. Cartter—I did it to cut you off, and all other amendments, and all discussion. [Great confusion, and cries of "Giddings" by the audience.]

After further discussion and confusion, a vote was taken on sustaining the call for the previous question, resulting as follows:

States.	Yeas.	Nays.	States.	Yeas.	Nays.
Maine	1	14	Missouri	0	18
New Hampshire	0	10	Michigan	8	4
Vermont	0	10	Illinois	14	8
Massachusetts	4	21	Texas	0	6
Rhode Island	0	8	Wisconsin	8	2
Connecticut	1	11	Iowa	2	6
New York	25	45	California	0	8
New Jersey	12½	1½	Minnesota	0	8
Pennsylvania	½	53½	Oregon	2	2
Maryland	0	11	*Territories.*		
Delaware	4	2	Kansas	0	6
Virginia	17	6	Nebraska	2	4
Kentucky	10	10	District of Columbia	0	2
Ohio	28	18			
Indiana	20	6		155	301

Mr. Giddings—Mr. President, I propose to offer, after the first resolution as it stands here, as a declaration of principles, the following:

That we solemnly reassert the self-evident truths that all men are endowed by their Creator with certain inalienable rights, among which are those of life, liberty and the pursuit of happiness [cheers]; that governments are instituted among men to secure the enjoyment of these rights.

The first resolution was as follows:

Resolved, That we, the delegated representatives of the Republican electors of the United States, in Convention assembled, in discharge of the duty we owe to our constituents and our country, unite in the following declarations.

The second section of the Platform as originally reported was in these words:

2. That the maintenance of the principles promulgated in the Declaration of Independence and embodied in the Federal Constitution, is essential to the preservation of our Republican institutions; and that the Federal Constitution, the rights of the States, and the Union of the States, must and shall be preserved.

Mr. Giddings made a short speech in favor of his amendment, concluding:

Now, I propose to maintain the doctrines of our fathers. I propose to maintain the fundamental and primal issues upon which the government was founded. I will detain this Convention no longer. I offer this because our party was formed upon it. It grew upon it. It has existed upon it—and when you leave out this truth you leave out the party.

Mr. Carter called for the reading of the second section of the platform. It was read. Giddings's amendment was voted down. The old man quickly rose, and made his way slowly toward the door. A dozen delegates begged him not to go. But he considered every thing but even honor. His Philadelphia Platform has not been reaffirmed. The "twin relics" were not in the new creed. And now the Declaration of Independence had been voted down! He must go. He got along as far as the New York delegation, where he was comforted by assurances that the Declaration would be tried again; but he left the Convention—actually seceded in sorrow and anger.

Mr. Wilmot of Pennsylvania—I move that the resolutions be adopted separately. [Cries of "No," and "Take them in a lot," etc.] I have an amendment to offer which I believe will commend itself to the good sense of every gentleman here. The amendment is this: In the fourteenth resolution we say "that the Republican party is opposed to any change in our Naturalization Laws, *or any State legislation* by which the rights of citizenship hitherto accorded to immigrants from foreign lands shall be abridged or impaired; and in favor of giving a full and efficient protection to the rights of all classes of citizens, whether native or naturalized, both at home and abroad." My amendment is to strike out the words "State legislation," because it conflicts directly with the doctrine in the fourth resolution, which reads thus:

"That the maintenance inviolate of the *rights* of the States, and especially the right of each State to order and control its own domestic institutions according to its own judgment exclusively, is essential to that balance of powers on which the perfection and endurance of our political fabric depends; and we denounce the lawless invasion, by armed force, of the soil of any State or Territory, no matter under what pretext, as among the gravest of crimes."

The resolution would then read. "That the Republican party is opposed to any change in our naturalization laws, by which the rights of citizenship hitherto accorded to immigrants from foreign lands shall be abridged or impaired."

It being explained that Mr. Wilmot was mistaken, in presuming that there was any assault on State Rights meditated, he withdrew his amendment. Carl Schurz however made a speech on the subject. He had insisted on having the very words in the platform that Wilmot had objected to. He said:

It has been very well said that it was not the purpose of this resolution to declare that no State has the right to regulate the suffrage of its citizens by legislative enactment, but it was the purpose to declare that the Republican party, in its national capacity, is opposed to any such thing in principle.

Mr. Hassaureck of Ohio made a thrilling little speech.

Mr. Curtis of New York obtained the floor and said:

I then offer as an amendment to the report, as presented by the committee, the following: That the second clause of the report shall read, "That the maintenance of the principles promulgated in the Declaration of Independence and embodied in the Federal Constitution"—and then, sir, I propose to amend by adding these words, "That all men are created equal; that they are endowed by their Creator with certain inalienable rights; that among these are life, liberty and the pursuit of happiness; that to secure these rights, governments are instituted among men, deriving their just powers from the consent of the governed"—then proceed—"is essential to the preservation of our Republican institutions; and that the Federal Constitution, the Rights of the States, and the Union of the States, must and shall be preserved." [Great applause, and many gentlemen struggling for the floor.]

[A point of order was raised that this amendment had been once voted down. The chair, under a misapprehension, sustained the point. Mr. Blair of Missouri proposed to appeal from the decision of the chair, but whereas it appeared that the amendment offered by Mr. Giddings had been the first clause, and that this amendment was offered to the second clause, it was pronounced in order.]

Mr. Curtis made a short speech. He said:

I have to ask this Convention whether they are prepared to go upon the record and before the country as voting down the words of the Declaration of Independence? [Cries of "No," "no," and applause.] I ask gentlemen gravely to consider that in the amendment which I have proposed, I have done nothing that the soundest and safest man in all the land might not do; and I rise simply—for I am now sitting down—I rise simply to ask gentlemen to think well before, upon the free prairies of the West, in the summer of 1860, they dare to wince and quail before the men who in Philadelphia, in 1776—in Philadelphia, in the Arch-Keystone State, so amply, so nobly represented upon this platform to-day—before they dare to shrink from repeating the words that these great men enunciated. [Terrific applause.]

This was a strong appeal and took the Convention by storm. It was a great personal triumph for Curtis. His classical features, literary fame, pleasing style as a speaker, and the force of his case, called attention to him, and gave him the ear of the Convention, and gave him the triumph. And the Declaration again became part of the platform of the Republican party.

THE PLATFORM

now stood :

Resolved, That we, the delegated representatives of the Republican electors of the United States, in Convention assembled, in discharge of the duty we owe to our constituents and our country, unite in the following declarations :

1. That the history of the nation during the last four years, has fully established the propriety and necessity of the organization and perpetuation of the Republican party, and that the causes which called it into existence are permanent in their nature, and now, more than ever before, demand its peaceful and constitutional triumph.

2. That the maintenance of the principles promulgated in the Declaration of Independence and embodied in the Federal Constitution, "That all men are created equal ; that they are endowed by their Creator with certain inalienable rights ; that among these are life, liberty and the pursuit of happiness ; that to secure these rights, governments are instituted among men, deriving their just powers from the consent of the governed," is essential to the preservation of our Republican institutions ; and that the Federal Constitution, the Rights of the States, and the Union of the States, must and shall be preserved.

3. That to the Union of the States this nation owes its unprecedented increase in population, its surprising development of material resources, its rapid augmentation of wealth, its happiness at home, and its honor abroad ; and we hold in abhorrence all schemes for Disunion, come from whatever source they may : And we congratulate the country that no Republican member of Congress has uttered or countenanced the threats of Disunion so often made by Democratic members, without rebuke and with applause from their political associates ; and we denounce those threats of disunion, in case of a popular overthrow of their ascendancy as denying the vital principles of a free government, and as an avowal of contemplated treason, which it is the imperative duty of an indignant People sternly to rebuke and forever silence.

4. That the maintenance inviolate of the rights of the States, and especially the right of each State to order and control its own domestic institutions according to its own judgment exclusively, is essential to that balance of powers on which the perfection and endurance of our political fabric depends ; and we denounce the lawless invasion by armed force of the soil of any State or Territory, no matter under what pretext, as among the gravest of crimes.

5. That the present Democratic Administration has far exceeded our worst apprehensions, in its measureless subserviency to the exactions of a sectional interest, as especially evinced in its desperate exertions to force the infamous Lecompton Constitution upon the protesting people of Kansas ; in construing the personal relation between master and servant to involve an unqualified property in persons ; in its attempted enforcement, everywhere, on land and sea, through the intervention of Congress and of the Federal Courts, of the extreme pretensions of a purely local interest ; and in its general and unvarying abuse of the power intrusted to it by a confiding people.

6. That the people justly view with alarm the reckless extravagance which pervades every department of the Federal Government ; that a return to rigid economy and accountability is indispensable to arrest the systematic plunder of the public treasury by favored partisans ; while the recent startling develop-

ments of frauds and corruptions at the Federal metropolis, show that an entire change of administration is imperatively demanded.

7. That the new dogma that the Constitution, of its own force, carries slavery into any or all of the Territories of the United States, is a dangerous political heresy, at variance with the explicit provisions of that instrument itself, with contemporaneous exposition, and with legislative and judicial precedent; is revolutionary in its tendency, and subversive of the peace and harmony of the country.

8. That the normal condition of all the territory of the United States is that of freedom : That as our Republican fathers, when they had abolished slavery in all our national territory, ordained that "no person should be deprived of life, liberty, or property, without due process of law," it becomes our duty, by legislation, whenever such legislation is necessary, to maintain this provision of the Constitution against all attempts to violate it; and we deny the authority of Congress, of a Territorial Legislature, or of any individuals, to give legal existence to slavery in any Territory of the United States.

9. That we brand the recent re-opening of the African slave-trade, under the cover of our national flag, aided by perversions of judicial power, as a crime against humanity and a burning shame to our country and age; and we call upon Congress to take prompt and efficient measures for the total and final suppression of that execrable traffic.

10. That in the recent vetoes, by their Federal Governors, of the acts of the Legislatures of Kansas and Nebraska, prohibiting slavery in those Territories, we find a practical illustration of the boasted Democratic principle of Non-Intervention and Popular Sovereignty embodied in the Kansas-Nebraska bill, and a demonstration of the deception and fraud involved therein.

11. That Kansas should, of right, be immediately admitted as a State under the Constitution recently formed and adopted by her people, and accepted by the House of Representatives.

12. That, while providing revenue for the support of the General Government by duties upon imports, sound policy requires such an adjustment of these imposts as to encourage the development of the industrial interests of the whole country ; and we commend that policy of national exchanges, which secures to the working men liberal wages, to agriculture remunerating prices, to mechanics and manufacturers an adequate reward for their skill, labor and enterprise, and to the nation commercial prosperity and independence.

13. That we protest against any sale or alienation to others of the Public Lands held by actual settlers, and against any view of the Free Homestead policy which regards the settlers as paupers or suppliants for public bounty ; and we demand the passage by Congress of the complete and satisfactory Homestead measure which has already passed the House.

14. That the Republican party is opposed to any change in our Naturalization Laws or any State legislation by which the rights of citizenship hitherto accorded to immigrants from foreign lands shall be abridged or impaired; and in favor of giving a full and efficient protection to the rights of all classes of citizens, whether native or naturalized, both at home and abroad.

15. That appropriations by Congress for River and Harbor improvements of a National character, required for the accommodation and security of an existing commerce, are authorized by the Constitution, and justified by the obligation of Government to protect the lives and property of its citizens.

16. That a Railroad to the Pacific Ocean is imperatively demanded by the interests of the whole country ; that the Federal Government ought to render immediate and efficient aid in its construction ; and that as preliminary thereto, a daily Overland Mail should be promptly established.

17. Finally, having thus set forth our distinctive principles and views, we invite the co-operation of all citizens, however differing on other questions, who substantially agree with us in their affirmance and support.

So it was adopted. The vote was taken about six o'clock, and upon the announcement being made a scene ensued of the most astounding character. All the thousands of men in that enormous wigwam commenced swinging their hats, and cheering with intense enthusiasm, and the other thousands of ladies waved their handkerchiefs and clapped their hands. The roar that went up from that mass of ten thousand human beings under one roof was indescribable. Such a spectacle as was presented for some minutes has never before been witnessed at a Convention. A herd of buffaloes or lions could not have made a more tremendous roaring.

As the great assemblage poured through the streets after adjournment, it seemed to electrify the city. The agitation of the masses that pack the hotels and throng the streets, and are certainly forty thousand strong, was such as made the little excitement at Charleston seem insignificant.

The Convention adjourned without taking a ballot for President, as the tally-sheets were not prepared.

The tactics of the Seward men in convention to-day were admirable. They made but one mistake, that of voting against the recommitment of the report of the committee on Credentials. They made a beautiful fight against Wilmot's proposition to examine into the constituencies of slave State delegations, putting forward men to strike the necessary blows who were not suspected of Sewardism. There was also a splendid fight on the subject of the two-thirds rule (as it was in effect), which was sought to be used to slaughter Seward. So perfect were the Seward tactics, that this rule, which his opponents had hoped to carry, was made odious, and defeated by a two-thirds vote. Then Giddings was anxious, beyond all description, to have the initial words of the Declaration of Independence in the platform. In attempting to get them in, he was snubbed by Seward's opponents most cruelly. He had been working against Seward, and was not without influence. Now a New York man took up and carried through his precious amendment. So confident were the Seward men, when the platform was adopted, of their ability to nominate their great leader, that they urged an immediate ballot, and would have had it if the clerks had not reported that they were unprovided with tally-sheets. The cheering of the thousands of spectators during the day, indicated that a very large share of the outside pressure was for Seward. There is something almost irresistible here in the prestige of his fame.

The New Yorkers here are of a class unknown to Western Republican politicians. They can drink as much whiskey, swear as loud and long, sing as bad songs, and "get up and howl" as ferociously as any crowd of Democrats you ever heard, or heard of. They are opposed, as they say, "to being too d—d virtuous." They hoot at the idea that Seward could not sweep all the Northern States, and swear that he would have a party in every slave State, in less than a year, that would clean out the disunionists, from shore to shore. They slap each other on the back with the emphasis of delight when they meet, and rip out "How *are* you?" with a "How are you boss?" style, that would do honor to Old Kaintuck on a bust. At night those of them who are not engaged at caucusing, are doing that which ill-tutored youths call "raising h—l generally."

Wherever you find them, the New York politicians, of whatever party, are a peculiar people.

The Seward men have been in high feather. They entertain no particle of doubt of his nomination in the morning. They have a champagne supper in their rooms at the Richmond House to-night, and have bands of music serenading the various delegations at their quarters. Three hundred bottles of champagne are said to have been cracked at the Richmond. This may be an exaggeration, but I am not inclined to think the quantity overstated, for it flowed freely as water.

The delegation here is a queer compound. There is a party of tolerably rough fellows, of whom Tom Hyer is leader, and there is Thurlow Weed (called Lord Thurlow by his friends), Moses H. Grinnell, James Watson Webb, Gov. Morgan, Gen. Nye, George W. Curtis, and others of the strong men of the State, in commerce, political jobbing, and in literature—first class men in their respective positions, and each with his work to do according to his ability. In the face of such "irrepressibles," the conservative expediency men—Greeley, the Blairs, the Republican candidates for Governor in Pennsylvania, Indiana, and Illinois—are hard pressed, sorely perplexed, and despondent.

THIRD DAY.

Proceedings opened by prayer by the Rev. Mr. Green of Chicago. Mr. Green said :

"O, we entreat thee, that at some future but no distant day, the evils which now invest the body politic shall not only have been arrested in its progress, but wholly eradicated from the system. And may the pen of the historian trace an intimate connection between that glorious consummation and the transaction of this Convention."

After adjournment on Thursday (the second day), there were few men in Chicago who believed it possible to prevent the nomination of Seward. His friends had played their game to admiration, and had been victorious on every preliminary skirmish. When the platform had been adopted, inclusive of the Declaration of Independence, they felt themselves already exalted upon the pinnacle of victory. They rejoiced exceedingly, and full of confidence, cried in triumphant tones, "Call the roll of States." But it was otherwise ordered. The chair announced that the tally-sheets had not been prepared, and that it would subject the clerks to great inconvenience to proceed to a ballot at that time. The Seward men expressed themselves greatly disgusted, and were still unwilling to adjourn. A motion was made to adjourn, however, and after an uncertain response, very little voting being done either way, the chair pronounced the motion for adjournment carried. The Seward men were displeased but not disheartened. They considered their hour of triumphing with brains and principle, over presumptions of expediency, as merely postponed. They did not fear the results of the caucusing that night, though they knew every hour would be employed against them. The opponents of Mr. Seward left the wigwam that evening thoroughly disheartened. Greeley was, as has been widely reported, absolutely "terrified." The nomination of Seward in defiance of his influence, would have been a cruel blow. He gave up the ship, as appears from the following despatch to the New York Tribune:

GOV. SEWARD WILL BE NOMINATED.

CHICAGO, Thursday, May 17—11:40 P. M.—My conclusion, from all that I can gather to-night, is, that the opposition to Gov. Seward cannot concentrate on any candidate, and that he will be nominated.   H. G.

I telegraphed, about the same time, the same thing to the Cincinnati Commercial; and every one of the forty thousand men in attendance upon the Chicago Convention will testify that at midnight of Thursday-Friday night, the universal impression was that Seward's success was certain.

The New Yorkers were exultant. Their bands were playing, and the champagne flowing at their head-quarters as after a victory.

But there was much done after midnight and before the Convention assembled on Friday morning. There were hundreds of Pennsylvanians, Indianians and Illinoisans, who never closed their eyes that night. I saw Henry S. Lane at one o'clock, pale and haggard, with cane under his arm, walking as if for a wager, from one caucus-room to another, at the Tremont House. He had been toiling with desperation to bring the Indiana delegation to go as a unit for Lincoln. And then in connection with others, he had been operating to bring the Vermonters and Virginians to the point of deserting Seward. Vermont would certainly cast her electoral vote for any candidate who could be nominated, and Virginia as certainly against any candidate. The object was to bring the delegates of those States to consider success rather than Seward, and join with the battle-ground States—as Pennsylvania, New Jersey, Indiana, and Illinois insisted upon calling themselves. This was finally done, the fatal break in Seward's strength having been made in Vermont and Virginia, destroying at once, when it appeared, his power in the New England and the slave State delegations. But the work was not yet done. The Pennsylvanians had been fed upon meat, such that they presented themselves at Chicago with the presumption that they had only to say what they wished, and receive the indorsement of the Convention. And they were for Cameron.* He was the only man, they a thousand times said, who would certainly carry Pennsylvania. They were astonished, alarmed, and maddened to find public opinion settling down upon Seward and Lincoln, and that one or the other must be nominated. They saw that Lincoln was understood to be the only man to defeat Seward, and thinking themselves capable of holding that balance of power, so much depended upon, and so deceptive on those occasions, stood out against the Lincoln combination. Upon some of the delegation, Seward operations had been performed with perceptible effect. The Seward men had stated that the talk of not carrying Pennsylvania was all nonsense. Seward had a good Tariff record, and his friends would spend money enough in the State to carry it against any Democratic candidate who was a possibility. The flood of Seward

---

* It has since appeared from a speech delivered by Mr Cameron at Harrisburg, that Seward was his first choice, and in his opinion could carry Pennsylvania. Nothing of the kind was heard of at Chicago.

money promised for Pennsylvania was not without efficacy. The phrase used was, that Seward's friends " would *spend oceans of money.*"

The Wade movement died before this time. It had a brilliant and formidable appearance for a while; but the fact that it originated at Washington was against it, and the bitterness of those delegates from Ohio, who would not in any event go for any man from that State other than Chase, and who declared war to the knife against Wade, and as a second choice were for Lincoln or Seward, stifled the Wade project.

It does not appear by the record that "old Ben. Wade" ever stood a chance for the place now occupied by "old Abe Lincoln." If his friends in Ohio could have brought the friends of Mr. Chase to agree, that the delegation should vote as a unit every time as the majority should direct, Wade might have been the nominee, and instead of hearing so much of some of the exploits of Mr. Lincoln in rail-splitting, when a farmer's boy, we should have information concerning the labors of Ben. Wade on the Erie Canal, where he handled a spade. While touching the Wade movement as developed in the delegation from Ohio, it is proper to give as an explanatory note the fact, that at least six gentlemen from Ohio, who were engaged in it, were understood to have aspirations for the Senate, and to be regarding Mr. Wade's chair in the Senate-chamber with covetous glances. These gentlemen were D. K. Cartter, Joshua R. Giddings, C. P. Wolcott, William Dennison, jr., Tom Corwin, and Columbus Delano.

The cry of a want of availability which was from the start raised against Seward, now took a more definite form than heretofore. It was reported, and with a well-understood purpose, that the Republican candidates for Governor in Indiana, Illinois and Pennsylvania would resign, if Seward were nominated. Whether they really meant it or not, the rumor was well circulated, and the effect produced was as if they had been earnest. Henry S. Lane, candidate in Indiana, did say something of the kind. He asserted hundreds of times that the nomination of Seward would be death to him, and that he might in that case just as well give up the canvass. He did not feel like expending his time and money in carrying on a hopeless campaign, and would be disposed to abandon the contest.

The Chicago Press and Tribune of Friday morning contained a last appeal to the Convention not to nominate Seward. It was evidently written in a despairing state of mind, and it simply begged that Seward should not be nominated. The Cameron men, discovering there was absolutely no hope for their man, but that either Seward or Lincoln would be nominated, and that speedily, and being a calculating company, were persuaded to throw their strength for Lincoln at such a time as to have credit of his nomination if it were made. There was much difficulty, however, in arriving at this conclusion, and the wheels of the machine did not at any time in Pennsylvania run smooth. On nearly every ballot, Pennsylvania was not in readiness when her name was called, and her retirements for consultation became a joke.

The Seward men generally abounded in confidence Friday morning. The air was full of rumors of the caucusing the night before, but the opposition of the doubtful States to Seward was an old story ; and after the distress of Pennsylvania, Indiana & Co., on the subject of Seward's availibility, had been so freely and ineffectually expressed from the start, it was not imagined their protests would suddenly become effective. The Sewardites marched as usual from their head-quarters at the Richmond House after their magnificent band, which was brilliantly uniformed—epaulets shining on their shoulders, and white and scarlet feathers waving from their caps—marched under the orders of recognized leaders, in a style that would have done credit to many volunteer military companies. They were about a thousand strong, and protracting their march a little too far, were not all able to get into the wigwam. This was their first misfortune. They were not where they could scream with the best effect in responding to the mention of the name of William H. Seward.

When the Convention was called to order, breathless attention was given the proceedings. There was not a space a foot square in the wigwam unoccupied. There were tens of thousands still outside, and torrents of men had rushed in at the three broad doors until not another one could squeeze in.

The first thing of interest was a fight regarding the Maryland delegation. A rule had been adopted that no delegation should cast more votes than there were duly accredited delegates. The Maryland delegation had not been full, and Mr. Montgomery Blair of that State now wanted to fill up the delegation. Three of the delegates, who were Seward men, opposed filling up the ranks with men, as one of them said, "God Almighty only knows where they come from." Here was another Seward triumph, for the Blairs were not allowed to add to the strength of their Maryland delegation. It might be said of the Blairs and the Maryland delegation as Thaddeus Stevens said of the Union and Constitutional Convention at Baltimore, "It was a family party—*it was all there.*"

Every body was now impatient to begin the work. Mr. Evarts of New York nominated Mr. Seward. Mr. Judd of Illinois nominated Mr. Lincoln. Mr. Dudley of New Jersey nominated Mr. Dayton. Mr. Reeder of Pennsylvania nominated Simon Cameron. Mr. Cartter of Ohio nominated Salmon P. Chase. Mr. Caleb Smith of Indiana seconded the nomination of Lincoln. Mr. Blair of Missouri nominated Edward Bates. Mr. Blair of Michigan seconded the nomination of William H. Seward. Mr. Corwin of Ohio nominated John McLean. Mr. Schurz of Wisconsin seconded the nomination of Seward. Mr. Delano of Ohio seconded the nomination of Lincoln. The only names that produced "tremendous applause," were those of Seward and Lincoln.

Every body felt that the fight was between them, and yelled accordingly.

The applause, when Mr. Evarts named Seward, was enthusiastic. When Mr. Judd named Lincoln, the response was prodigious, rising and raging far beyond the Seward shriek. Presently, upon Caleb B. Smith seconding the nomination of Lincoln, the response was absolutely terrific. It now became the Seward men to make another effort, and when Blair of Michigan seconded his nomination,

> "At once there rose so wild a yell,
> Within that dark and narrow dell;
> As all the fiends from heaven that fell
> Had pealed the banner cry of hell."

The effect was startling. Hundreds of persons stopped their ears in pain. The shouting was absolutely frantic, shrill and wild. No Camanches, no panthers ever struck a higher note, or gave screams with more infernal intensity. Looking from the stage over the vast amphitheatre, nothing was to be seen below but thousands of hats—a black, mighty swarm of hats—flying with the velocity of hornets over a mass of human heads, most of the mouths of which were open. Above, all around the galleries, hats and handkerchiefs were flying in the tempest together. The wonder of the thing was, that the Seward outside pressure should, so far from New York, be so powerful.

Now the Lincoln men had to try it again, and as Mr. Delano of Ohio, on behalf "of a portion of the delegation of that State," seconded the nomination of Lincoln, the uproar was beyond description. Imagine all the hogs ever slaughtered in Cincinnati giving their death squeals together, a score of big steam whistles going (steam at 160 lbs. per inch), and you conceive something of the same nature. I thought the Seward yell could not be surpassed; but the Lincoln boys were clearly ahead, and feeling their victory, as there was a lull in the storm, took deep breaths all round, and gave a concentrated shriek that was positively awful, and accompanied it with stamping that made every plank and pillar in the building quiver.

Henry S. Lane of Indiana leaped upon a table, and swinging hat and cane, performed like an acrobat. The presumption is, he shrieked with the rest, as his mouth was desperately wide open; but no one will ever be able to testify that he has positive knowledge of the fact that he made a particle of noise. His individual voice was lost in the aggregate hurricane.

The New York, Michigan and Wisconsin delegations sat together, and were in this tempest very quiet. Many of their faces whitened as the Lincoln *yawp* swelled into a wild hozanna of victory.

The Convention now proceeded to business. The New England States were called first, and it was manifest that Seward had not the strength that had been claimed for him there. Maine gave nearly half her vote for Lincoln. New Hampshire gave seven out of her ten votes for Lincoln. Vermont gave her vote to her Senator Collamer, which was understood to be merely complimentary. It appeared, however, that her delegation was hostile or indifferent to Seward, otherwise there would have been no complimentary vote to another. Massachusetts was divided. Rhode Island and Connecticut did not give Seward a vote. So much for the caucusing the night before. Mr. Evarts of New York rose and gave the vote of that State, calmly, but with a swelling tone of pride in his voice—"The State of *New York* casts her *seventy votes* for *William H. Seward!*" The seventy votes was a plumper, and there was slight applause, and that rustle and vibration in the audience indicating a sensation. The most significant vote was that of Virginia, which had been expected solid for Seward, and which now gave him but eight and gave Lincoln fourteen. The New Yorkers looked significantly at each other as this was announced. Then Indiana gave her twenty-six votes for Lincoln. This solid vote was a startler, and the keen little eyes of Henry S. Lane glittered as it was given. He was responsible for it. It was his opinion that the man of all the land to carry the State of Indiana, was Judge John McLean. He also thought Bates had eminent qualifications. But when he found that the contest was between Seward and Lincoln, he worked for the latter as if life itself depended upon success. The division of the first vote caused a fall in Seward stock. It was seen that Lincoln, Cameron and Bates had the strength to defeat Seward, and it was known that the greater part of the Chase vote would go for Lincoln.

FIRST BALLOT.

States.	Seward.	Lincoln.	Wade.	Cameron.	Bates.	McLean.	Reed.	Chase.	Dayton.	Sumner.	Fremont.	Collamer.
Maine	10	6										
New Hampshire	1	7						1			1	
Vermont												10
Massachusetts	21	4										
Rhode Island					1	5	1	1				
Connecticut		2	1		7			2				
New York	70											
New Jersey									14			
Pennsylvania	1½	4		47½		1						
Maryland	3				8							
Delaware					6							
Virginia	8	14		1								
Kentucky	5	6	2			1		8		1		
Ohio		8				4		34				
Indiana		26										
Missouri					18							
Michigan	12											
Illinois		22										
Texas	4				2							
Wisconsin	10											
Iowa	2	2		1	1	1		1				
California	8											
Minnesota	8											
Oregon					5							
Territories.												
Kansas	6											
Nebraska	2	1		1				2				
Dist. of Columbia	2											

The Secretary announced the vote:

William H. Seward, of New York...173½
Abraham Lincoln, of Illinois..102
Edward Bates, of Missouri..48
Simon Cameron, of Pennsylvania...50½
John McLean, of Ohio...12
Salmon P. Chase, of Ohio...49
Benjamin F. Wade, of Ohio..3
William L. Dayton, of New Jersey...14

John M. Reed, of Pennsylvania................................... 1
Jacob Collamer, of Vermont 10
Charles Sumner, of Massachusetts................................. ... 1
John C. Fremont, of California...................................... 1
Whole number of votes cast, 465 ; necessary to a choice, 233.

The Convention proceeded to a second ballot. Every man was fiercely enlisted in the struggle. The partisans of the various candidates were strung up to such a pitch of excitement as to render them incapable of patience, and the cries of "Call the roll" were fairly hissed through their teeth. The first gain for Lincoln was in New Hampshire. The Chase and the Fremont vote from that State were given him. His next gain was the whole vote of Vermont. This was a blighting blow upon the Seward interest. The New Yorkers started as if an Orsini bomb had exploded. And presently the Cameron vote of Pennsylvania was thrown for Lincoln, increasing his strength forty-four votes. The fate of the day was now determined. New York saw "checkmate" next move, and sullenly proceeded with the game, assuming unconsciousness of her inevitable doom. On this ballot Lincoln gained seventy-nine votes! Seward had 184½ votes ; Lincoln 181.

SECOND BALLOT.

States.	Seward.	Lincoln.	Bates.	Cameron.	McLean.	Chase.	Dayton.	C. Clay.
Maine...........................	10	6	...	...	...	...	...	...
New Hampshire	1	9	...	...	...	...	...	...
Vermont.........................	...	10	...	...	...	...	...	...
Massachusetts...................	22	4	...	...	...	...	...	...
Rhode Island....................	...	3	...	...	2	3	...	...
Connecticut.....................	...	4	4	...	...	2	...	2
New York.......................	70	...	...	...	...	...	...	...
New Jersey.....................	4	...	...	...	...	...	10	...
Pennsylvania...................	2½	48	...	1	2½	...	...	...
Maryland.......................	3	...	8	...	...	...	...	...
Delaware.......................	...	...	6	...	...	...	...	...
Virginia........................	8	14	...	1	...	...	...	...
Kentucky.......................	7	9	...	...	...	6	...	...
Ohio............................	...	14	...	...	3	29	...	...
Indiana.........................	...	26	...	...	...	...	...	...
Missouri........................	...	...	18	...	...	...	...	...
Michigan	12	...	...	...	...	...	...	...
Illinois.........................	...	22	...	...	...	...	...	...
Texas...........................	6	...	...	...	...	...	...	...
Wisconsin.......................	10	...	...	...	...	...	...	...
Iowa............................	2	5	...	...	½	½	...	...
California	8	...	...	...	...	...	...	...
Minnesota	8	...	...	...	...	...	...	...
Oregon.........................	...	...	5	...	...	...	...	...
Territories.								
Kansas	6	...	...	...	...	...	...	...
Nebraska.......................	3	1	...	...	...	2	...	...
District of Columbia.	2	...	...	...	...	...	...	...

(Great confusion while the ballot was being counted.)
The Secretary announced the result of the second ballot as follows:

148

For William H. Seward of New York, 184½ votes. [Applause.]
For Abraham Lincoln of Illinois, 181 votes. [Tremendous applause, checked by the Speaker.]
For Edward Bates of Missouri, 35 votes.
For Simon Cameron of Pennsylvania, 2 votes.
For John McLean of Ohio, 8 votes.
For Salmon P. Chase of Ohio, 42½ votes.
For William L. Dayton of New Jersey, 10 votes.
For Cassius M. Clay of Kentucky, 2 votes.
Whole number of votes cast, 465; necessary to a choice, 233.

It now dawned upon the multitude, that the presumption entertained the night before, that the Seward men would have every thing their own way, was a mistake. Even persons unused to making the calculations and considering the combinations attendant upon such scenes, could not fail to observe that while the strength of Seward and Lincoln was almost even at the moment, the reserved votes, by which the contest must be decided, were inclined to the latter. There, for instance, was the Bates vote, thirty-five; the McLean vote, eight; the Dayton vote, ten—all impending for Lincoln—and forty-two Chase votes, the greater part going the same way.

THIRD BALLOT.

States.	Seward.	Bates.	Chase.	Lincoln.	McLean.	Dayton.	C. M. Clay.
Maine	10			6			
New Hampshire	1			9			
Vermont				10			
Massachusetts	18			8			
Rhode Island	1		1	5	1		
Connecticut	1	4	2	4			1
New York	70						
New Jersey	5			8		1	
Pennsylvania				52	2		
Maryland	2			9			
Delaware				6			
Virginia	8			14			
Kentucky	6		4	13			
Ohio			15	29	2		
Indiana				26			
Missouri		18					
Michigan	12						
Illinois				22			
Texas	6						
Wisconsin	10						
Iowa	2		½	5½			
California	8						
Minnesota	8						
Oregon	1			4			
Territories.							
Kansas	6						
Nebraska	3		2	1			
District of Columbia	2						
Total	180	22	24½	231½	5	1	1

While this ballot was taken amid excitement that tested the nerves, the fatal defection from Seward in New England still further appeared —four votes going over from Seward to Lincoln in Massachusetts. The latter received four additional votes from Pennsylvania and fifteen additional votes from Ohio. It was whispered about—"Lincoln's the coming man—will be nominated this ballot." When the roll of States and Territories had been called, I had ceased to give attention to any votes but those for Lincoln, and had his vote added up as it was given. The number of votes necessary to a choice were two hundred and thirty-three, and I saw under my pencil as the Lincoln column was completed, the figures $231\frac{1}{2}$—one vote and a half to give him the nomination. In a moment the fact was whispered about. A hundred pencils had told the same story. The news went over the house wonderfully, and there was a pause. There are always men anxious to distinguish themselves on such occasions. There is nothing that politicians like better than a crisis. I looked up to see who would be the man to give the decisive vote. The man for the crisis in the Cincinnati Convention—all will remember—was Col. Preston of Kentucky. He broke the Douglas line and precipitated the nomination of Buchanan, and was rewarded with a foreign mission. In about ten ticks of a watch, Cartter of Ohio was up. I had imagined Ohio would be slippery enough for the crisis. And sure enough! Every eye was on Cartter, and every body who understood the matter at all, knew what he was about to do. He is a large man with rather striking features, a shock of bristling black hair, large and shining eyes, and is terribly marked with the small-pox. He has also an impediment in his speech, which amounts to a stutter; and his selection as chairman of the Ohio delegation was, considering its condition, altogether appropriate. He had been quite noisy during the sessions of the Convention, but had never commanded, when mounting his chair, such attention as now. He said, "I rise (eh), Mr. Chairman (eh), to announce the change of four votes of Ohio from Mr. Chase to Mr. Lincoln." The deed was done. There was a moment's silence. The nerves of the thousands, which through the hours of suspense had been subjected to terrible tension, relaxed, and as deep breaths of relief were taken, there was a noise in the wigwam like the rush of a great wind, in the van of a storm—and in another breath, the storm was there. There were thousands cheering with the energy of insanity.

A man who had been on the roof, and was engaged in communicating the results of the ballotings to the mighty mass of outsiders, now demanded by gestures at the sky-light over the stage, to know what had happened. One of the Secretaries, with a tally sheet in his hands, shouted—"Fire the Salute! Abe Lincoln is nominated!" As the cheering inside the wigwam subsided, we could hear that outside, where the news of the nomination had just been announced. And the roar, like the breaking up of the fountains of the great deep that was heard, gave a new impulse to the enthusiasm inside. Then the thunder of the salute rose above the din, and the shouting was repeated with such tremendous fury that some discharges of the cannon were absolutely not heard by those on the stage. Puffs of smoke, drifting by the open doors, and the smell of gunpowder, told what was going on.

The moment that half a dozen men who were on their chairs making motions at the President could be heard, they changed the votes of their States to Mr. Lincoln. This was a mere formality, and was a cheap way for men to distinguish themselves. The proper and orderly proceeding would have been to annouce the vote, and then for a motion to come from New York to make the nomination unanimous. New York was prepared to make this motion, but not out of order. Missouri, Iowa, Kentucky, Minnesota, Virginia, California, Texas, District of Columbia, Kansas, Nebraska and Oregon, insisted upon casting unanimous votes for Old Abe Lincoln before the vote was declared.

While these votes were being given, the applause continued, and a photograph of Abe Lincoln which had hung in one of the side rooms was brought in, and held up before the surging and screaming masses. The places of the various delegations were indicated by staffs, to which were attached the names of the States, printed in large black letters on pasteboard. As the Lincoln enthusiasm increased, delegates tore these standards of the States from their places and swung them about their heads. A rush was made to get the New York standard and swing it with the rest, but the New Yorkers would not allow it to be moved, and were wrathful at the suggestion.

When the vote was declared, Mr. Evarts, the New York spokesman, mounted the Secretaries' table and handsomely and impressively expressed his grief at the failure of the Convention to nominate Seward—and in melancholy tones, moved that the nomination be made unanimous.

Mr. Andrew of Massachusetts seconded the motion in a speech, in which his vanity as a citizen of the commonwealth of Massachusetts was ventilated, and he said it had not been for old Massachusetts to strike down William Henry Seward, concluding by a promise to give the nominee of that Convention one hundred thousand majority.

Carl Schurz, on behalf of Wisconsin, again seconded the motion, but not so effectively in his speech as his reputation as an orator would have warranted us in expecting. There was a little clap-trap and something of anti-climax in shouting "Lincoln and victory," and talking of "defying the whole slave power and the whole vassalage of hell."

M. Blair of Michigan made the speech of the hour. He said:

"Michigan, from first to last, has cast her vote for the great Statesman of New York. She has nothing to take back. She has not sent me forward to worship the rising sun, but she has put me forward to say that, at your behests here to-day, she lays down her first, best loved candidate to take up yours, with some beating of the heart, with some quivering in the veins [much applause]; but she does not fear that the fame of Seward will suffer, for she knows that his fame is a portion of the history of the American Union; it will be written, and read, and beloved long after the temporary excitement of this day has passed away, and when Presidents themselves are forgotten in the oblivion which comes over all temporal things. We stand by him still. We have followed him with an eye single and with unwavering faith in times past. We martial now behind him in the grand column which shall go out to battle for Lincoln."

After a rather dull speech from Mr. Browning of Illinois, responding in behalf of Lincoln, the nomination was made unanimous, and the Convention adjourned for dinner. The town was full of the news of Lincoln's nomination, and could hardly contain itself. There were bands of music playing, and processions marching, and joyous cries heard on every hand, from the army of trumpeters for Lincoln of Illinois, and the thousands who are always enthusiastic on the winning side. But hundreds of men who had been in the wigwam were so prostrated by the excitement they had endured, and their exertions in shrieking for Seward or Lincoln, that they were hardly able to walk to their hotels. There were men who had not tasted liquor, who staggered about like drunkards, unable to manage themselves. The Seward men were terribly stricken down. They were mortified beyond all expression, and walked thoughtfully and silently away from the slaughter-house, more ashamed than embittered. They acquiesced in the nomination, but did not pretend to be pleased with it; and the tone of their conversations, as to the prospect of electing the candidate, was not hopeful. It was their funeral, and they would not make merry.

A Lincoln man who could hardly believe that the "Old Abe" of his adoration was really the Republican nominee for the Presidency, took a chair at the dinner-table at the Tremont House, and began talking to those around him, with none of whom he was acquainted, of the greatness of the events of the day One of his expressions was, "Talk of your money and bring on your bullies with you!—the immortal principles of the everlasting people are with Abe Lincoln, of the people, by —." "Abe Lincoln has no money and no bullies, but he has the people by —." A servant approached the eloquent patriot and asked what he would have to eat. Being thus recalled to temporal things he glared scornfully at the servant and roared out, "Go to the devil—what do I want to eat for? Abe Lincoln is nominated, G— d— it; and I'm going to live on air—the air of Liberty by —." But in a moment he inquired for the bill of fare, and then ordered "a great deal of every thing"—saying if he must eat he might as well eat "the whole bill" He swore he felt as if he could "devour and digest an Illinois prairie." And this was one of thousands.

During the dinner recess a caucus of the Presidents of delegations was held, and New York, though requested to do so, would not name a candidate for the Vice-Presidency. After dinner we had the last act in the drama.

The nomination of Vice-President was not particularly exciting. Cassius M. Clay was the only competitor of Hamlin, who made any show in the race; and the outside pressure was for him. At one time a thousand voices called "Clay! Clay!" to the Convention. If the multitude could have had their way, Mr. Clay would have been put on the ticket by acclamation. But it was stated that Mr. Hamlin was a good friend of Mr. Seward. He was geographically distant from Lincoln, and was once a Democrat. It was deemed judicious to pretend to patronize the Democratic element, and thus consolidate those who were calling the Convention an "old Whig concern." They need not have been afraid, however, of having it called an old Whig affair, for it was not "eminently respectable," nor distinguished for its "dignity and decorum." On the other hand, the satanic element was very strongly developed.

FIRST BALLOT FOR VICE-PRESIDENT.

States.	Cassius M. Clay.	Banks.	Reeder.	Hickman.	Hamlin.	Reed.	H. W. Davis.	Dayton.	Houston.
Maine................................	....	....	....	....	16	....	....	....	....
New Hampshire...................	....	....	....	....	10	....	....	....	....
Vermont	....	....	....	....	10	....	....	....	....
Massachusetts.....................	....	20	1	1	1	....	....	....	....
Rhode Island.......................	....	....	....	....	8	....	....	....	....
Connecticut.........................	2	1	....	2	5	....	....	....	....
New York...........................	9	4	2	11	35	1	8	....	....
New Jersey.........................	1	....	7	....	6	....	....	....	....
Pennsylvania.......................	4½	2½	24	7	11	....	....	8	....
Maryland............................	2	....	....	1	8	....	....	....	....
Delaware............................	3	....	....	1	2	....	....	....	....
Virginia..............................	23	....	....	....	....	....	....	....	....
Kentucky...........................	23	....	....	....	....	....	....	....	....
Ohio..................................	0	....	....	....	46	....	....	....	....
Indiana..............................	18	....	....	....	8	....	....	....	....
Missouri.............................	....	9	....	9	....	....	....	....	....
Michigan............................	4	....	....	....	8	....	....	....	....
Illinois...............................	2	....	10	2	2	....	....	....	....
Texas................................	....	....	....	....	....	....	....	....	6
Wisconsin...........................	5	....	....	....	5	....	....	....	....
Iowa..................................	....	1	1	....	6	....	....	....	....
California...........................	....	....	....	8	....	....	....	....	....
Minnesota..........................	1	....	....	1	6	....	....	....	....
Oregon..............................	....	1	....	3	1	....	....	....	....
Territories.									
Kansas..............................	....	....	....	6	....	....	....	....	....
Nebraska...........................	1	....	....	5	....	....	....	....	....
District of Columbia............	2	....	....	....	....	....	....	....	....
Total..............	101½	38½	51	58	194	1	8	8	6

SECOND BALLOT FOR VICE-PRESIDENT.

States.	Hamlin.	Clay.	Hickman.
Maine	16		
New Hampshire	10		
Vermont	10		
Massachusetts	26		
Rhode Island	8		
Connecticut	10		2
New York	70		
New Jersey	14		
Pennsylvania	54		
Maryland	10	1	
Delaware	6		
Virginia		23	
Kentucky		23	
Ohio	46		
Indiana	12	14	
Missouri	13	5	
Michigan	8	4	
Illinois	20	2	
Texas		6	
Wisconsin	5	5	
Iowa	8		
California	7	1	
Minnesota	7	1	
Oregon	3		2
Territories.			
Kansas	2	1	3
Nebraska			6
District of Columbia	2		
Total	367	86	13

During this ballot the name of N. P. Banks was withdrawn. As this was done, Gen. Nye of New York cried out, "That's a good thing done—one of the conspirators gone to h—, thank God!"

The fact of the Convention, was the defeat of Seward rather than the nomination of Lincoln. It was the triumph of a presumption of availability over pre-eminence in intellect and unrivaled fame—a success of the ruder qualities of manhood and the more homely attributes of popularity, over the arts of a consummate politician, and the splendor of accomplished statesmanship.

Now that the business of the Convention was transacted, we had the usual stump speeches, and complimentary resolutions, and the valedictory from the chairman, and the "three times three" upon adjournment for the candidate.

The city was wild with delight. The "Old Abe" men formed processions, and bore rails through the streets. Torrents of liquor were poured down the hoarse throats of the multitude. A hundred guns were fired from the top of the Tremont House. The Chicago Press and Tribune office was illuminated. That paper says:

"On each side of the counting-room door stood a *rail*—out of the

three thousand split by 'honest Old Abe' thirty years ago on the Sangamon River bottoms. On the inside were two more, brilliantly hung with tapers."
I left the city on the night train on the Fort Wayne and Chicago road. The train consisted of eleven cars, every seat full and people standing in the aisles and corners. I never before saw a company of persons so prostrated by continued excitement. The Lincoln men were not able to respond to the cheers which went up along the road for "old Abe." They had not only done their duty in that respect, but exhausted their capacity. At every station where there was a village, until after two o'clock, there were tar barrels burning, drums beating, boys carrying rails; and guns, great and small, banging away. The weary passengers were allowed no rest, but plagued by the thundering jar of cannon, the clamor of drums, the glare of bonfires, and the whooping of the boys, who were delighted with the idea of a candidate for the Presidency, who thirty years ago split rails on the Sangamon River—classic stream now and for evermore—and whose neighbors named him "honest."

CONSTITUTIONAL DEMOCRATIC CONVENTION AT RICHMOND.

The address issued by distinguished Southern Congressmen, urging that the Richmond Convention should not transact any business, but adjourn to Baltimore and make there a final effort to preserve the harmony and unity of the Democratic party by the defeat of Mr Douglas, had the effect of preventing a large representation of the Southern wing of the party at Richmond. Instead of attempting to make the Richmond Convention an affair of substantive importance, the aim of those who had it in charge, was to so manage the preliminaries that it should transact no business. The people of Richmond were not much interested in it, and no preparations whatever were made for it until the Saturday before the Convention assembled, when a hall was engaged.

FIRST DAY.

The Convention assembled at Metropolitan Hall at noon on Monday, the 11th of June. Lieut. Gov. Lubbock of Texas was called to the chair, as temporary chairman. He acknowledged the compliment in becoming terms—said they met in the same spirit in which they had met in Charleston. He said:

"We have met here to-day, as we did there, to carry out our principles, whatever may be the result. [Applause.] I trust we have come here for no compromises of the Constitution. [Applause.]

"If we cannot succeed in sustaining those principles, we must create—no, we will not 'create' a new Democratic party, but we will simply declare ourselves the true Democratic party, and we will unfurl our banner, and go to the country upon true Democratic principles." [Applause.]

The States were called for delegates, and New York answering by a young man in a corner, produced a sensation. The following are the documents presented by the State of New York, and they are curiosities in their way:

NEW YORK, June 8, 1860.

This is to certify, that at a meeting of the Trustees of the National Democratic Hall of the State of New York, held in the city of New York, they recommended to the association the following names as delegates and alternates to represent them at the Richmond Convention, for the nomination of candidates for President and Vice-President of these United States, with power to add to their number, or fill vacancies:

Delegates--Col. Baldwin, Isaac Lawrence, Jas. B. Bensel, James Villiers.
Alternates--Neare Drake Parson, James S. Selby, M. Dudley Bean, Alfred W. Gilbert.

NEW YORK, June 8th, 1860.

This is to certify, that Hon. Gideon J. Tucker, and Dr. Charles Edward Lewis Stuart, were, at a meeting of the above association, made delegates at large from the association.

SAMUEL B. WILLIAMS, Chairman of Trustees.
WM. BEACH LAWRENCE, Jr., Chairman of Ex. Com.
THADDEUS P. MOTT, Chairman of Association.

Secretary of Trustees, M. DUDLEY BEAN.
Secretary of Executive Committee, JAS. B. BENSEL.
Secretary of Association, J. LAWRENCE.

Mr. Fisher of Virginia responded for that State, producing loud applause. He was the only Virginian who seceded, and hence was a lion at that moment.

A despatch was received, saying Florida delegates were coming. The following is the list of delegates made out this day by the Secretaries:

ALABAMA.—A B. Meek, W. L. Yancey, D. W. Baine, F. S. Lyon, R. G. Scott, J. W. Portis, N. H. R. Dawson, T. J. Burnett, Eli S. Shorter, D. W. Williams, J. C. B. Mitchell, Wm. C. Penick, A. S. Van Degraaf, John Erwin, John E. Moore, E. W. Kennedy, Robt. T. Scott, R. Chapman, Winfield Mason, W. P. Browne, D. W. Bozeman.

MISSISSIPPI.— Geo. H. Gordon, E. Barksdale, W. F. Barry, H. C. Chambers, Jos. R. Davis, Beverly Matthews.

LOUISIANA.— A. Martin, John Tarleton, Richard Taylor, Emile LaSere. F. H. Hatch, E. Lawrence, A. Talbot, B. W. Pearce, R. A. Hunter, D. D. Withers, Charles Jones, J. A McHutton.

SOUTH CAROLINA.—*Principals:* Hon. R. B. Rhett, Hon. A. C. Garlington, Hon. J. J. Middleton, A. Bush, J. A. Dargan, Col. W. S. Mullins, Gen. W. E. Martin, C. M. Furman, Gen. D. F. Jamison. Col. A. P. Aldrich, W. D. Simpson, D. B. Waldo, Hon. A. P. Calhoun, William Choice, Col. E. Jones, Maj A. H. Boykin. *Alternates:* Hon. W. D. Porter, Col. John S. Sloan, Col. Allen McFarlan, Hon. G. A. Trenholm, Henry McIvor, J. G. Pressly, Hon. J. E. Carew, S. W. Barker,

Hon. J. Townsend, Hon. E. Martin, J. D. Nance, D. W. Aiken, W. K. Easely, Gen. S. R. Gist, R. A. Springs, Maj. N. R. Eames.
GEORGIA.—Henry L. Benning, Nelson Fitt, E. J. McGeehee, John A. Jones, John C. Nichols.
TEXAS.—G. M. Bryan, F. S. Stockdale, H. R. Runnels, J. F. Crosby, F. R. Lubbock.

Mr. Mott of New York undertook to explain to the Convention the position of the delegation from that State. He said the National Democratic Association of New York had held a meeting, and appointed them delegates and alternates, and that fifteen out of sixteen members of the State Central Committee were in favor of a representation of the Democracy at Richmond. He closed, according to the custom of the country, with something about the Union. His remarks were received respectfully, but incredulously. It was singular that a delegation should arrive from New York, when such a thing as a movement in that State regarding the Richmond Convention had not been heard of. Motions were carried to form committees on Organization and Credentials. Those committees were organized as follows:

COMMITTEE ON PERMANENT ORGANIZATION—Mississippi, W. L. Barry; Louisiana, R. A. Hunter; Alabama, Robt. G. Scott; Tennessee, W. T. Helms; Texas, J. F. Crosby; Georgia, John A. Jones; Virginia, M. W. Fisher; South Carolina, A. P. Calhoun; Arkansas, Van H. Manning; New York, Thaddeus P. Mott.

COMMITTEE ON CREDENTIALS—South Carolina, John J. Middleton; Tennessee, George W. Brodfield; Alabama, D. W. Bain; Georgia, Dr. Edmund J. McGeehee; Louisiana, F. H. Hatch; Texas, T. S. Stockdell; Mississippi, Beverly Matthews; Arkansas, Van H. Manning.

SECOND DAY.

Mr. Smith of Alabama desired to have his name recorded. Agreed to. The Florida delegates had now arrived. Mr. Calhoun of South Carolina—son of John C. Calhoun—chairman of the committee on Organization, submitted the following report:

Your committee respectfully report the name of the Hon. John Erwin of Alabama as permanent President of your Convention, and the following named persons as Vice-Presidents:
H. R. Runnels of Texas, W. S. Featherston of Mississippi, M. W. Fisher of Virginia, Hon. R. G. Scott of Alabama, N. B. Burrows of Arkansas, B. F. Wardlaw of Florida, Gen. A. C. Garlington of South Carolina, D. H. Cummings of Tennessee, P. Tracy of Georgia, E. LaSere of Louisiana.

And the following as Secretaries:
H. H. Tyson of Mississippi, Dr. A. C. Smith of Virginia, G. W. Bradfield of Tennessee, A. S. Vandergriff of Alabama, Chas. Dyke of Florida, John Cobb of Georgia, Henry McIver of South Carolina, D. D. Withers of Louisiana, Van H. Manning of Arkansas.

The committee would further recommend the rules adopted at Cincinnati in 1856, as the rules for the government of this Convention.

Your committee beg leave to report, as a basis of representation, that where a State is represented as a whole, the delegation present shall cast the entire vote of said State, according to the Congressional basis; and in such cases as there are delegates from a district of the State present, said delegate or delegates shall be entitled to cast the vote of said district.

ANDREW E. CALHOUN.

Mr. Erwin upon taking the chair made a brief speech. He said they were there to vindicate the Constitution and assert the rights of the South under it. He said further:

"At Charleston we exerted ourselves assiduously, earnestly, for days and weeks, hoping that we might agree—that we might concur with the majority of that body—that they would concede to us what seemed, to our apprehension, to clearly belong to us. But, governed by objects of self—of personal aggrandizement—they sternly refused. We had no alternative left but to pursue the course that we did pursue, and we are happy now to announce that our conduct has been approved by our constituents. [Great applause.]

"It is proposed here, as I understand, that we shall not act definitely —that we shall make one more attempt at reconciliation. Gentlemen, I neither commend nor condemn that course. Every gentleman will be governed by his own views of what is right. But we must yield nothing, whether we remain here, or whether we go elsewhere. Wherever we go, we must demand the full measure of our rights. [Applause.] The serpent of 'Squatter Sovereignty' must be strangled. [Vehement applause.] What! are we to be told that we are not to go into the Territories and enjoy equal rights, when that principle has been settled by the Supreme Court of our country?"

Mr. Middleton of South Carolina stated the case of the New York Commissioners. He said:

"Mr. President, in going into this matter the committee was informed that the gentlemen therein named did not claim seats in this body as delegates and alternates, but came here simply as commissioners to advise with this body as to the course of its proceeding."

This it was proclaimed was done in "entire courtesy," but it was a quiet way of getting rid of the New Yorkers who were now, by resolution, invited to take seats upon the floor of the Convention.

Mr. Hatch—Mr. President, after consulting with the large number of delegates from the different States, I beg leave to offer the following resolutions, which, I believe, will accomplish the general purposes and wishes of this Convention:

1. *Resolved*, That as the delegations from all the States represented in this Convention are assembled upon the basis of the platform recommended by a majority of the States at Charleston, we deem it unnecessary to take any further action upon that subject at the present time.

2. *Resolved*, That when this Convention adjourn, it adjourn to meet in this city on Monday, the 25th inst.; provided that the President of this Convention may call it together at an earlier or later day, if it be deemed necessary.

An attempt was made to have it declared that that Convention indorsed the majority report of a platform made at Charleston, but this was overruled, on the ground that it had, upon consultation by an informal committee, been determined to take no action whatever. A motion to raise a select committee to consider what should be done, was met by the assurance that an informal committee had gathered the sense of the Convention, and that it was agreed nothing was to be done. Mr. Hunter of Louisiana said in this connection, upon the proposition to indorse the majority platform reported at Charleston :

"I was desirous that not one word should be said upon this subject, when the resolutions were reported, but that we should accept them in the spirit of harmony which has characterized our deliberations so far. I hope the amendment will not be pressed. There is no difficulty except upon one point, and I hope that amendment will not be pressed, for we desire earnestly that no discussion should take place in regard to the matter. We are satisfied with the resolutions, and will accept them; we do not desire to go further."

Some conversational debate occurred on the proposition to give the President of the Convention discretionary power in calling it together upon adjournment. Mr. Jones of Georgia, in the course of a speech, said:

We want other States to come in with us and have their voices heard in this important matter; we ought not to preclude them by any declarations in advance. That is all. What is fair, is fair. We ask Virginia, North Carolina, Maryland, Tennessee and Kentucky to come in here.

A Voice—Missouri and Delaware.

Mr. Jones—Yes, Missouri and Delaware unite with us in counsel.

The first resolution was agreed to, and Mr. Mullins of South Carolina moved that the second resolution be amended by striking out "25th" and inserting "21st." South Carolina called for the vote by States—that that State might appear upon the record as opposed to adjournment. He withdrew his call, however, and the resolution was adopted by acclamation.

The committee on Credentials was now called upon for a report, and reported that the following States and districts are represented in this Convention, to wit:

Alabama, Arkansas, Texas, Louisiana, Mississippi, Georgia, South Carolina, Florida, Second Congressional District of Tennessee, Seventh Electoral District of Virginia.

The Convention was proceeding to adjourn, when Mr. Baldwin of New York, an elderly gentleman with immense green-goggles, begged to be allowed to state the true position of New York in that Convention. He caused a very florid and inconsequential letter to be read. It concluded as follows:

"Here as Commissioners of Conference on a mission for party peace, and in national love, we are also here to give the assurance that should the crisis arise to test us, you may reckon on noble evidence, in the Empire State, of a loyalty which cannot be shaken in its allegiance to the Golden Rule of Democracy, and can never be corrupted in the good faith which should ever bind the true of the North to the true of the South."

He proceeded to talk of the great danger in which the country found itself, and was doing tolerably well in the way of a union speech, when he was called to order for talking on matters that the delegates had declined to talk about. He said he was there at the mercy of the Convention, and was told to go on. He was again talking of the horrors of disunion, when Mr. Barry of Mississippi called him to order by saying he had abused the courtesy of the Convention; and while the commissioner was begging forgiveness in the most abject manner, the Convention adjourned.

NATIONAL DEMOCRATIC CONVENTION AT BALTIMORE.

The Democratic politicians assembled in great force in Washington City the week before the Convention was called to meet in Baltimore, and caucused the matter in the usual way.

On the Saturday before the meeting of the Convention, the politicians concentrated in Baltimore, where a much greater crowd than that at Charleston came together. It was not, however, numerically so great, by many thousands, as that at Chicago. The weight of the outside pressure was for Mr. Douglas. The talk about the hotels was principally favorable to Mr. Douglas, whose friends were full of confidence and determination. It was evident that he could not be nominated without the division of the party, and placing two tickets in the field; yet his friends gave no symptoms of flinching from taking any responsibility. The hostile feeling between the factions of the Democracy was even more embittered than at the time of the adjournment at Charleston, and the more the points of difference were caucused, the more intense was the warfare. The debate in the Senate during the recess—the speeches of Douglas and Pugh on the one hand, and Benjamin and Davis on the other—had served to deepen and exasperate the controversy, and make it more personal in its nature, and therefore more incapable of compromise. The friends of Mr. Douglas, encouraged by the presence and support of Soule of Louisiana, Forsyth of Texas, and other strong Southern men, assumed an arrogance of tone that precluded the hope of amicable adjustment of difficulties. As at Charleston, every person and passion and prejudice was for or against Mr. Douglas. The opinion was almost universal that the friends of Mr. Douglas would be able to nominate him, and they were certainly resolved to give him the nomination at any hazard or sacrifice. There was no question, however, that the New York delegation had the fate of the Convention in its keeping; and while it was understood that the strength of Mr. Douglas in the delegation had been increased, during the recess, by the Fowler defalcation (the substitute for Mr. Fowler being reported to be a Douglas man), and by the appearance of regular delegates who were for Douglas, and whose alternates had been against him at Charleston, it was obvious that the action of the politicians of New York could not be counted upon in any direction with confidence. Rumors were circulated before the meeting of the Convention, that a negotiation had been carried on in Washington, by the New Yorkers with the South, the object of which was to sell out Douglas, the Southerners and the Administration offering them their wh le strength for any man New York might name, provided that State would slaughter Douglas. On the other hand, it appeared that Dean Richmond, the principal manager of the New Yorkers, had been engaged in private consultations with Mr. Douglas and his fast friends, and had pledged himself, as solemnly as a politician could do, to stand by the cause of Douglas to the last.

FIRST DAY.

MORNING SESSION.

The Convention assembled at ten o'clock, in the Front Street Theatre, the parquet and stage having been fitted up for the delegations, the dress circle reserved for the ladies, and the upper circles assigned to spectators, who were admitted by tickets, of which each delegation had a supply in proportion to its numbers. There was some delay about calling the Convention to order, owing to a misunderstanding as to the hour of meeting.

The delegates entitled to seats all presenting themselves at a quarter past eleven o'clock, the Convention was called to order by the President, and opened with prayer by the Rev. John McCron, whose prayer was very touching and beautiful.

THE PRESIDENT'S ADDRESS.

At the conclusion of the prayer, the President stated the condition of business before the Convention in a clear, sharply-defined address, speaking so distinctly that every man in the Convention heard every word. He said:

GENTLEMEN OF THE CONVENTION :—Permit me, in the first place, to congratulate you upon your being reassembled here for the discharge of your important duties in the interests of the Democratic party of the United States; and I beg leave, in the second place, to communicate to the Convention the state of the various branches of its business, as they now come up for consideration before you.

Prior to the adjournment of the Convention, two principal subjects of action were before it. One, the adoption of the doctrinal resolutions constituting the platform of the Convention; the other, voting upon the question of the nomination of a candidate for the Presidency.

In the course of the discussion of the question of a platform, the Convention adopted a vote, the effect of which was to amend the report of the majority of the committee on the Platform, by substituting the report of the minority of that committee; and after the adoption of that motion, and the substitution of the minority for the majority report, a division was called for upon the several resolutions constituting that platform, being five in number. The 1st, 3d, 4th and 5th of those resolutions were adopted by the Convention, and the 2d was rejected. After the vote on the adoption of the 1st, 3d, 4th and 5th of those resolutions, a motion was made in each case to reconsider the vote, and to lay that motion of reconsideration upon the table. But neither of those motions to reconsider or to lay on the table was put, the putting of these motions having been prevented by the intervention of questions of privilege, and the ultimate vote competent in such case, to wit, of the adoption of the report of the majority as amended by the report of the minority, had not been acted upon by the Convention. So that at the time when the Convention adjourned, there remained pending before it these motions, to wit: To reconsider—the resolutions constituting the platform, and the ulterior question of adopting the majority as amended by the substitution of the minority report. Those questions, and those only, as the chair understood the motions before the Convention, were not acted upon prior to the adjournment.

After the disposition of the intervening questions of privilege, a motion was made by Mr. McCook of Ohio to proceed to vote for candidates for President and Vice President. Upon that motion the Convention instructed the chair (not, as has been erroneously supposed, in the recess of the Convention, the chair determining for the Convention, but the Convention instructing the chair) to make no declaration of a nomination except upon a vote equivalent to two-thirds in the Electoral College of the United States, and upon that balloting, no such vote being given, that order was, upon the motion of the gentleman from Virginia (Mr. Russell), laid on the table for the purpose of enabling him to propose a motion, which he subsequently did, that the Convention adjourn from the city of Charleston to the city of Baltimore, and with a provision concerning the filling of vacancies embraced in the same resolution, which resolution the Secretary will please to read.

The Secretary read the resolution, as follows:

Resolved, That when this Convention adjourns to-day, it adjourn to reassemble at Baltimore, Md., on Monday, the 18th day of June, and that it be respectfully recommended to the Democratic party of the several States to make provision for supplying all vacancies in their respective delegations to this Convention when it shall reassemble.

The President—The Convention will thus perceive that the order adopted by it provided, among other things, that it is respectfully recommended to the Democratic party of the several States to make provision for supplying all vacancies in their respective delegations to this Convention, when it shall reassemble. What is the construction of that resolution?—what is the scope of its application?—is a question not for the chair to determine or to suggest to the Convention, but for the Convention itself to determine.

However that may be, in the preparatory arrangement for the present assembling of this Convention, there were addressed to the chair the credentials of members elected, or purporting to be elected, affirmed and confirmed by the original Conventions, and accredited to this Convention. In three of those cases, or perhaps four, the credentials were authentic and complete, presenting no question of controverting dele-

11

gates. In four others, to wit, the States of Georgia, Alabama, Louisiana and Delaware, there were contesting applications. Upon those applications the chair was called to determine whether it possessed any power to determine *prima facie* membership of this Convention. That question was presented in its most absolute and complete form in the case of Mississippi, where there was no contest either through irregularity of form or of competing delegations, and so also in the cases of Florida, Texas and Arkansas. In those four States, there being an apparent authenticity of commission, the chair was called upon to determine the naked abstract question whether he had power, peremptorily and preliminary, to determine the *prima facie* membership of alleged members of this Convention. The chair would gladly have satisfied himself that he had this power, but upon examining the source of his power, to wit, the rules of the House of Representatives, he was unable to discern that he had any authority, even *prima facie*, to scrutinize and canvass credentials, although they were such as, upon their face, were free from contest or controversy either of form or of substance, and therefore he deemed it his duty to reserve the determination of that question to be submitted to the Convention. And in due time the chair will present that question as one of privilege to this body.

And now, gentlemen, having thus presented to you the exact state of the questions pending or involved in the action of the Convention when it adjourned, the chair begs leave only to add a single observation of a more general nature. We assemble here now at a time when the enemies of the Democratic party—when, let me say, the enemies of the Constitution of the United States, are in the field [applause] with their selected leaders, with their banners displayed, advancing to the combat with the constitutional interests and party of the United States; and upon you, gentlemen, upon your action, upon your spirit of harmony, upon your devotion to the Constitution, upon your solicitude to maintain the interests, the honor and the integrity of the Democratic party as the guardians of the Constitution—upon you, gentlemen, it depends whether the issue of that combat is to be victory or defeat for the Constitution of the United States. [Renewed applause.]

It does not become the chair to discuss any of the personal or political demands of that question. It may be permitted, however, to exhort you in the spirit of our community, of party interests, in the faith of our common respect for the Constitution, in the sense of our common devotion to the interests and honor of our country; I say to exhort you to feel that we come here this day not to determine any mere technical questions of form, not merely to gain personal or party triumphs, but we come here in the exercise of a solemn duty, in a crisis of the condition of the affairs of our country such as has never yet befallen the United States. Shall we not all enter upon this duty in the solemn and profound conviction of the responsibilities thus devolved upon us, of our high duty to our country, to ourselves, and to the States of this Union ? [Applause.] Gentlemen, the Convention is now in order for the transaction of business.

This is an admirable statement of the condition of the business before the question.

Mr. Howard of Tennessee introduced the following resolution:

Resolved, That the President of this Convention direct the Sergeant-at-Arms to issue tickets of admission to the delegates of the Convention as originally constituted and organized at Charleston.

Mr. Cavanagh moved to lay the resolution on the table, and called the vote by States.

Mr. Russell of Virginia wished to inquire of the chair what he had done in the way of determining the rights of delegations to seats.

The President—The chair will then state, in response to the inquiry of the gentleman from Virginia (Mr. Russell), that the chair did not undertake to judge any thing, neither to decide that there were or were not vacancies. All the chair undertook to say, was, that the gentlemen borne upon its roll as members of this Convention at the time of its adjournment at Charleston, were entitled to recognition of membership precisely to-day as they would had the Convention adjourned yesterday. [Applause.] To have gone beyond this point would have been to enter into the canvass of conflicting credentials upon new elections of members. The chair was thoroughly convinced that he had no power to enter into that inquiry of conflicting credentials of persons alleging to have been elected to this Convention by State Conventions held since the adjournment of this Convention at Charleston. The chair will suggest to the gentleman from Virginia that the question did not present itself in the form of simplicity and unity in which his inquiry would suppose, inasmuch as several States to which he refers, did assume that the resolution in the adjournment created vacancies to be filled by new action of the respective States; and if the chair had entered into any inquiry of the new credentials, as, for instance, to discriminate upon the question whether these credentials came from a new State Convention called anew, and that Convention vacating anterior commissions; or whether they emanate from a Convention called anew and simply confirming anterior commissions;—in either case, if the chair had gone into the question, it would have been necessary for him to hold hearings and investigations of credentials and of facts in regard to eight States of the Union, as to which he had no more power under the rules of the House of Representatives than any other member of the Convention.

Whilst the chair is disposed to exert the whole power, in any contingency, of the Speaker of the House of Representatives—having entered upon the discharge of this most unwelcome and responsible duty with a determination to act without favor and also without fear—yet the chair knows that it is impossible that he shall maintain order in this Convention, that the deliberations of this Convention shall go on in any system of regularity, unless the chair takes care to walk carefully and rigorously in the simple line of routine and of technical authority. [Applause.] Within the line of technical authority, and upon the rules of the House of Representatives, as constituting the guide of the chair, the chair will take leave to decide all questions as they may arise, in or out of the Convention. But the chair does not propose to assume any judicial or quasi-judicial authority in regard to the canvass of credentials and the authenticity of membership; an authority manifestly not conferred upon the presiding officer, according to precedent and the uniform usage of the two houses of the Congress of the United States, never preliminarily determined by the presiding officer of either house of Congress. In issuing tickets to the gentlemen borne on the roll of the Convention, already sufficiently authenticated by the proceedings of the Convention itself, at the time of adjournment, the chair did that at least which was in the sphere of the duties of the chair; and in doing that he in no degree involved or prejudiced the question of what was the right of any gentleman—that depending upon the action of this Convention. The chair, as he before intimated, will now make this, the first question, a question of privilege, that the Convention may instruct the chair regarding his duty concerning the delegations of the other States.

Mr. Church of New York offered the following resolution, as an amendment to that of Mr. Howard—Mr. Cavanagh, who had moved to table Howard's resolution, yielding for that purpose:

Resolved, That the credentials of all persons claiming seats in this Convention made vacant by the secession of delegates at Charleston, be referred to the committee on Credentials, and said committee is hereby instructed, as soon as practicable, to examine the same and report the names of persons entitled to such seats, with the district—understanding, however, that every person accepting a seat in this Convention is bound in honor and good faith to abide by the action of this Convention, and support its nominations.

The resolution was received with shouts of tumultuous applause, originating with members of the Convention, and taken up and repeated by the spectators in the galleries.

It was erroneously understood at this time, that the resolution of Mr. Church, was the proposition of a majority of the New York delegation, and the sensation was very great. The applause in the galleries caused the chair to become indignant, and he fiercely stated his purpose of preserving order and prevent the galleries from participating by indications of approbation or disapprobation in the proceedings.

An unimportant debate on points of order followed. Mr. Church called the previous question on his resolution. During the conversational discussion:

Mr. Russell of Virginia—I ask that this Convention will allow me to make a friendly, candid and sincere appeal to the gentleman who made the call for the previous question (Mr. Church of New York) to withdraw his call.

The President—The chair has no authority over that question.

Mr. Russell—I ask the chair to appeal to the gentleman to allow fair play in this Convention.

Mr. Stuart of Michigan—I insist that the chair preserve order.

The President—The gentleman from Virginia (Mr. Russell) is not in order.

Mr. Russell—If we are to be constrained to silence, I beg gentlemen to consider the silence of Virginia as somewhat ominous. [Applause and hisses.]

The question was stated to be upon seconding the demand for the previous question. Being taken *viva voce*,

The President stated that the noes appeared to have it.

Mr. Richardson of Illinois doubted the announcement, and asked that the vote be taken by States, which was ordered.

Mr. Brodhead of Pennsylvania stated that the gentleman from New York (Mr. Church) was willing to withdraw his call for the previous question.

Mr. Montgomery of Pennsylvania—The vote having been ordered to be taken by States, it is not now in order to withdraw the call for the previous question.

A motion was made to adjourn until four o'clock. A call for the vote by States was made. While this was being taken, a controversy occurred in the Minnesota delegation, a part of which has become hostile to Douglas, a fact which irritates his friends beyond measure. After consuming nearly an hour's time of the Convention, the delegation temporarily settled the difference.

The vote on adjournment was:

YEAS—Maine $1\frac{1}{4}$, New Hampshire $\frac{1}{2}$, Connecticut 1, New Jersey 5, Pennsylvania 6, Delaware 3, Maryland 6, Virginia 15, North Carolina 10, Missouri $6\frac{1}{4}$, Tennessee $8\frac{3}{4}$, Kentucky 3, Minnesota $1\frac{1}{2}$, California 4, Oregon 3—$73\frac{1}{2}$.

NAYS—Maine $6\frac{3}{4}$, New Hampshire $4\frac{1}{2}$, Vermont 5, Massachusetts 13, Rhode Island 4, Connecticut 5, New York 35, New Jersey 2, Pennsylvania 21, Maryland 2, Arkansas 1, Missouri $2\frac{1}{4}$, Tennessee $3\frac{1}{4}$, Kentucky 9, Ohio 23, Indiana 13, Illinois 11, Michigan 6, Wisconsin 5, Iowa 4, Minnesota $2\frac{1}{2}$—$178\frac{1}{2}$.

Some of Douglas's friends here absurdly claimed the nays to indicate positively their strength.

The Convention now refused, objection being made, to hear a communication from the State of Mississippi.

The question was then taken on seconding the demand for the previous question, upon the proposition of Mr. Church. It was not agreed to. Yeas $107\frac{3}{4}$, nays $140\frac{3}{4}$, as follows:

YEAS—Maine 6, New Hampshire 5, Vermont $4\frac{3}{4}$, Massachusetts $4\frac{1}{2}$, Connecticut $3\frac{1}{2}$, New Jersey $2\frac{1}{2}$, Pennsylvania $9\frac{3}{4}$, Maryland 2, Missouri $2\frac{1}{4}$, Tennessee 3, Kentucky $1\frac{3}{4}$, Ohio 23, Indiana 13, Illinois 11, Michigan 6, Wisconsin 5, Iowa 4, Minnesota $2\frac{1}{2}$—$107\frac{3}{4}$.

NAYS—Maine 2, Vermont $\frac{1}{2}$, Massachusetts $4\frac{1}{2}$, Rhode Island 4, Connecticut 2—one absent, New York 35, New Jersey $4\frac{1}{2}$, Pennsylvania $16\frac{1}{2}$, Delaware 2, Maryland 6, Virginia 15, North Carolina 10, Arkansas 1, Missouri $6\frac{3}{4}$, Tennessee 8, Kentucky $10\frac{1}{4}$, Minnesota $1\frac{1}{2}$, California 4, Oregon 3—$140\frac{3}{4}$.

On calling the roll, the New York delegation asked permission to retire for consultation, and during the interim there was an entire cessation of business. The power of the State of New York was made quite apparent in this vote, and it also appeared that the course she would take was among the uncertainties. Some considered the vote to indicate the determination of New York not to sustain Douglas. There were evidences, however, that it was a piece of New York tactics not at all incompatible with friendliness toward Douglas. New York judged it unwise to stifle debate—that was all.

The question was then stated to be upon the amendment to the amendment.

Mr. Gilmor of Pennsylvania offered the following amendment to Mr. Church's resolution:

Resolved, That the President of the Convention be directed to issue tickets of admission to seats in the Convention to the delegates from the States of Texas, Florida, Mississippi and Arkansas, in which States there are no contesting delegations.

A motion to adjourn to ten o'clock, Tuesday, was now negatived by a vote of 85 to 216. A motion to take a recess until five o'clock in the evening, was carried *viva voce*.

EVENING SESSION.

The chair gave notice of the possession of documents regarding contested seats.

Mr. Gilmor has his amendment read again, having slightly modified it:

Resolved, That the President of the Convention be authorized to issue tickets of admission to seats in this Convention to the delegates from the States of Arkansas, Texas, Florida and Mississippi, in which States there are no contesting delegations, and that in those States, to wit, Delaware, Georgia, Alabama and Louisiana, where there are contesting delegations, a committee on Credentials shall be appointed, by the several delegations, to report upon said States.

Mr. Clark of Missouri obtained, after encountering some objections, the reading for information of a proposition which he considered of immense altitude.

It was: Strike out the proviso in the amendment of Mr. Church of New York, and add the following:

Resolved, That the citizens of the several States of the Union have an equal right to settle and remain in the Territories of the United States, and to hold therein, unmolested by any legislation whatever, their slaves and other property; and that this Convention recognizes the opinion of the Supreme Court of the United States in the Dred Scott case as a true exposition of the Constitution in regard to the rights of the citizens of the several States and Territories of the United States upon all subjects concerning which it treats; and that the members of this Convention pledge themselves, and require all others who may be authorized as delegates, to make the same pledge, to support the Democratic candidates, fairly and in good faith, nominated by this Convention according to the usages of the National Democratic party.

The debate now opened upon the proposition of Mr. Gilmor, Mr. Randall of Pennsylvania obtaining the floor. Mr. Randall however addressed himself to the amendment of Mr. Church. He said:

The amendment of the gentleman from New York imposes a condition upon the returning members of the several States that seceded at Charleston. I deny the power of this Convention to impose any such condition. The right of their constituents is unqualified, and beyond the power of this Convention, to send their representatives to this body without condition and without limitation. [Applause and hisses] It is an interference with the right of the constituents of seven seceding

States to impose any qualification upon the representatives of this body. I deny its equity or its justice.

It is said in the amendment that it is "understood." Understood! an apology for the broad declaration of a naked invasion of the rights of freemen. Not that the members of this body thus admitted have denied the right, but it is understood that they are pledged to do what other members are not pledged to do—to conform to the decision of the majority. Mr. President and gentlemen, I invoke you to look at the injustice of every such qualification—a qualification which no honorable man, except under very peculiar circumstances, could ever submit to; a qualification which it is known that the representatives of these seven seceding States will never submit to. [Applause and hisses.] But, Mr. President and brethren of the great Democratic family, who are now contending for the success of the Democratic cause, I ask you to halt, not simply upon the ground of right and justice, but of policy. Not a member of this body but knows that the representatives of those States will not give any such pledge [applause and hisses]; that it is tantamount to a declaration of expulsion from the body. [Applause and hisses.]

Mr. Hoag of Virginia:

I rise to a question of privilege. I desire to ascertain, once for all, whether, when a gentleman like that from Pennsylvania is addressing the Convention, he is to be exposed to the cowardly insult of hisses from the gallery? [Applause, and calls to order by the chair.] I ask if citizens of Virginia are to endure the ignominy and insult of hearing honorable gentlemen hissed from the galleries for uttering sentiments in accordance with our own? If there is to be an outside pressure brought to bear upon this body, I, for one, will deem my personal honor sacrificed if I remain here without being protected against the outrage and insult of these hisses. [Applause.]

The chair was properly indignant at the outsiders. Mr. Randall made the usual appeals for harmony (which meant the sacrifice of Douglas) and the preservation of the unity of the party and the integrity of the Union.

Mr. Richardson of Illinois replied. He was opposed to the adoption of the amendment of Mr. Gilmor. He said:

It declares that the President of the Convention shall issue his tickets to the delegates from Florida, Mississippi, Texas and Arkansas. Talking, the other day, in the city of Washington, with a delegate from the State of Florida, who was at Richmond, I learned from him the fact that they were not accredited to this Convention. The gentleman from Pennsylvania proposes by his amendment to elect delegates from the State of Florida, that the people have not accredited. To that I am opposed. We are not so hard driven yet as to be compelled to elect delegates from States that do not choose to send any here. It is true, the delegate with whom I talked, said to me that if this Convention invited them—I believe his words were, "extended the olive branch" to them—they would come here. I want no delegates here who have not been accredited here. I do not propose to sit side by side with delegates who do not represent the people; who are not bound by any thing, when I am to be bound by every thing. [Applause.]

I know, so far as I have heard, that there is no contest about the seats from Mississippi. By placing them here, in connection with the others, it is impossible that the sense of this Convention can be fully expressed. I shall vote against the amendment, because it brings delegates in here who have not been sent here; because it decides a controversy in another State without a hearing; because I have not heard whether in the State of Mississippi they have been sent here or not. I think that in all these cases the usages of the Democratic party require that they should be investigated by a committee before any of them are admitted upon this floor. [Applause.]

Mr. Richardson's speech received the most marked attention, for the reason, he was known to be peculiarly the spokesman of Douglas. He was always deeply in earnest, and his tone was that of the utmost degree of resolution.

Mr. Cochrane of New York made a speech, quite impressive in voice and manner, but not containing much matter. He was not in favor of either proposition before the house in its integrity.

Mr. Russell of Virginia made a speech in which he said that Virginia intended to cling to the Democracy of the South, and see that they had fair play at least. He had seen that day she would have fair play. He urgently appealed for the admission of Southern delegates, regarding whose seat there was no contest. As to the merits of the proposed test, he said: I suppose we all come here to be bound by the obligations of gentlemen. If we are not gentlemen—if we are such knaves that we cannot trust one another—we had better scatter at once, and cease to make any effort to bind each other. [Applause.

Montgomery of Pennsylvania now made his sensation speech.

Mr. Montgomery of Pa.—I regret that the previous question was not sustained this morning. I regret that the time of this Convention has been taken up in this discussion; but as it has progressed thus far, it is due to those who are opposed to the resolution offered by my colleague, that they should explain their views upon it. My colleague (Mr. Randall) has said that we are under no pledges. I differ with him. There is not a Democrat upon this floor who is not under the most solemn pledges of his honor as a man, and of his integrity as a Democrat, to abide by the nominations that we may make. [Applause.] And I say to my colleague that if he thinks that he is not bound by those honorable obligations, the sooner he retires from the Convention, the sooner he will relieve the Democracy from the imputation which he has sought to cast upon it. Any man who comes into the Convention of a party is bound by its decisions. You turn the party back into chaos if you do not acknowledge that obligation. [Loud applause.]

Now what is it we propose that these delegates shall do? It is simply that they shall give that honorable pledge, and declare, in taking their seats, that they will not countenance a Seceders' Convention in another place. [Enthusiastic applause, in which the galleries participated.]

The President—The gentlemen will suspend. The proceedings of the Convention have again been interrupted by loud clapping and noises from the gallery.

Many Voices—On the floor.

A Delegate—And in the gallery.

The President—And in the gallery also, distinctly seen and heard by me.

Mr. Johnson of Maryland—As a delegate from Maryland, I ask that representatives of this State may be cleared from the imputation cast upon them by the disorder in the gallery. Those joining in the disorder there are not the people of Baltimore. I ask of the chair that the galleries may be cleared. [Cries from all parts of the house—"No," "No," "No"—and hisses.

Mr. Montgomery—We have heard this before at Charleston. I have had to sit silent when an honorable delegate from the far South was hissed by a whole gallery for casting his vote as he had the right to do as the representative of a sovereign State, and the indignation and manifestation of feeling as exhibited here to-day nowhere exhibited itself then. [Applause.] I do not justify the applause, but I am here in defense of my rights, as that man was there in defense of his. Let us have even-handed justice.

The President—The chair begs leave to remind the gentleman from Pennsylvania that on that occasion the hissing was about to produce a clearing of the gallery, and it was at the special request of Mr. Perry of South Carolina that the Convention desisted from that act.

Mr. Wright of Pennsylvania—We were hissed time and again at Charleston.

[The manner of Mr. Montgomery in referring to the hissing of Mr. Perry from the Convention at Charleston, was perfectly ferocious. A grizzly bear could not have presented a more formidable appearance, or growled with more ravenous rage.]

We are situated, peculiarly, Mr. President. We are situated to-day as no Democratic Convention has never been in before, in the history of the party. From the day that the first Democratic Convention assembled, up to this hour, we never have had a scene presented to us like this. For the first time in the history of the Democratic party, a number of delegations of sovereign States relinquished and resigned, by a solemn instrument in writing, their places as delegates upon the floor of the Convention. They went out with a protest, not against a candidate, but against the principles of a party, declaring that they were not their principles—that they did not hold them, and they would not indorse and support them. There, sir, was the divorce of which my colleague has spoken, They declared it. It was not our act, but theirs. They put themselves from us, and not we from them. And not only that, but they called a hostile Convention, in the city of Charleston, and sat side by side with us, deliberating upon a nomination of candidates and the adoption of a platform. Principles hostile to ours were asserted, and a nomination hostile to ours was threatened. Our Convention was compelled, under the circumstances, in order to have those sovereign States represented, to adjourn. We did adjourn. What became of the gentlemen who seceded? They adjourned to meet at Richmond at another time. They did meet at Richmond. It is said by honorable gentlemen that they seek to come back and sit upon this floor with us. Now what did they do at Richmond? They adjourned that Convention, and to-day they hold it in terrorem over us if we do not come to their terms. [Applause.]

We adjourned for what? For the purpose of enabling those States in the South, whose delegates had seceded, to fill up the places of those who had left us. Now, I appeal to the magnanimity, to the Democracy, to the manhood of any delegate here, if such was not your declaration sent greeting to all those States? We told them—" Fill up your delegations and send us back new men." They have filled them up, and they have sent delegates who claim to represent the people of those States. * * *

But the gentleman from Virginia tells us that from the State of Florida the delegates have come to inform us that they have their original authority which constituted them delegates to the National Convention at Charleston. But he forgets that these same delegates, by a paper which remains on file in this Convention, resigned their places and abandoned them. They declared that they were no longer delegates to this Convention, and they filed a protest against its proceedings. And not only that, they were now in a hostile organization to ours. Now, I am in favor, under these circumstances, and their peculiar situation (one which has never existed before), of requiring that those delegates shall declare, when they are admitted to seats upon this floor, that they are honorably bound by our action, and by the nominations that we may make. We owe that to ourselves, to the party, to the country, and to the Union, which they tell us is to be preserved by the action of those very delegates. Do we require it of one side? Not at all—but of all sides. My colleague (Mr. Randall) says he is in favor of perpetuating our glorious Union. So am I. God knows I love the Star Spangled Banner of my country as dearly as he can, and it is because I love the country and the Union that I am determined that any man who arrays himself in hostility to it shall not, by my consent, take a seat in this Convention. [Applause.] I am opposed to disunion, and I am opposed to the advocates of it. [Applause.] And I am opposed to secession, either from this Union or from the Democratic Convention. [Applause.] But when men take this responsibility upon themselves—when they file among the records of this Convention their determination to have nothing more to do with its action—when they make speeches in our hearing, declaring that the principles of the party are not their principles, and that they will not be bound to support them—then I say it is high time, if they ask to come back, that they shall declare that they have changed their minds. [Applause.] What is the history of the past? Is this a novel feature in the proceedings of National Conventions? No, sir—it is a part of the history of our party that in all such contests we have always required such pledges. The gentleman from New York (Mr. Cochrane) felt the pressure of this same practice when he referred to his own delegation. Only at your last National Convention in Cincinnati, a contest existed between the two wings of the party in the State of New York. And it was required of the delegates from that State, before they had an examination upon their credentials, that they should pledge themselves to abide by the action of the Convention and support the nominees of the Convention. [Applause.] Are you going to insult the empire State of New York? Are you willing to make an exception against New York in favor of the South? [Cries of "No!" "no!"] Even-handed justice is all I am asking for. I ask that we shall adhere to the precedents of the past. [Applause.]

This was the speech of the day. It was considerably more than red hot, and by the time he had concluded, the political atmosphere was at the temperature it reached in Charleston just before the explosion. The speech was that of a bold man with a rude sort of ability, and zeal developed out of proportion to his discretion. Still it raised every body's estimate of "Bill Montgomery."

Mr. Ewing of Tennessee—I ask you, gentlemen of this Democratic Convention from all portions of this country, what do you mean? Have you no enemy in front? Have you any States to spare? Have you any States to give up? If you have, I have not yet learned it from the history of the past, or from the position of parties and of men at the present moment. We are pursued in front by a remorseless enemy, advancing step by step, squadron by squadron, until the field is almost irretrievably lost. And yet from all quarters and all sides of this Convention come exclamations of bitterness and words that burn, with a view to open the breach in our ranks wider and wider, until at last, Curtius-like, we will be compelled to leap into it to close it. What advantage will this give you? Who will be benefited by it?

And so on, begging for conciliation—which means, cut the throat of Douglas! He said:

It seems to me that gentlemen forgot that this is a voluntary Convention for the purpose of selecting a Democratic candidate for the Presidency. And how do you expect to succeed? Suppose, you Democrats of the North, you nominate your candidate, do you expect to receive the votes of Florida, Mississippi, Texas and Arkansas, by keeping them out of this Convention, and keeping up a constant fire of invective and reproach upon them? Can you afford to lose their votes?

I invoke this Convention to admit Florida, Mississippi and Texas—strike out Arkansas if there is any contest—and if there is to be a committee on Credentials, let them report, let the Convention decide, and then we will be prepared to go on with the nominations. But as matters now stand, the Convention is losing its whole power and frittering away its time upon these little and formal technicalities. I tell you that if this Convention does not nominate before long—within a few days—I believe that we shall become utterly and irretrievably demoralized and lost.

Mr. Loring of Massachusetts, who had not been at the Charleston Convention, his substitute being there, said:

Now, as I surveyed the doings of this Convention at Charleston, what did I see? When the platform of principles was discussed there, I saw a portion of my party driven, honestly driven, by the declarations therein made, from that Convention, to take their stand upon what they believed to be their constitutional rights. [Applause.]

And when I come here to-day what do I see? Why, I see those gentlemen presenting themselves here, and, as I insist, only claiming those rights which they have no power to resign to this Convention. They claim their right to sit here as members delegated by their sovereign States, and answerable to their sovereign States for their doings here. Is that not so? Has this Convention any power to expel or retain, to bind or loose? Has it any power to accept my resignation? Am I not answerable to my constituency, and to them alone—to the party organization that sent me here? And when I see those gentlemen presenting themselves at the doors of this Convention, the first impulse of my heart is, not to stand here quibbling upon questions of technical right, but to open my arms and welcome them in here [applause], and congratulate the Democratic party of this country.

Now, sir, when I hear judgment passed here upon any one of these States; when I hear it said that delegates from any one of these States have seen fit to present themselves at the doors of another Convention; when I hear the judgment passed upon them that they have not been reaccredited to this Convention, I am astonished—I am appalled. I do not understand such a position. I say that these delegates do not need any reaccrediting. The power they formally possessed is still theirs, and I beg and implore this body to give them their seats here, cordially and freely, and receive them here as members of this body. Sir, what is your nomination without that? I have heard, for the first time in a Democratic Convention, declarations made that there are sections in this country. I had thought I must go elsewhere for that. I have heard enough of that in Massachusetts.

I beg this Convention to interpose no obstacle to the admission of these gentlemen. I beg this Convention to invite and assist them to come back; and let me not be compelled now to vote upon a question which by a single technical point can in any way throw obstacles in their way. I never wish to vote upon it; but it must come. If I must cast my vote upon it, it shall be for that proposition, whatever it may be, which shall open the doors of this Convention, and allow our brethren freely to come in. [Renewed applause.]

* * * Gentlemen, let me tell you, that if the declaration I have heard here this afternoon, that the State of Florida presents no delegates to this Convention, is carried out by a vote of this body, and if it is made in that way a represensation of only a portion of the States of this Union, I will resign my seat, and never be bound by its action. [Loud applause from Southern delegates.]

Mr. King of Missouri made a sensation speech—the most unreserved yet in handling delicate subjects. He said:

An amendment is offered by the gentlemen from Pennsylvania to select some four States, in which he says there is no contest, and to give to delegates of those States certificates accrediting them to this Convention on an equal footing with other delegates. Now, I deny that that is democratic. If there never had been a whisper that these men have a roving commission in their pockets to go here or yonder, and play fast and loose with this Convention [laughter]—if they came here with clean papers, and nobody disputing that they were delegates, their credentials ought to go to a committee. That is the usage of the party.

* * * * * * *

If I find, from the report of the committee, that they are accredited to a Convention antagonistic to this—and if I find they have been there and elected their officers and taken a recess, and have come here like the man who went to a camp-meeting because he had the right to go there, then the amount of it is that they are not entitled to seats here. They have come here for mischief. [Applause.]

Now, if I have no authority, still I verily believe that they intend, if they cannot have things as they want them here, to go back to Richmond, and the powers of heaven and earth will be invoked to bring into condemnation the acts of this Convention. And they intend to put in nomination some man who has neither heels nor bottom enough to get the nomination here, and put him up against the nomination of the Democratic party. [Applause.] And if it turns out, as I believe the facts to be, in reference to their credentials, that they have no right here, so help me God, they will never get my vote. [Applause.] But if the majority of the Convention overlook all that, and let them in, I will greet them, because they are entitled to my respect.

Now, as regards Florida, they throw themselves upon their dignity, like South Carolina. [Laughter.] They scouted the idea of coming here, and they are not accredited to come, and yet these gentlemen want to bring them in. I say it is the height of absurdity. South Carolina, I am sorry to have it to say, is the only State that has preserved her dignity. [Laughter.]

Let any man study the history of Barnwell Rhett and his coadjutors in the days of Jackson, and he will find that they would rather dissolve the Union than keep it together. [Applause.] Look at the tone of the Charleston Mercury since the Charleston Convention. It is independent enough to tell the truth, and it does tell the truth. Those delegates who come here from the seceding States are the associates of those men who say that while the Democratic party has kept its organization together nationally it was a stumbling block to disunion. I wonder, when they come to Richmond, if they will try to keep themselves from being made an entering wedge to render it asunder. I do not know, but I trust they will indulge in no such scheme.

* * * * * * *

But these secessionists tell us that Virginia will go, and then as a matter of course, her daughters, Tennessee and North Carolina, would follow their mammy. And even Kentucky, Maryland and Missouri would take the same course. They then say, if you nominate Douglas it will be a sectional nomination as much as that of Seward or Lincoln, and it would not be long before you would call us Free-Soilers, and even the veriest Abolitionists. Even now it is said that we are a bogus Convention. High legal authority at Washington (the Attorney General, I suppose), [laughter], says we are *functus officio*. So I suppose if they do not succeed in disorganizing us, and go to Richmond, then they will call us a bogus concern. In conclusion, he called upon the Convention to hold on to the national organization. He did not believe, if eight or ten men could destroy the Union, it was worth preserving. [Applause.]

He further remarked, that if the delegates from Southern States who would not abide the decision of the Convention were to go out, there were other men from the same States just as good, ready to come in.

Mr. West of Connecticut proceeded to review the speech of Mr. Loring:

A portion of delegates have seceded, have withdrawn. Has a man from Connecticut? has a man from New England? has a man from the North declared that if certain things were not done they would withdraw from the Convention? No, sir; not one. We come here in good faith, with our preferences, it is true, and determined to vote and act like freemen. If you vote us down we will go home and hurrah for your candidate the best we can. [Applause.] Delegates have withdrawn; the Hon. gentleman from Massachusetts (Mr. Loring), with whom I have not the honor of an acquaintance, says that they were driven from this Convention. I ask, in the name of God, how driven? Has any thing been done here that has not been done in accordance with the principles and usages of the party? Yet these gentlemen have left upon the records of this Convention their solemn protest when they withdrew. And for what did they withdraw? Simply because the majority would not bow down and give them the platform they desired; such a platform, too, as four years ago they did not ask. [Applause.] I ask the indulgence of this Convention while I read a single sentence from the protest of the Mississippi delegation, although the gentleman from Massachusetts (Mr. Loring) rises in his place and informs the members here that those delegates were driven out of the Convention:

"As the representatives of Mississippi, knowing her wishes; as honorable men regarding her commands; we withdraw from the Convention, and, as far as our action is concerned, *absolve her from all connection with this body, and all responsibility for its action.*"

Who did that? Did the North do it?

You came together with us in common council in Cincinnati, and there you gave your unanimous vote for the platform adopted there. Four short years have gone their round, and now you ask us to turn about and place ourselves in a position which would be absolute death to our whole Democratic party of the North. [Applause.] We have fought the Black Republicans at home; we have been denounced from the pulpit and from the press, and been hissed in the street. And now when we come here and ask you to reaffirm the same principles which every leading man of your party in Congress—in the House of Representatives and the Senate of the United States—have proclaimed, you even turn around and taunt us with being Black Republicans. ["That is too true," and applause.]

Gentlemen talk of the vote of the South being necessary to carry forward and elect the candidate for President. Are not also the votes of the North necessary to do that? Change places with us; let us make our platform, revive us with life, being and vigor, send our representatives to Congress, return our Senators and elect Governors while you go down and fight the enemy, as we have done, and see how you would like it. [Applause.]

If you are determined to rend this party and the Union, our homes amid the hills of New England are as safe and as sacred as yours upon your sunny plains with your thousands of slaves around you. [Applause.] And we simply ask that you shall not take a position, and force use to take a position, which will be tantamount to absolute ruin when we return to our constituents. As to your taunts and threats we heed them not.

The gentleman from Massachusetts (Mr. Loring) asks, "Will you be bound?" Certainly; shackle us by your party trammels; make your decrees here, simply give us the right to speak when we have that right; give us the right to vote in common with you, and I pledge you my word you will never hear the word "secession" from the North. [Applause.]

An old-fashioned gentleman from Missouri, Mr. Hunter, now gave his colleague, Mr. King, some attention. Mr. Hunter stated that Gov. King was not a Democrat, but a sort of Benton man. Mr. Hunter further remarked:

When he was told, in Charleston, that Mr. Douglas would not stand upon a certain platform, he had said this Union could get along just as well if five hundred Douglases were dead and out of the way. [Applause.] If Mr. Douglas were to die to-night, there were five hundred men in the Democratic party who would make just as good a President as he. Mr. Douglas had done and was doing exactly what Benton had done for the party in Missouri; divided and broken them up. The contest between Benton and the people of Missouri, had been upon the Jackson resolution. His colleague (Mr. King) was Governor of Missouri when that resolution was first introduced, and was supposed to be in favor of it. But before the end of the session, he turned against it, and has been with Col. Benton ever since.

The old gentleman's quaint remarks put the Convention in a good humor.

Mr. Avery of North Carolina—The remarks that have fallen from the gentleman from Pennsylvania (Mr. Montgomery), and from Illinois (Mr. Merrick), require a reply at my hands. The speeches of the gentlemen, I suppose, indicate the sentiments of their hearts, a sentiment I would not entertain toward my Northern brethren to be President of the United States. It looks to us at the South as if it were the settled purpose to drive us from this Convention. But there is got to be more said than has been said, before they can drive me from this Convention.

Mr. Avery was but very imperfectly heard, but the spirit of his remarks was such as to irritate the Convention again.

Mr. Atkins of Tennessee appealed for harmony in the usual way, and with the common meaning, and called the previous question. The call was sustained by an almost unanimous vote, only Illinois and Michigan voting against it. The Convention then adjourned.

It was felt at the close of this long and warm debate (it occupied near six consecutive hours), that the general effect had been to damage Mr. Douglas, whose enemies took courage. The friends of Mr. Douglas, however, gathered in great strength with their bands of music about the streets, and concentrated in front of the residence of Hon.

Reverdy Johnson, one of their head-quarters, with their bands of music, and there were soon many thousands packed together there.

The first speech was by Mr. Powell of New York, who was for Douglas. But a large portion of the crowd was against Douglas, and swayed over toward the Gilmore House, where deafening and persistent cries of "Yancey," "Yancey," were raised. Ex-Senator Soule was the principal speaker from the steps of Mr. Johnson's house, though Claiborne of Missouri made a violent speech. Judge Meek of Alabama and Barry of Mississippi spoke to the Southern crowd. So there were two mass meetings of the Democracy side by side, both in full blast for about three hours, and the speakers of each substantially in effect, and sometimes in express words, reading the opposing crowd out of the party. The Southerners were the longest winded, and kept up a torrent of speaking and roar of shouting for four hours. It was surprising to see that so much of the outside pressure was against Douglas. There was such a tremendous and incessant yelling for Yancey, that a few minutes before twelve o'clock, that gentleman appeared and made one of his handsome silver-toned speeches, which satisfied the crowd. For the last hour of the Southern meeting, the Douglasites congregated on the opposite side of the square, and gave three cheers for Douglas at short intervals and kept a band of music playing lively airs. This conflict of jurisdiction was for the most part good-humored. There was a surprising number of people in the streets during the early part of the night; the strangers in the city being numbered by tens of thousands, whilst citizens swarmed forth enjoying the pleasant air, the excellent music discoursed by half a dozen bands, and the excitement of the politicians who were in fervent heat and violent commotion.

SECOND DAY.

Tuesday, June 19th, 1860.

Convention met, with the expectation on the part of those who had not been informed as to the action taken in caucus, of proceeding at once to vote upon the amendment of Mr. Gilmor. Mr. Church asked unanimous consent for the purpose of making a motion that would harmonize the Convention. It was given. Mr. Church had had a consultation with Mr. Gilmor and said:

Mr. Gilmor of Pennsylvania has consented to withdraw entirely his amendment, to my amendment, to Mr. Howard's original resolution, and I am prepared to do away with the latter portion of my amendment as offered yesterday, and make it only a reference to the committee on Credentials.

Mr. Gilmor of Pennsylvania arose and announced in person that he would withdraw his amendment.

Mr. Church again arose and withdrew the latter portion of his amendment, asking that it be read by the Secretary as modified.

The Convention now came to a vote upon the naked proposition to refer all contested seats to the committee on Credentials, and there was no dissenting voice. The resolution as amended and adopted is as follows:

Resolved, That the credentials of all persons claiming seats in this Convention, made vacant by the secession of delegates at Charleston, be referred to the committee on Credentials, and said committee are hereby instructed, as soon as practicable, to examine the same, and report the names of persons entitled to such seats.

Some changes were announced by the various delegations in the committee on Credentials, which committee is constituted as follows:

Maine—C. D. Jameson.	Louisiana—Vacancy.
New Hampshire—A. P. Hughes.	Mississippi— do.
Vermont—Stephen Thomas.	Texas— do.
Massachusetts—Oliver Stevens.	Arkansas— do.
Rhode Island—George H. Brown.	Missouri—Judge Crum, Chairman.
Connecticut—James Gallagher.	Tennessee—W. H. Carroll.
New York—Del. De Wolf.	Kentucky—G. F. Wood.
New Jersey—A. R. Speer.	Ohio—Mr. Steedman.
Pennsylvania—H. M. North.	Indiana—S. A. Hall.
Delaware—John H. Bradley.	Illinois—W. Allen.
Maryland—W. S. Gittings.	Michigan—J. G. Parkhurst.
Virginia—E. W. Hubbard.	Wisconsin—Mr. Smith.
North Carolina—R. R. Bridges.	Iowa—Mr. Finch.
South Carolina—G. B. F. Perry.	Minnesota—H. H. Sibley.
Georgia—Vacancy.	California—Mr. Gregory.
Florida— do.	Oregon—Gov. Stevens.
Alabama— do.	

There was some difference of opinion as to the time to which an adjournment should be taken, there being, of course, no business which could be transacted in the absence of the committee on Credentials, with the cases of half a dozen delegations pending. An adjournment was carried to five o'clock.

EVENING SESSION.

A great deal of difficulty was experienced by the delegates in obtaining admission to the Convention. A new set of tickets had been issued, because the old ones had been counterfeited, and crowds obtained admission who had no business among the delegates. But the two sets of tickets were greatly mixed. A good many delegates had not understood the order for a change of tickets, and there was an immense amount of trouble and botheration outside. When the Convention was called to order, Mr. Fisher of Virginia rose to a question of privilege, and denounced the trained bands at the doors of the Convention and the officers of the Convention. He talked of secession from the Convention and a dissolution of the Union, in case delegates were not better treated. Mr. Stetson of New York quietly ridiculed the gentleman of Virginia for his portentous speech about a small matter. The chair stated the imperative necessity that existed for guarding the doors. A communication from the committee on Credentials was read. It was badly written and badly read; and as read, it desired the Convention to continue its sessions. The chair said he would state the substance of the communication; and this was received with roars of laughter.

The communication was, of course, that the committee wanted time, and that it requested to be permitted to continue its sessions There being no business before the Convention, it adjourned in good humor. During the evening the politicians were full of excitement about the proceedings in the committee on Credentials, a personal difficulty between Messrs. Hindman and Hooper of Arkansas, having given them a high flavor.

At the time the Convention adjourned there was a heavy shower, and a great many people remained in the theatre ; there were several persons called out to amuse the crowd. Mr. Fisher of Virginia was called out by Marshal Rynders, who led the foolishness. Mr. Fisher got along tolerably well until he pronounced emphatically *emfat-a-li*—something being troubling his vocal organs. Upon this he was cheered down. Then citizen Work of Mississippi—known here as the man with the scarlet vest—was called out, and had much to say of this degenerate age. Even the Democracy was degenerating. The old gentleman swung his hat and cane about his head, scattering his papers far and wide, and told of his friendship for Andrew Jackson, making mention of the fact that there were no Jacksons in this degenerate age.

THIRD DAY.

WEDNESDAY, June 20th, 1860.

The theatre was greatly crowded this day, and thousands swarmed about the various public places of the city, discussing the crisis. There was a slight controversy between Messrs. Clark and King, of Missouri, about Col. Benton's democracy; and a communication was read from the Florida delegation, protesting that they were not seeking admission into the Convention. [The fact is they were waiting to be asked, and rather solicitous than otherwise on the subject of an invitation.]

Mr. Ludlow of New York stated the committee on Credentials would not be ready to report until 5 o'clock in the afternoon, and the Convention took a recess until that time, when Mr. Stuart of Michigan stated the committee would not be able to report until next day ; and the Convention adjourned. The city was meanwhile full of rumors about the action of the committee on Credentials, and probable results; and the controversies between the opposing factions were becoming more embittered every hour.

FOURTH DAY.

THURSDAY, June 21st, 1860,

There was an immense crowd in attendance upon the Convention this day. All the circles of the theatre were densely filled, and the floor allotted to delegates was encumbered by outsiders. Soon after the call to order, the floor in the centre of the Convention gave way. The accident was not serious in itself, but the panic was dangerous. Delegates rushed in masses to the windows, and climbed, nimbly as monkeys, over the chairs of the reporters seeking, according to appearances, to place themselves under the protection of the President. As soon as quiet was restored, another sensation was produced by a person in the gallery spreading his umbrella, and suspending it over a chandelier in which the gas was burning, as the day was quite dark. There was danger that the umbrella would take fire; and in case it did, all felt that a dreadful alarm would spread throughout the building. A hundred voices ordered the man with the umbrella to withdraw it from the gas, but he stretched his neck to see what the row was about, and was astonished to see every body looking at him. He heard the call at last, and obeyed the multitudinous commandment. The Convention now took a recess of an hour for the repair of the floor. Delegates were ordered to give up their tickets upon re-entering the hall, that the masses of intruders could be kept out.

Upon reassembling, the reports were received from the committee on Credentials. Mr. Krum of Missouri presented the majority report, as follows:

MAJORITY REPORT.

To the President of the National Democratic Convention:

SIR—The committee upon Credentials respectfully report, that prior to the adjournment of this Convention at Charleston, on the 3d of May last, the following resolution was adopted:

"*Resolved,* That when this Convention adjourns to-day, it adjourn to reassemble at Baltimore, Md., on Monday, the 18th day of June, and that it be respectfully recommended to the Democratic party of the several States to make provision for supplying all vacancies in their respective delegations to this Convention when it shall reassemble."

On the reassembling of this Convention at Baltimore, the following resolution was adopted:

"*Resolved,* That the President of the Convention be authorized to issue tickets of admission to seats in this Convention to the delegates from the States of Arkansas, Texas, Florida, and Mississippi, in which States there are no contesting delegations; and that in those States, to wit, Delaware, Georgia, Alabama, and Louisiana, where there are contesting delegations, a committee on Credentials shall be appointed, by the several delegations, to report upon said States."

By the further order of the Convention, the claims of all other persons claiming seats were also referred to your committee. Your committee, thus instructed, have proceeded to examine the claims of all persons which have been brought before them. Your committee found that the delegations of the several States of Alabama, Mississippi, Louisiana, Texas, and Florida had become wholly vacant by reason of the secession of the entire original delegations from this Convention; the delegations of the States of Georgia, Arkansas, and Delaware had become vacant in part only from the same cause. In no other State had there been any secession; but individual seats were contested in the delegations from the States of Massachusetts and Missouri.

Aside from the above, no question contesting the seats of delegates was brought to the notice of your committee. After patient and full investigation, your committee are of opinion that the persons hereinafter named in the resolutions, which are herewith submitted as a part of this report, are severally entitled to seats as delegates in this Convention, and they respectfully recommend that they be so received by this Convention.

From the State of Florida, no credentials of any delegates were presented to your committee. From the States of Mississippi and Texas, no contesting claimants appear. From Alabama, Louisiana, Georgia, and Arkansas, there appeared contesting claimants for all the vacant seats. Of the four votes to which the State of Arkansas is entitled, the now sitting delegates represent and vote one. The seats representing the remaining three votes had become vacant by the secession of the original delegates. These seats were all contested, one set of contestants consisting of six persons, and the other set consisting of three persons. Your committee are of opinion, that all of these contestants should be admitted to seats as delegates, with the power of voting as hereinafter declared in the resolution herewith reported in that behalf.

In the Fifth Congressional District of Massachusetts, it appears that B. F. Hallett and another person were appointed as delegates to this Convention, and K. S. Chaffee and another person were appointed substitutes. That Mr. Hallett, not being able to attend at Charleston, notified Mr. Chaffee of that fact, who thereupon proceeded to Charleston, presented his credentials, and was duly admitted to his seat, which he continued to fill at the time of the adjournment of this Convention to Baltimore. At the reassembling of the Convention at Baltimore, Mr. Hallett appeared, claimed the seat which had been awarded to Mr. Chaffee, and receiving the entrance ticket from the chairman of the Massachusetts delegation, actually took possession of the seat. Your committee were of opinion that, when Mr. Hallett had notified Mr. Chaffee that he could not fulfill his duty as delegate, and Mr. Chaffee, repairing to Charleston, had been duly admitted to this Convention, his rights to his seat became absolute, and not subject to be superseded at the pleasure of Mr. Hallett, and that Mr. Chaffee is now the rightful delegate to this Convention.

In the Eighth Electoral District of Missouri the facts are precisely parallel to the above Massachusetts case. The only difference is in terms. Johnson B. Clardy having been elected delegate, and John O'Fallan, Jr., having been elected alternate. Your committee, for reasons above stated, are of opinion that Mr. O'Fallan is now the rightful delegate.

In regard to the contesting claimants from Georgia, your committee have to report that the evidence adduced before your committee by the respective parties presented a great variety of novel as well as complexed facts and questions, touching the rights of either parties to seats. Your committee, in attempting to solve these difficulties, encountered embarrassments on every hand. After a most patient consideration of the whole matter, it seemed to your committee that the only way of reaching a satisfactory adjustment, is to admit to seats both delegations, with power to each of said delegations to cast one-half of the vote of the State, in the manner expressed in the resolution herewith submitted. This solution seems equitable to your committee, and therefore they recommend the adoption of said resolution. All of which is respectfully submitted.

JOHN W. KRUM, *Chairman.*

1. *Resolved,* That George H. Gordon, E. Barksdale, W. F. Barry, H. C. Chambers, Joseph R. Davis, Beverly Matthews, Charles Clark, Wm. L. Featherston, P. F. Slidell, C. G. Armistead, Wm. F. Avant, and T. J. Hudson are entitled to seats in this Convention, as delegates from the State of Mississippi.

2. *Resolved,* That Pierre Soule, F. Coltman, R. C. Wickliffe, Michael Ryan, Manuel White, Charles Brenveneau, Gustavus Leroy, J. E. Morse, A. S. Herron, M. D. Colmar, J. N. T. Richardson, and J. L. Walker are entitled to seats in this Convention, as delegates from the State of Louisiana.

3. *Resolved,* That R. W. Johnson, T. C. Hindman, J. P. Johnson, Leroy Caroll, J. Gould, and John A. Jordan be admitted to seats, as delegates from the State of Arkansas, with power to cast two votes; and that Thos. H. Bradley, M. Hooper, and D. C. Cross be also admitted to seats, as delegates from the same State, with power to cast *one vote;* and in case either portion of said delegates shall refuse or neglect to take their said seats, or to cast their said votes, the other portion of said delegates, taking seats in this Convention, shall be entitled to cast the entire three votes of said State.

4. *Resolved,* That Guy M. Brinn, F. R. Lubbock, F. S. Starkdale, E. Greer, H. R. Runnels, Thos. P. Ochiltree, M. W. Covey, Wm. H. Parsons, R. Ward, J. F. Crosby, B. Burrows, and Van H. Manning are entitled to seats, as delegates from Texas.

5. *Resolved*, That James A. Bayard and Wm. G. Whiteley are entitled to seats from the county of New Castle, Delaware.
6. *Resolved*, That R. L. Chaffee, who was duly admitted at Charleston as a delegate from the Fifth Congressional District of Massachusetts, is still entitled to said seat in this Convention, and that Benjamin F. Hallett, who has assumed said seat, is not entitled thereto.
7. *Resolved*, That John O'Fallon, Jr., who was duly admitted at Charleston as a delegate from the Eighth Congressional District of Missouri, is still entitled to said seat in this Convention ; and that John B. Clardy, who has assumed said seat, is not entitled thereto.
8. *Resolved*, That R. A. Barker, D. C. Humphrey, John Forsyth, Wm. Garrett, J. J. Seivels, S. C. Posey, L. E. Parsons, Joseph C. Bradley, Thomas B. Cooper, James Williams, O. H. Bynum, Samuel W. Wheatley, L. V. B. Martin, John W. Warrack, W. R. R. Wyatt, Benjamin Harrison, Thomas M. Mathews, and Norment McLeod are entitled to seats in this Convention, as delegates from the State of Alabama.
9. *Resolved*, That the delegation from the State of Georgia, of which H. L. Benning is chairman, be admitted to the Convention, with power to cast one-half of the vote of said State ; and that the delegation from said State, of which Col. Gardner is chairman, be also admitted to the Convention, with power to cast one-half of the vote of said State ; and if either of said delegations refuse or neglect to cast the vote as above indicated, that in such case the delegates present in the Convention be authorized to cast the full vote of said State.

Mr. Stevens of Oregon presented the

MINORITY REPORT.

To the President of the Democratic National Convention:

SIR—We, the undersigned, members of the committee on Credentials, feel constrained to dissent from many of the views and a large portion of the action of the majority of the committee in respect to the rights of delegates to seats referred to them by the Convention, and to respectfully recommend the adoption of the following resolutions :

1. *Resolved*, That B. F. Hallett is entitled to a seat in this Convention as a delegate from the 5th Congressional District of Massachusetts.
2. *Resolved*, That Johnson B. Clardy is entitled to a seat in this Convention as a delegate from the 8th Congressional District of the State of Missouri.
3. *Resolved*, That James A. Bayard and W. G. Whiteley are entitled to seats in this Convention as delegates from the State of Delaware.
4. *Resolved*, That the delegation headed by R. W. Johnson are entitled to seats as delegates in this Convention from the State of Arkansas.
5. *Resolved*, That the delegation of which Guy N. Bryan is chairman, are entitled to seats as delegates in this Convention from the State of Texas.
6. *Resolved*, That the delegation of which John Tarleton is chairman, are entitled to seats in this Convention as delegates from the State of Louisiana.
7. *Resolved*, That the delegation of which L. P. Walker is chairman, are entitled to seats in this Convention from the State of Alabama.
8. *Resolved*, That the delegation of which Henry L. Benning is chairman, are entitled to seats in this Convention from the State of Georgia.
9. *Resolved*, That the delegation from the State of Florida, accredited to the Charleston Convention, are entitled to take seats in this Convention, and cast the vote of Florida.

The principles involved in these resolutions, and the facts on which they rest, are of such gravity and moment, that we deem it due to the Convention and to ourselves to set them forth with care and particularity. We differ radically from the majority of the committee, both in much of the action we recommend to the Convention and the principles which should control such action. It is a question not simply of the integrity, but the existence of the Democratic party in several States of this Union. It is a question whether the Democratic party in said States shall be ostracised and branded as unworthy of affiliation with the national organization.

It is a question whether persons irregularly called, or withdrawing from the regular Convention, shall have the sanction of the National Convention to raise the flag of rebellion against their respective State organizations. It is a question whether the Convention itself shall repudiate its own deliberate action at Charleston. We do not magnify the importance of these questions when we assert that upon their proper solution depends the fact as to whether there shall be a National Democratic party or not. The task will not be difficult to show that the action recommended by the majority of the committee is grossly inconsistent, and should be reprobated and condemned by this Convention. But to the task, without further preamble.

Reserving to the closing portion of this report the cases of contested seats in the Massachusetts and Missouri delegations, we come at once to the cases of the delegates who withdrew from the Charleston Convention. This Convention, on the eve of its adjournment at Charleston, and in the great cause of the restoration of harmony to our distracted party, "respectfully recommended to the Democratic party of the several States to make provision for supplying all vacancies in their respective delegations to this Convention when it shall reassemble." We call particular attention to the wording of the resolution. Certain delegates had withdrawn. They had placed on the Convention the reasons of their withdrawal.

They still, however, were the representatives of the Democratic party of their several States. Their withdrawal was not a resignation. It was not so considered by the Convention. The vacancies referred to had reference to the contingency of vacancies *at the time of reassembling*, and the resolution proposed to provide for supplying them. The Convention did not presume to touch the question as to whether the withdrawal of the delegates constituted a resignation, nor had it any right to interfere in the matter. A resignation must be made to the appointing power, and to be complete and final must be accepted by the appointing power. It was well known on the adjournment of the Convention at Charleston, that the withdrawing delegates desired the instruction of their several constituencies before deciding on their future course.

Such was the spirit and purpose of their deliberations at Charleston. They consulted their respective constituencies. In every case except the case of South Carolina, their constituencies directed or authorized them—their constituencies being filled as contemplated in the resolution of the Convention—to repair to Baltimore, and there in earnest efforts with their brethren of the Convention, to endeavor once more to unite their party, and promote harmony and peace in the great cause of their country. The resolution of the Convention did not prejudge the question, since so strenuously raised, that their withdrawal was a resignation, but left the whole question to the said delegates, and their respective constituencies, to the end that every State of this Union might be represented in Baltimore.

The committee has passed resolutions, declaring by a vote of 16 to 9, that the delegation from Louisiana headed by Pierre Soule, by a vote of 14 to 11, that the delegation from Alabama headed by Parsons, by a vote of 13 to 10, and that half of each delegation claiming seats from Georgia, are entitled to seats in the Convention. The resolutions recommended by the undersigned to the Convention, declare the right of the delegations elected to Charleston, with vacancies supplied, as contemplated in the resolution of the Convention to which reference has been made, and accredited to Baltimore, to said seats. The committee which thus recommend the irregular delegates from these three States, have rejected the irregular delegates from Delaware, and admitted the Charleston delegates.

It has admitted irregular delegates from Arkansas, and rejected a portion of the Charleston delegates, as modified by the filling of vacancies. It has admitted the (Charleston) delegates from Mississippi, by a vote of 23 to 2, and the (Charleston) delegates from Texas, by a vote of 19 to 6. The fact that delegations are not contested, does not establish the right to seats in the Convention. There may be irregular delegates without contest, and there may be a contest between two sets of irregular delegates. The right of persons to seats as delegates is to be determined by the fact as to whether they were appointed by the constituency which they claim to represent, and appointed according to the usages of said constituency. Wanting these essential prerequisites, they are not entitled to seats, even if there be no contestants; and having these, their right to seats is not impaired or affected by contestants.

The committee, in deciding by a vote of 23 to 2, that the Charleston delegates from Mississippi are entitled to seats in the Baltimore Convention, have decided rightly, just because they were duly accredited to Charleston, have never since resigned, and have received instructions from the State of Mississippi, through a Convention called of the Democratic Executive Committee of the State, to return to Baltimore.

The Charleston delegates, both from Alabama and Georgia, stand in precisely the same position. They were also duly accredited to Charleston. They withdrew, and never resigned. They returned to their respective constituencies. The Executive Committees in these States, as in the case of Mississippi, called a Convention of the party. The Conventions met. The delegates, as in the case of Mississippi, submitted their action to the Conventions, and these Conventions approved their course, continued their powers, and accredited them to Baltimore. Their rights stand on precisely the same basis, and are sustained by the same authority, as in Mississippi. The contestants were appointed by nobody authorized to meet according to the usages of the party in these States, and are not entitled to any consideration whatever.

In the case of Alabama, the Convention assembled on the call of the Democratic Executive Committee (addressed to the Democracy of the State), was very largely attended, nearly every county in the State having been represented. A small number of persons, however, issued a notice, which was published in only three newspapers in the State—in two papers the notice was without signers, and in the third paper (Mobile Register), it was signed by John Forsyth and thirty-five others. The notice in one paper called upon all Democrats and *all other persons*—in the second paper upon Democrats and *all conservatives*, and in the third paper (Mobile Register), upon *the people of Alabama* to hold county meetings and send delegates to a State Convention to be held in Montgomery or Selma, the 4th day of June, to appoint delegates to Baltimore.. Twenty-eight counties only out of fifty-two were represented.

It was the coming together of persons from all parties outside of the regular organization to strike down the Democracy of the State. It was a call without any official authority whatsoever. We thus find the Democracy of the State assembling in Convention according to the usages of the party, and we find at the same time persons assembling at the call of unauthorized individuals. In the former case the whole State was represented. In the latter about half of the State. Yet the majority of the committee have indorsed the action of the Democracy of Alabama and have repudiated, contrary to all precedent, usage, right and justice, the action of the former; not only this, they have repudiated the principles of their own action in the case of the Mississippi delegation.

But the action of the majority of the committee in the case of Georgia has gone one step further in its disregard of the acknowledged principles of the party. The Convention which the committee put on an equality with the regularly authorized Convention, consisted in great part of persons who just participated in the regular Democratic Convention of the State. The regular called Convention consisted of nearly four hundred delegates, representing nearly all the counties of the State. The resolutions of the Convention having been adopted by a vote of 290 to 41, these latter withdrew from the Convention and organized anew. Thus the majority of your committee have exalted the pretensions of less than one-eighth of the delegates of the State Convention to an equality with the rights of seven-eighths of the Democracy of the State.

In the case of Louisiana, the old Convention, which originally appointed the delegates to Charleston, was reassembled, on the call of the Executive Committee of the State, and by a decisive majority accredited the Charleston delegates to Baltimore. The reasons for this action have their parallels in the case of Texas and Delaware, which have received the sanction of the committee. In Texas, the delegates come back accredited by the Democratic Executive Committee simply—it being a manifest impossibility, from want of time, to assemble the party in a State Convention; and in Delaware, under the usages and rules of the party, the old Convention was reassembled. In Louisiana there was time to assemble the old Convention, but not to order an election of delegates in the several parishes to meet a new Convention. The Executive Committee did every thing it could to get the expression of the views of the State. It reassembled the old Convention, nearly every parish in the State being represented, and accredited the Charleston delegates to Baltimore.

But the Convention whose delegates to Baltimore have been indorsed by the majority of your committee, was called at the instance of two local organizations, and of Dr. Cottman, a former member of the National Executive Committee of the party. The calls were somewhat conflicting. The notice did not reach many parishes in the State. Only twenty parishes out of thirty-nine are pretended to be represented, and in several of these there is no reason to doubt the fact that the delegates did not leave behind them a single constituent agreeing with them in sentiments. In not a single parish was this call responded to by a majority of the Democratic voters. The Convention only represented a very small portion of the party—it was totally irregular, besides.

The majority of the committee object to the action of the old Convention on its reassembling at the call of the Executive Committee, on the ground that it was defunct and could not be brought to life. Yet it indorses the action of the other Convention on the call in part of the equally defunct member of the National Committee, Dr. Cottman. Following the usage of Delaware, by the Executive Committee of Louisiana, though manifestly a necessity for the reasons stated, has no weight as a precedent with this majority. Conceding their ground of its being irregular, seats as delegates should be given to the body called by the regular authority and not to the body assembled by no responsible authority whatever, and especially when the former represented the great body of the party and the latter did not. All these considerations, however, have been disregarded by the majority of the committee, who have persisted, by a vote of 16 to 9, to award the seats as delegates to the representatives of the disorganizing minority Convention.

In the case of Arkansas, the majority of the committee propose to divide out the seats to all applicants. In this State the Democratic party were about assembling in their District Conventions, consisting of delegates from the several counties of the State, for the nomination of members of Congress, when their delegates returned from Charleston. As in Texas, there was not time for the assembling of a State Convention. In these District Conventions, delegates were selected to represent the party at Baltimore. A call was however issued in a Memphis paper, without any signature whatever, calling upon the people of the Northern District to assemble in mass meeting at Madison, to elect delegates to Baltimore.

Some four or five hundred men from ten to twelve counties thus assembled and appointed three delegates to Baltimore. The majority of the committee propose to allow these men to vote in the Convention. There are twenty-seven counties and twenty-five thousand voters in the district. Col. Hindman, a delegate, elected by the District Convention, to Baltimore, was elected to Congress, in 1858, by eighteen thousand majority, and was unanimously renominated by the Convention which selected him as a delegate to Baltimore. These facts show the significance of the action of the District Convention in electing delegates to Baltimore as representing truly the sentiment of the Democratic party of the district, and they exhibit the utter insignificance of the anonymously called Convention, for it will be borne in mind that it was held at a central point, at the western terminus of the railroad from Memphis, and where several stage and wagon routes meet. They were elected as delegates generally from the State to the National Convention, with the hope that they might get in without any definite claim.

In Massachusetts and Missouri, the contest is between principals now holding their seats and substitutes who held their places at Charleston. In each case the principal was detained at home by sickness in his family. In each case the principal gave notice to his substitute that he should take his seat at Baltimore. The majority of the committee hold that the principals, elected as such by the proper Conventions, are not entitled to their seats and have reported accordingly. We hold that a substitute is appointed simply to act in the absence of the principal, and that his authority ceases whenever the principal makes his appearance and takes his seat. We emphatically declare that such has been the invariable usage in all Conventions of the party, whether National or State, and that it is based on reason and the representative principle.

All which is respectfully submitted.

ISAAC I. STEVENS, Oregon.
A. R. SPEER, New Jersey.
H. M. NORTH, Pennsylvania.
JNO. H. BEWLEY, Delaware.
E. W. HUBBARD, Virginia.
R. R. BRIDGERS, North Carolina.
WM. H. CARROLL, Tennessee.
GEO. H. MORROW, Kentucky.
D. S. GREGORY, California.

In the points of difference between the majority and minority reports of the committee on Credentials, I concur in the conclusions of the minority report in the cases of Georgia, Alabama, Missouri and Massachusetts.

AARON V. HUGHES, New Hampshire.

Mr. Stevens—It will be observed that the committee are nearly unanimous, and the two reports agree in the case of Texas, Missouri and Delaware. I am requested to state that the delegate from Tennessee dissents from a portion of the conclusion of the committee, but votes under instruction of his co-delegates; also that the gentleman from New Hampshire agrees with the report of the minority, in the case of Georgia, Alabama, Massachusetts and Missouri.

Mr. W. S. Gittings of Maryland also made a report, which he subsequently withdrew. Mr. Krum took the floor, and after a few remarks yielded it to Mr. Stevens. He was appealed to, at this moment, to move the previous question on the report. The question then was whether he had yielded temporarily or entirely to Mr. Stevens, and whether he could resume the floor. There was a long contest on the point of order, ending by Mr. Stevens moving the previous question. He could well afford to do this, as his report was universally acknowledged to be a remarkably strong document, presenting the case of the seceders in the clearest possible light and with singular skill. It at once became evident that New York was shaky. Several of her delegates made appeals for an adjournment, that New York might have time for consultation While the Convention was struggling toward an adjournment, Mr. Butler of Mass. announced that the tickets furnished delegates had been forged, and that crowds of intruders admitted by forged tickets were on the floor of the Convention.

In order to accommodate New York, the committee took a recess until half-past four o'clock. The demand of New York for time to consider, was a surprise, as it was known that she had been in caucus on the very point regarding which she was undecided, and had concluded, by a small majority, to sustain the majority report. At the hour to which the Convention took a recess, the theatre was crowded in every part except the seats of the New Yorkers, which were vacant. Mr. Ludlow presently appeared and apologized for New York, and asked more time.

In a hopeless sort of way the Convention adjourned. The Douglas men were rather disheartened. They would have voted against an adjournment, but it would have been useless. New York was profoundly anathematized for her dishonest and cowardly procrastination. The immediate impression was that the New Yorkers were at the last moment proposing to slaughter Douglas. The streets were full of excited men, and the atmosphere electric with a personal war-spirit. Just before the adjournment, Mr. Montgomery, member of Congress from Pennsylvania, made a disturbance about tickets of admission to the hall, and Mr. Randall of Pa., questioning his statements, he spoke of Mr. Randall in a very sneering way as "This poor old man." A sensation scene followed. After adjournment, a son of Mr. Randall waited for Mr. Montgomery on the street, and rushing up, dealt him several severe blows in the face, causing the blood to flow profusely. Montgomery, a powerful man, recovering from the shock of the assault, knocked Randall, a slender little fellow, down. The crowd then separated them. There was intense excitement throughout the evening. Rumors as to the action of the New York delegation were constantly circulated. About nine o'clock it became understood that New York had agreed to sustain the majority report. Her delegation had divided upon the several propositions of the report, and had sustained them all by a considerable majority. This news greatly reassured the friends of Mr. Douglas, and they became exultant. They had been, however, gradually for a couple of days thinning out, and the outside pressure turning against them. However, they rallied as usual in Monument Square, and were more noisy and arrogant than ever. The Southerners also congregrated and, according to custom, cried "Yancey," "Yancey." The Plugs also turned out strong, and diversified the exercises by many times giving "Three cheers for Bell and Everett."

These mass meetings at night did much to exasperate the pending controversy. They were held side by side, and the prevailing sentiment in each was hostility to the other. The friends of Douglas denounced the others as disorganizers, bolters, traitors, and disunionists. The Southerners called the Douglasites a sneaking species of Abolitionists. Douglas delegates from Pennsylvania declared that, if any of the delegation from that State, or any other Northern State, refused to confirm the nomination of Douglas, or joined the Seceders' Convention, they would not dare return to their families. At the steps in front of the residence of Reverdy Johnson, the true test of Democracy would appear to be devotion to Douglas. At the balcony of the Gilmore House, the test seemed to be hostility to Douglas. It was the habit of hundreds of noisy fellows to appear every night in the square and cry "Yancey," "Yancey," at the top of their voices for hours. Yancey on two occasions responded. He said he was neither for the Union *per se*, nor against it *per se*, but he was for the Constitution. He denounced the friends of Douglas as small men, with selfish aims—as corrupt and abolitionized. They were ostrich-like—their head was in the sand of squatter sovereignty, and they did not know their great, ugly, ragged abolition body was exposed.

Mr. Hunter of Louisiana, in announcing the action of the committee on Credentials, said there were men on that committee who should not cross his threshold—and a lady of his family should not speak to them. They were men without honor or decency. The Douglas men had blowed and bragged about their honor, and in so doing they lied, and now they lied. They talked of carrying the cotton States. The Louisiana delegation was ready to enter into bonds to bet one million of dollars that Douglas could not carry one of those States. He dared Douglas men who had talked of betting to face the music of that proposition. He spoke of Douglas and his followers as bankrupts in pocket and principle, as profligates and impostors and cowards. The Douglas orators were all the while proclaiming the greatness and honor of their candidate—and assuming that all opposition to him was treason to the party, and must be ranked as Southern disunionism or Northern Abolitionism. On the outskirts of the mass meetings every evening were to be seen scores of groups of men, crowding close and talking, not loudly, but with deep emphasis, every group concentrating and intensifying the greater antagonism of the mass meetings. The Southerners would be claiming "all the rights of the slaveholding States as co-equal States," and the Northerners by turns beseeching their opponents for a living chance for success, and threatening them with an Abolition President. The controversies would become personal. A Douglasite would sneeringly ask: "What office has old Buchanan given you?" And the response would be: "What office has Douglas promised you?" Meanwhile personal difficulties were occurring at short intervals, and the cauldron boiled and bubbled more and more. There was the Hindman and Hooper difficulty, the Whiteley and Townsend difficulty, and the Montgomery and Randall difficulty, and fifty others of less note.

FIFTH DAY.

BALTIMORE, *Friday*, June 22d.

Definite action was expected this morning, and there was an immense crowd in the circles of the theatre, while the floor, by the adoption of precautions against interlopers, was tolerably clear.

The President stated that the Convention had, on the previous day, ordered "the main question to be now put." The majority and minority reports from the committee on Credentials were now read. Mr. Gittings of Maryland withdrew the report which he had offered. Mr. Krum of Missouri, as chairman of the committee on Credentials, was allowed to close the debate upon it, and made a reply to Stevens's minority report. It was ineffectual, however, entirely failing to break the force of the document by the gentleman from Oregon.

The Hon. Bedford Brown of North Carolina now attempted a speech. He said it would give him "infinite pleasure to pour oil upon the agitated waves"—when Mr. Gorman of Minnesota called him to order. Mr. Stevens of Oregon wished to utter a single sentence, but Stuart of Michigan objected, and insisted upon proceeding to business.

The first question was upon the proposition of Mr. Stevens of Oregon, which was moved as a substitute for the report of the committee. Just here occurred an illustrative specimen of the style of ruling by Mr. Cushing. On the motion of Mr. Stevens, the chair said:

The chair understands that motion to be equivalent to a motion to strike out and insert, and although the chair feels that there may be some doubt as to what should be the construction of a case like this, of indeed what is the true construction of the universal rule that a motion to strike out and insert is indivisible, without going into the question whether that universal declaration applies to that motion itself or what is behind the motion, the chair has on reflection come to the conclusion to rule that this motion to strike out and insert is indivisible, and therefore unless overruled by the Convention, he will be prepared to put the question to the Convention upon the series of resolution in block.

Having come to that conclusion upon of course a *prima facie* reflection upon the subject, subject to being overruled, the chair had conceived that if the resolution offered by the gentleman from Oregon should be adopted on a motion to strike out and insert, then they would be divisible, and the separate propositions contained in the report of the minority would be susceptible of being voted upon separately; or if the motion of substitution should be rejected, then upon the Convention being brought to a vote upon the resolutions presented by the gentleman from Missouri (Mr. Krum), those propositions would be separable.

Mr. Cochrane of New York appealed from the decision of the chair and made a speech on the point, and then withdrew his appeal. There were now loud cries of "Question," "question." The vote was taken on the substitution of the minority for the majority report. At this moment the chair made a suggestion, that in the declaration of the vote "being of a momentous character in its party relations," involving much interest and emotion, there should not be any manifestations of approbation. The chair remarked:

If the Convention will itself set that example of dignified decorum in the gravest of all possible questions in which any of us can be placed, it will be surely for the advantage of the Convention and of our common public interests.

The vote was as follows:

AYES—Maine 2½, New Hampshire ½, Vermont 1½, Massachusetts 8, Connecticut 2½, New Jersey 4, Pennsylvania 17, Delaware 2, Maryland 5¾, Virginia 14, North Carolina 9, Arkansas ¼, Missouri 5, Tennessee 10, Kentucky 10, Minnesota 1½, California 4, Oregon 3—100½.

NAYS—Maine 5½, New Hampshire 4½, Vermont 3½, Massachusetts 5, Rhode Island 4, Connecticut 3½, New York 35, New Jersey 3, Pennsylvania 10, Maryland 2½, Virginia 1, North Carolina 1, Arkansas ½, Missouri 4, Tennessee 1, Kentucky 2, Ohio 23, Indiana 13, Illinois 11, Michigan 6, Wisconsin 5, Iowa 4, Minnesota 2½—150.

While the States were called on this vote, there was the most profound and solemn silence. The decisive vote of New York was given promptly, and caused a fluttering, as it was known to decide the result of the contest at that point.

The resolutions of the regular report of the committee were now reported and read by the Secretary in their order.

The vote was then taken on the first resolution admitting the regular delegation from Mississippi, and it was adopted by ayes 250, nays 2½. The nays were, Pennsylvania 2, Iowa ½.

Mr. Rynders of New York—Mississippi having been admitted, I ask if she is not entitled now to vote?

Mr. Cochrane of New York said that until the last branch of the resolutions had been disposed of the whole question had not been put and determined.

The vote was then taken on the second resolution, admitting the Louisiana contestants, and it was adopted by yeas 153, nays 98, as follows:

YEAS—Maine 5¼, New Hampshire 4½, Vermont 3½, Massachusetts 5, Rhode Island 4, Connecticut 3½, New York 35, New Jersey 2½, Pennsylvania 10, Maryland 2¾, Virginia 1, North Carolina 2, Arkansas ½, Missouri 4, Tennessee 2, Kentucky 2, Ohio 23, Indiana 13, Illinois 11, Michigan 6, Wisconsin 5, Iowa 4, Minnesota 2½—153.

NAYS—Maine, 2¾, New Hampshire ½, Vermont ½, Massachusetts 8, Connecticut 2½, New Jersey 4½, Pennsylvania 17, Delaware 2, Maryland 5¼, Virginia 13, North Carolina 8, Arkansas ½, Missouri 5, Tennessee 10, Kentucky 10, Minnesota 1⅓, California 4, Oregon 3—98.

There was no longer any doubt about the disruption of the Convention. It was merely a question of time, and the time short. Some of the delegates seemed singularly pleased; their good humor was admirable. Others took it hard, and pursed up their brows, twisted their mouths in the firmest possible attitude, and looked at once fierce and sad. Dean Richmond was the pivotal personage. There was not a minute but some one was whispering in his ear. Peter Cagger found something funny all the while, and laughed until his face was red as the heart of a beet.

The vote having been declared in the Louisiana case, the third resolution was read as follows:

Resolved, That R. W. Johnson, T. C. Hindman, J. P. Johnson, De Rosey Carroll, J. Gould, F. W. Hoadley and John A. Jordan be admitted to seats as delegates from the State of Arkansas, with power to cast *two* votes, and that Thomas H. Bradley, M. Hooper and D. C. Cross be also admitted to seats as delegates from the same State, with power to cast *one* vote; and in case either portion of said delegates shall refuse or neglect to take their said seats or to cast their said votes, the other portion of said delegates taking seats in this Convention shall be entitled to cast the entire three votes of said State.

The question was then taken on the first part of the resolution, admitting R. W. Johnson and five others of Arkansas, to seats in the Convention, with power to cast *two* votes, and it was adopted by yeas 182, nays 69, as follows:

YEAS—Maine 5½ New Hampshire 5, Vermont 5, Massachusetts 13, Rhode Island 4, Connecticut 6, New York 35, New Jersey 7, Pennsylvania 10, Delaware 2, Maryland 2¾, North Carolina 1, Missouri 9, Tennessee 11½, Ohio 23, Indiana 13, Illinois 11, Michigan 6, Wisconsin 5, Iowa 3½, Minnesota 4—182.

NAYS—Maine 2¼, Pennsylvania 17, Maryland 5¼, Virginia 15, North Carolina 9, Tennessee 1½, Kentucky 12, Iowa 1½, California 4, Oregon 3—69.

The vote was then taken on the second branch of the resolution, and resulted ayes 150, nays 100½, as follows:

YEAS—Maine 5½, New Hampshire 5, Vermont 4½, Massachusetts 5, Rhode Island 4, Connecticut 3½, New York 35, New Jersey 2½, Pennsylvania 10, Maryland 2, Virginia 1, North Carolina 1, Missouri 4, Tennessee ½, Kentucky 2, Ohio 23, Indiana 12, Illinois 11, Michigan 6, Wisconsin 5, Iowa 4, Minnesota 2½—150.

NAYS—Maine 2½, Vermont ½, Massachusetts 8, Connecticut 2½, New Jersey 4½, Pennsylvania 17, Delaware 2, Maryland 6, Virginia 14, North Carolina 9, Missouri 5, Tennessee 11, Kentucky 10, Minnesota ½, California 4, Oregon 3—100½.

Arkansas declined to vote.

The remainder of the resolution was adopted without a vote by States.

The 4th resolution was read, which is as follows:

Resolved, That Guy M. Bryan, F. R. Lubbock, F. S. Stockdale, E. Greer, H. R. Runnels, Thos. P. Ochiltree, M. W. Covey, Wm. H. Parsons, R. Ward, J. F. Crosby, H. Burrows and Van H. Manning are entitled to seats as delegates from Texas.

The resolution was agreed to—yeas 250, nays 2½.

The 5th resolution was read as follows:

Resolved, That James A. Bayard and Wm. G. Whiteley are entitled to seats from the county of New Castle, Del.

It was adopted.

The 6th resolution was then read, as follows:

Resolved, That R. L. Chaffee, who was duly admitted at Charleston as a delegate from the Fifth Congressional District of Massachusetts, is still entitled to said seat in this Convention, and that Benjamin F. Hallett, who has assumed said seat, is not entitled thereto.

The question being taken upon this resolution by States, it resulted —yeas 138, nays 112½—as follows:

YEAS—Maine 5½, New Hampshire 2½, Vermont 3, Massachusetts 3, Rhode Island 4, Connecticut 3½, New York 35, New Jersey 1½, Pennsylvania 9½, Maryland 2½, Missouri 4, Ohio 23, Indiana 13, Illinois 11, Michigan 6, Wisconsin 5, Iowa 3½, Minnesota 2½—138.

NAYS—Maine 2½, New Hampshire 2½, Vermont 2, Massachusetts 8½, Connecticut 2½, New Jersey 4½, Pennsylvania 17½, Delaware 2, Maryland 5½, Virginia 15, North Carolina 10, Arkansas 1, Missouri 5, Tennessee 12, Kentucky 12, Iowa 1½, Minnesota 1½, California 4, Oregon 3—112½.

The resolution was accordingly adopted.

Mr. Stuart of Michigan—I move to reconsider the vote just taken, and to lay that motion upon the table.

The President—The chair will receive and enter the motion, to be disposed of at a future time.

Mr. Stuart—I make the same motions upon each of the other votes that have preceded, including the vote upon the minority report, in order that the motions may be entered as distinct motions.

The President—The chair receives the motions to reconsider and to lay on the table, and the Secretary will enter them, and note the propositions to which they apply.

The 7th resolution was then read, as follows:

7. *Resolved*, That John O'Fallon, Jr., who was duly admitted at Charleston as a delegate from the Eighth Congressional District of Missouri, is still entitled to said seat in this Convention; and that John B. Clardy, who has assumed said seat, is not entitled thereto.

The question being then taken by States upon the resolution, it resulted—yeas 138½, nays 112—as follows:

YEAS—Maine 5½, New Hampshire 2½, Vermont 3, Massachusetts 5, Rhode Island 4, Connecticut 3½, New York 35, New Jersey 1½, Pennsylvania 10, Maryland 2½, Arkansas ½, Missouri 1½, Ohio 23, Indiana 13, Illinois 11, Michigan 6, Wisconsin 5, Iowa 3½, Minnesota 2½—138½.

NAYS—Maine 2½, New Hampshire 2½, Vermont 2, Massachusetts 8, Connecticut 2½, New Jersey 5½, Pennsylvania 17, Delaware 2, Maryland 5½, Virginia 15, North Carolina 10, Arkansas 1½, Missouri 6, Tennessee 12, Kentucky 12, Iowa 1½, Minnesota 1½, California 4, Oregon 3—112.

The resolution was accordingly adopted.

Mr. Cessna of Pennsylvania moved that the vote just taken be reconsidered, and that the motion to reconsider be laid upon the table.

The motion was received and ordered to be entered upon the journal.

The 8th resolution was then read, as follows:

8. *Resolved*, That R. A. Barker, D. C. Humphrey, John Forsyth, Wm. Garrett, J. J. Seivels, S. C. Posey, L. E. Parsons, Joseph C. Bradley, Thomas B. Cooper, James Williams, O. H. Bynum, Samuel W. Wheatley, L. V. B. Martin, John W. Warrack, W. R. R. Wyatt, Benjamin Harrison, Thomas M. Mathews and Norment McLeod, are entitled to seats in this Convention as delegates from the State of Alabama.

The question being then taken by States upon this resolution, it resulted—yeas 148½, nays 101½—as follows:

YEAS—Maine 5½, New Hampshire 2½, Vermont 4½, Massachusetts 5, Rhode Island 4, Connecticut 3½, New York 35, New Jersey 3, Pennsylvania 10, Maryland 2, Virginia ½, North Carolina 1½, Arkansas ½, Missouri 4, Tennesssee 2, Kentucky 1½, Ohio 23, Indiana 13, Illinois 11, Michigan 6, Wisconsin 5, Iowa 4, Minnesota 2½—148½.

NAYS—Maine 2½, New Hampshire 2, Vermont ½, Massachusetts 8, Connecticut 2½, New Jersey 4, Pennsylvania 17, Delaware 2, Maryland 6, Virginia 14½, North Carolina 8½, Arkansas ½, Missouri 5, Tennessee 10, Kentucky 10½, Minnesota 1½, California 4, Oregon 3—101½.

New Hampshire ½ declined voting.

The resolution was accordingly adopted.

Mr. Cessna of Pennsylvania moved to reconsider the vote just taken, and that that motion be laid upon the table.

The motion was received and ordered to be entered upon the journal.

The 9th and last resolution of the series was then read, as follows:

9. *Resolved*, That the delegation from the State of Georgia, of which H. L.

Benning is chairman, be admitted to the Convention, with power to cast one-half of the vote of said State; and that the delegation from said State, of which Col. Gardner is chairman, be also admitted to the Convention, with power to cast one-half of the vote of said State, and if either of said delegations refuse or neglect to cast the vote as above indicated, that in such case the delegates present in the Convention be authorized to cast the full vote of said State.

There was a contest as to whether this resolution was divisible. The chair ruled that it was divisible.

Mr. Atkins of Tennessee—I trust the Convention will proceed to consummate its work. [Applause.] We have nearly completed this work, and I hope that no gentleman opposed to these resolutions will interpose any thing to delay the work of this Convention. [Applause and hisses.] The man that hisses is a viper and a coward. [Applause.]

Mr. Seward of Georgia attempted to obtain the floor, and presented a letter which he wished read. Objections were made and it was not read.

[It was understood that the letter was from Col. Gardner, the chairman of the contesting delegation from the State of Georgia, notifying the Convention that they withdrew from all further contest.]

Mr. Jones of Tennessee—At the request of several gentlemen I withdraw my call for a division of the question.

The President stated the question to be upon agreeing to the entire resolution, as originally reported by the Secretary to the Convention.

The question being then taken by States upon the resolution, it was rejected—yeas $106\frac{1}{2}$, nays 145—as follows:

YEAS—Maine 4, New Hampshire 2, Vermont $3\frac{1}{4}$, Massachusetts 5, Rhode Island 4, Connecticut $3\frac{3}{4}$, New Jersey 2, Pennsylvania $9\frac{1}{2}$, Maryland 2, Virginia 1, North Carolina 1, Arkansas $\frac{1}{2}$, Missouri 4, Ohio 23, Indiana 13, Illinois 11, Michigan 6, Wisconsin 5, Iowa 4, Minnesota $2\frac{1}{2}$—$106\frac{1}{2}$.

NAYS—Maine 4, New Hampshire 3, Vermont $1\frac{3}{4}$, Massachusetts 8, Connecticut $8\frac{1}{4}$, New York 35, New Jersey 5, Pennsylvania $17\frac{1}{2}$, Delaware 2, Maryland 6, Virginia 14, North Carolina 9, Arkansas $\frac{1}{2}$, Missouri 5, Tennessee 12, Kentucky $11\frac{3}{4}$, Minnesota $1\frac{1}{2}$, California 4, Oregon 3—145.

During all this voting the Convention was strangely silent. "Not a drum was heard, nor a funeral note." There was not a rattle of applause nor a hiss for an hour and a half.

The vote of New York—"thirty-five no," in the case of Georgia, caused a buzz of astonishment.

Mr. Church of New York said his delegation had no opportunity to vote on the admission of delegates from Georgia, as they deemed right, and they now proposed to make a motion that the delegates from Georgia, of which Mr. H. L. Benning is chairman, be admitted to seats in the Convention.

Mr. Hallett of Massachusetts (author of the Cincinnati Platform) got the floor and made a speech, though Stuart of Michigan raised points of order on him. The parliamentary contest was highly interesting. Mr. Hallett had, however, voted with the majority on the ninth proposition, and had moved to reconsider. In the midst of the confusion, the main question was put on the resolution admitting the delegation, of which Mr. Benning of Georgia was chairman, to seats, and it was adopted.

Mr. Hallett was again recognized on the floor, and made his speech, explaining the circumstances of the contest for his seat. He entered into the general subject, saying:

And you are now upon the eve of what? After having severed your Convention from eight of the Southern States, you are now upon the very verge—are about to consummate that blow—which shall send out the other six or seven States, and then what is this Convention? Nay, what is the great Democratic party of this Union? Nay, in God's name, what is the Union itself?

He appealed to New York to come forward and save the country. He said:

When the great question is, shall you have any Union to which we can give a President, and shall you have any Democratic party to elect a President, why not then come forward, young men, and sustain this measure of reconciliation and sustain the Union? Let it not be broken up. I say to you this is no light matter. I say to you the impending crisis is only the more awful because it is silent. It is hushed, it is true, but it is here all around me. You know, sir, every honorable man knows, that if the resolutions of that committee which I am now desiring to be reconsidered prevail in this Convention, that you have a dissevered Convention. The States that are standing knocking at your doors will never come in and pass under the yoke. Southern chivalry will prevent that. [Applause.] The States that are here now will adhere to the Democratic Union, or they will adhere to their own South. They will never stay here to the disgrace of their brother States outside. [Applause.]

And then what will you do? Make a nomination?—a nomination which, tendered to any man, is but the ruin of that man, and the ruin of that party which desires it. I stand here to-day a personal friend of the man whose friends are about to sacrifice him, as I view it. [Laughter and applause.] Ah, I would rather see him elevated to the Presidency than any other man in this Union, if it could be done without the destruction of this party—without the dissolution of this Convention. But no—men here say, let us have this man or none; we will have no other but him. Where is the discriminating justice which shall impel you to the adjustment of this great question?

Mr. Hallett moved that the Convention take a recess until five o'clock.

Mr. Stuart of Michigan moved to lay the motions to reconsider upon the table. This was a movement to consummate the action of the Convention on the report from the committee on Credentials.

Mr. Russell, chairman of the Virginia delegation—Mr. President, I wish, before the Convention adjourns, to make an announcement in behalf of the Virginia delegation. I wish to do it at the proper time. [Sensation.]

This was the announcement of Virginia that she was about to lead the column of the new secession.

A motion, that when the Convention adjourn it be to meet at five o'clock in the afternoon, was put, the vote taken by States, and lost—yeas 82¼, nays 168.

Mr. Cessna of Pennsylvania called up the several motions to reconsider, with the accompanying motions to lay on the table.

The President stated the first question to be upon laying upon the table the motion to reconsider the vote by which the Convention refused to substitute the resolutions reported by the minority of the committee on Credentials for those reported by the majority of said committee.

Upon this question the State of Tennessee demanded a vote by States, which was ordered.

The question being then taken by States, the motion to lay on the table was not agreed to—yeas 113¾, nays 138½—as follows:

YEAS—Maine 5¼, New Hampshire 3, Vermont 4½, Massachusetts 5, Rhode Island 4, Connecticut 3½, New Jersey 3¼, Pennsylvania 10, Maryland 2, North Carolina 1, Arkansas ¼, Missouri 4½, Kentucky 2, Ohio 23, Indiana 13, Illinois 11, Michigan 6, Wisconsin 5, Iowa 4, Minnesota 2½—113½.

NAYS—Maine 2½, New Hampshire 2, Vermont ½, Massachusetts 8, Connecticut 2½, New York 35, New Jersey 3½, Pennsylvania 17, Delaware 2, Maryland 6, Virginia 15, North Carolina 9, Arkansas ½, Missouri 4½, Tennessee 12, Kentucky 10, Minnesota 1¼, California 4, Oregon 3—138½.

And so at the last moment New York flinched from the consummation of the work preparatory to the division of the Convention. Her vote, cast in the negative on this ballot, left the question still open, that is, the action taken by the Convention might be reconsidered. There was an intense sensation in the Convention, and a recess until seven o'clock in the evening was immediately taken.

During this recess, the interest of the thousands of politicians concentrated in Baltimore, and indeed of the whole country within reach of the telegraph, was wrought up to the highest pitch. The New York delegation was denounced on every side as composed of tricksters and bargainers. The friends of Douglas lost faith in them, and emulated the Southerners in showering epithets upon them.

A rumor of a despatch from Douglas to Dean Richmond, virtually withdrawing his name, leaked out. Its existence was fiercely denied by the straight Douglas men. Richardson was very emphatic in saying there was not one word of truth in the report; and many disbelieved it, because they believed Richardson to be the only medium through which Douglas would communicate with the Convention. Friends of Richardson said it would be a personal insult to him, if Douglas should despatch to Dean Richmond. There was a despatch, however, as afterward appeared. It was as follows:

WASHINGTON June 22d—9½ A. M.

To DEAN RICHMOND, Chairman of Delegation, Baltimore:

The steadiness with which New York has sustained me will justify a word of counsel. The safety of the cause is the paramount duty of every Democrat. The unity of the party and the maintenance of its principles inviolate are more important than the election or defeat of any individual. If my enemies are determined to divide and destroy the Democratic party, and, perhaps, the country, rather than see me elected, and if the unity of the party can be preserved, and its ascendancy perpetuated by dropping my name and uniting upon some other reliable Non-intervention and Union-loving Democrat, I beseech you, in consultation with our friends, to pursue that course which will save the party and the country, without regard to my individual interests. I mean all this letter implies. Consult freely and act boldly for the right.

(Signed)   S. A. DOUGLAS.

It would appear that this was sent to Richmond, because a letter containing similar suggestions, had been forwarded to Richardson, who kept it in his pocket. Douglas finding that Richardson would not communicate his wish to withdraw to the Convention, telegraphed to Richmond, who suppressed the despatch, as Richardson had suppressed the letter.

It was asserted in Baltimore, and believed in political circles, that during this recess New York offered to reconsider her vote on the Louisiana case, and make up the Convention out of the original materials, with the exception of the Alabama delegation. They could not agree to admit Yancey & Co. But the seceders and their friends would not bear to any such proposition. They scorned all compromise, assuming that their rights were undoubted and their title clear; they would not bargain away any portion whatever of their claims.

EVENING SESSION.

The long looked-for "Crisis" a hundred times postponed, arrived at last. The Convention was called to order a few minutes after seven o'clock.

The President stated the pending question to be upon reconsidering the vote by which the Convention refused to substitute the resolutions submitted upon the part of the minority of the committee on Credentials in place of the resolutions submitted by the majority of said committee.

The question being taken by States, the motion to reconsider was not agreed to—yeas 113, nays 139—as follows:

YEAS—Maine $2\frac{1}{2}$, New Hampshire 2, Vermont 1, Massachusetts 8, Connecticut $2\frac{1}{2}$, New Jersey $4\frac{1}{2}$, Pennsylvania 17, Delaware 2, Maryland 6, Virginia 15, North Carolina 9, Arkansas $\frac{1}{2}$, Missouri $4\frac{1}{2}$, Tennessee 10, Kentucky 10, Minnesota $1\frac{1}{2}$, California 4, Oregon 3—113.

NAYS—Maine $5\frac{1}{2}$, New Hampshire 3, Vermont 4, Massachusetts 5, Rhode Island 4, Connecticut $3\frac{1}{2}$, New York 35, New Jersey $2\frac{1}{2}$, Pennsylvania 10, Maryland 2, North Carolina 1, Arkansas $\frac{1}{2}$, Missouri $4\frac{1}{2}$, Tennessee 2, Kentucky 2, Ohio 23, Indiana 13, Illinois 11, Michigan 6, Wisconsin 5, Iowa 4, Minnesota $2\frac{1}{2}$,—139.

New York's "Thirty five votes no" given in the quick sharp tones of Peter Cagger, settled this as all other contested questions. The motions to reconsider the votes by which the resolutions of the majority report had been adopted, and to lay those motions on the table, were now in order. Upon those motions being carried the action in each case was final and irrevocable.

The motion to lay on the table the motion to reconsider the vote by which the Convention adopted the resolution of the majority report of the committee, on the State of Mississippi, was carried without a division.

The next question was upon the motion to lay upon the table the motion to reconsider the vote by which the Convention adopted the majority resolution in relation to delegates from Louisiana.

The question being taken by States, the motion to lay on the table was agreed to—yeas 150½, nays 99—as follows:

YEAS—Maine 5¼, New Hampshire 4½, Vermont 4½, Massachusetts 5, Rhode Island 4, Connecticut 3¼, New York 35, New Jersey 2¼, Pennsylvania 10, Maryland 2, North Carolina 1, Arkansas ½, Missouri 4, Tennessee 2, Kentucky 2, Ohio 23, Indiana 13, Illinois 11, Michigan 6, Wisconsin 5, Iowa 4, Minnesota 2½—150½.

NAYS—Maine 2½, New Hampshire 1½, Vermont ½, Massachusetts 8, Connecticut 2½, New Jersey 4½, Pennsylvania 17, Delaware 2, Maryland 6, Virginia 15, North Carolina 8¼, Arkansas 1½, Missouri 4¼, Tennessee 10, Kentucky 10, Minnesota 1½, California 4, Oregon 3—99.

The next question was upon laying upon the table the motion to reconsider the vote by which the Convention adopted the majority resolution in relation to delegates from Arkansas.

The question being taken, the motion was agreed to.

The next question was upon same motion in relation to Texas.

The question being taken, the motion to reconsider was laid upon the table.

The next question was upon the same motion in relation to Delaware, and the motion to lay upon the table was agreed to.

The same with regard to the resolution in relation to Massachusetts, and the resolution in relation to Missouri.

The next question was upon the motion to lay upon the table the motion to reconsider the vote upon the resolution in relation to Alabama—the motion was agreed to.

The same with regard to the vote of the Convention, rejecting the resolution of the majority in relation to Georgia.

The same with regard to the resolution of Mr. Church of New York, admitting original delegation from Georgia.

Mr Cessna of Pennsylvania—I now offer the following resolution:

Resolved, That this Convention do now proceed to nominate candidates for President and Vice-President of the United States,

And on that resolution I call the previous question.

Mr. Stansbury of Maryland moved to adjourn *sine die.*

Mr. McKibben of Pennsylvania seconded the motion. New York demanded a vote by States. The motion was withdrawn.

Mr. Russell of Virginia had been for some time standing, very pale, nervous and solemn, in his chair, and now obtained the ear of the chair and the Convention, and desired to make an "announcement." Mr. Gorman of Minnesota objected to the gentleman's proceeding, and emphatically refused to withdraw his objection. The President desired to hear what proposition it was that the gentleman from Virginia had to make. Mr. Russell at length said:

I understand that the action of this Convention upon the various questions arising out of the reports from the committee on Credentials, has become final, complete and irrevocable And it has become my duty now, by direction of a large majority of the delegation from Virginia, respectfully to inform this body that it is inconsistent with their convictions of duty to participate longer in its deliberations.

There was a mingled din of applause and hisses, cries of order, of a highly sensational character. The greater tumult, so far as the galleries were concerned, seemed to be that of approbation—the Douglas outside pressure having for some days subsided rapidly. The chair ordered the galleries cleared. He did not, however, attempt to enforce the order. The disorder lasted some minutes.

Mr. Russell remained standing, and when his voice could be heard, said that all of the delegates to whom tickets of admission had been issued, who were regarded as National Democrats by the Democracy of Virginia, would refuse to enter the hall. The reasons which impelled the representatives of the State of Virginia to leave the Convention, would be rendered to the Democracy of Virginia, and to them alone. The Virginians, with a few exceptions, when Mr. Russell ceased speaking, rose in a body, and passing into the aisles, proceeded to leave the theater, shaking hands and bidding personal friends good by, as they retired.

Mr. Moffatt, one of those who remained, commenced a speech, but gave way to Mr. Lander of North Carolina, who announced that eight out of the ten votes of that State retired. He said:

The rights of sovereign States and of gentlemen of the South, have been denied by a majority of this body. We cannot act, as we conceive, in view of this wrong.

Mr. Ewing of Tennessee announced that ten out of the twelve votes of that State retired to consult. He spoke of the disposition of the Tennessee delegation to harmonize. "They were the first, when the majority platform was not adopted, to seek for some proposition for compromise—something that would enable us to harmonize. They have a candidate that was dear to them. They cast away his prospect for the sake of harmony. They have yielded all that they can."

Col. Caldwell, chairman of the Kentucky delegation, asked leave to retire to consult. Mr. Stuart of Michigan objected, for the reason that business could not be transacted while a State was absent by permission of the Convention. It being understood that the delegation wished to retire but for a few minutes, Mr. Stuart withdrew his objection.

Mr. McKibben—Mr. President, I want to understand if the gentleman from Michigan is the manager of the theatre? [Laughter.]

[The point of this inquiry was the fact that the Douglas men followed implicitly the directions and suggestions of Mr. Stuart, who was so sharp a parliamentarian and adroit manager, that even the chairman (Cushing) was believed to regard him with something of dread. It is certain that Mr. Cushing always gave attention to Mr. Stuart, and usually yielded to him on contested points. Mr. Stuart's points of order were almost always admirably taken.]

Mr. Johnson of Maryland made a speech withdrawing half the delegation from that State. He said:

We have made all sacrifices for the grand old Democratic party, whose mission it has been to preserve the Constitution and to cure for the Republic for more than sixty years, until it now seems as if you were going to substitute a man in the place of principle. [Calls to order.] I desire to be respectful. I desire to say that the action of the majority of the late Convention—a majority created by the operation of a technical unit rule imposed upon the Convention, contrary to Democratic precedent and usage—States have been disfranchised and districts deprived of their rights, until, in our opinion, it is no longer consistent with our honor or our rights, or the rights of our constituents, to remain here.

Mr. Glass of Virginia withdrew himself from the Convention.

Mr. Waterson of Tennessee, one of the delegates from that State who had declined to secede, said there were some gallant spirits from the land of Jackson who would remain. He had no fears that the Convention would refuse to indorse the Cincinnati Platform.

Mr. Jones of Tennessee hoped that the delegates of that State who had retired to consult, would find their way back into the Convention. Mr. Jones said he had been a Democrat ever since he first drew milk from his mother's breast.

Mr. Smith of California said:

While I cannot say with the gentleman from Tennessee (Mr. Jones) that my Democracy dates back to that time of which I have no recollection, yet I can say that it is as unspotted as the vault of heaven. California is here with melancholy faces. [Laughter.] California is here with a lacerated heart, bleeding and weeping over the downfall and destruction of the Democratic party. [Applause and laughter.] Yes, sir, the destruction of the Democratic party, consummated by assassins now grinning upon this floor. [Loud cries of "Order," "order," "Put him out," and great confusion.]

Mr. Smith, "in no spirit of braggadocia," said that "if any one took exceptions, he knew his remedy." He proceeded:

This Convention has properly been held in a theatre, and upon that stage a play has been enacted this evening that will prove a tragedy of which the Democratic party will be the victim. [Mingled hisses and applause.] I then do state that there have been wrongs perpetrated upon the Democracy of that deep and damning character that it does not permit California longer to participate in the proceedings of this irregular organization. [Laughter.] Irregular! and why irregular? Irregular because there has not been a single affirmative proposition carried through this body that has not been done through a resolution that cannot be characterized by any other term than that used by a delegate from Illinois—a trick. [Loud cries of "Order," "order," and great confusion.]

Mr. Merrick of Illinois demanded the name of the delegate referred to from that State, and what he said. After a protracted scene of confusion, Mr. Smith remarked that the Convention acted very much like a child taking medicine. He said:

I will repeat, without the fear of the slightest contradiction, that the resolution passed at Charleston, known as the "Cessna resolution," by virtue of which the minority of this Convention have been enabled to cast the majority vote, and thus beating down or carrying through and enacting every measure that has been so repulsive to the delegates who have withdrawn—I say that that resolution was acknowledged in substance to me to be a deliberate, willful, premeditated trick.

This was received with roars of disorder. There was wild excitement, and a tempest of calls to order. Mr. Smith yelled that he would say what he had to say, and the Convention should hear him. Mr. Merrick of Illinois was upon a chair, crying, "Name the delegate from Illinois"—"tell us what he said." The chair declared Smith out of order. His time under the fifteen minute rule had expired. He insisted that the time taken up in interruptions should not come out of his time. He was as hard to choke off as a bull-dog, but all the Douglas men in the house, aided by the President, succeeded in getting him down, when he retired at the head of the Oregon delegation.

Mr. Stevens of Oregon rose. He had "a most melancholy duty to perform." He had not allowed his feelings to get the better of his judgment. He concluded by saying:

We did hope, when this Convention reassembled at Baltimore, that it would bring together the Democratic party in every sovereign State.

We find ourselves grievously mistaken. By your action to-day, gentlemen as much entitled to seats as ourselves, in our opinion, are excluded from the floor. We do not mean to impugn the motives of others, but are conscious that a most grievous wrong and insult has been given to sovereign States. These States are the weak parties in this contest, and we have resolved to stand by them and assert their rights. I now announce that the delegation from Oregon have come to the conclusion to withdraw from the deliberations and take no further part in them.

Mr. Moffat of Virginia, who had sought the floor for some time, now obtained it. He made an eloquent speech, saying of the representatives of Virginia—"We were thirty when we came in—now we are but five." He said he would stand by that Convention through weal and through woe. He said:

I am an out-and-out pro-slavery man. I believe in the institution all the time. I believe it is right morally, socially and politically. I have fought in my State for the extension of pro-slavery views. I am a Southern man, and interested with the people of Virginia in having protection for our property. I ask you who are true to us in the North, not to desert us, but to stand by and defend us henceforth as you have done in times past [voices, "We'll do it,"], and so help me God, I will defend you as long as I have confidence in you. [Loud applause, and cries of "Good," "good."] I will never fight my friends.

In the name of common sense, have not we enough of higher law, revolutionary, abolition scoundrels in the North to fight, without fighting our friends? [Applause.] Must we fight the men who stood on the platform at Cincinnati in 1856, and kick them off and break up the Democratic party?

Mr. Davis of Virginia made a speech. He was a Henry A. Wise

man. He said he could not see how Judge Douglas could be the nominee of the Convention. He came to Baltimore to try to prevent it, at any rate. He meant to fight inside the Democratic party. He believed Gov. Wise, if nominated, could carry Virginia by 30,000 votes. He would be for Wise first, last, and all the time, if he were permitted to present his name, but he was not so authorized.

Here a motion was made to adjourn and a vote by States called on it. Ayes 18½—nays 210½.

Mr. Cessna of Pennsylvania—I now ask the chair to ascertain from the Convention whether or not there is a second to my demand for the previous question upon the resolution to proceed to ballot for candidates for the Presidency and Vice Presidency.

Mr. Clark of Missouri asked permission for a portion of the delegation of that State to retire and consult. He also asked for an adjournment.

Mr. Cessna of Pennsylvania was willing to adjourn when the previous question on his motion should be seconded and the main question ordered to be now put.

After some consultation, it was concluded that the demand for the previous question had been seconded. This was a mistake, but it made no difference as it was received as authority by common consent.

Mr. Craig of Missouri said he was not willing to follow his distinguished friend Clark out of a Democratic Convention. Whereupon Mr. Clark announced that his purpose was fixed to remain in the Convention.

Senator Saulsbury of Delaware was instructed by the delegation of that State to announce that they desire to be excused from voting on any further ballots or votes, unless circumstances should alter this determination. He said: It is our desire to be left free to act or not act, our desire being to leave the question open for the consideration of our constituents after we return home.

Mr. Gaulden of Georgia made his Charleston slave-trade and slave-breeding speech again. He announced himself a slave breeder. He had not joined his fortunes to either the house of York or the house of Lancaster. He said:

I have felt that the experiment of man for self-government was about to prove a failure here, and that the genius of liberty was about shrieking to leave the world.

I am an advocate for maintaining the integrity of the National Democratic party; I belong to the extreme South; I am a pro-slavery man in every sense of the word, aye, and an African slave-trade man. [Applause and laughter.] This institution of slavery, as I have said elsewhere, has done more to advance the prosperity and intelligence of the white race, and of the human race, than all else together. I believe it to be founded upon the law of nature and upon the law of God; I believe it to be a blessing to all races. I believe that liberty would not truly exist in this Western World except by maintaining the integrity of the great National Democratic party. [Applause.]

He spoke of the " slave-breeding and slave-trading State of Virginia," when a delegate from Virginia called him to order for casting an imputation upon the State of Virginia. Gaulden thought he had been paying Virginia a high compliment. He said:

Well, I will say the slave-breeding State of Georgia, then. I glory in being a slave-breeder myself. [Loud laughter.] I will face the music myself, and I have got as many negroes as any man from the State of Virginia. And as I invited the gentlemen of this Convention at Charleston to visit my plantation, I will say again that if they will come to see me, I will show them as fine a lot of negroes, and the pure African, too, as they can find any where. And I will show them as handsome a set of little children there as can be seen [laughter], and any quantity of them, too. [Renewed laughter.] And I wish that Virginia may be as good a slave-trading and slave-breeding State as Georgia; and in saying that, I do not mean to be disrespectful to Virginia, but I do not mean to dodge the question at all.

I think I shall live to see the day when the doctrines which I advocate to-night will be the doctrines of Massachusetts and of the North, for

> "Truth crushed to earth will rise again,
> The eternal years of God are hers;
> While error, wounded, writhes in pain
> And dies amid her worshipers."

I say I go for non-intervention in the broadest sense of the term.

Mr. Gaulden's speech was generally laughed at, but he was in sober and resolute earnest. He is quite a Yankee in appearance, tall, straight, sharp-nosed and keen-eyed, and vigorous as a black-snake. Nothing delights him more than to tell of the swarms of young niggers on his plantation.

Mr. Ewing of Tennessee here announced: Mr. President, the majority of the delegation from Tennesssee, who asked the indulgence of this Convention to retire for consultation, have done so, and as the result of their deliberations I have to announce that nineteen out of twenty-four representatives have decided to retire, and five to remain.

Mr. Steele of North Carolina had not seen cause for going out of the Convention.

Mr. Claiborne of Missouri made a speech. He said:

To-day, for the first time in the history of Democracy, I have seen the mother of States starting madly from a National Convention. I am a Southern man, born and raised beneath the sunny sky of the South. Not a drop of blood in my veins ever flowed in veins north of Mason's and Dixon's line. My ancestors for 300 years sleep beneath the turf that shelters the bones of Washington, and I thank God that they rest in the graves of honest slaveholders. [Applause.]

He had once in his life bolted from a Convention, and it came very near proving his political death. He found that he had fallen about seventeen hundred feet in the estimation of his constituents when he returned home, and he predicted that a similar fate awaited all who should secede from this National Convention.

He spoke in the most enthusiastic manner of Mr. Douglas. He talked of the Scottish Chieftain, Lord James of Douglas, carrying to the man of Palestine the heart of Bruce encased in a golden box, throwing it into the ranks of the enemy and fighting his way to it. Even so Stephen A. Douglas, with the Constitution, would go into the ranks of the enemy. He said: Sir, if there is any thing the Southern Democracy dislike, it is the fossil remains of Whiggery and Know-Nothingism [laughter]; and I tell you when it is known to the people of the South that it is the design of the Seceders to defeat the old time-honored Democracy in this way, they will dodge them as they dodge lightning. [Laughter.] He promised twenty-five thousand majority for Douglas in Missouri.

After some remarks by Mr. Clark of Missouri, who wished to consult, there were cries of question; and the motion, "Shall the main question be now put," to go into a nomination of candidates for President and Vice-President, was carried.

The President—The motion has been carried. Will the Convention now vote upon the main question?

Mr. Cessna of Pennsylvania—I move an adjournment.

Cries of "No, no."

Mr. Clarke—I will claim the right to make the statement I proposed in the morning.

The President—A motion to adjourn has been made. All who are in favor of it will vote aye, etc.

The vote being taken *viva voce*, the President decided that the question had been determined in the affirmative, whereupon the Convention, at 10:30 P. M., adjourned.

SIXTH DAY.

BALTIMORE, June 23d.

We had from this time forth a divided Convention—one sitting in the theatre, and one in the Maryland Institute. Both claimed regularity, and to be the National Democratic Convention. The controversy was animated as that respecting Townsend's Sarsaparilla. Perhaps the record will show the facts. There seemed to be a lull in the excitement after adjournment on the fifth day. The deed was done. The disruption of the Convention was a fixed fact. The case was beyond the power of medicine or surgery. Consequently there was a comparative calm.

There was the usual double-headed mass meeting in Monument Square, but its spirit had evaporated. The private cursing was not loud but deep. The public speaking was rather loud than deep. The meeting was adjourned by a crowd of Baltimoreans with "Three cheers for Bell and Everett."

IN THE THEATRE

This morning, the first thing in order after prayers, was the report of the decision of the Kentucky delegation. Col. Caldwell stated the determination arrived at in very gentlemanly and respectful terms, and withdrew the name of James Guthrie. A communication from Mr.

James G. Leach of Kentucky was read. It stated his reasons for withdrawing, and was couched in terms that reflected severely upon the action of the Convention.

Mr. Payne of Ohio considered the communication insulting. Several other gentlemen thought the Convention had been insulted.

Mr. Leach said he had intended no disrespect to the Convention, and he thought it a morbidly sensitive body to take offense.

The following gentlemen from the Kentucky delegation, N. W. Williamson, G. A. Caldwell, delegates for the State at large, W. Bradley, Samuel B. Field, Thos. J. Young, presented a series of resolutions, setting forth that without intending to vacate their seats, and hoping, for the restoration of unity and harmony, they would decline to participate longer in the action of the Convention and would not hold themselves or constituents bound by its action.

The following was also presented:

Resolved, That the chairman of our delegation be instructed to inform the Convention in our behalf that in the present condition of that body we deem it inconsistent with our duty to ourselves and our constituents to participate further in its deliberations. Our reasons for so doing will be given to the Democracy of Kentucky.

Jno. Dishman,	L. Green,
J. S. Kindrick,	R. M Johnson,
Jos. B. Beck,	Cal. Butler,
D. W. Quarles,	R. McKee,
Colbert Cecil,	Jas. G. Leach.

Mr. Reed of Kentucky was happy to say there were nine delegates from that State, who saw no cause for the disturbance of the harmony of the Convention. He said:

I read in the history of the ancient city of the plain that an angel of the Lord was sent to inquire whether there were any righteous men to be found that that city might be saved, the promise being that if five could be found it should not be destroyed. [Applause.] I am happy to say that from Kentucky there are not only five but nine men who will stand by this Convention. [Applause.] It is a Democratic Convention. It belongs to the Democratic party. We, of Kentucky, stand here opposing secession and sectionalism North and South. We will stand with you as a wall of fire in opposing both extremes. I am not going to abandon the Convention because it is apparent that one of our glorious chieftains is not likely to receive the nomination. [Applause.] No, I have gratitude in my heart to the man whose pathway from the city of Washington to his house in the far West is lighted by his own effigies. [Applause.] We in Kentucky owe to him, and to the North and West, our homes and firesides. Gentlemen who own a hundred slaves each, say I am right. I will go home to my constituents and to the campaign, and camp-fires will be lighted in the mountains and valleys, and in less than seventy days you will hear a shout that will turn the course of affairs and set things right. [Applause.] We will take this matter out of the hands of politicians and the Administration and return it to the people. He concluded by putting in nomination again "Mr. Guthrie, Kentucky's favorite son."

Mr. Clark of Missouri announced that two of the delegation of that State had concluded to retire from the Convention. Mr. Clark reiterated his fixed purpose of remaining in the Convention, if it followed in its action "the usages of the Democratic party."

Mr. Hill of North Carolina retired from the Convention, because he held a seat under the same circumstances as Mr. Hallett of Massachusetts had held his. As Mr. Hallett had been ousted, he could not in honor remain, though his alternate did not claim his seat.

Mr. Moore of Delaware was anxious to make some remarks.

Mr. McCook of Ohio objected.

Mr. Jones of Tennessee said that instead of 19 only 13 of the delegates from that State had retired from the Convention.

Several leading Douglas men now insisted upon choking off debate, and as the main question had been ordered to be now put, nothing could be said without general consent. The President had received two papers, and deemed it his duty to communicate them to the Convention. One paper was signed by Mr. Stirman of Arkansas. The other was from the delegation of Georgia.

Mr. Stirman of Arkansas desired to state why he retired from the Convention. Objection was made and insisted upon.

Mr. Cessna of Pennsylvania called for the vote upon his resolution to ballot for candidates for President and Vice-President.

The President—Gentlemen of the Convention, a motion has been made by the gentleman from Pennsylvania (Mr. Cessna), to the consideration of which the chair will now proceed.

But before doing so, I beg the indulgence of the Convention to say that whilst deeply sensible of the honor done me by the Convention in placing me in this chair, I was not less deeply sensible of the difficulties, general and personal, looming up in the future to environ my path. Nevertheless, in the solicitude to maintain the harmony and union of the Democratic party, and in the face of the retirement of the delegations of several States, I continued at my post, laboring to that end, and in that sense had the honor to meet you, gentlemen, here in Baltimore. But circumstances have since transpired which compel me to pause. The delegations of a majority of the States of this Union have, either in whole or in part, in one form or another, ceased to participate in the deliberations of this body. At no time would any consideration of candidates have affected my judgment as to my duty. And I came here prepared, regardless of all personal preferences, cordially to support the nominations of this Convention, whosoever they might be. But under the present circumstances I deem it a duty of self-respect, and I deem it still more a duty to this Convention as at present organized—I say I deem it my duty in both relations, whilst tendering my most grateful acknowledgements to gentlemen of all sides, and especially to those gentlemen who may have differed with me in opinion in any respect, whilst tendering my most grateful acknowledgments to all gentlemen for the candid and honorable support which they have given to the chair, even when they differed in opinion upon rulings, and whilst tendering also to the gentlemen present my most cordial respects and regards, not knowing a single gentleman upon this floor as to whom I have other than sentiments of cordiality and friendship—I deem it my duty to resign my seat as presiding officer of this Convention. [Applause.] I deem it my duty to resign my place as presiding officer of this Convention in order to take my seat on the floor as a member of the delegation of Massachusetts, and to abide whatever may be its determination in regard to its further action in this Convention. And I deem this above all a duty I owe to the members of the Convention as to whom my action would no longer represent the will of the majority of the Convention.

When Mr. Cushing used the words "but before doing so" the whole Convention knew what was coming, and every word he uttered was heard by all. The occasion was a severe trial for even the well-trained nerves of Mr. Cushing, and there was, for a moment, slight embarrassment of manner. The North-western delegates cheered him violently as he retired from the chair, and hundreds of spectators cheered him also. The North-westerners wished to express their joy in getting rid of him. The spectators desired to show that they approved his course.

Gov. David Todd of Ohio, one of the Vice-Presidents, took the chair, and as he rapped to order, the friends of Mr. Douglas, seeing their way clear (through the Convention), cheered enthusiastically. Gov. Todd said, as soon as he could be heard:

As the present presiding officer of this Convention by common consent of my brother Vice-Presidents, with great diffidence I assume the chair. When I announce to you that for thirty-four years I have stood up in that district so long misrepresented by Joshua R. Giddings, with the Democratic Banner in my hand [applause], I know that I shall receive the good wishes of this Convention, at least, for the discharge of the duties of the chair. If there are no privileged questions intervening, the Secretary will proceed with the call of the States.

Mr. Butler of Massachusetts was now anxious to obtain the floor, the object being to withdraw the majority of the delegation of his State. The Douglas men flew into a tempest of passion, and shouted "order," and "object." Todd thought it his business to force a vote instantly, and insisted that the Secretary should proceed to call the States—consequently the Secretary shrieked out the names of States, in the din of an indescribable confusion. There were partial responses from some of them which could hardly be heard, and the Convention seemed rapidly becoming a roaring mob. Gavit, chairman of the Indiana delegation, jumped up and moved that the Convention give Massachusetts leave to retire, and give her three cheers for going.

When the State of Massachusetts was called for a vote, however, Mr. Butler had the opportunity of stating the desire of the majority of the Massachusetts delegation to withdraw. He said:

We have not discussed the question, Mr. President, whether the action of the Convention, in excluding certain delegates, could be any reason for withdrawal. We now put our withdrawal before you, upon the simple ground, among others, that there has been a withdrawal in part of a majority of the States, and further (and that, perhaps, more personal to myself), upon the ground that I will not sit in a Convention where the African slave-trade—which is piracy by the laws of my country—is approvingly advocated.

The Convention laughed at the virtue of Mr. Butler on the subject of the slave trade. He passed out shaking hands right and left, and was loudly cheered on his way. A good many hard things had been said of Mr. Butler, but he had provided himself with a body-guard in the person of Price, the Boston prize-fighter, who stood near with a bulldog expression of countenance, while Mr. Butler was striving for the floor, and speaking.

Mr. Stevens, one of the remaining delegates of Massachusetts, said it was his conviction that he could not leave that Convention without meeting the deepest reprobation of his constituents.

Mr. Brent of Maryland had something to say. Mr. Jones of Pennsylvania insisted sharply, when Mr. Dick of North Carolina commenced a speech, that gentlemen should not make stump speeches in explaining their votes. Dick said his constituents had sent him there, knowing that he would vote for Douglas. Speaking of the parties opposed to the Democracy, he said:

True, one is but a small army, with no ammunition, and with old rusty guns long since condemned. [Laughter.] But the other is a foe to be dreaded. They are falling into line and advancing. They have an experienced chieftain, and above their heads waves the banner of treason and disunion, stained with the blood of Virginia's sons. [Applause.]

A point of order was raised on Mr. Dick by Mr. Jones of Pennsylvania.

Mr. Yost of Virginia threatened to leave the Convention, "as a Douglas man," if Southern delegates were not allowed to explain their votes, and make a record to go before their constituents upon.

The President ruled that Mr. Dick could proceed in spite of objection. It was explained that Mr. Dick was a District Attorney of the United States. Mr. Dick concluded his speech, and cast one vote from North Carolina for Douglas.

Mr. Gaulden of Georgia read a card from the Georgia delegation, stating that he (Gaulden), "in assuming to act as a delegate from the State of Georgia, has violated the instructions of his State, and his *personal pledges* to his colleagues, and has caused mortification and disgust to the delegation from Georgia." Mr. Gaulden had "as much pity and contempt for them, as they could possibly have for him." In concluding, Mr. Gaulden excused himself from voting.

Mr. Parsons of Alabama, in casting the vote of Alabama, said:

You will find a response come up from the Gulf States—the Cotton States—such as never before has been heard since this Republic was established. [Applause.] You have been told by distinguished gentlemen from our State that we do not speak the sentiments of our people. We appeal to the verdict of the ballot-box. We made the issue with them in 1850 and 1851, and we tell them to take warning from the result of that issue.

Pierre Soule now made the speech of the Convention. His rolling, glittering, eagle eye, Napoleonic head and face, sharp voice, with a margin of French accent, and piercing, intense earnestness of manner, commanded profound attention, and fascinated all who saw and heard. His speech was a brilliant and noble effort, and was rapturously applauded to the echo. The effect of this speech was to greatly animate and reassure the friends of Douglas. He said :

I have not been at all discouraged by the emotion which has been attempted to be created in this body, by those who have seceded from it. We from the furthest South were prepared ; we had heard around us the rumors which were to be initiatory of the exit which you have witnessed on this day, and we knew that conspiracy which had been brooding for months past, would break out on this occasion, and for the purposes which are obvious to every member. Sirs, there are in political life men who were once honored by popular favor, who consider that the favor has become to them an inalienable property, and who cling to it as to something that can no longer be wrested from their hands—political fossils so much incrusted in office that there is hardly any power that can extract them. [Applause.] They saw that the popular voice was clearly manifesting to this glorious nation who was to be her next ruler. More than eight or ten months before this Convention assembled, the name of that future ruler of these States had been thrown into the canvass and was before the people. Instead of bringing a candidate to oppose him ; instead of creating before the people issues upon which the choice of the nation could be enlightened ; instead of principles discussed, what have we seen ? An unrelenting war against the individual presumed to be the favorite of the nation [applause]—a war waged by an army of unprincipled and unscrupulous politicians, leagued with a power which could not be exerted on their side without disgracing itself and disgracing the nation. [Renewed applause]

Mr. Soule declared secession meant disunion. He said, however, the South had backed out from its threat made on the California question. He said further :

John C. Calhoun, when the famous compromise tendered by Mr. Clayton of Delaware was being discussed in the United States Senate—John C. Calhoun considered that the proffer to place in the hands of one federal tribunal the question of the extent of power in the Territories was to the South a sufficient guarantee to make acceptable the compromise tendered ; and where Calhoun could stand a Southern man need not fear to stand.

He declared the people of the South would not respond to the call made upon them by the Secessionists. He said Louisiana was unwilling to risk her future, and the future of the Union, upon impracticable issues and merely theoretical abstractions.

Mr. Stirman of Arkansas here withdrew from the Convention. He was sorry to go, but under his instructions, had no alternative.

Mr. Flournoy of Arkansas explained how he happened to be instructed to vote for Breckenridge. He then proceeded in the following eloquent strain :

I am a Southern man, born and reared amid the institution of slavery. I first learned to whirl the top and bounce the ball with the young African. Every thing I own on earth is the result of slave labor.

The bread that feeds my wife and little ones is produced by the labor of slaves. They live on my plantation with every feeling of kindness as between master and slave. Sir, if I could see that there is any thing intended in our platform unfriendly to the institution of slavery—if I could see that we did not get every constitutional right we are entitled to, I would be the last on earth to submit in this Union; I would myself apply the torch to the magazine and blow it into atoms before I would submit to wrong. [Applause.] But I feel that in the doctrine of non-intervention and popular sovereignty are enough to protect the interests of the South.

Mr. Dodge of Iowa made a speech in which he praised Judge Douglas and Col. Richardson extravagantly, and wondered at the hostility displayed toward them by the South.

Before the result of the ballot was announced, Mr. Stoughton challenged the vote of Vermont. He had declined to vote, and yet the whole vote of the State had been cast. Mr. Smith of Vermont contended that, according to instructions, he had the right to cast the whole vote of the State.

As the name of Horatio Seymour had been mentioned and a vote cast for him, Mr. Bissell of New York withdrew the name of Seymour, reading a letter of declension from that gentleman. Mr. Seymour said in his letter:

"I do not suppose my name will be presented on that occasion, but if it is I request that you will, as a delegate from this district, withdraw it from their consideration. I cannot, under any circumstances, be a candidate for the office of President or Vice-President."

Mr. Bissell said:

It is due to Mr. Seymour to say that he has ever expressed to me, his neighbor and friend, the same feeling. Gentlemen have entertained different views; and a paper in New York (I regret to pollute my lips with its name), the New York Herald, has insisted all the time that Mr. Seymour was not honest; but, as his friend and neighbor, I withdraw his name.

A Maryland delegate withdrew his vote for Breckenridge and declined to vote.

RESULT OF THE FIRST BALLOT.

The Secretary here announced the result of the first ballot as follows:

```
Whole vote cast..................................190½
For Douglas.....................................173½
For Guthrie.....................................   9
For Breckenridge................................   5
For Seymour.....................................   1
For Hocock......................................   1
For Wise........................................   ½
For Dickinson...................................   ½
```

FIRST BALLOT.

States.	Douglas.	Breckenridge.	Wise.	Bocock.	Dickinson.	Guthrie.	Seymour.
Maine	5½						
New Hampshire	5						
Vermont	5						
Massachusetts	10						
Rhode Island	4						
Connecticut	3½	1					
New York	35						
New Jersey	2½						
Pennsylvania	10	3				3	1
Maryland	2½		½				
Virginia	1½			1	½		
North Carolina	1						
Alabama	9						
Louisiana	6						
Arkansas	1	½					
Missouri	4½					1½	
Tennessee	3						
Kentucky						4½	
Ohio	23						
Indiana	13						
Illinois	11						
Michigan	6						
Wisconsin	5						
Iowa	4						
Minnesota	2½	½				1	
Total	173½	5	½	1	½	10	1

Mr. Church of New York offered a resolution. Objections were made. Many delegates wanted another ballot before a resolution was introduced. The resolution was read as follows:

Resolved, That Stephen A. Douglas, of the State of Illinois, having now received two-thirds of all the votes given in this Convention, he is hereby declared, in accordance with the rules governing this body and in accordance with the uniform custom and rules of former Democratic National Conventions, the regular nominee of the Democratic party of the United States for the office of President.

Mr. Church made a speech in favor of his resolution. He said:

We have yielded every thing but personal honor in order to heal up the divisions of this Convention. One question after another has been presented to us, and we have been asked to yield this point, and that point, and the other point, and we have never failed to respond whenever we have been asked until we were required to yield up every thing which distinguishes our manhood—nay, more, every thing which distinguishes the manhood of the 200,000 Democrats behind us. [Applause.] When we came to that point—though we say it with pain, and sorrow, and anguish—when we were asked to admit, without question or examination, the whole body of seceders who came here to our doors—not repentant, not determined to abide by our action, but demanding the surrender of our principles into their hands—when we were asked to do that, and, besides, to give up our candidate and the candidate of the choice of the Democracy of New York—a candidate who will sweep New York as with a whirlwind [applause]—when we were asked to do all that, we said firmly we cannot in honor comply with your demands.

Mr. Church said of the adoption of the two-thirds rule in the shape it took in Charleston, that it was "outrageous, undemocratic, despotic, wrong"—but New York had submitted to it for the sake of harmony.

Mr. Gittings of Maryland rose to most solemnly protest against the proposed action. He said:

The gentleman from New York (Mr. Church), says in one breath that New York has always desired to offer the olive-branch; and in the next breath he throws a fire-brand in the midst of the Democratic party which will create a flame no power on earth can quench. The two-thirds rule is one of the cardinal principles for the government of Democratic Conventions; and better not make a nomination at all than rescind a rule for the purpose of making any one man a candidate.

After some further debate, Mr. Church withdrew his resolution for another ballot.

Mr. Flournoy of Arkansas voted for Douglas this time.

Mr. Becker stated that himself and two of his colleagues had come to the conclusion to withdraw from the Convention. They were ready to meet all the responsibility for so doing. The following is the result of the

SECOND BALLOT.

States.	Douglas.	Breckenridge	Guthrie.
Maine	7		
New Hampshire	5		
Vermont	5		
Massachusetts	10		
Rhode Island	4		
Connecticut	3½	½	
New York	35		
New Jersey	2½		
Pennsylvania	10	7	2½
Maryland	2½		
Virginia	3		
North Carolina	1		
Alabama	9		
Louisiana	6		
Arkansas	1½		
Missouri	4½		1½
Tennessee	3		
Kentucky	3		1½
Ohio	23		
Indiana	13		
Illinois	11		
Michigan	6		
Wisconsin	5		
Iowa	4		
Minnesota	4		
Total	181½	7½	5½

Whole number of votes, 194½.
The increased vote on this ballot was from Pennsylvania.
Mr. Hoge of Virginia wanted to move the unanimous nomination of Douglas. Mr. Clark of Missouri, who had voted against Douglas, said it was his purpose to second the motion of Mr. Hoge. Mr. H. now said:

I now beg leave to submit the following resolution, being the same as that offered by the gentleman from New York (Mr. Church), with a slight modification that he and I have made:

Resolved unanimously, That Stephen A. Douglas, of the State of Illinois, having now received two-thirds of all votes given in this Convention is hereby declared, in accordance with rules governing this body, and in accordance with the uniform customs and rules of former Democratic National Conventions, the regular nominee of the Democratic party of the United States for the office of President of the United States.

Mr. Sayles of Rhode Island made a speech about the late Democratic victory in that State, and said he had been told in Charleston that they were hardly better than Black Republicans.

Mr. Seymour of New York enthusiastically indorsed Douglas, though he had heretofore opposed him.

Mr. Mason of Kentucky made a speech, in which he doubted whether the fires would blaze so high upon the mountain-tops as had been asserted. He thought the resolution of Mr. Church injudicious, and proposed an amendment as follows:

Now, if you will not say in the resolution that this is the rule which has heretofore governed the Democratic party—because you voted at Charleston, that it was not, and for our accommodation; if you will not make this new construction, but simply declares that, under all the circumstances, Mr. Douglas ought to be the unanimous nominee of this party. I should not be surprised if the State of Kentucky would agree with you, and that quite likely you may get the vote of that State, though I cannot say it with certainty.

Mr. Richardson of Illinois—There has never been a nomination for President under any other construction than that made by my friend from New York in his resolution. It is true you agreed at Charleston that you would not do it this time, but always heretofore you have nominated the candidate by a two-third vote. Mr. Stevenson of Virginia, in 1848, when the New York delegation was excluded, and Gen. Cass was nominated, declared that 170 votes were two-thirds. The action of the Convention has been uniform upon this subject.

Mr. Craig of Missouri—Is there any objection to withdrawing the resolution and declaring the nomination unanimous by a big, old-fashioned Democratic yell? [Laughter and cries of "Question," "question."]

The question being taken on the resolution of Mr. Church, it was adopted by an unanimous aye.

Now a storm of cheers went up. The banner of the Keystone State was hung out from the upper gallery, and somebody produced on the stage a flag on which it was written "Pennsylvania good for 40,000 majority for Douglas."

The President said: Gentlemen of the Convention, as your presiding officer I declare Stephen A. Douglas, of Illinois, by the unanimous vote of this Convention, the nominee of the Democratic party of the United States for President. [Here Captain Rynders led off with three hearty cheers.] And may God, in his infinite mercy, protect him, and with him this Union!

Mr. Dawson, chairman of the Pennsylvania delegation, was called on for a speech. The following paragraphs embody its substance:

Mr. President and gentlemen of the Convention, it is scarcely necessary for me to say that, at no time during the sittings of this body, did Judge Douglas receive the united vote of the delegation from Pennsylvania. And, I may further add, that in the consideration of a platform a majority of us united with our Southern friends, ready to give them all that we believed them entitled to under the Federal Constitution. In our judgment they asked for nothing more, and we were not willing to give them less. [Applause.] In our actions then we have been overruled by a decided majority of this body, and, for Pennsylvania, I am free to say that, attached as we are to the Democratic party, its principles, its discipline, its organization, standing true forever, in the eloquent language of the President in his opening speech at Charleston, "Standing as perpetual sentinels upon the outposts of the Constitution," we will, I trust, abide by its decisions and support its nominees. [Cheers.]

Judge Douglas is a man of acknowledged talent, and everywhere regarded as the accomplished statesman, skilled in the art of ruling. Born under a New England sun, yet by adoption a citizen of the West, honored and cherished in the valley of the Ohio and on the slopes of the Atlantic, he now should be of the whole country. [Cheers.] Untrained, to some extent, in early life, in the learning of the schools, the deficiency, if any exists, has been largely compensated by the generous measure in which nature has bestowed upon him her choicest gifts of intellect and character. [Applause.] Like Henry of the Revolution, like Peel of England, these noble qualities have made him the architect of his own fortune. [Cheers.]

Mr. Shepley of Maine spoke next. He had not been for Douglas at first, but he indorsed his nomination and said, in concluding his remarks:

I have only one word to say in conclusion. We represent 55,000 Democrats in the State of Maine, and although it has been urged here that there is no Northern Democracy in the coming election, we will show those men of the lowlands who have said it, that

"There are hills beyond Pentland,
There are friths beyond Forth,
If there are lords in the Southland,
There are chiefs in the North."

Mr. Cochrane of New York made a handsome harmony speech. He had been against Douglas, but now congratulated the Convention and the whole country. He said:

But the time has arrived when these differences of opinion are to be merged in the authoritative decree of the great Democratic party, and as that decree is here announced to the people of the United States, I for one, lend the feeble volume of my voice to those winds and currents that are now bearing to every portion of the Union the honored, illustrious, impregnable name of Stephen A. Douglas. [Loud cheers.]

He declared further that "the reluctance of the past should be compensated by the cordiality of the future," and said in conclusion: "Patriotism and honesty require that those who have been sent here as delegates are in strict honor bound by the action of this Convention. [Applause.] But above and beyond the obligations of honor there is a volition that will expand from these walls to the whole country, which will resound in huzza upon huzza for Stephen A. Douglas."

The Convention took a recess until seven o'clock in the evening.

EVENING SESSION.

The first thing was an explanation from Mr. Harrington of Illinois, who was the man alluded to by Mr. Smith of California as having acknowledged that the Cessna resolution was a trick. He said that, on the contrary, he had denied that that resolution was a trick. He accounted for Mr. Smith's statement by saying that he (Smith) had been almost insane from excitement.

The following was named as the National Executive Committee:

Sylvanus R. Lyman, of Portland, Maine; Alfeus F. Snow, of Claremont, New Hampshire; Charles G. Eastman, of Montpelier, Vermont; Frederick C. Price, of Boston, Massachusetts; Jacob Babbitt, of Bristol, Rhode Island; Wm. F. Converse, of Norwich, Connecticut; Auguste Belmont, of New York, New York; Jacob Van Nosdale, of Newark, New Jersey; Richard Haldeman, of Harrisburg, Pennsylvania; Thos. M. Lanahan, of Baltimore, Maryland; John A. Harman, of Staunton, Virginia; Rob't E. Dick, of Greensborough, North Carolina; Wm. B Gaulden, of Huntsville, Georgia; W. W. Moore, of Jacksonville, Florida; Oatley H. Bynum, of Portland, Alabama; Thos. Cottman, of Donaldsonville, Louisiana; Thomas Flournoy, of Arkansas; James Craig, of St. Joseph's, Missouri; C. Knox Walker, of Memphis, Tennessee; Henry C. Harrison, of Covington, Kentucky; Hugh J. Jewett, of Zanesville, Ohio; H. W. Harrington, of Madison, Indiana; Murray McKunncl, of Jacksonville, Illinois; Benj. Follett, of Michigan; John K. Sharpstein, of Milwaukee, Wisconsin; Wm. H. Merrick, of Cedar Rapids, Iowa; Henry H. Sibley, of Minnesota; James A. McDougal, of San Francisco, California.

Mr. Gaulden of Georgia desired to decline, but was not allowed to do so, and accepted "as a private citizen of Georgia."

In the report of the committee on Rules and Regulations, it was provided that the place of holding the next National Convention should be in the discretion of the National Committee.

Mr. Sibley of Minnesota said: It was held by the presiding officer that the term of office of the National Executive Committee expired upon the assembling of the Convention, and serious inconveniences have resulted in consequence of that ruling. I now move that the Executive Committee shall remain in existence and continue its functions until its successors are elected and qualified.

The motion was agreed to.

After it had been provided that Mr. G. Parkhurst, Recording Secretary, should prepare the proceedings for publication, and cause 10,000 copies to be printed,

Mr. Jones of Tennessee said : Mr. President, the Southern delegates in their Convention have conferred together and have agreed unanimously to nominate for Vice-President of the United States the Hon. Benjamin Fitzpatrick, of the State of Alabama. [Applause.]

Mr. Clark of Mo. seconded the nomination. He said that a better one could not have been made, and that the name of Mr. Fitzpatrick would be a tower of strength.

Telegraphic despatches were read announcing the reception of the nomination of Douglas at various points.

The President (after calling the Convention to order repeatedly)— Gentlemen, you all know that the chair feels so much disposition to join in these yells that *he* can't keep order.

At the call of States for the vote on the Vice-Presidential nomination, Mr. Fitzpatrick received 198¼ votes, and one vote was given William F. Alexander of New Jersey. Mr. Alexander's name was authoritatively withdrawn when it was mentioned—a delegate from Pennsylvania voting for him—by Mr. Whitburn of New Jersey.

The following committee, upon motion of Mr. Ludlow, was appointed to inform Messrs. Douglas and Fitzpatrick of their nomination : William H. Ludlow of New York, J. L. Seward of Georgia, J. L. Dawson of Pennsylvania, Robert C. Wickliffe of Louisiana, W. A. Gorman of Minnesota, T. V. Flournoy of Arkansas, A. A. King of Missouri, Bion Bradbury of Maine, R. P. Dick of North Carolina.

Mr. Payne of Ohio—It is generally understood that the platform was adopted at Charleston. I understand a distinguished member from Louisiana (Mr. Wickliffe) desires to present a resolution relating to the platform, and I hope he will be allowed to do so.

Gov. Wickliffe of Louisiana—In behalf of the committee on Resolutions, I beg leave to present the following. The adoption of it will give to Stephen A Douglas forty thousand votes in two of the Southern States of this Union :

Resolved, That it is in accordance with the interpretation of the Cincinnati Platform, that during the existence of the Territorial Governments the measure of restriction, whatever it may be, imposed by the Federal Constitution on the power of the Territorial Legislature over the subject of the domestic relations, as the same has been or shall hereafter be finally determined by the Supreme Court of the United States, should be respected by all good citizens and enforced with promptness and fidelity by every branch of the General Government.

The resolution was received with loud expressions of approbation.

Mr. Payne—Mr. President, I undertake to say that no fair-minded man, North or South, can find fault with one word of that resolution. [Several voices, "Not a word."]

Mr. Payne moved the previous question. Mr. Davis of Virginia rose with excitement, said it was unfair, and wanted to be heard. Mr. Payne withdrew the previous question.

Mr. Davis thought the subject of a platform was already sufficiently complicated. He did not want Fitzpatrick sacrificed by the introduction of that resolution, particularly as it did not mean any thing at all. He was for the Cincinnati Platform alone. He said:

"If we can't get what we want, let us have nothing but the Cincinnati Platform and abide by that and wait our time. By and by the Democratic party will give protection, I believe, and that is the reason why I was elected as a protective man. I am a protective man here to-day. I think we have got one protective man on the ticket. If not, I am terribly deceived. I don't want him sacrificed by the introduction of this resolution. You won't hear me to-night. I stand ready to refute the fallacy of squatter or popular sovereignty whenever I can be listened to. All I will say here then is that this resolution complicates the subject and involves the South worse and worse, and I protest, in the name of my constituency, against its adoption.

The resolution was adopted *viva voce*, with one or two dissenting voices.

The Hon. William A. Richardson made a short speech reviewing the controversy between those who had seceded from, and those who remained in the Convention. He said:

I am going to make an announcement that will account for the currency of a rumor prevalent here the other day. Judge Douglas will accept the nomination. [Loud cheers and applause.] But Judge Douglas was prepared, for the harmony of the party, for the success of the party, for the preservation of the government, always and at all times, to withdraw his name from the Convention. [Applause.] I mean those gentlemen shall meet that issue when they go home. I have had in my possession, since the session of this Convention here, his authority placed in my hands to withdraw his name, to be used by his friends whenever they deemed it necessary to do so. [Great applause.] And I now send to the Secretary's desk a letter which, though marked "private," I ask may be read to this Convention.

In this letter Mr. Douglas reiterated his doctrine of "Non-intervention," and said:

"But while I can never sacrifice the principle, even to attain the Presidency, I will cheerfully and joyfully sacrifice myself to maintain the principle. If, therefore, you and my other friends, who have stood by me with such heroic firmness at Charleston and Baltimore, shall be of the opinion that the principle can be preserved and the unity and ascendancy of the Democratic party maintained and the country saved from the perils of Northern abolitionism and Southern disunion by withdrawing my name and uniting upon some other non-intervention and Union-loving Democrat, I beseech you to pursue that course.

* * * * *

"The action of the Charleston Convention in sustaining me by so large a majority on the platform, and designating me as the first choice of the party for the Presidency, is all the personal triumph I desire. This letter is prompted by the same motives which induced my despatch four years ago, withdrawing my name from the Cincinnati Convention."

Mr. Richardson resuming, said:

So anxious was my friend, the nominee of this Convention, that this should be impressed upon the minds of all his friends here that he telegraphed the gentleman from New York (Mr. Richmond) on yesterday, I believe, to the same effect. I trust that no person who knows me believes that I would be guilty of manufacturing evidence for an occasion of this sort. [Cries of "No," "no."] I have borne this letter with me for three days, but those gentlemen who have seceded from this Convention placed it out of my power to use it. And the responsibility, therefore, is on them.

* * * * * * *

We in the North have one sectional party to fight, and intend to whip them. You have an equally sectional party to fight in the South, and we expect you to whip them. When the election comes on in November next, we shall carry a majority of the electoral vote of the North, and we expect you to carry a majority of the electoral vote of the South.

Mr. Cessna of Pennsylvania—We were informed upon the opening of this Convention in this city, by our late highly respected and most lamented presiding officer [laughter], that when we adjourned at Charleston there were pending three motions to reconsider, and three motions to lay those motions to reconsider on the table. I move that the question be now taken upon those motions.

The motion was agreed to, and accordingly the several motions to reconsider were laid on the table.

The usual votes of thanks were passed. Hon. David Todd was thanked. Railroads were thanked for half-fare tickets. The police of Baltimore were thanked.

Then Mr. Warwack of Alabama returned thanks for the nomination made for Vice-President, and pledged the electoral vote of Alabama for the nominees of the Convention. It was here announced that four States had seceded from the Seceders' Convention. The announcement was received with much applause. It was, however, a mistake. No such secession had occurred.

Mr. Stuart of Michigan proposed to adjourn, go into the field where the enemy were and "conquer them in a hand-to-hand fight."

The President returned thanks for the vote of thanks, and concluded :

We have only to continue firmly, nationally, sternly, fairly, honorably in the discharge of our duties, as we have done since we met at Charleston, to crown our efforts with entire success.

Wishing you all a safe return to your homes, to your wives and children, and God grant that you may all have them at home waiting for you, I now declare this Convention adjourned, and bid you adieu.

The hour was fifteen minutes to ten P. M.

INSTITUTE HALL ("SECEDERS") CONVENTION.

After the retirement of Mr. Cushing from the Presidency of the Convention in the theatre, the public lost interest in that body. There were several sensation scenes in the morning, the most remarkable of which was Mr. Cushing dropping the gavel and leaving the chair, and Mr. Todd taking his place, with the Convention cheering heartily. But when it was evident to all that the Convention would nominate Douglas, as soon as the remaining delegates should exhaust themselves in speech-making, the public turned toward the Maryland Institute (or Market) Hall. The Hall is three hundred and twenty feet long, and seventy broad, with galleries running entirely around, and contains, when full in every part, eight thousand persons. The galleries, and the space on the floor set apart for outsiders, were quite full when the Convention was called to order.

The Baltimore Sun says of the feeling of the Seceding delegates, in coming together: "The members of the respective delegations entered freely into conversation. All restraint of feeling had disappeared, and a spirit of the most cordial unanimity and harmony characterized every man and every feature. The change of manner, expression and sentiment was complete, and would have been striking and remarkable, but that it was consistent with general experience, in a Democratic Convention undisturbed by factitious influences. None could possibly fail to realize the perfect restoration of that geniality of intercourse which is alone the earnest of a harmonious result."

Mr. Ewing of Tennessee called the Convention to order, and announced Mr. Russell of Virginia as temporary chairman of the Convention. Messrs. Featherson of Mississippi and Stevens of Oregon were appointed a committee to escort Mr. Russell to his seat. Mr. Russell made a speech, in which he said:

The Convention assembled elsewhere, and from which you have withdrawn, has lost all title to the designation of national. [Applause.] It cannot longer continue to perform the functions of a National Democratic Convention, and every one believes that all true Democrats will unite to declare it unsound in national relations. You and those who you represent are a majority of the people of the Democracy and of the Democratic States. [Applause.] They will look to you to perform the functions of a National Democratic Convention, and you will be so recognized alike by the North and the South, the East and the West. [Cheers.]

On motion of Mr. Ewing, Messrs. Crosby of Oregon and Johnson of Maryland were selected as temporary Secretaries.

Mr. Walker of Alabama moved the appointment of a committee of 15 on Permanent Organization. Carried unanimously.

Senator Bayard of Delaware moved reconsideration, as the number (15) looked sectional. At his suggestion, the committee was made 5 instead of 15.

There was some talk about filling up the delegates' seats, there being a good many more chairs than delegates. This was quieted, however. The following was reported as the committee on Organization :

Walker of Alabama, McHenry of Pennsylvania, Stevens of Oregon, Williams of Massachusetts, and John Dishman of Kentucky.

The Convention took a recess, and there were cries among the spectators for a speech from Yancey.

EVENING SESSION.

The chairman of each delegation was requested to hand to the Secretary a list of the delegates from his State.

The Secretary proceeded to call the roll of the States, when the following responses were made :

Maine, New Hampshire, Rhode Island, Connecticut, Ohio, Indiana, Illinois, Michigan, Wisconsin and Minnesota—no delegates.

Vermont—One delegate.
Massachusetts—Sixteen delegates. [Immense cheering.]
New York—Two delegates. [Cheers.]
Pennsylvania—Please pass Pennsylvania for the present—she is here. [Cheers.]
New Jersey—No representative.
Delaware is here—pass her for the present.
Virginia—She is here with twenty-three delegates.
North Carolina—She is here with sixteen delegates. [Applause.]
Alabama is here with a full delegation—thirty-six delegates.
Mississippi—A full delegation of fourteen.
Louisiana—A full delegation ; fourteen.
Texas—All here ; eight delegates.
Arkansas—A full delegation, nine in number.
Missouri—Two delegates.
Tennessee—We have nineteen delegates here.
Kentucky—Ten delegates.
Iowa—Mr. H. H. Heath presented a document with relation to a representation of that State on the floor of this Convention. [Cheers.]
California—The entire delegation of that State is here as a unit.
Oregon—She is here as a unit.
Maryland—Maryland is here with nine of her delegation.
South Carolina—No representatives.
Florida—Six delegates. [Applause.]

Mr. Johnson stated he was authorized to state in behalf of the Hon. Senator Bayard of Delaware, who was called to Washington on pressing business, that he was with this Convention in sentiment and heart, and would cordially sustain its nominee. [Applause.]

There was so much confusion in the hall, that the process of calling delegations was tedious. There were many prominent Southern men in the hall, among them Senator Toombs, whose dark, lowering face seemed for once lit up with good cheer. The leading Southerners of the delegations smiled radiantly. I had not seen them look so happy during the sixteen weary days of the Convention, and the two days' episode at Richmond. Yancey, who always wears a surface smile, twisted about in his seat with the unrest of intolerable felicity, laid his head first upon one shoulder and then upon the other, and glowed with satisfaction. Garnett, of Virginia, whose countenance is usually grave as Don Quixote's, seemed pleased as a school-boy with new boots. The great body of those collected as spectators were manifestly favorable to the movement. The same public feeling apparent at Charleston in favor of the Seceders, came out in less degree here. It was a feeling of sectional pride, and a loyalty to the Southern leaders, that is superior to convictions of either principle or expediency.

Mr. Walker of Alabama, from the committee on Organization, was authorized to report the following as the permanent officers of this Convention :

PRESIDENT.
Hon. CALEB CUSHING, of Massachusetts.

VICE-PRESIDENTS.

V. L. Bradford, Pennsylvania.
O. R. Funsten, Virginia.
A. P. Denison, Oregon.
J. E. Dresbit, California.
J. O. C. Atkins, Tennessee.
J. S. Kenrick, Kentucky.
Bradford Brown, North Carolina.
W. F. Featherston, Mississippi.
H. S. Benning, Georgia.

H. E. Stoughton, Vermont.
M. J. McElhaney, Missouri.
Richard Tayler, Louisiana.
R. G. Scott, Alabama.
Josiah Gould, Arkansas.
W. P. Bowie, Maryland.
W. H. Ross, Delaware.
H. M. Runnels, Texas.
B. F. Wardlaw, Florida.

SECRETARIES—W. H. Crosley, Oregon ; W. P. Cooper, Virginia ; E. S. F. Hardcastle, Maryland ; N. H. R. Dawson, Alabama ; Thos. P. Ochiltree, Texas ; J. J. Williams, Florida ; F. West, Georgia ; F. W. Hoadley, Arkansas; W. G. Whiteley, Delaware ; David Fist, Pennsylvania ; C. J. Armistead, Mississippi ; S. W. Humphrey, North Carolina ; D. D. Withers, Tennessee.

The name of Caleb Cushing was received with applause that reminded me of Chicago Hats and handkerchiefs were waved all around the great circle of the galleries, and over the heads of the crowds upon the floor. A committee was appointed to wait upon Mr. Cushing. The committee did not have far to proceed to find that gentleman, and in a few minutes were seen escorting him down the long passage, fenced from the multitude with settees leading from the door to the seats reserved for the delegates and the platform. Cushing's person has, during his Presidency over the deliberations of the Convention, become very well known. He was therefore instantly recognized by hundreds, and his familiar blue coat and brass buttons, his Websterian garments and Cæsarian head, were hailed with extraordinary acclamation. He marched through a lane of yelling Southerners, hats whirling, and handkerchiefs waving over his head, while the occupants of the galleries leaned forward, and shouted and clapped their hands, swung their hats, fluttered handkerchiefs, and as he mounted the platform, Mr. Russell of Virginia took him by the hand, the Convention and crowd gave him three cheers, and Mr. R. mentioned that he "*resumed*" his seat as chairman of the National Democratic Convention.

Mr. Cushing, after anxiously inquiring of the Secretaries how many States were represented, said:

Gentlemen of the Convention—we assemble here, delegates to the National Democratic Convention [applause], duly accredited thereto from more than twenty States of the Union [applause], for the purpose of nominating candidates of the Democratic party for the offices of President and Vice-President of the United States—for the purpose of announcing the principles of the party, and for the purpose of continuing and re-establishing that party upon the firm foundation of the Constitution, the Union and the co-equal rights of the several States. [Applause.] Gentlemen, the Convention is in order for business.

Every word rung through the immense hall, and the familiar sound of his voice certainly gave the Convention the tone of regularity.

Mr. Loring of Massachusetts moved that a committee of one from each State be appointed as a committee on Credentials to decide the qualification of members to seats on this floor.

Mr. Johnson of Maryland moved as an amendment, that the credentials be referred to the committee on Credentials as that committee stood at the last meeting of this Convention. [Applause.]

Mr Loring—I accept the amendment. I had forgotten. I move, therefore, that the committee on Credentials be requested to examine and report on the credentials of members.

A communication was received from H. H. Heath of Dubuque, Iowa, and John Johns of Davenport, Iowa. These gentlemen were desirous that the National Democracy of Iowa should have a representation on that floor. They did not claim to be regular delegates, but asked seats on the floor with "the right of mutual conference and consultation." The document was referred to the committee on Credentials.

Mr. Atkins of Tennessee wanted business despatched. There was no reason why all the business could not be accomplished before adjourning.

Mr. Butler of Massachusetts moved that the members of the committee on Resolutions be requested to report a platform forthwith. He resigned his place on the committee, and Hon. B. F. Hallett ("Author Cincinnati Platform") was substituted.

Mr. Johnson of Maryland moved the adoption at once, without reference to a committee, of that which was known as the majority platform reported at Charleston.

Mr. Lubbock of Texas deprecated these hasty proceedings. The committee on Credentials had not reported. Care should be taken to do the work well. He conscientiously believed the nominees of that Convention would be elected President and Vice-President of the United States.

Mr. Hunter of Louisiana presented the following resolution:

Resolved, That the delegates to the Richmond Convention be requested to unite with their brethren of the National Democratic Convention, now assembled at the Maryland Institute Hall, on the same platform of principles with themselves, if they feel authorized to do so.

Mr. Loring of Massachusetts moved that the resolution be amended so as to read "the delegates from South Carolina and Florida accredited to Richmond," and he did so at the request of those delegates. [Applause.]

Mr. Russell suggested a committee of one from each State, to name candidates for President and Vice-President, to be voted for by the Convention.

Mr. Howard of Tennessee objected—and Mr. Russell withdrew his motion.

Mr. Fisher of Virginia offered the following resolution:

Resolved, That a committee be appointed by the President of the Convention, consisting of five members, to address the Democracy of the Union upon the principles which have governed this body in making the nomination of President and Vice-President, and in vindication of the principles of the party.

Mr. Howard of Tennessee moved that the President of this Convention be chairman of that committee. Mr. Howard put the question, and declared it carried unanimously. [Applause.]

The President—I will appoint the committee at my earliest convenience.

It was suggested, that while the report of the committee on Credentials was being prepared a little business might be done. So it was decreed that a "National Executive Committee of the Democratic party" should be appointed, and that the next Convention should be held in the city of Philadelphia.

Mr. Stevens of Oregon, chairman of the committee on Credentials, reported the following duly accredited members as in attendance:

VIRGINIA.

Charles W. Russell, Arthur R. Smith, John J. Kindred, M. W. Fisher, George Booker, James Barbour, John Seddon, Lewis E. Harvie, William F. Thompson, Henry P. Garnett, Wm. A. Buckner, John Blair Hoge, O. R. Funston, Walter D. Leake, Wm. P. Cecil, Robert Crockett, John Brannon, Henry Fitzhugh, Robert A. Coghill, P. B. Jones, E. W. Hubard, Walter Coles, Wm. H. Clark, R. H. Glass.

GEORGIA.

Henry R. Jackson, J. T. Irwin, Henry L. Benning, Solomon Cohen, John W. H. Underwood, Frederick H. West, T. Butler King, Julian Hartridge, Hugh M. Moore, John A. Jones, James M. Clark, Nelson Tift, T. J. McGehee, J. C. Gibson, F. Tracey, E. L. Strohecker, Thomas W. O. Hill, Wm. Phillps, James M. Barnwell, G. J. Fain, Lewis Tumlin, James Hoge, Mark Johnston, H. B. Thomas, James Jackson, James A. Sledge, Osborn T. Rogers, John A. Cobb, David C. Barrow, W. C. Fulton.

NEW YORK.

Augustus Schell, —— Bartlett.

[NOTE.—*Several of the delegates from the State of New York are in attendance, in cordial sympathy with the objects and course of this Convention; but as many of their colleagues have left the city, and as they feel themselves precluded by the unity rule of their State Convention, they do not feel authorized to participate as delegates in the proceedings of this body.]

CALIFORNIA.

Austin E. Smith, D. S. Gregory, John A. Dreibelbis; Chas L. Scott, proxy for G. W. Patrick; R. F. Langdon, proxy for L. R. Bradley; G. L. Dudley, proxy for John Raans; Calhoun Beahaam, proxy for John S. Dudley. John Bidwell appointed S. J. Heasley his proxy, but neither of them are here.

MARYLAND.

William T. Hampton, John Contee, Levin Woolford, John R. Emory, E. L. F. Hardcastle, Daniel Fields, Bradley T. Johnson, William D. Bowie, Harville Stansbury.

PENNSYLVANIA.

W. M. Reilly, V. L. Bradford, Geo. M. Henry, E. C. Evans, Geo. H. Martin, H. A. Guensey, H. Laser, H. H. Dent, A. J. Glossbrenner, Arnold Plummer, H. B. Swarr, David Fister.

LOUISIANA.

R. A. Hunter, Richard Taylor, E. Lawn, John Tarleton, F. H. Hatch, D. D. Withers, R. C. Downs, J. G. Pratt, F. H. Knapp, J. H. New, R. Milzken.

* This is the note of the Reporter of the Baltimore American.

MISSISSIPPI.

George H. Gordon, Charles Clark, E. Barksdale, W. S. Barry, W. S. Wilson, W. S. Featherston, H. C. Chambers, Joseph W. Mathews, C. G. Armistead, B. Matthews, P. F. Liddell, Joseph R. Davis, Wirt Adams Alexander M. Clayton.

OREGON.

Lansing Stout, J. F. Lamerick, Isaac Stevens, Justis Steinberger, H R. Crosbee, A. P. Dennison.

MINNESOTA.

R. M. Johnson.

NORTH CAROLINA.

Wm. Landis, W. W. Avery, Lotte W. Humphreys, John Walker, Samuel Hargrave, James Fulton Samuel P. Hill, T. J. Green, Columbus Mills, W. S. Ashe, C. H. Foster, Bedford J. Brown, R. R. Bridges, W. A. Moore, W. S. Steele.

FLORIDA.

James B. Owens, W. D. Barnes, Joseph John Williams, B. F. Wardlaw, Geo. W. Call, Charles E. Dyke, N. Baker.

TENNESSEE.

Samuel Milligan, Wm. A. Quarles, J. D. C. Atkins, W. L. McClelland, Alfred Robb, James D. Thomas, Daniel Donelson, Thomas Meniers, John D. Riley, J. B Lamb, H. F. Cummins, R. Matthews, F. C. Dunnington, John McGavoch, H. W. Wall, Andrew Ewing, R. D. Powell, John K. Howard, C. Vaughne.

MASSACHUSETTS.

Caleb Cushing, James S. Whitney, W. C.

N. Swift, P. W. Leland, Alexander Lincoln, Bradford L. Wales, Isaac H. Wright, James Riley, Benjamin F. Hallett, George B Loring, E. S. Williams, George Johnson, Benjamin F. Butler, Abijah W. Chapin, David W. Carpenter, Reuben Noble.

ARKANSAS.

J. P. Johnson, De Rosig Carroll, Robert W. Johnson, T. C. Hindman, John A. Jordan, John J. Stirman, Josiah Gould, Van H. Manning, F. W. Hoadley.

KENTUCKY.

Richard M. J. Mason, Lafayette Green, James G. Leach, John Lishman, Colbert Cecil, James B. Beck, D. W. Quarles. Robert Gale, Robert M. Kean, John S. Kendicks.

ALABAMA.

L. P. Walker, A. B. Meck, H. D. Smith, W. L. Yancey, F. S Lyon, W. M. Brooks, R. G. Scott, J W. Portis, N. H. R. Dawson, T. J. Burnett, Eli S Shorter, J. C. B. Mitchell, W. C. Penick, A. S. Van de Graff L M. Stone, John Erwin, G. D. Johnston, F. G. Norman, John E. Moore, E. W. Kennedy, Robert T. Scott, R. Chapman, Winfield Mason, Alexaider Snodgrass, J. T. Bradford, W. P. Browne, W. H. Forney, D. W. Bozeman.

TEXAS.

Guy M. Bryan, H. R. Runnels, F. S. Stockdale, F. R Lubbock, J. F. Crosby, Tom. P. Ochiltree.

MISSOURI.

C. J. Carwin, W. J. McIlhiney.

It was recommended that the delegates from Iowa have complimentary tickets to the Convention, without leave to participate in its proceedings. The Credential report was adopted unanimously.

Mr. Avery of North Carolina, from the committee on Platform, reported the following, being the majority Platform of the Charleston committee:

Resolved, That the platform adopted by the Democratic party at Cincinnati, be affirmed, with the following explanatory resolutions:

1st. *Resolved*, That the government of a Territory organized by an act of Congress, is provisional and temporary; and during its existence, all citizens of the United States have an equal right to settle with their property in the Territory, without their rights either of person or property being destroyed or impaired by Congressional or Territorial legislation.

2d. *Resolved*, That it is the duty of the Federal Government, in all its departments, to protect, when necessary, the rights of persons and property in the Territories, and wherever else its constitutional authority extends.

3d. *Resolved*, That when settlers in a Territory having an adequate population, form a State Constitution, the rights of sovereignty commences, and, being consummated by admission into the Union, they stand on an equal footing with the people of other States; and the State thus organized ought to be admitted into the Federal Union, whether its constitution prohibits or recognizes the institution of slavery.

4th. *Resolved*, That the Democratic party are in favor of the acquisition of the Island of Cuba, on such terms as shall be honorable to ourselves and just to Spain, at the earliest practicable moment.

5th. *Resolved*, That the enactments of State Legislatures to defeat the faithful execution of the Fugitive Slave law, are hostile in character to and subversive of the Constitution, and revolutionary in their effect.

6th. *Resolved,* That the Democracy of the United States recognizes it as an imperative duty of this Government to protect naturalized citizens in all their rights, whether at home or in foreign lands, to the same extent as its native-born citizens.

And whereas, one of the greatest necessities of the age, in a political, commercial, postal and military point of view, is speedy communication between the Pacific and Atlantic coasts, therefore be it

7th. *Resolved,* That the National Democratic party do hereby pledge themselves to use every means in their power to secure the passage of some bill to the extent of the constitutional authority of Congress for the construction of a Pacific Railroad from the Mississippi River to the Pacific Ocean, at the earliest practicable moment.

Mr. Avery moved the previous question upon this platform, and it was adopted without dissent.

Mr. Mathews offered the following resolution, which was adopted:

That the National Committee shall not issue tickets to the floor of the Convention in any case where there is a *bona fide* contestant.

Mr. Greene of North Carolina moved "That all Constitutional Democrats of such States as are not at present represented, be requested to unite in the organization, and form an Electoral College in favor of the election of the nominees of this Convention."

Mr. Henderson moved to strike out the word "Constitutional," and substitute "National," which was agreed to.

Mr. Barksdale moved to proceed to the nomination of candidates for the Presidency and Vice-Presidency.

So the Convention went on, harmoniously as a Republican Convention where the party is in a minority. The pressure to transact business was overpowering.

If a delegate spoke for five minutes, he would see many anxious indications of impatience, that would not long tolerate him. The only clog upon business was a difference of opinion as to the casting of votes. The question was whether a delegate from a Congressional District, whose colleague was absent, should cast one vote or one-half a vote.

The rule of voting adopted at Charleston and Cincinnati prevailed.

The President stated that a telegraphic message had just been put into his hands from the members of the State of Minnesota at the Charleston Convention, desiring that Richard M. Johnson should cast their vote. The despatch was signed by Messrs. Baker and Egerton.

The committee on Credentials had recommended "that the rules and regulations adopted by the National Democratic Convention of 1852 and 1856, be adopted by this Convention for its government, with this qualification—that no nomination shall be considered as made unless the candidate receives two-thirds of the votes of the States represented by this Convention."

The committee had further recommended "that each delegate cast the vote to which he is entitled in this Convention, and each State shall only cast the number of votes to which it may be entitled by actual representation in this Convention."

Under these rules the Convention proceeded to the nomination of candidates for the Presidency and Vice-Presidency. Mr. Loring of Massachusetts made a speech. He said:

We have seen the statesmen of Mississippi coming into our own borders, and fearlessly defending their principles, aye, and bringing the sectionalism of the North at their feet by their gallantry. We have admiration for this courage, and I trust to live by it and be governed by it. Among all these men to whom we have been led to listen, and admire, and repeat, there is one standing pre-eminently before this country—a young and gallant son of the South.

And he named John C. Breckenridge, which name was received with a grand uproar of applause that signified his nomination.

Mr. Denny of Pennsylvania seconded the nomination.

Mr. Ward of Alabama begged leave "to put in nomination a distinguished son of the old commonwealth of the State of Virginia—R. M. Hunter—as our representative man. He has fought the battle for twenty-five years, and has stamped the impress of principle upon the great Democratic party of his country."

Mr. Ewing of Tennessee put in nomination Daniel S. Dickinson of New York, and said:

Mr. Webster, who was opposed to him, said he could not leave the Senate without paying a tribute to the patriotism and dignity of character, as a gentleman and as a statesman, of Mr. Dickinson. Webster now sleeps with his fathers, but his judgment remains, and it was the impartial judgment of a man who was able to judge, and who was an opponent.

Mr. Stevens of Oregon named the "Marion of the Mexican War." He said:

We have tried him, and know him as a statesman and as a man of honor—we know him as a man of experience, and we know him as a man ruled by the Constitution under which we live. I beg leave, therefore, to present to this Convention the name of General Joseph Lane of Oregon.

Mr. Matthews of Mississippi spoke of "the orator, warrior, statesman and lawyer, Jefferson Davis," but for the sake of harmony withheld his name.

Mr. Russell of Virginia, after consulting with his delegation, requested Alabama to withdraw the name of Hunter.

Mr. Ward of Alabama complied, expressing his "profound admiration" for the bearing of Virginia.

The roll of States was then called. The result was:

For Breckenridge—Vermont ½, Massachusetts 8, Pennsylvania 4, Maryland 1½, Virginia 11½, Georgia 10, Florida 3, Alabama 9, Louisiana 6, Mississippi 7, Texas 4, Arkansas 4, Kentucky 4½, Minnesota 1, California 4, Oregon 3—81.

For Dickinson—New York 2, Maryland 3, North Carolina 8½, Missouri 1, Tennessee 9½—24.

The States that had voted for Dickinson one after another changed to Breckenridge, who was then declared unanimously nominated.

During the ballot for a candidate for the Presidency, Mr. Bartlett of New York said:

I came into the delegation of the State of New York, under the rule passed by the Democratic State Convention of that State. But it did not take me long to discover what the game was, after one day's session in that delegation. I was satisfied in my own mind that the slate had been filled, and, therefore, I was placed, like many others of my colleagues, in the minority of that delegation; and upon all questions, and especially upon the adoption of the majority report on Credentials, in which we had a long contest, the line was strictly drawn, and there was thirty on one side and forty on the other.

He also made an eloquent appeal for the Union.

Mr. Green of North Carolina rose and proposed Hon. Joseph Lane of Oregon, as Vice-President, which was seconded by the California delegation, and, on a call of the States, unanimously agreed to.

When the cheering subsided, there was a general call for "Yancey" "Yancey"—and that gentleman stepped forward upon the platform, and had a reception of the most flattering character. He is a square built middle-sized gentleman, with a decided stoop in the shoulders. His hair is a light brown, and his eyes large and gray. His face is peculiar, and without striking features, though closely observed it is seen to be the face of an intense and powerful man, having an expression of concentration, and a good-natured sort of pluck. His style of dress is that of a tidy business man, and his manners frank and unassuming as those of a boy. There is not the slightest symptom of the fanatic about him. His convictions are evidently not disturbed for a moment, nor is his confidence in himself by any means depressed by the vicissitudes of a doubtful controversy. In the midst of the most exciting scenes he is placid in appearance and so thoroughly conversant with his purpose, that he is at perfect ease. The smile that he wears amid the acclamations of a multitude of admirers would hardly darken a shade at the hootings of an exasperated mob. But you do not know him until you have heard him speak. His voice is clear as a bugle-note, and at the same time singularly blended with its music is a sharp high metallic ring, like that of a triangle of steel. This peculiar voice, always clear and sharp, pierces to a great distance, and would instantly command attention in any assembly. He speaks with great animation of gesture with his arms, meanwhile walking quietly up and down the platform. Upon commencing a particular branch of his subject, he straightens himself with an effort, stands perfectly erect, and pulls up his coat-sleeves. As he proceeds in the demonstration, he moves toward the edge of the platform and leaning forward, indicates the progress he is making by exclamation points given with the index finger of his right hand upon the palm of the left. As he clinches the proposition he leans forward until poised upon the toes of his boots, his right arm extended and pointing into the heart of the matter, and then usually as he rebounds, he throws off sportively as it were a graceful climax of rhetoric; and is ready for the next point.

Mr. Yancey commenced his speech on this occasion, by saying: Mr. President and Gentlemen of the Convention—The storm clouds of faction have drifted away, and the sunlight of principle, under the Constitution, and of the Union under the Constitution, shines brightly upon the National Democracy. He declared that the Democracy, the Constitution, and through them the Union, were yet safe. In defining his position in regard to the Union, he said : I am, however, no worshiper at the shrine of the Union. I am no Union shrieker. I meet great questions fairly, on their own merits. I do not try to drown the judgment of the people by shrieking for the Union. I am neither for the Union nor against the Union—neither for disunion nor against disunion. I urge or oppose measures upon the ground of their constitutionality and wisdom or the reverse.

He said of Mr. Douglas : But I will let Mr. Douglas rest where his friends have placed him, contending, however, that they have buried him to-day beneath the grave of squatter sovereignty. The nomination that was made (I speak it prophetically), was made to be defeated and it is bound to be defeated.

Mr. Yancey reviewed very clearly, the scriptural and historical references made in the Douglas Convention by Mr. Green of Ky., respecting the few righteous men of Sodom, and by Mr. Claiborne of Missouri, who introduced the story of Lord James Douglas and the heart of Bruce.

And with all Mr. Yancey's power, it is due the truth to say that he was guilty of that terrible offense on such an occasion—too much speaking—and contrived to use up very handsomely the brilliant reputation with which he came to Baltimore, as an orator of the first order, and a man of wonderful ability, perfect tact, and fascinating address. He has great and glittering qualities, but the Baltimoreans had over-estimated him. His speech was a disenchanter. He was not calculated to assist his party at all, but rather to place embarrassments in its way. He denied being a disunionist, but his talk respecting the Union did not indicate any warmth of affection for our common nationality. It was very calculating, and to the man who loves the Union for itself, and entertains a sentiment of national pride, which has its origin rather in the warm emotions of the heart, than the cold reason of the head, was offensive and distressing. He proceeded to elaborate the same argument made by Mr. Stevens in his minority report, and did not improve it at all by his redundancy of words. He had the bad taste, too, to enter largely into Alabama politics, and gave details of matters purely local in their nature. The people left the hall by hundreds; yet he spoke on, as if unconscious that instead of captivating the multitudes he was boring them. Cushing became uneasy, nervous and fidgety. Yancey was speaking the people out of the hall, and using up all the time with Alabama matters. It had been intimated that Burnett of Kentucky should respond to the nomination of John C. Breckenridge, but now there was no time for Burnett. Yancey was interrupted once, delicately as possible, to attend to some necessary business, but he could not or would not take the hint, but resuming, talked on and on—most injudiciously irritating the nerves of the people, and tampering with the patience of all who would have been glad to have heard all he had to say on another occasion. He was doing another thing that was undesirable. By talking so loud and long then and there, and putting himself and Alabama so prominently forward, he was identifying his name, and the ultraism of Alabama, too intimately and conspicuously with the movement represented in that hall. When he concluded it was evident that there would not be any more speech making. If the eloquence of Yancey had become a weariness, who should dare propose to stand up before the jaded crowd, sick, as all were, of the very sound of the human voice.

Mr. Avery of North Carolina offered a resolution of thanks to Mr. Cushing, who, on rising to acknowledge the compliment, was received with extravagant applause. He said:

Gentlemen of the Convention—I beg you to accept the expression of my heartfelt acknowledgment of your thanks. I do not intend to say any thing more, except to congratulate you upon the most felicitous termination of your labors, both in the adoption of platform, and in the nomination of your candidates.

A motion, by Judge Meek, that the President have power to appoint committees, was adopted. And at eleven o'clock the Convention adjourned *sine die*.

THE CONTEST AT BALTIMORE—THE SPIRIT OF THE SPLIT.

When the Seceders appeared at Baltimore, pursuant to the programme of the Southern Congressmen, advertised in their manifesto and perfected at Richmond, the contest between the antagonisms which had been fully developed at Charleston, resolved itself into a simple one on credentials, between the original Charleston delegates, and the delegations from several States, provided to fill up the gaps caused by secession, with the deciding vote in the hand of Dean Richmond, chairman of the New York delegation. Richmond & Co., while able to say whether the Convention should be consolidated by admitting the original Southern delegates, or disrupted by excluding the seceders, could not say, in case of consolidation, who should be the nominee. The friends of Douglas were without confidence in Richmond ("the Dean"), and were only prevented from denouncing him, by the appreciation of their dependence upon him. If he slaughtered Douglas, they had the power and the will to slaughter his man, and would have prevented the nomination of any candidate for whom he, in connection with the South, might have thrown his influence. Hence the hesitation of New York—her long consultations—her vascillation, and retrograde movements. She struggled for a compromise, but both sides were so fierce that compromising was out of the question. The Southerners thought they had compromised enough in coming to Baltimore, and condescending to ask admission into the Convention from which they had seceded. The friends of Douglas could not be expected to throw away the last chance for their candidate, by making up the Convention, so far as possible, out of its original materials. Such a compromise as that would have been, not a capitulation, but a surrender at discretion. They did, at the solicitation, indeed the dictatorial demand of New York, back out from two propositions, and were sorry for it afterward. They had taken the ground that no delegate accredited to the Richmond Convention, should be allowed to enter that at Baltimore. They were drawn from this point by the strong case of Mississippi. They had also declared the necessity of a pledge or understanding, that all delegates entering the Convention, should make or assent to, to the effect that they would support the nominees of the Convention. After urging this for a few hours, and observing the explosive excitement engendered by it, they withdrew it. They also, or rather New York, succumbed respecting their delegation from Georgia. Yet it was impossible to satisfy the demands of the South and preserve the unity of the Convention, without passing under the yoke of Yancey, and they could not consent to that humiliation.

The friends of Mr. Douglas finding their boasted availability in candidate and platform repudiated, and themselves treated as "property," rather than Sovereign, became infuriated. They were animated by passions whose force is terrible. There was in the first place an unappeasable hungering for the spoils, common, I suppose, to all politicians. They had long been placed on short allowance. In yielding to the demands of the South, and following their leaders ambitious of national eminence, they had been deserted by the greater portion of the people of their own localities. They had long been stung by the taunts of their Republican neighbors, that they were serfs of Southern masters, and in the new demands and arrogant intolerance of the South, they felt that they were regarded as inferiors, and treated accordingly. They had assumed that the South was under obligations to them for fighting battles for Slavery, and were exasperated upon discovering that no such obligation was recognized as having existence. They found, in short, that they could not be "sound" on the slavery question, without yielding up their most profound convictions, and all manly instincts. They were prepared to say that slavery should be tolerated—they could even go so far as to say that they did not care whether it was voted up or down—in or out of a Territory—but they were not willing to vote it up, and glorify it as a good thing, and especially acknowledge its political pre-eminence. And behind all this, they represented the purposes of Mr. Douglas, and had taken up his quarrel with the Lecompton wing of the party, and it became their fixed resolution to use every atom of power they could acquire, to vindicate the position of Mr. Douglas and his regularity in the party, and if possible, to assert by authority his control over the organization.

They proceeded to Baltimore in a state of stimulated enthusiasm, and partial blindness. They did not know the power and desperation of the South, and were foolish enough to believe the opposition to them in that quarter would quietly subside. They were, however, met in a spirit more intolerant than their own. Virginia, upon whom they had depended to give Douglas the nomination, in the spirit of harmony and according to Democratic usages, was the first to make threats, and finally led the seceding column—the mother of Democracy thus becoming chief of the seceders.

The appearance of the Seceders at Baltimore, and their evident purpose and power to control the Convention or destroy it, produced ex tremely hostile feeling on the part of the North-west. The immediate friends of Douglas became rancorous. Their temper was not improved by the fact that in the most conspicuous case, and on the vital point, they were manifestly worsted in argument. The report of Mr. Stevens of Oregon from the committee on Credentials, displays the strength, according to the usage of the party, of the case of the seceders. There was no way of proceeding to business, which to them had a single point—the nomination of Douglas—but to blow up the Convention. If a single one of the Douglas delegations from the Gulf States should be admitted, the explosion would take place just as if all were admitted. The compromising and trading New Yorkers found an absence of available material for obtaining advantages in political stock gambling. They were alternately bulls tossing up the Douglas stock and bears tearing it down, and yet, through all the fluctuations, they were unable to make a sale or a purchase on which any thing could be realized. The North-west was as determined and impracticable regarding one scheme as the South was regarding another. The Democracy of the North-west rose out of the status of serfdom. There was servile insurrection, with attendant horrors, and Baltimore became a political St. Domingo.

The South was amazed to hear its favorite threat of secession despised and hooted at. The seceders were sneeringly asked why they came back? and told that they had no business there—that Richmond was the place for them. Yancey had said it would be dishonorable for seceders to sneak back and beg to be allowed to re-enter the Convention. Now, why were they sneaking back? What had they done with their honor? The double-headed mass-meetings held every night for a week, constantly inflamed every antagonism within the party. Every old feverish sore was rent open by speakers from one stump or the other, and the want of unity in the party was so manifest that feeble efforts to make speeches in the old time strain of "conciliation, harmony, every thing for the man, nothing for the principle," were received with derision and remarks abundantly garnished with profanity, that there was no occasion for that sort of twaddle.

Just in the crisis of the Convention Mr. Douglas lost his nerve, and wrote by mail and telegraph to his most confidential and influential friends, beseeching them to save the party, if it could be done by withdrawing his name from the contest. It was too late, however. He was the implement of a revolution, and it was necessary that he should be used. He had raised a greater tempest than he had imagined. He had stirred up the storm but could not control the whirlwind.

After the Conventions, the feeling between the people of the Theatre and those of the Institute was so fiercely belligerent, that they could not talk in good humor. The fact that a family quarrel is of the most remorseless character, was manifest in the conversation of every group of ten persons to be seen on the streets or about the hotels. Each faction accused the other in the most harsh terms, of being factionists, bolters, traitors, incendiaries, etc., etc.—epithets conveying imputations offensive, in a political sense, being exhausted in vain efforts on both sides to do justice to the subject.

The North-western delegates, on their return home, congratulated themselves upon the presumption, that if they had ripped up the Democratic party, they had shown the Republicans that they, as Democrats, were not doughfaces. The reflection that they were no more to be reproached as serfs of the South, seemed sweet and ample consolation for all the struggles and perils through which they had passed, and the pangs they had suffered in the dissolution of the party. They talked all the way over the mountains to this effect : " Well, there is one thing of which we can't be accused any more. There was not a doughface shown in the North-west." The fact is the South was never before quite so well matched in her own game of brag and intolerable arrogance. They never before met in Convention face to face, with oath to oath, and menace for menace, and told with as much vehemence as they threatened to secede, that they might "do it and be d—d."

I shared a railroad seat, when crossing the mountains, with a North-western delegate, one of the most zealous of the partisans of Douglas. He was in a bad humor with the South. I asked what was the matter. He said : " I have been vexed. After all the battles we have fought for the South—to be served in this manner—it is ungrateful and mean."

He wanted the South to be made sweat under an Abolition President. He was glad Seward was not the Republican candidate, for he would be too easy on the South. He hoped Lincoln would make them sweat. The Southerners had been ruling over niggers so long they thought they could rule white men just the same. The South should not go out of the Union either. The would stay in and sweat. The fugitive slaves might go to Canada or to the devil in welcome, and their masters after them. He never would trouble his head about them any more. He did not care whether the Fugitive Slave law was enforced or not. He declared the South had alienated her best friends forever, and must now do the best she could for herself. He was also disposed to disparage the Southern country, depreciate the resources of the South, and magnify the evils that beset her.

And this conversation, I am convinced, represents the feeling with which the North-western delegates crossed the mountains returning home. The extent and bearings of the political revolution, of which this is one of the indications, may be further illustrated from the bar-room talk at Baltimore. One delegate from Indiana was happy to tell the Seceders that the valley of the Wabash was worth more than all the country between the Potomac and the Rio Grande, niggers included. And then an Ohioan boasted that there was " one town in a corner of Ohio, called Cincinnati, worth more than the whole d—d State of Alabama. Another assured the Seceders that he thought more of Black Republicans than of such fellows as they were, and that if there was to be a fight between sections, he was for his own side of the Ohio.

THE SECOND RICHMOND CONVENTION.

During the session of the Baltimore Convention, the South Carolina delegates remained at Richmond, and after the 21st, the day to which they had adjourned, they adjourned from day to day.

On the evening of Tuesday, the 26th, a number of the Southern delegates were in the city, among others, Messrs. Scott and Yancey of Alabama, and the Convention assembled in Metropolitan Hall. Col. Irwin, the President, called the Convention to order.

Mr. Middleton of South Carolina made a report from the committee on Credentials on the New York case (the New York Commissioners). The committee found that those commissioners had been "duly elected as delegates from the third, fourth, fifth, sixth, seventh and eighth Congressional Districts of New York to the Richmond Convention."

After some discussion the whole matter was laid on the table by the following vote:

AYES—Virginia ½, South Carolina 7½, Florida 3, Alabama 9, Mississippi 7—27.

NOES—North Carolina ½, South Carolina ½, Georgia 10, Louisiana 6, Texas 4—21.

Mr. Dargam of South Carolina then offered the following resolution:

Resolved, That this Convention approve of the Platform of Principles recommended by the majority report at the Charleston Convention.

The question was put, and the resolution was adopted unanimously, amid loud cheering.

Mr. Furman of South Carolina, on behalf of his delegation, offered the following resolution:

Resolved, That John C. Breckenridge of Kentucky, and Joseph Lane of Oregon, are, and they are hereby declared to be the choice, unanimously, of this Convention, for President and Vice-President of the United States.

There were a few votes of thanks, as usual on such occasions, and the Convention adjourned *sine die*.

The Richmond Enquirer says:

"The galleries during the session were thronged, and whilst there was great enthusiasm, there was no one occasion, in the slightest degree, to disturb good order. All the proceedings were conducted with a calmness, dignity and decorum which we have never seen excelled."

The lesson to the Nation of the PRESIDENTIAL CAUCUSES of 1860 is the necessity for the abolition of the Caucus System, which, in whatever party organization operative, is a system of swindling, by which the people are defrauded out of the effective exercise of the right of suffrage. There is no honesty in caucuses, no sound principle or good policy, except by accident; and the accidents that furnish the exception are rare indeed.

The revenues of King Caucus are corruption funds—and his government costs the country at least fifty million dollars annually—his platforms of principles are elaborations of false pretenses—his nominees are his obsequious viceroys—and he is the power behind the chairs of our chief magistrates, and under the tables of our cabinets, far more potent than those who visibly assume authority.

If a Republican form of government is to be preserved in our confederacy, the people must make a bonfire of his throne.

The official reports from which this compilation has been largely made up, appeared in the following journals: The Mercury and the Courier of Charleston; the Press and Tribune of Chicago; the Baltimore Clipper (for the "Constitutional Union" Convention); the Baltimore American and Sun, for the National Democratic Conventions; and the Richmond Enquirer for the Convention held in that city.

www.ingramcontent.com/pod-product-compliance
Lightning Source LLC
Chambersburg PA
CBHW021807230426
43669CB00008B/660